STRATEGIC PROCESSES
IN MONSOON ASIA'S
ECONOMIC DEVELOPMENT

# THE JOHNS HOPKINS STUDIES IN DEVELOPMENT

Vernon W. Ruttan and T. Paul Schultz,
*Consulting Editors*

# STRATEGIC PROCESSES

# IN MONSOON

# ASIA'S ECONOMIC

# DEVELOPMENT

Harry T. Oshima

THE JOHNS HOPKINS UNIVERSITY PRESS

*Baltimore and London*

The Johns Hopkins University Press
2715 North Charles Street
Baltimore, Maryland 21218-4319
The Johns Hopkins Press Ltd., London

**Library of Congress Cataloging-in-Publication Data**

Oshima, Harry T. (Harry Tatsumi)
   Strategic processes in monsoon Asia's economic development / Harry T. Oshima.
     p.     cm.—(The Johns Hopkins studies in development)
   Includes bibliographical references and index.
   ISBN 0-8018-4479-7 (alk. paper)
   1. East Asia—Economic conditions.   2. Asia, Southeastern—Economic
conditions.   3. East Asia—Economic policy.   4. Asia, Southeastern—Economic
policy.   5. Monsoons—Economic aspects—East Asia.   6. Monsoons—Economic aspects—
Asia, Southeastern.   I. Title.   II. Series.
HC460.5.O863   1993
338.95—dc20                                        92-33545

A catalog record for this book is available from the British Library.

# CONTENTS

# FIGURES

# TABLES

# PREFACE AND
# ACKNOWLEDGMENTS

Most of the articles on which these chapters are based were written before my retirement in 1983 from the Rockefeller Foundation, which I had represented since 1973 at the School of Economics, University of the Philippines, Diliman, Quezon City. I am grateful to the foundation for allowing me ample time for writing and research and for funding research assistance. I have received much help from my former students, Mina T. Paz and Elizabeth de Borja, and my wife, Chiye, who not only diligently compiled the data and edited the manuscripts but also offered numerous, valuable comments. My secretary, Gloria D. Lambino, undertook the composition of the tables and the typing of the chapters. I am most grateful to Randolph Barker of Cornell University and Vernon Ruttan of the University of Minnesota for their efforts in getting this volume published.

The chapters have been circulated for discussion in various conferences and seminars and among my friends. Chapter 2 was discussed at the Asian Economic Association meetings in late October 1988. Chapters 3 and 4 were commented on by Hiroshi Kakazu of the International University of Japan and by Dean José Encarnacion of the School of Economics, University of the Philippines. Chapter 5 was discussed at the Asian and Pacific Development Center's full-employment strategy seminar in mid-July and late September 1988 and at the student-faculty seminar of the Faculty of Economics, Thammasat University, in early December 1988. Chapter 6 was discussed in Jakarta at Bappenas and chapter 7 in Seoul around mid-April 1987 at the Rural Economic Research Institute.

Chapter 8 was commented on by Ernesto Pernia and Malcolm Dowling of the Asian Development Bank and by Hans Arndt of the Australian National University; it was presented at the Human Resource Workshop of the Asian Development Bank in November 1988. Chapter 9 was examined by Hakchung Choo of the Asian Development Bank and presented at its conference in Beijing in early September 1989. The first half of chapter 10 was discussed at a seminar of the Economics Department, the University of Hawaii, in March 1987 and the latter half at a Tokyo conference jointly sponsored by the Institute of Developing Economies and the Asian and Pacific Development Centre. At Hitotsubashi University in Tokyo, where I based my lectures on the manuscript in 1991–92, I received many valuable comments from Toshiyuki Mizoguchi. I am grateful to all for their assistance.

STRATEGIC PROCESSES
IN MONSOON ASIA'S
ECONOMIC DEVELOPMENT

# CHAPTER I

# Introduction

Encouraged by the favorable reception of my previous book, *Economic Growth in Monsoon Asia: A Comparative Survey* (University of Tokyo Press, 1987), I am here extending that study, with special attention to the way East Asia—Japan, South Korea, Taiwan, Hong Kong, and Singapore—grew more rapidly than other countries of monsoon Asia.

Geographers include in monsoon Asia Japan, Taiwan, Hong Kong, China, and North and South Korea in East Asia; Vietnam, Cambodia, Laos, Thailand, Singapore, Burma, Malaysia, the Philippines, and Indonesia in Southeast Asia; and Bangladesh, Sri Lanka, India, Nepal, Bhutan, Sikkim, and Pakistan in South Asia. But I shall frequently refer to other designations that have come into wide use. Taiwan, South Korea, Hong Kong, and Singapore have come to be known as the NIEs, or the newly industrializing economies. Thailand, Malaysia, Indonesia, the Philippines, Burma, and Singapore have been referred to as the ASEAN, or the Association of South East Asian Nations. It is convenient to exclude the last two countries and refer to the others as the ASEAN Four and, unlike the geographers, to include Singapore with Japan, Taiwan, Hong Kong, and South Korea (but not China and North Korea) in East Asia.

The first section of this chapter reviews parts of the previous volume relating to the present one, with some updating; the second section previews the chapters in this volume.

ECONOMIC GROWTH IN MONSOON ASIA

## The Nature of Strategic Processes

The previous volume dealt with binary comparisons, with emphasis on the historical background of the postwar growth of Asian economies. My purpose in that volume was mainly to obtain insights into the processes contributing to the different speeds at which countries grew. It was necessary to discuss how they grew—that is to say, the processes and mechanism of development. But this was done briefly and only in passing. In the present volume, I examine

1

these processes in detail through comparisons across several countries, with special attention to how Japan and the NIEs performed better than the ASEAN Four and how the latter did better than South Asia, China, and Pakistan.

Because many processes are involved in such complex phenomena as economic growth, one needs to be selective. I identify a process as strategic if it has operating within it the main factors underlying growth, namely, capital, technology, institutions, and human resources. Moreover, the processes and mechanisms should be controllable and subject to policy manipulation; for example, it is useful to discuss how the development of human resources in the NIEs substituted for the lack of natural resources.

### The Significance of Strategic Processes

In order to benefit from East Asia's rapid growth—or more specifically, to replicate that experience—we need to go beyond determining factors and learn more about the processes. Certain processes are not easy to replicate, as some basic forces underlying growth are difficult to change and manipulate. For example, in *Economic Growth in Monsoon Asia,* I point out that social values and beliefs from the prewar past were important in the differential postwar performances of East, South, and Southeast Asia. These social values are difficult to change, because they are deeply rooted in traditions and persist in present institutions. Given enough time, they could change through "moral" education courses.

This volume seeks a better understanding of the factors underlying growth by analyzing processes.[1] Regression analyses of the determinants of productivity growth have not produced satisfactory results. R. C. O. Matthews and his associates note that the "results of the econometric fitting of production functions have exhibited marked instability in the face of major modifications in data, specification, observation, period, and estimation method."[2] The difficulties may occur because growth involves movements from one disequilibrium to another. In a long-term phenomenon such as growth, causes become consequences, and consequences become causes in the unending chain of events. The causes underlying productivity growth become consequences in the next instance, and the self-sustaining nature of productivity growth is difficult to understand if the process as a whole is not examined.

It may be better to study the behavior of the factors within particular processes, because their behavior and impact on growth may vary with processes at various stages of development. A small amount of capital spent on irrigation and diversified cropping during the early stages of development may have just as much impact on growth as a much larger amount invested in the iron and steel industry. Returns to a given piece of land can be doubled with multiple cropping. Returns to investment in factories can be enhanced by operating the factories at full capacity with full employment. Education spent on a farmer cultivating a multiple-crop farm may have a higher payoff than the same amount of education spent on a farmer tilling a one-crop rice farm. Women's education may be the main factor in reducing fertility in the early stages of the demographic transition, but it is the full-time employment of housewives that is important in the later stage of the transition.

In nuclear physics, particles interact, transform, or disappear within certain processes, and the character of particles cannot be grasped outside such processes. A compression of the forces underlying long-term productivity growth into a few equations may do violence to the extreme complexity of the phenomenon. Unlike in the distant past, the forces of technology and institutions changed rapidly and incessantly in the twentieth century. Nor are the conventional factors of production today as simple as those in the early nineteenth century, when they were listed by the classical economists as land, labor, and capital. In the twentieth century, with the acceleration of technological progress, the varieties of technologies may number into the hundreds of millions, not in the hundreds as in the nineteenth century. This increase implies that labor cannot be classified simply as skilled or unskilled, as a variety of specialized skills are needed to operate the enormous range of technologies incorporated in equipment. Along with the acceleration of technological progress, capital came to be made up of a wide variety of equipment and buildings, whose respective contributions to growth varied widely. Innumerable institutions intervene to bring together, coordinate, and manage these interacting factors to reproduce a bewildering variety of outputs.

My previous book did not discuss policies in detail; in contrast, each chapter in this volume discusses the implications for policies. It does not, however, discuss policy design, which is best done by government economists, who specialize in the designing and implementation of policies: academic economists can merely point out the general directions for policy to take.

### The Nature of a Monsoon Economy

The theme of both this volume and my previous book is the nature of a monsoon economy.[3] Heavy monsoon rains fall for six months of the year, while there is very little rain during the other six months, giving rise to an agriculture different from that of the West and other regions—namely, paddy rice cultivation, which over the centuries has become very labor-intensive. For maximum yields, many workers are needed to prepare the seedling beds, dig up the seedlings, and transplant them. But after the harvest, in the dry half of the year, this enormous labor force is unable to find sufficient work. Some find work in handicrafts and services, also highly labor-intensive. As population increased faster than available land, farm size diminished and densities rose to be the greatest in the world by the end of the nineteenth century. If Asia is to escape from the stagnation and poverty imposed by the seasonality of its rains and its great rural population densities, it has to find a way to operate all year at high levels of employment.

High year-long employment cannot be found by pulling Asians out of agriculture and into industries, as early development economists such as Ragnar Nurkse, Arthur Lewis, and others recommended. The poverty of those remaining in agriculture would hinder the development of a market for industrialization. There is no choice but to provide more and better productive activities during the dry season, such as multiple cropping of nonrice products (fruits, vegetables, beans, and feeds for animals, which require less water than rice), animal husbandry, and fishery—but these call for the construction of rural infrastructure, such as irrigation and roads. The processing of the crops, in turn, provides off-farm jobs after harvesting.

With plenty of work opportunities during the slack months resulting in higher annual incomes and purchasing power in the rural areas, the demand for urban production rises. All of these factors eventually lead to a full-employment economy. This is the strategic turning point for a monsoon economy. Without full employment and rising real wages, capital-labor substitution and technological progress are slow, and productivity gains are minimal in agriculture, industry, and services. And if productivity does not rise, structural change is slow, and rural densities continue to rise as population increases with the expansion of the demand for labor. This vicious circle was shattered for the first time in monsoon Asia in East Asia.

*The Impact of the Technological Revolution on Monsoon Asia*

Although the civilizations of China and India were second to none during most of the first millennium A.D. and into the first half of the second millennium A.D., they began to fall behind the West, which made rapid progress during the mercantile, agricultural, and industrial revolutions. The technologies of these revolutions failed for various reasons to take root in Asia, and by the end of the nineteenth century, Asia became one of the poorest regions in the world, densely packed with tiny farms and traditional handicrafts and, eventually, falling prey to the stronger West, whose farms were much larger and whose industries more mechanized.

But things began to change after World War I in Japan and then after World War II in the rest of East Asia. The second industrial revolution in the West (in contrast to the first) brought forth mechanized technologies more suitable for the tiny farms and small industries of Asia.[4] Electric-powered machines and gas-powered internal combustion engines were suitable for small industries and farms because of their size, cheapness, efficiency, and the ease with which electric power could be brought into workshops. The steam-powered engines of the first industrial revolution require large boilers, shafts, transmission lines, and other equipment, which only large factories can afford to install.

The internal combustion engines of the twentieth century can be inserted into small cultivators and used to run the small harvesters of Asian farms, which are too small for big tractors and combines. Experimental stations and agricultural research brought forth higher yielding varieties of rice, while chemical industries created new and more potent fertilizers and insecticides. The agricultural innovations of the West in the previous centuries were, in contrast, almost entirely irrelevant to monsoon agriculture. Moreover, before Asia's population explosion in the twentieth century, all of its rural labor force was needed in the rice paddies during the monsoon season and could not be spared year-round for the factories of the first industrial revolution. Asian handicraft shops, using inexpensive tools and equipment, could hire farm workers during the dry months as part-time workers.

Japan was the first Asian country to take advantage of the technologies of the second industrial revolution. Its growth was slow after emerging from feudalism in the 1880s, but around the turn of the century its growth began to speed up. With comprehensive institutional changes enacted after World War II and the opening of Western markets in the 1950s and 1960s, Japan experienced rapid growth, which contributed to the growth of the Taiwanese and South Korean economies. The record of their growth, together with that of Hong Kong and Singapore, is exceptional in the annals of two centuries of modern economic growth and unmatched by any Western industrialized economy. It is all the more notable because the pattern of growth had a favorable impact on social development. Although South Asia did not do well, the ASEAN Four grew fairly well, with growth rates between those of East Asia and South Asia. Japan completed the first economic transition from a predominantly agricultural economy to a predominantly industrial one by the early 1960s, when the industrial labor force began to exceed the agricultural labor force. Taiwan completed the transition by the early 1970s, and South Korea by the early 1980s. By the early 1980s, Japan was the only country to complete the second transition, in which the service sector labor force begins to exceed the industrial labor force. The ASEAN Four was mid-way into the transition, but most of South Asia (and China) was still in the early stages.

These changes had demographic implications. With rapid mechanization and technological changes, parents realized that their children must be educated for their future employment and well-being. Because educating a large family would be costly, parents began to limit the number of children. Moreover, the availability of machines and power-driven equipment lessened the usefulness of children in the home, on the farm, and in other family businesses, since equipment could be substituted for children's help. In the factories and workshops, also, the substitution of machines for unskilled labor lowered the demand for young, untrained workers, and full-employment economies enabled housewives to find jobs outside the home, raising the opportunity cost of rearing children at home.

Thus, the mechanization of monsoon economies not only laid the basis for the transition from a predominantly agricultural to predominantly industrial economy but also contributed to the demographic transition from high to low fertility and from large to small families.

It is the purpose of this volume to discuss the details of some postwar growth processes. I pay special attention to a mechanism in these processes that was central to initiating the sustained growth in East Asia—the mechanism through which, with multiple cropping and off-farm jobs, underemployed workers became fully employed during the dry season. The expanding purchasing power of these workers allowed urban industries to raise employment. With the continuation of this process, real wages rose faster than returns on capital; as labor became scarce, substitution of capital for labor accelerated, and pro- ductivity per worker rose with technological progress. This mechanism was essential in raising productivity per worker. As long as the economy was far from the technological frontier, full-employment growth was not inflationary. On the farms, machines substituted for workers who migrated to industry for higher paying jobs, and when migration slowed, machines embodying new technologies substituted for older machines.

*A Review of Economic Growth in the 1980s*

In the 1980s, both East Asia and the ASEAN Four were affected by the slowdown in the industrialized West, with which they traded a great deal; South Asia did somewhat better relative to its previous performance. But as a whole, the 1980s were generally a continuation of past trends, with East Asia leading the way (table 1.1). The big surprise was the performance of China, which registered close to double-digit rates of growth of net material product. World Bank estimates of GDP show that China registered the highest growth rate in Asia in 1980–88. The liberalization of Communist institutions unleashed the energies of the Chinese peasantry, who not only raised yields on their farms but established rural enterprises and earned off-farm incomes (as Japan and Taiwan had in previous decades). But the greater purchasing power of the peasant was not met by corresponding increases in urban output: prices rose when the urban state enterprises could not raise output. These enterprises must also be liber- alized if rapid growth is to be sustained. And if peasants are to be induced to improve the productivity of their farms—with terracing, irrigation, drainage, leveling, and other land improvements—ownership of the land must be trans- ferred to the peasantry in place of short-term leases. But instead of instituting greater liberalization and democratization, Chinese leaders tightened control and centralization.

Despite Japan's slow growth in the 1980s, its 4.1 percent was higher than that of the West. Singapore was hit hard in 1985 and 1986 by the stagnant economies of the ASEAN Four. Hong Kong, Taiwan, and South Korea did

TABLE 1.1

Growth of Gross Domestic Product, 1950s to 1990 (percent)

| Country | 1950s–1970s | 1980–1990 |
|---|---|---|
| Nineteen industrialized countries[a] | 3.7[b] | 3.1 |
| Japan | 8.0 | 4.1 |
| South Korea | 7.7 | 9.7 |
| Taiwan | 8.7 | 7.5 |
| Hong Kong | 9.5 | 7.1 |
| Singapore | 8.1 | 6.4 |
| Malaysia | 6.0 | 5.2 |
| Thailand | 7.1 | 7.6 |
| Indonesia | 5.2 | 5.5 |
| Philippines | 6.0 | 0.9 |
| India | 3.6 | 5.3 |
| Bangladesh | 3.8 | 4.3 |
| Sri Lanka | 4.2 | 4.0 |
| Nepal | 2.5 | 4.6 |

*Source:* Asian Development Bank, *Key Indicators;* World Bank, *World Development Report;* Harry Oshima, *Economic Growth in Monsoon Asia: A Comparative Survey* (Tokyo: University of Tokyo Press, 1987).

*Note:* Asian regions are unweighted.

[a] Ireland, Israel, Spain, Belgium, the United Kingdom, Italy, Australia, the Netherlands, Austria, France, Canada, the United States, Denmark, Germany, Norway, Sweden, Japan, Finland, and Switzerland. The 1980–90 growth rate for the United States, the United Kingdom, France, Germany, and Italy was 2.6 percent.

[b] 1965–80.

exceptionally well as they shifted to high-technology production for exports. Hence, East Asia continued to lead not only monsoon Asia but also the world in the pace of growth. The ASEAN Four dragged behind East Asia, as it had in the past. Its poor performance was largely due to the unfavorable prices received for its basic commodity exports (coconut, sugar, palm oil, and rubber) and the troubles it encountered with its heavy industries—into which Indonesia, Malaysia, and the Philippines had poured large investments from easily obtainable loans from the Middle East. This was not the case with Thailand, which wisely resisted the temptation to borrow. Instead, it diversified its export markets to include East Asia and the industrialized countries. As earlier, Thailand had the best performance among the ASEAN Four. In the closing years of the 1980s, as full employment neared, Thailand's GNP still grew at near double-digit rates.

The Philippines faltered badly, showing the lowest growth rate in the entire region. Marcos's corruption and mismanagement were the main but not the only reasons: the Aquino government was apparently not able to reduce corruption and improve management, dominated as it was by a combination of landlords and import-substitution industrialists who have been primarily responsible for the lethargy of the Philippine economy throughout the postwar era. Malaysia, like Thailand, has been the beneficiary of foreign investments, especially from Japan, Taiwan, and South Korea, whose labor-intensive industries have become increasingly noncompetitive as currencies have been revaluated and wages have risen.

In South Asia, India and Sri Lanka made major changes in strategy: shifting from capital-intensive to labor-intensive industrialization and paying greater attention to agriculture. There were only marginal changes in Bangladesh and Nepal, both of which remained stagnant. Despite these and other changes and the willingness of their elites to learn from Southeast Asia and East Asia, South Asia grew slowly in the late 1980s, even by the standards of Southeast Asia. The notion has been presented that the better showing of Southeast Asia is due to the Chinese residents of these countries. But while there is no denying that the Nanyan Chinese have been responsible for the vigor of the urban sector, the main reason for the good performance of Thailand, Malaysia, and Indonesia in the 1960s and 1970s was the contribution of the agricultural sector—the work of Thai peasants in Thailand, of Indian workers on British plantations and of Malay peasants in Malaysia, and of Javanese peasants in Indonesia. In contrast, the Philippines, with a large number of Chinese *mestizos,* did badly. Perhaps it was Confucian social values that were responsible for the faster growth of East Asia and Southeast Asia compared to South Asia, whose Islamic and Hindu social values may have been less suitable for modern economic growth.

India, the Philippines, and China, seeing the troubles they were having with their capital-intensive industries and the regulations needed to protect them, began to shift to labor-intensive industrialization, agricultural development, deregulation, and privatization. But the incubus of the past could not be easily overcome, and the vested interests that had grown up around the capital-intensive industries (with protectionism) began to assert their power, slowing the shift. China was most successful in making the shift. The situation is not bright for India and the Philippines. The Philippines' only hope is to turn to foreign investors and entrepreneurs, who may furnish enough competition to the monopolies that dominate the Philippine economy to make them more competitive. There is also an urgent need for agrarian reform that can bring about better working arrangements to furnish more employment.

In contrast, South Korea, Taiwan, Hong Kong, and Singapore are easily making the shift to capital intensity, high technology, and deregulation. These small nations grew most rapidly, despite the potentials of large mass markets in the larger Asian nations. It may be that these countries were forced to raise efficiency quickly through labor-intensive industries in order to export, while large countries, relying on domestic markets, went in for the scale economy of heavy industries. The latter requires costly and sophisticated technology and skills (which in turn require long experience) before becoming efficient enough to export.

The basic problem with both Indonesia and Bangladesh is that Java (with two-thirds of the Indonesian population) and Bangladesh have the highest rural population densities in the world. For hundreds of years, Bangladesh—with plenty of water—served as the "rice bowl" of the Indian continent, beginning with the Mughal conquerors of India in the sixteenth century, who took rice from Bangladesh to feed their armies in India. Under the British, the peasants paid rice as land revenue not only to their landlord but to the British conquerors. To produce all this and their own sustenance, the paddies had to be cultivated intensively, so that population densities rose.[5] The Dutch in Java forced the peasantry to produce cash crops such as coffee, sugar, and tea, which were exported to Europe to bolster the crumbling Dutch Empire. To produce the commercial crops for the Dutch and food for their families, the Javanese peasantry had to raise larger families to have enough manpower.[6] Java eventually found itself with too many people on too little land.[7]

After World War II, Bangladesh, as part of Pakistan, became separated from India, but after two decades of stagnation it seceded from Pakistan because it found few advantages as an appendage to that country. After secession in 1972, independent Bangladesh began the task of nation building; its natural resources were meager and it had to be supported with large doses of foreign aid. After centuries of exploitation, decades of war, instability, difficulties with the Hindus (who were brought in by the British as administrators and traders), and independence and internal struggles, there was little opportunity to establish social and physical infrastructures, such as irrigation and drainage systems, which were badly needed to support a large population. Land reform was attempted but resulted in land divided into patches too small to raise per capita incomes, since population grew faster than food supply. Schools had to be built, since the population was almost completely illiterate, and industries had to be established to process jute, cotton, and other raw materials. Family planning programs had to be started to hold down population increases. With so many problems and so few resources, progress was slow.

Indonesia fared better after World War II but only after nearly two decades of turmoil: a war of liberation against the Dutch, who attempted to reassert their control, and battles to force Sumatra and Sulawesi to remain in the Indonesian Republic. Not long after the islands were unified, internal struggles within Java broke out, with Communists attempting a takeover. When stability was finally achieved in the mid-1960s, the government found that it could not get the nation moving. The Dutch had done very little for Indonesian education; schools had to be built and teachers had to be trained. To become self-sufficient in rice and to conserve foreign exchange for industrialization, the productivity of the peasantry had to be raised with modern rice cultivation methods. The bureaucracy had to be built up with Indonesian officials. Finally, Indonesia, like India, had to contend with ethnic, communal, regional, and religious diversity before it could achieve national solidarity. Thus, unlike the Philippines and Sri Lanka, which started on the road to development immediately after World War II, Indonesia and Bangladesh took nearly two decades to get started.

However, after attaining stability, Indonesia (unlike Bangladesh) registered good rates of GDP growth, averaging 5.2 percent between 1950 and 1980. This was partly due to the discovery of oil and the rehabilitation of commercial crop plantations, whose output was exported at good prices in the 1970s. But prices fell in the 1980s, and growth slowed. Moreover, the government made some bad investments in establishing large capital-intensive industries (iron and steel, paper and pulp, automobiles, heavy machinery, etc.), which lost heavily, since they were difficult to manage. Indonesia began to show balance of payments deficits as exports slowed and large payments had to be made to service the foreign debts incurred for the big industries.

With the labor force expanding rapidly as a result of the population explosion in the 1960s and the education of women, the young people in the rural areas were unable to find jobs on the tiny farms of Java and had to move into the cities, where employment was also difficult to find. Unemployment in the cities and underemployment in rural areas emerged as problems for Indonesia. There is hope that after full employment is reached in Malaysia and Thailand, foreign investments may turn increasingly to Indonesia.

Unlike these countries—with too many people on insufficient land—the small mountain kingdoms of the Himalayas—Nepal, Bhutan, and Sikkim—are sparsely settled. Nevertheless, rice paddies in the scattered valleys are insufficient to support the people in the densely populated hills. The hostile mountain climate (except in the lowlands of Nepal), despite plenty of monsoon rain, keeps productivity and per capita income low. The villages are widely separated, transportation and communication between villages are difficult, and literacy and education are minimal, leaving the population backward and poorly fed. Under these circumstances, absolute monarchies and aristocracies remain powerful, ruling serfs and even slaves in feudal economies. Some progress has been made with land reform, and curtailment of the power of kings and nobles, and the establishment of modern institutions such as schools, hospitals, and roads, but these improvements take time to be implemented effectively in these inaccessible Himalayan kingdoms. They are still a century behind those countries that restricted the power of the nobility and monarchy some time ago.

Asia also contains large areas not reached by the monsoons. They are found in the northern and western parts of China, western India, western Pakistan, and eastern Indonesia. Having no monsoon rains and rice paddies, Manchuria, Mongolia, and Tibet are sparsely settled, with the population subsisting on wheat, barley, buckwheat, potatoes, and other root crops. Most parts of arid Pakistan in the west grow wheat with water from the Indus River, which starts in the north and runs down the length of Pakistan. This water comes from the monsoons reaching the mountain range of the Pamirs in the north. Extensive irrigation provides waters to both sides of the Indus River in much the same way that the Nile irrigates the dry lands of Egypt. But because wheat farms do not support as many people per acre as monsoon rice paddies, Pakistan is sparsely settled.

There is enough rain to feed a large population in monsoon Asia but not enough in nonmonsoon Asia, despite large tracts of flatland. There is plenty of rain in the mountain kingdoms of the Himalayas but not enough farmland to support a large population. In Java and Bangladesh, historical forces have concentrated too many people on too small farms. And where the rains fall heavily all year round, as in most parts of Sumatra, Kalimantan, and Sulawesi, uninhabitable rain forests grow.

In Japan, Taiwan, South Korea, and Thailand, the monsoons do not bring excessive nor insufficient rain, as in Tibet, Mongolia, and Pakistan; nor did Heaven impose on them the towering Himalayas, which block the rains in Tibet; nor did history deposit so many people, as in Java and Bangladesh.

PREVIEW OF CHAPTERS

Underlying the productivity growth of East Asia were high rates of capital formation, technological progress, and savings, full employment, multiple cropping, off-farm employment, the development of human resources, the alleviation of income disparity and poverty, and governments that served and promoted these processes.

In part 1, comprising chapters 2, 3, and 4, productivity is a major concern because productivity growth underlies per capita income growth and is necessary if the growth of the economy is to be self-sustaining. According to Engel's law, smaller portions of the increasing incomes are spent on food, and if this law is generalized to include other consumption items, national savings rise with increasing incomes from productivity growth. In chapter 2 I compare the record of productivity changes, quantify the increment to GNP from productivity gains, and estimate the amount saved from the increments. I find that productivity rose faster and a larger share of productivity gains was saved in the East Asian countries than in other monsoon Asian countries.

East Asia also promoted productivity through technological progress, which was slower in South and Southeast Asia. Also, with fewer natural resources than in other countries, East Asian countries were compelled to export in order to import natural resources; to export, they had to improve their competitiveness in the international market by raising the efficiency of their capital through better technologies and a trained labor force. In the efficiency with which technologies were selected, imported, adapted, and disseminated in the 1950s and 1960s, Japan led the way by means of government intervention. The other East Asian countries followed suit. Technological experience was necessary to

Japan's shift from the importation to the generation of technology when the technological frontier was reached in the late 1970s.

Chapter 4 takes up personal savings and consumption. Since there is a limit to foreign borrowing, which must be repaid sooner or later, internal savings, in the long run, sustain capital formation, and personal savings contribute the most to internal savings. The share saved was largest in East Asia, which adopted an export-led strategy, resulting in the slow growth of consumption despite the rapid growth of personal income. Because of the emphasis on education in Confucian ethics, parents saved for their children's future education so that they would get a good start in life and in building family fortunes (to please the ancestors). Since social security benefits and loans for housing were insufficient, they saved for their old age and retirement and for buying homes. To save more, consumption had to be reduced: it can be said that East Asian families targeted the maximization of savings and consumed the residual, and not the other way around. By the 1980s, these countries were saving more than their domestic investment needs, and the excess was flowing abroad to finance investment.

An important process by which capital and technology were accumulated and productivity was raised in East Asia was by reaching and sustaining full employment, which, in turn, accelerated capital-labor substitution. This was not possible without the reduction of underemployment (taken up in chapter 5). The most difficult problem in monsoon Asia, with its many months of dry weather, is the reduction of underemployment, which is of double-digit magnitude in most countries of South Asia and Southeast Asia. Chapter 5 shows how East Asia dealt with the problem of underemployment. Chapter 6 takes up in detail multiple cropping as one process by which underemployment was reduced. Multiple cropping enables farm families to cultivate more than one crop of rice and, after rice self-sufficiency, to move into nonrice crops: vegetables, fruits, and animal feeds. This process took place most rapidly in East Asia; the construction of extensive irrigation and other rural infrastructure was the key step, together with an efficient farm extension system, cooperation, land reform, and credit (especially in Japan and Taiwan).

Moreover, diversified crops require more processing than rice; this together with packing, storing, marketing, and transporting, contributed to employment in the rural sector. Diversification represented structural change in the agricultural sector and initiated the shift of the labor force to industries and services. Industrial and service wages, together with off-farm incomes, raised the incomes of farm families, giving them greater buying power and savings, which in turn expanded urban industries and services, which hired more rural laborers. For the first time in the long history of monsoon Asia, the rural population was reduced.

In chapter 7, it is noted that, even when farms are provided with irrigation for dry season cultivation, farmers still have time for more work. East Asian countries (Japan in the 1950s and Taiwan in the 1960s) began to expand opportunities for farmers with off-farm work in food processing and industry. The growth of off-farm jobs enabled East Asian countries to reach full employment throughout the year, as farm incomes nearly doubled and purchasing power for urban goods and services expanded. When shortages of urban labor occurred, smaller industries in the cities sought labor in the rural sector and relocated to small cities and towns. Off-farm employment was more extensive among small farms with large amounts of surplus labor, and thus income disparities lessened. With more income and less labor, farms had to purchase machines and equipment, which contributed to higher productivity per worker. But in South Asia and Southeast Asia, off-farm incomes were insufficient, and underemployment persisted, preventing the full labor force from contributing to production (with the exception of Thailand in the late 1980s).

Chapter 8 deals with the role of human resources in productivity. In heavily populated Asia, it is not the quantitative but the qualitative aspects of human resources that are important. If the quality is not improved and the efficiency of human resources raised, not enough people can be employed. Densely populated East Asia was able to relieve population pressure through human resource development. Confucian ethics, like Protestant ethics, were favorable for East Asian growth (although in China, Communist institutions constrained the realization of Confucian teachings, and campaigns against Confucius were conducted). South Asia's Islamic and Hindu social values were not helpful to modern development; Theravada Buddhism in Sri Lanka and Burma also did not help development, although it did not prevent growth in Thailand. Nor were Catholicism in the Philippines and Islam in Indonesia appropriate for development. Besides religion, other dimensions in the cultural heritage of South Asia and Southeast Asia were not favorable to development.

In the postwar decade, East Asia continued its large investments in education and developed a formidable work force—well educated and highly trained in vocational skills. Other countries in Asia, especially China and South Asian countries, began the postwar era with meager educational stocks and had to build schools. The exceptions were Sri Lanka and the Philippines, which started with high levels of general education but which had neglected vocational training.

In chapter 9, I show that poverty incidence in Asia declined in the 1970s and the early 1980s, as the economy raised employment levels. Japan and Taiwan eradicated poverty and raised low incomes with multiple cropping and off-farm jobs, especially on the smallest farms, plus plentiful work in the urban sector. Sustained full employment raised not only the level of employment but also the wages of unskilled workers, as labor shortages occurred in the lower occupations. Low-income families—with prospects for jobs, food, housing, and health facilities—were motivated to work hard to raise themselves out of poverty. Growth in East Asia affected not only the affluent but also the lower class, which sought to educate its children and move into the middle class. This meant that productivity in marginal industries and occupations rose, thereby improving income inequality.

Chapter 10 presents the record of government activities in the form of expenditures for various functions, among which educational expenditures are very important in the growth of productivity. The other important task of government is the building of physical and institutional infrastructures. East Asian government expenditure patterns appear more appropriate than those of other monsoon Asian governments for enhancing productivity and economic growth, and these countries carried out their policies with a better trained and more diligent bureaucracy.

With the decline of communism in Europe, there may be a rejuvenation in the West, and the twenty-first century may see two economic centers, one in the Pacific and another in the Atlantic, peacefully competing for economic supremacy. Governments will play a major role in the realization of what may be the Pacific century. East Asian countries, besides investing in the industries of Southeast Asia, should open their markets to these countries' exports. In turn, Southeast Asia should liberalize their policies to improve the climate for foreign investments. Japan will play a crucial role in providing the initiative in technological and institutional transfers, trade and investment, and regional cooperation.

Figure 1.1 summarizes the strategic processes in monsoon Asia's productivity growth and changes in income distribution. Central to the processes is full employment, through which East Asia was able to accelerate growth and pull ahead of the rest of Asia in the postwar era. Reaching full employment in the rural sector by multiple cropping and off-farm activities, they raised wages, sped up capital-labor substitution, and increased productivity. At the same time, with incomes rising as unemployment diminished, savings rose, making available more capital for the capital-labor substitution process and for education and food consumption. Both as causes and consequences, structural change and export earnings accelerated.[8] The other countries of monsoon Asia, with large pools of idle labor, were unable to move into a full employment growth path, and growth was much slower than in the past decades.

The message of this volume is that other monsoon Asian countries should give top priority to employment generation. Since these countries are far from the technological frontier, full employment will speed the process of importing technologies from abroad. In the 1990s, with Thailand and Malaysia leading the way, other South and Southeast Asian countries will, it is hoped, follow in the footsteps of East Asia.

Many studies have searched for the causes of the exceptional growth of East Asian countries. The rationale for yet one more study is that this study looks for causes beyond the proximate, such as exports, productivity, and capital accumulation, into more distal processes and mechanisms, such as employment

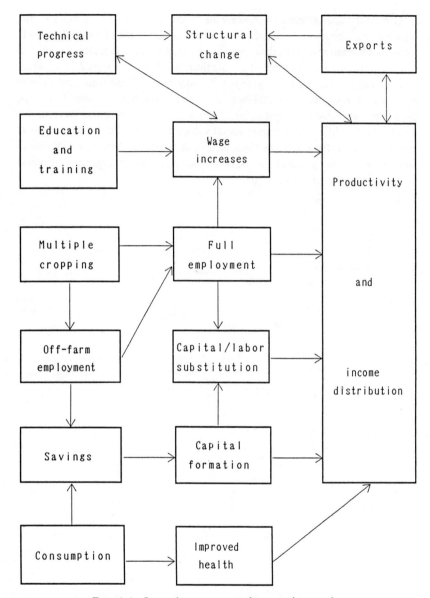

FIG. 1.1. Strategic processes and economic growth.

generation, multiple cropping, social values, and human resource development. It is not helpful to tell countries anxious to learn from East Asia that they must raise savings, productivity, and exports, as has been done in the past. They have to know how savings, productivity, and exports can be increased.

One final question remains. Among the processes singled out in this volume, which one is the most strategic for monsoon Asia? It may be tautological to single out human resources development as the most strategic; after all, human resources are the basic source of production, and human beings do the saving and investing, innovate and create new technologies, till the land, and work in factories, stores, and offices. Hence, the more developed the labor force, the greater the efficiency of capital, land, and technology. But going beyond this generality, the differences among social values may underlie the differences in growth between the countries discussed in this volume. Strong social values were behind the long hours of work—and the consumption forgone—by workers and entrepreneurs in East Asia.

# PART I

## Productivity and Proximate Processes

# CHAPTER 2

# Differential Productivity Trends

PRODUCTIVITY AND ECONOMIC GROWTH

Fundamental to economic growth is productivity growth, that is, the rise of per worker product. Without productivity gains, the growth of per capita incomes and exports, for example, cannot be sustained. Per capita product may be related to the demand side of GNP, and per worker product to the supply side. The difference between the two concepts is the inclusion of the dependent population in the denominator of per capita product and its exclusion in per worker product.[1] When per worker product rises, per capita product rises too unless it is offset by a proportionate rise in the number of dependents.

With the slowing of population growth in East Asia, there is a tendency for the growth of per worker and per capita product to converge—but not always. For example, with output constant, if the number of dependents are falling but the size of the work force is rising, per capita product rises even though per worker product falls. In terms of levels, as distinct from changes, high levels of labor force participation rates such as in Thailand and China imply that per capita product is higher than per worker product relative to countries where labor force participation rates are low. Thus in 1986, the productivity of the Thais, with the highest labor force participation in Asia (76 percent), had the same per worker productivity as the Filipinos ($1,550), but per capita product was much higher in Thailand ($810, compared to $560 in the Philippines). Since higher participation rates are due to the higher propensity of Thai women to work outside the home, productivity growth may be slower than otherwise because women workers tend to be less educated or trained and tend to work fewer hours per day than male workers.[2]

The importance of productivity in economic growth is shown by the fact that productivity growth accounted for about 80 percent of the growth of per capita product in Western countries during the century before 1960.[3] During the first half of the twentieth century, when Britain was losing its industrial supremacy, its growth rate of labor productivity was less than 1 percent per year.[4] During that same time period, this rate was more than 2 percent in the other industrialized countries and was 2.5 percent in Japan. The increase in GDP as a result of productivity gains averaged about 40 percent of total GDP in the postwar decades in East Asia, 30 percent among the ASEAN Four, and 20 percent in South Asia.

In what follows, no attempt is made to measure the various sources of productivity growth, as many have done. Nor is there an attempt to assign values to capital and labor to see how much each contributed to the growth of GNP, as is done by the Solow growth equations. Not only are the necessary data unavailable in most Asian countries, but some of the methods of measuring the contribution are somewhat arbitrary and unsatisfactory. Much can be learned by a comparative account of the factors contributing to differential productivity growth without measuring specific contributions. In the chapters that follow, the importance of savings, investment, technology, natural resources, employment, education, and so on is assessed. But more than factor inputs (both their quantity and quality) go into productivity changes: balance in the allocation of resources and such nonquantifiable forces as political stability are also important.

I use labor productivity (or product per employment or worker) as the measure of productivity. It would be preferable to use total factor productivity, but data on total capital stock for the earlier period are not available for most of the countries.[5] In any case, I take into account the contributions of capital and technology (using investment and other approximations) and the contributions of the quality of the labor force (using education and other data).

Estimates of GDP (the numerator of product per worker) are taken from the official national accounts. I use GDP instead of GNP as I am interested not in the welfare of residents but in the capability of both residents and nonresidents to work and produce. It would have been better to work with net domestic product or national income concepts, but depreciation estimates are likely to be somewhat arbitrary. As a measure of current production, GDP or GNP estimates have certain defects: they do not adequately take into account improvement in the quality of products over time or social costs such as pollution and environmental degradation. They also exclude many social benefits, such as housewives' services and the services of consumer durables, although social costs and benefits tend to roughly cancel each other out.

These conceptual problems are less important than statistical problems in South and Southeast Asia. Generally, GDP is figured from the output side, where total production originating in each industry is converted into gross product by deducting input purchased from the other industries in order to eliminate duplications. For rice agriculture and organized industry, there is sufficient information, but several countries do not have adequate data on nonrice crops and on animal, fishery, and forestry products except from decennial agricultural censuses. Even for the years when industrial and commercial censuses and surveys were undertaken, the information on smaller units— industries, retail and wholesale shops, taxis, personal service units, and so on—are not available. These are by no means of negligible importance.

Problems exist in the deflation of product originating. The wholesale price for each detailed product and the price of each input purchased in the process of production are needed, but except for Japan, Taiwan, and South Korea, the data are insufficient. These difficulties are greater for the earlier years, when sources of data were scarce. Despite these flaws, the estimates on product originating are the best in the national accounts of most nations, and they are usable for establishing long-run trends, even though small changes may not be reliable for Southeast and South Asia, where data sources are less plentiful and less reliable than for East Asia.

There are also conceptual and statistical difficulties in the employment data, which are derived from the decennial population censuses and labor force surveys. Those included in the labor force must be ten years old and older for most South Asian countries and fifteen years and older for East Asia, with ten to fourteen years as the cutoff age for Southeast Asian countries. More important is the definition of housewives in the labor force: some countries define a minimum standard of work hours for housewives to be included in the labor force (twenty hours per week in Thailand), but others do not, leaving it up to the respondents to determine their status.

The major statistical issues are frequency of the surveys and extent of under-employment. Census data are taken one time in the censual years, usually in the slack time of the monsoon season, and thus do not represent the employment situation during the busier months, perhaps understating employment for the year. Conversely, if the census is taken in a busy month, there may be an overstatement. Labor force surveys, usually taken each quarter in South and Southeast Asia, represent better the year-round situation, but not as adequately as the monthly surveys of East Asia. Frequency of the surveys is important for the data on hours of work. Usually, labor force surveys consider a worker to be employed if he or she works at least one hour in the reference week of the survey. Hence, the employment data include all those in the labor force working from one hour a week to fifty-five or more hours. This issue is different from the one relating to hours that housewives work a week. Population censuses do not collect data on hours of work—nor did the earlier labor force surveys. If they did, the denominator of productivity estimates could be annual aggregate hours of work instead of the cruder measure, employment.

Estimates of per capita product converted into U.S. dollars overstate Japanese levels of purchasing power compared to U.S. and other countries' per capita income. Prices in Japan are much higher than in the United States because of low productivity per worker in Japanese agriculture and services, which are dominated by tiny units of production. Japanese per capita dollar income also may overstate Japanese purchasing power over that of other Asian countries, especially those with overvalued exchange rates, such as the Philippines, India, and China.[6]

The significance of productivity increases lies primarily in the increased savings made possible by the higher incomes (higher wages and property incomes) from productivity gains. Much of the higher property incomes are saved, and these savings are invested in material and human capital and contribute to the rise in productivity in the future. The greater the gain in productivity, the larger the amount that can be invested in material and human capital, and the greater the rise in future productivity. Hence, the importance of productivity gains is that the potential for the future growth of per capita product is raised, contributing to a self-sustaining process in economic growth. Some part of productivity gains paid out to workers in higher wages may also be saved, although most of the gains are probably consumed. Increased wages enhance the incentive to work and motivate workers to improve labor productivity in the future.

In the early period of an agroindustrial transition, savings are scarce, which constrains future growth so that the larger the amount saved, the greater the impact on future growth. This may not be the situation after an economy has passed through its transition and is well on its way to being a service economy, as in the case of Japan and Taiwan, where internal savings tend to exceed domestic capital needs. Service sectors require much less capital than industrial sectors.

PRODUCTIVITY STATISTICS

In table 2.1 growth rates of productivity in Asian countries are shown, beginning for most countries in the 1960s, since population censuses and labor force surveys were not begun until the late 1950s or early 1960s. The faster growth of product per capita over product per worker reflects the slower growth of population (i.e., in the dependent population) compared to that of the labor force, except in South Korea, Thailand, Pakistan, and China, where population grew faster than the labor force, given the GDP growth rate. If population growth and labor force growth are equal, then product per capita and product per worker are equal.

The East Asian growth rate of product per worker of 5.4 percent over two and a half decades is unusually high. It is nearly twice the rates of the ASEAN Four. If hourly productivity is used, productivity growth may be more than twice as high, since average hours may have been declining faster (or increasing more slowly) in East Asia than in Southeast Asia. (Figures for the ASEAN Four are not reliable.)

Japan led East Asian productivity growth in the 1960s. Beginning in the 1970s, there was a slowdown, as Japan approached the technological frontier and could not import technologies as readily as before. Productivity growth was high in Japan and Taiwan (and probably in Hong Kong) during the 1950s (about 4 percent), when other East Asian countries had barely begun the development

TABLE 2.1

Growth of Productivity per Worker, 1960s to 1980s (percent)

| Country | 1960s | 1970s | 1980s | Average 1960s–80s | Product per Capita 1960s–80s | Product Gains as % of GDP 1955–84 |
|---|---|---|---|---|---|---|
| Japan | 9.3 | 4.0 | 2.8$^a$ | 5.6 | 5.9 | 37.6 |
| Taiwan | 6.7 | 6.0 | 4.7 | 5.8 | 6.4 | 43.7 |
| South Korea | 6.5$^b$ | 5.5 | 6.1 | 6.0$^c$ | 4.7 | 39.1 |
| Hong Kong | 5.6$^d$ | 5.8$^e$ | 4.8$^f$ | 5.4$^g$ | 6.1$^h$ | 41.0 |
| Singapore | 7.0$^i$ | 3.9 | 4.7 | 5.1$^j$ | 6.5 | 43.8 |
| Philippines | 2.3 | 2.0 | −2.2 | 0.8 | 1.5 | 24.5 |
| Thailand | 5.2 | 3.8$^k$ | 2.5$^f$ | 4.0 | 3.9 | 36.1 |
| Malaysia | 3.8$^m$ | 5.4 | 2.0 | 3.8$^n$ | 4.1 | 32.0 |
| Indonesia | 2.3$^d$ | 3.8$^e$ | 0.5$^a$ | 2.3 | 3.2 | 28.9 |
| India | 4.3 | 0.8 | | 2.5$^r$ | | 20.8 |
| Burma | | 2.3$^k$ | 1.6 | 1.9$^q$ | 2.2 | 20.8 |
| Bangladesh | | 4.1$^r$ | −1.9$^f$ | 1.1$^s$ | 2.5$^s$ | 15.9 |
| Pakistan | | 1.5 | 3.8$^a$ | 2.5$^t$ | 2.4$^t$ | 28.7 |
| United States | 1.4 | −0.7 | 1.1 | 0.5 | 1.9$^u$ | |

*Source:* Official national accounts and yearbooks; Asian Development Bank, *Key Indicators;* International Labor Organization, *Yearbook of Labor Statistics;* United Nations, *Yearbook of National Accounts;* World Bank, *World Tables;* Harry Oshima, *Economic Growth in Monsoon Asia: A Comparative Survey* (Tokyo: University of Tokyo Press, 1987); United States, *Economic Report of the President 1986.*

*Note:* The decades show ten years' of data except where indicated: $^a$1980–81, $^b$1963–69, $^c$1963–88, $^d$1961–71, $^e$1971–79, $^f$1980–86, $^g$1961–88, $^h$1960–86, $^i$1966–70, $^j$1966–88, $^k$1972–79, $^m$1962–67, $^n$1962–88, $^p$average of 1960s and 1970s, $^q$1972–88, $^r$1973–79, $^s$1973–86, $^t$1970–87, $^u$1980–85.

process. But these others were not far behind, and East Asian growth rates were similar. Among the ASEAN Four, on the other hand, Thailand grew steadily throughout the postwar period, but the Philippines, which started out well in the 1950s, faltered thereafter.

Table 2.2 shows data on growth rates of product per worker for the three broad sectors, agriculture (crops, forestry, fishing, and livestock), industry (mining, manufacturing, utilities, transport, storage, and communication), and services (commerce and private and public services). Productivity in agriculture, if computed by man-hours of work in the denominator, may be higher than in the table, because many farm workers spend part of their time during the slack months of farming in the industrial and service sectors. To the extent that these workers are included in agriculture ($A$), their contributions to output in the other two sectors ($I$ and $S$) are included in the numerators of $I$ and $S$ productivity estimation, thereby overstating the productivity of workers in $I$ and $S$. These biases may, over the decades, be substantial for Japan and Taiwan, where incomes of farm families from off-farm employment have risen substan-

TABLE 2.2
Sector Productivity Growth per Worker, 1960s to 1980s (percent)

| Country | Agriculture | | | | Industry | | | | Services | | | |
|---|---|---|---|---|---|---|---|---|---|---|---|---|
| | 1960s | 1970s | 1980s | Average | 1960s | 1970s | 1980s | Average | 1960s | 1970s | 1980s | Average |
| Japan | 6.3 | 3.8 | 2.6 | 4.2 | 8.9 | 4.9 | 2.6 | 5.5 | 6.9 | 2.8 | 2.0 | 3.9 |
| Taiwan | 4.2[a] | 4.3 | 1.7 | 3.4 | 7.5[a] | 4.8 | 5.4 | 5.9 | 3.7[a] | 4.0 | 2.6 | 3.4 |
| South Korea | 5.9[b] | 4.3 | 9.0 | 6.4 | 7.5[b] | 7.0 | 5.4 | 6.6 | 3.3[b] | 1.8 | 2.1 | 2.4 |
| Hong Kong | 8.3 | 4.9 | | 6.6 | 2.8 | 3.0 | | 2.9 | 7.6 | 4.7 | | 6.2 |
| Singapore | 10.1 | 6.9 | 9.1 | 8.7 | 5.3 | 4.7 | 5.5 | 5.2 | 5.5 | 2.8 | 4.6 | 4.3 |
| Thailand | 3.9 | 2.6 | 4.0 | 3.5 | 4.6 | 0.2 | 0.6 | 1.8 | 5.6 | 2.0 | -0.2 | 2.5 |
| Philippines | 3.0 | 1.0[c] | 0.2 | 1.4 | 2.7 | 5.8[c] | -3.3 | 1.7 | -2.9 | -1.4[c] | -11.8 | -5.4 |
| Malaysia | 6.1 | 4.1 | 3.2 | 4.5 | 4.9 | 3.1 | 1.6 | 3.2 | 3.4 | 2.9 | 0.7 | 2.3 |
| Indonesia | 1.9 | 2.3 | 0.1 | 1.4 | 1.2 | 4.6 | -2.5 | 1.1 | 0.3 | 0.4 | 1.9 | 0.9 |
| India | 2.9 | 0.4 | | 1.7 | 5.4 | 1.1 | | 3.2 | 4.9 | 0.7 | | 2.8 |
| Sri Lanka | 1.6 | 0.3 | | 1.0 | 4.9 | 1.5 | | 3.2 | 4.2 | 2.6 | | 3.4 |

Source: See table 2.1

Note: The decades show ten years' of data except where indicated.

[a] 1961–69.

[b] 1963–69.

[c] 1970–78.

tially. The biases are reduced to the extent that housewives and schoolchildren, who are not part of the labor force, help out during the busy periods of planting and harvesting. This may not be important for Japan, South Korea, and Taiwan, where children are not required to help and are urged to study, but may be substantial for other countries. The bias is also reduced when workers classified in the $I$ and $S$ sectors help out with farm work during the busy months. The data to correct these biases for and against agriculture are not available for any of the countries, but the impression is strong that for countries where off-farm work is large (Japan, Taiwan, South Korea, Thailand, and Malaysia), productivity growth in agriculture is understated and is overstated in the other two sectors.

A major reason for the high growth of overall productivity in East Asia is the good performance of all three sectors. Among the ASEAN Four, the $I$ and $S$ sectors had a poor showing. This suggests that the factors underlying productivity gains in East Asia, such as favorable social values and the education and training of the labor force, cut across sectors—in contrast to technological progress, which may be more applicable to the $I$ sector than to the $A$ and $S$ sectors. Southeast Asian productivity gains are unexpectedly lower in the $I$ sector than in the $A$ sector. Even in East Asia, where industrial productivity rose rapidly, agriculture did as well or better. One would expect that, because of the slow rise of yield per hectare, the difficulty of achieving higher economies of scale in Asia with severely limited supply of land, and the long gestation period or production run of crops (due to the biological nature of production), productivity in agriculture would rise more slowly than that in the $I$ sector. Moreover, given the output per hectare (or land productivity), the size of farmland cultivated per worker determines labor productivity.[7] And farm size is smallest in East Asia (and Bangladesh and Java).

One expects productivity in the industrial sector to grow more rapidly than productivity in the other two sectors because of the wider applicability of Western technologies to the process and product of the $I$ sector and their shorter production runs compared to the $A$ sector—in addition to the greater potentials for scale economies. And since the $I$ sector deals with exportable and importable goods, it is subjected to greater competition and, therefore, faster capital-labor substitution. Japan's and Taiwan's $I$ sector productivity grew more rapidly in the 1950s than in later decades; it was very slow in South Korea, which made up for it in later decades.

The $S$ sector growth was substantial in East Asia, especially compared to Southeast Asia. This sector plays a major role in a modern economy, and it is misleading to regard it as unproductive (as Marxian literature does). This is most clearly seen in Hong Kong and Singapore, whose $S$ sectors played a crucial role in finding markets for industrial output, sources for buying inputs, and credit for financing production for small and medium-sized industries.[8]

TABLE 2.3
Productivity Gains in Gross Domestic Product, 1955 to 1984

| Country | 1955–1959 Amount (billions of currency) | 1955–1959 Shares (percent) | 1960–1964 Amount (billions of currency) | 1960–1964 Shares (percent) | 1965–1969 Amount (billions of currency) | 1965–1969 Shares (percent) | 1970–1974 Amount (billions of currency) | 1970–1974 Shares (percent) | 1975–1979 Amount (billions of currency) | 1975–1979 Shares (percent) | 1980–1984 Amount (billions of currency) | 1980–1984 Shares (percent) | Simple Average 1955–1984 Amount (billions of currency) | Simple Average 1955–1984 Shares (percent) |
|---|---|---|---|---|---|---|---|---|---|---|---|---|---|---|
| Japan | 6,943 | 38.5 | 16,584 | 58.7 | 24,864 | 52.0 | 22,908 | 32.1 | 21,913 | 22.9 | 25,007 | 21.1 | 19,703 | 37.6 |
| Taiwan | 71 | 35.3 | 123 | 42.7 | 218 | 48.8 | 366 | 51.3 | 580 | 50.2 | 585 | 33.5 | 324 | 43.7 |
| South Korea | 496 | 20.2 | 861 | 27.8 | 2,159 | 48.9 | 3,401 | 48.6 | 5,663 | 62.2 | 4,294 | 26.4 | 2,812 | 39.1 |
| Hong Kong | | | 8.6 | 30.2ᵃ | 16 | 41.4 | 25 | 42.9 | 47 | 51.0 | 56 | 39.5 | 30 | 41.0 |
| Singapore | | | 0.5 | 21.9ᵇ | 2.1 | 58.3 | 3.5 | 57.9 | 3.7 | 37.6 | 6.2 | 43.1 | 3.2 | 43.8 |
| Malaysia | | | 2.1 | 25.8ᵇ | 3.2 | 29.8 | 4.8 | 33.8 | 7.1 | 36.1 | 9.6 | 34.2 | 5.3 | 32.0 |
| Thailand | 14 | 28.3 | 29 | 41.7 | 46 | 44.6 | 54 | 34.9 | 87 | 39.2 | 85 | 27.6 | 52 | 36.1 |
| Indonesia | | | 319 | 13.3ᵇ | 957 | 23.2 | 2451 | 42.9 | 2896 | 34.7 | 3427 | 30.1 | 2010 | 28.9 |
| Philippines | 7.5 | 29.5 | 7.4 | 22.4 | 11 | 26.3 | 15 | 28.4 | 23 | 32.5 | 6.5 | 7.6 | 11 | 24.5 |
| India | | | 62 | 20.9ᵇ | 49 | 14.2 | 40 | 10.0 | 93 | 30.7 | 161 | 27.9 | 81 | 20.8 |
| Bangladesh | | | 8.7 | 22.0ᵇ | 6.2 | 13.4 | 0.5 | 2.7 | 14 | 26.2 | 10 | 15.0ᶜ | 8.1 | 15.9 |
| Sri Lanka | 2.2 | 18.9 | 3.3 | 22.6 | 4.9 | 26.1 | 3.9 | 16.9 | 9.8 | 33.5 | 9.7 | 26.3 | 5.6 | 24.1 |
| Pakistan | | | 5.1 | 26.1ᵇ | 9.3 | 35.4 | 9.6 | 27.3 | 14 | 30.6 | 14 | 24.1ᶜ | 10 | 28.7 |

Source: See table 2.1.

ᵃ1962–64.
ᵇ1961–64.
ᶜ1980–83.

PRODUCTIVITY AND STRUCTURAL CHANGES

Simon Kuznets, after discussing the nature of productivity changes in modern economic growth, noted that "while economic analysis may never reach down to the basic levels of production and spread of new knowledge and innovations, we may be able, through examining structural changes, to infer some of the ways by which efficiency was improved."[9] Structural changes have been exceptionally rapid in East Asia. In Japan, half of the labor force was in agriculture in the early part of the postwar era, but this dropped to one-tenth in 1980; in Taiwan, two-thirds were in agriculture in 1950 and only one-fifth in 1980; in South Korea, the agricultural labor force fell from two-thirds to one-third. In Southeast Asia, there were three-fourths in the earlier period, one-half in 1980. In South Asia, shifts were minimal, and most of the region still has nearly three-fourths of its population in agriculture.

Accordingly, the most important indirect impact of sector productivity gains on economic growth is through structural shifts, especially from the lower per capita income $A$ sector to the higher income $I$ and $S$ sectors. This shift will be difficult in the early stage of the transition if higher labor productivity in agriculture does not produce sufficient food for the urban sector, since food requirements rise in the earlier stages of the transition, when mechanization of the $I$ and $S$ sectors tends to be limited. Later in the transition, food needs lessen with the widespread substitution of electric-powered machines for muscle-powered tools. Of course, with higher incomes, domestic demand for clothing, housing, and other consumption goods rises. If productivity gains do not increase their output, prices rise, and nominal wages in the urban sector rise to squeeze profits—in the Ricardian fashion.

The shift from agriculture to industry is also difficult if there are insufficient savings to finance the purchase of the raw materials needed to occupy new workers and new equipment. Moreover, urban occupations in factories, stores, and offices tend to be education-intensive, and savings are needed to finance schooling. Thus even more important than consumption, savings are needed for structural shifts. Through increased consumption and savings, productivity gains contributed to rapid structural changes and growth in the East Asian economies. In table 2.3, the portion of GDP contributed by productivity gains, as a share of total GDP, is higher in East Asia than in Southeast Asia, and higher in the latter than in South Asia. The best years for most countries in Asia were the 1960s and 1970s; the worst were the 1980s, with the slowdown in the world economy.

Japan attained its largest shares in the 1960s. In Taiwan and Korea, it was in the 1970s. In these years, these countries moved toward full employment, with a sharp reduction in underemployment in the rural sector and accelerated substitution of machines for labor. In Southeast Asia, Thailand's share of productivity gains was the highest and most stable; the Philippines' share was the lowest.

TABLE 2.4

Educational Spending from Productivity Gains in Gross Domestic Product, 1955 to 1984 (percent)

| Country | 1955–1959 | 1960–1964 | 1965–1969 | 1970–1974 | 1975–1979 | 1980–1984 | Simple Average, 1955–1984 |
|---|---|---|---|---|---|---|---|
| Japan | 16.3 | 17.5 | 15.3 | 24.0 | 19.9 | | 18.6 |
| Taiwan | 4.4 | 4.7 | 6.2 | 8.0 | 9.0 | 6.3 | 6.4 |
| South Korea | 3.2 | (0.2) | 3.6 | 2.5 | 2.0 | | 2.2 |
| Hong Kong | | | | 0.8[a] | 0.4 | 0.3[b] | 0.5 |
| Singapore | | 8.3[c] | 7.8 | 11.4 | 10.8 | 16.7[b] | 11.0 |
| Thailand | | | 0.6 | 0.4 | 0.4 | 0.7 | 0.7 |
| India | | 1.2[c] | | 2.2[a] | 0.4 | 0.9[b] | 0.6 |
| Sri Lanka | | | | 4.8[a] | 1.3 | 1.8[b] | 1.8 |

Source: Official national accounts.

Note: Data used for computation were Japan, miscellaneous; Taiwan, recreation, entertainment, education, and cultural services; South Korea, miscellaneous services, excluding entertainment and recreation; Singapore, recreation and education; Thailand, other services, such as education, legal and funeral services; Hong Kong, India, and Sri Lanka, education only.

[a] 1971–74.

[b] 1980–83.

[c] 1961–64.

In South Asia and in Asia as a whole, Bangladesh and India performed the poorest. These results agree with the analysis of growth rates in the postwar decades.

In most countries, the part of GDP attributed to productivity gains is used more for consumption than for savings in the earlier stages of the agroindustrial transition, especially in the form of food. (See chapter 6 for a discussion of food consumption.) But in the later stages of the transition, the demand for capital goods increases because of the greater needs for investment in factories and machines—far greater than in agriculture and services. In the second transition—the passage from an industrial to a service economy—the demand for secondary and higher education increases, since jobs in service industries require more education than jobs in the other sectors.[10]

Gross domestic fixed investment per worker tends to be higher in the industrial than in the other sectors, partly because manufacturing, the main part of the industrial sector, requires more capital in the form of plant and equipment than do retail and wholesale trade (including restaurant services) and personal services. The highest need for capital is in public utilities (including transport and communication), where the infrastructure for distribution of output is costly. The lowest demand for capital is in agriculture, which does not need plants or buildings and in which machine use is minimal.

As the economy moves toward the completion of the first transition and enters the industrial-service transition, the increasing capital intensity of industry, the widespread commercialization of agriculture, and in particular, the rise of the service sector begin to require a more highly educated labor force (table 2.4). Occupations in the service subsectors of finance, education, health, and government are highly education-intensive. The labor forces' years of schooling averaged about 25 percent more in the $S$ sector than in the $A$ and $I$ sectors in Japan in 1979, about 20 percent greater in Taiwan, South Korea, Hong Kong, Singapore, and Malaysia, and about 15 percent greater in Thailand, the Philippines, and Indonesia. The lower differential in schooling is due to the smaller size of the $S$ sector and its relatively simple nature in less developed countries. Thus as the industrial-service transition is completed, low food requirements and the declining need for savings to finance plant and equipment investment by industries are offset by an acceleration in the demand for education.

Japan's share of savings from productivity gains rose to high levels from the latter 1960s, as industrialization emphasized heavy industries, but by the 1980s, with the completion of the basic infrastructure for industrialization, Japan's gross national savings began to exceed gross domestic investment. A similar situation occurred in Taiwan, with the difference that in Taiwan, which is a much smaller country, the whole range of heavy industries with their large scale-economies was not feasible. In both countries, the excess of national savings over domestic investment was sent abroad for investment. In South Korea, after a slow start, industrialization was pushed rapidly in the 1970s, with large loans from Middle Eastern petrodollars, and in the mid-1980s South Korea began to save and to earn enough foreign exchange to start repaying its foreign borrowings. The Philippines, after a fast start, ran into considerable trouble in the two decades of Marcos's rule, ending up with a negative savings share.

In Japan, the percentage spent on education from productivity gains rose as Japan began to move into an *S* economy. Japanese educational shares were high throughout all the postwar decades, reflecting the high regard the Japanese have for education. The same situation is true for Singapore. Hong Kong grew labor-intensively with the use of migrants from the Chinese continent, so there was less need to spend on education. South Korea's low education spending levels are puzzling, since education has always had a strong place in Korean social values. The extremely low education spending levels in Southeast and South Asia reflect the heavily agrarian nature of these economies and their low per capita incomes.

In sum, the rapid growth of East Asian economies reflects the large productivity gains during the postwar decades as well as the huge savings from the additional incomes derived from such gains, which were used for future productivity and growth. In the next section, I turn to some of the forces related to productivity growth.

### CIRCUMSTANCES BEARING ON EAST ASIAN PRODUCTIVITY GROWTH

In the prewar colonial period, East Asia (unlike Southeast Asia) gained considerable experience in modern rice growing and, to a lesser extent, in industrialization. Japan, of course, was far ahead of the others by more than half a century of scientific rice growing and industrialization. In the early decades of the twentieth century Japan began to modernize Korean and Taiwanese rice growing; in the 1930s Japan introduced industrialization as its labor supply dropped along with its concentration on the effort to conquer China. The Western colonial powers were interested in the tropical crops produced by the plantations and in the colonial markets for selling their manufactures.[11] With the defeat of Japan in World War II, Korea and Taiwan were able to get a head start in developing their agriculture and industries. Land reform and other institutional changes after World War II contributed to the widening of the local market. And when the rapidly growing U.S. economy of the 1950s and 1960s opened its doors wide to imports, East Asia was able to quickly send its industrial exports to the United States. With expanding domestic and external markets, East Asia was able to achieve full employment: Japan and Hong Kong in the 1950s and Taiwan and South Korea in the 1960s.

The tightening of the labor markets with full employment under extensive competition was crucial to the acceleration of the growth of productivity in East Asia. Real wages rose as labor became scarce, and entrepreneurs substituted capital, especially mechanized technologies, for labor. With accelerated mechanization, the scale of production rose and there was a further rise in productivity. Rising real wages and full employment meant that the incomes of lower income families were rising and income disparities were declining. None of the countries of Southeast and South Asia attained full employment, and real wages rose slowly, if at all. Except in the largest farms and firms, mechanization spread slowly, so that productivity gains were small. The exception was West Malaysia in 1984, but when prices of plantation crops began to drop in 1985, unemployment there began to increase. In the late 1980s, Thailand's high growth rates enabled it to reach full employment.

Large agricultural productivity gains in East Asia were related to the sharp fall in the denominator of the productivity ratio, or the shift of farm workers to the industrial and service sectors. In Japan, employment declined in the 1950s. It accelerated in the 1960s and 1970s in Japan and Taiwan, in Korea in the late 1970s, and in Thailand toward the end of the 1980s. The increase in agricultural productivity with declines in employment was made possible by a series of institutional changes (of which land reform was the most important) and new technologies, both biological and mechanical, with the former raising yields and the latter substituting for labor in plowing, planting, and harvesting. In Japan, the need for deep plowing of paddy rice brought on mechanization. With the ensuing shortage of labor, younger workers left for the cities. Later, these machines were brought into Taiwan and, still later, into South Korea.[12] The large increases in agricultural productivity in Hong Kong and Singapore were due to the shift away from crops to livestock and fish raising, as the price of labor rose with full employment and as land prices increased with urbanization. In these noncrop sectors of agriculture, production runs are shorter and the application of Western technologies easier than in crop production.

The importance of the use of machines in raising agricultural productivity can be seen in Thailand during the 1980s, when productivity nearly doubled over the two previous decades. Thai farmers began to substitute machines for buffaloes, reducing time for cultivation; in the mid-1980s machines began to substitute for human labor, as migration accelerated with the tightening of the urban labor market. Power tillers rose from 370,000 in 1978 to 1 million in 1983 and 1.7 million in 1988. Mechanized threshers rose from 216,000 in 1978 to 594,000 in 1983 and 736,000 in 1988.

In the Philippines the sales of agricultural machinery declined between the 1970s and the 1980s, because of high unemployment in the 1980s. Malaysia's good performance was largely due to the plantation sector, which did far better than Sri Lanka's plantation sector, which paid high taxes to pay for that country's extensive welfare programs. India's agriculture did poorly, because public resources were largely used up in constructing a large number of very costly heavy industries and later in operating the deficit-ridden plants and rehabilitating them.[13] Also important to full employment was the increase in multiple cropping in Japan during the 1950s, in Taiwan during the 1950s and 1960s, and in Korea during the 1970s and 1980s. Since the denominator is not measured in annual man-hours, the increase in the number of crops produced in a given twelve-month period raises the numerator without changing the denominator of the productivity ratio. After the rice crop is harvested, another crop (either rice or nonrice) can be planted, weather and water availability permitting.

In Japan, the multiple-cropping index (ratio of planted area to physical area) reached 150 in the mid-1960s. It rose to 186 in Taiwan and 153 in South Korea in the late 1960s. These are the highest in Asia, with Southeast Asia averaging around 130 and South Asia, 115.[14] The index was lower in Japan and South Korea because of their cold winter months, compared to Taiwan, a subtropical country where most crops can grow throughout the year. Hence, Taiwan's cropping index is most comparable to those of South and Southeast Asia, most of which are in the tropics.

Asian farmers mainly produce nonrice products during the second and third cropping (after the rice harvesting), as water is insufficient to fill the paddies. Nonrice crops usually require processing, which opens up employment for farm family members in nearby agribusinesses. This income supplements on-farm income, raising total farm family income and purchasing power for industrial products, which in turn leads to the growth of rural industries catering to farmers' needs. Off-farm income in Japan rose nearly 400 percent and in Taiwan was 200 percent of on-farm incomes by the 1980s.[15]

In monsoon agriculture, without other work after the rice harvest, there would be extensive underemployment of the rural labor force, since the rainfall is insufficient for crops. In Japan, underemployment was reduced from 15 percent of the labor force in the mid-1950s to 8 percent in the mid-1970s; in Taiwan it dropped to 2 percent, and in South Korea to 10 percent through multiple cropping and off-farm employment. In Thailand, it fell to 10 percent by the end of the 1980s. Elsewhere, underemployment continued to be much greater, with about 25 percent in the Philippines and Bangladesh in the 1980s and about 15 percent in Malaysia, Indonesia, and Sri Lanka. Thus, multiple cropping and off-farm employment contributed substantially to productivity gains in East Asia's rural economies in two ways: directly, through greater output of the labor force, and indirectly, through mechanization via full employment and faster capital-labor substitution.

As to the industrial sector, similar circumstances led to greater increases in productivity in East Asia compared to Southeast and South Asia. With full employment in Japan in the latter 1950s, industrial productivity rose 10 percent per year in the 1950s, 8 percent in Taiwan in the 1960s, and 8 percent in South Korea during the late 1960s and early 1970s. There was a shift from low productivity sectors, such as handicrafts, to mechanized industries. The rise in efficiency as productivity rose made it possible for these countries to export to the West, raising economies of scale. The low rates for Hong Kong in the 1960s and 1970s were due to the large influx of labor from the Chinese mainland, where industry was labor-intensive. In Southeast Asia, the decline in the prices of agroindustrial products and the poor performance of capital-intensive industries in the 1980s contributed to negative productivity gains, as excess capacities emerged. In India and Sri Lanka, publicly owned capital-intensive industries stagnated in the 1960s and 1970s, and productivity gains were small.

The rise in $S$ sector productivity was larger in East Asia than in the ASEAN Four because of labor shortages and greater mechanization in Japan and Taiwan after full employment was reached. There was a shift of the labor force from low-paying services, such as domestic work, to modern services as wages rose.[16] In higher paying services such as banks and insurance companies, the use of computers and telecommunication technology raised productivity substantially. In Southeast Asia, young workers leaving agriculture found jobs difficult to get in the slow-growing $I$ sector, and many of them ended up as disguisedly unemployed in the overstaffed $S$ sector. The slow growth of productivity in Southeast Asia's $I$ and $S$ sectors contributed to the insufficient growth of industrial exports, which in turn led to unemployment in the urban sector— while the failure to shift to multiple cropping contributed to underemployment in the $A$ sector.

Besides the increased use of capital in place of labor, productivity was enhanced by improved technologies embodied in or related to capital. Rough indicators of this are found in the horsepower per worker in manufacturing, since faster and more powerful machines require more electricity. In Japan it rose sharply, from an average of one horsepower per worker in the 1930s and 1940s to sixteen horsepower in the 1970s. In Taiwan, the average rose from one horsepower in the 1950s to four horsepower in the 1970s, and in South Korea from one in the 1950s to three in the 1970s.[17] Part of the increase represents the substitution of capital for workers, but another part reflects the substitution of faster, more powerful, and more efficient machines for those previously used, since by 1970 most of the factories in East Asia were fully mechanized. The import statistics are indicative of better machines introduced to replace those in use. Countries tend to import machinery and equipment whose technology they do not possess or make. Japan illustrates this: the import of machinery, mainly from the United States, slowed in the 1970s, when the technological frontier was reached and there were fewer machines of higher technology to import from the West. But Taiwan and South Korea continued to increase their purchases throughout the 1970s, as they were far from the technological frontier. The slower progress of technology in Southeast Asia is shown by the lower levels of machinery imports: in 1980, its per capita imports of machinery was only $100, compared to Taiwan's $300. The work force in East Asia used the increasingly complex machines and other technologies effectively and efficiently. Average years of schooling completed by the East Asian labor force was 7 years (Japan's was 10 years) in 1970. This compares with 4.5 years for Southeast Asia.[18]

Note the low growth of productivity in table 2.1 in the United States. As in other postindustrial economies, its economy is dominated by the service sector, which employs more than two-thirds of the labor force. And productivity growth is low in the service sector because of the limited applicability of mechanized labor-saving technologies, especially in trade, restaurants, hotels, and other personal services. Moreover, with the *A* and *I* sectors not only fully mechanized but with machines at the very frontier of technology, productivity could not be raised quickly by more mechanization nor could new technologies be easily brought in, since it takes time to generate new ones. But even in Japan, which by the mid-1980s was at the edge of the technological frontier in most industries, imports of technologies were still high, and payments for technologies from abroad rose from about $1–2 billion in 1975 to well over $2 billion in 1984. This was because there were many small industries in Japan with low levels of mechanization; as they grew, they were able to use more and larger equipment.

U.S. gross domestic private capital formation during the 1970s and 1980s averaged 16.6 percent of GNP (in constant prices), much lower than Japan's gross domestic private capital formation of 26.8 percent.[19] This is in part due to lower savings, especially personal savings.[20] If Japanese households accumulate as many assets—such as homes, durables, cars, and entitlements in old age—as U.S. households do, the desire to save may be weakened. This, in turn, may have an unfavorable impact on propensity to work, as the need to save impels people to work long hours to maximize their earnings and be able to save. Annual working hours in manufacturing in 1989 were about 10 percent higher in Japan over the United Kingdom and the United States and 25 percent higher than in Germany and France.[21] Weekly hours of work in industry and services in 1987 were 25 percent higher in Japan than in the United States.[22] Even though 1988 productivity *levels* for the economy as a whole, including agriculture, were 30 percent lower in Japan than in the United States (because of the low productivity of small farms and service units, which are much more extensive in Japan than in the West), the much higher *growth* of productivity in Japan over the United States will determine these levels in the years to come. As long as productivity growth remains low in the United States, real wage rates per hour will be stagnant. This together with the refusal of American workers to work longer hours will keep U.S. savings too low to finance large capital formation.[23]

## PRODUCTIVITY AND EXPORTS

Productivity also underlies the ability to export. The ups and downs within export trends may be influenced by market changes abroad, but the trends themselves are related mainly to the domestic growth of productivity, which is essential to meet foreign competition. In turn, greater exports contribute to larger economies of scale and the earning of foreign exchange to purchase more machinery and technologies from abroad. But in the crucial early stages of the transition, internal efficiency sets the stage for the external takeoff, even though benefits from exports help in the subsequent acceleration and sustenance of exports.

The unprecedented growth of Japanese industrial productivity during the 1950s enabled manufacturing exports to expand. Textile and machinery exports more than doubled in value, from 400 to 900 billion yen between 1955 and 1960. From 1950 to 1955, the textile production index more than doubled (2.3 times), but employment increased by only 15 percent; in machinery, production also more than doubled (2.4 times), while employment rose 20 percent. Both industries were characterized by minimal scale economies and were labor-intensive, and foreign exchange earnings were used in the 1960s to develop heavy industries, not textiles and machinery.[24] In the 1960s, iron and steel, heavy machinery, petrochemicals, and paper and pulp led industrial productivity, with double-digit increases in product per worker, paving the way for the large exports of heavy industrial products from the early 1970s.[25]

The growth rate of Taiwanese agricultural productivity was highest during the 1950s, which enabled Taiwan to export agricultural products (70 percent of total exports in the 1950s). Since scale economies were minimal in the 1950s, the growth of domestically induced productivity was responsible for export growth. In the 1960s, the export of textiles and food manufactures spearheaded the export drive. In the 1950s, textile and food production doubled, with employment increasing by 15 percent. Similarly, before the big rise of textile exports, food and textile manufactures in South Korea doubled between 1955 and 1965, while employment increased by 25 percent. In Japan, Taiwan, and South Korea, there was sufficient internal demand for industrial production to keep most industries expanding for many years.[26]

In scale-economic industries such as the iron and steel industry in Japan, Taiwan, and South Korea, productivity grew before exports. Only after productivity rose in the earlier periods were they able to sell abroad. In the Japanese automobile industry, productivity grew in the 1970s before large increases of exports took place in the 1980s. The situation was different in Hong Kong and Singapore, with limited local markets. In both of these city-states, export industries had to be developed by experienced foreign investors. The growth of these city-states (which don't have large domestic markets) can be called export-led growth in the sense that their economies were driven by exports from the outset. But exports from Japan, Taiwan, and South Korea were led by internal demand, fueled by agricultural productivity gains. However, it is not clear what exactly is meant by *export-led growth*. If it refers to the growth of an economy that was stagnant prior to the rise of exports and was driven to expand because of exports, Taiwanese and South Korean growth cannot be said to be export led because these economies were already growing during the 1950s and into the early 1960s with agricultural development and import substitution. But if it refers to the acceleration of growth due to the rise in exports in the latter 1960s, then Taiwanese and South Korean growth may be said to be export led since the latter 1960s. But perhaps it may be more accurate to call this *export-led growth acceleration,* in contrast to China's *productivity-led acceleration* in the 1980s.

Malaysia's growth in the 1960s and 1970s can be said to be even more export led, since it was the demand for tires in the West that sparked the growth of exports, although it was the efficiency of British-managed plantations that enabled Malaysian rubber producers to sell much more rubber than rubber producers in Indonesia and Ceylon. Moreover, when Western growth slowed in the 1980s, the newly industrialized economies of East Asia continued to do well by shifting their production and markets. Here, only the accelerated portion of GDP was export led. In contrast, in the Philippines and Indonesia, when foreign demand for their plantation products fell in the 1980s, their overall growth rates fell sharply. Thus their growth in the 1970s was export led. In the late 1980s, productivity growth accelerated over that in the early 1980s, as the global economy improved. The largest gains were recorded in Southeast Asia, South Korea, Taiwan, Hong Kong, and Singapore, but substantial gains were also made in India and Pakistan.[27]

POLICY IMPLICATIONS

The experience of East Asia points to the importance of full-employment policies if capital-labor substitution and the adoption of better technologies are to be sped up. It is better to promote labor-intensive industries than capital-intensive ones in the earlier phases of the agroindustrial transition and then gradually move toward more capital- and technology-using industries. Productivity in agriculture is crucial to food supply, farm family savings, farm family purchasing power, and the release of farm workers for the growing urban sectors. Attempts to increase productivity in publicly supported capital-intensive industries are likely to be unsuccessful, as the experience of India, China, Sri Lanka, Bangladesh, the Philippines, Indonesia, and Malaysia demonstrates. And artificially raising wages with high minimum wage laws may do more harm than good, as the experience of Singapore and the Philippines indicates.

The state should vigorously promote competition, keeping markets open to new entries willing to bring in new technologies. Liberalized trade and the promotion of exports expose entrepreneurs to the outside, which works better than prolonged protection and subsidization, as in India, the Philippines, and elsewhere. Industrial estates and research into technologies to improve productivity should be encouraged. In the beginning of industrialization, there may be a need for an industrial policy to target the establishment of new industries.

## PRODUCTIVITY TRENDS IN CHINA

Table 2.5 gives productivity trends in China. China's official estimates are given as net material product, a concept that excludes certain services (6–7 percent of GDP). The main disadvantage of this Marxian concept is that it is not easily divisible into total consumption, investment, and government expenditures.

There was an increase in the growth of product per worker in the 1980s over the previous decades. Although much remained unchanged, such as controls on grain production, various changes contributed to the faster growth of productivity. In launching the Great Leap Forward in the 1950s, Mao mistakenly identified rural underemployment as disguised unemployment. In contrast, Deng's strategy aimed for the rapid expansion of off-farm employment to reduce underemployment in the dry months. Disguised unemployment, defined to be people working but not producing, existed mainly in industrial enterprises, where workers could not be dismissed even if they were not productive.

Agricultural product grew in the 1980s more than twice over that of 1965–80 (7.9 percent against 3 percent), which enabled the industrial product to grow at the double-digit rate of 12.5 percent, and service product at 9.4 percent (in 1980–85).[28] With greater production of diversified products (cotton, sugar, fruits, vegetables, and animal products), more material inputs were available for the food processing and textile industries, and the increase in transporting, marketing, financing, and servicing raised the activities of the service sector. Moreover, the purchasing power of the peasants rose, as monthly family in-

TABLE 2.5
Growth Rates, China, 1965 to 1985 (percent)

| Year | Gross Domestic Product | Population | Gross Domestic Product per Capita | Labor Force | Gross Domestic Product per Worker |
|---|---|---|---|---|---|
| 1965–80 | 6.4 | 2.2 | 4.2 | 2.4 | 4.0 |
| 1980–85 | 9.8 | 1.2 | 8.6 | 2.5 | 7.3 |
| 1965–85 | 7.2 | 2.0 | 5.2 | 2.4 | 4.8 |

*Source:* World Bank, *World Development Report.*

comes doubled from 191 yuan in 1980 to 398 in 1985 (current prices). Not only farm production but the expansion of off-farm activities in small factories contributed to the rapid rise of family incomes, especially in the mid-1980s, when agriculture slowed.[29]

In 1988, industrial liberalization began, but because public enterprises were not experienced with market operations, the market mechanism did not work well. Nor did industrial efficiency improve, since Communist cadres were reluctant to give a free hand to technicians and management, and the firing of inefficient workers was difficult. Prices rose with mounting liberalization, perhaps mainly because the management of the public enterprises was not up to the task of expanding production fast enough. Chinese economists have suggested that privatization of enterprises is necessary before the market can work better and productivity can improve. Nevertheless, there has been some modest rise in the growth of industrial production, from an annual growth of 10 percent in 1965–80 to 12.5 percent in 1980–85, representing a faster growth of output over employment. This may be attributed to the large increase in gross domestic investment, which rose at an annual rate of 19.3 percent in 1980–86, compared to 10.5 percent in 1965–80. The 1980–86 rate was by far the highest in Asia, with South Korea trailing in second place at 9.6 percent and Taiwan at 9.5 percent. Much of this investment went into the industrial sector, where investments rose from 275 million to 446 million yuan between 1980 and 1985. It may also be due to the linking of wages to productivity increases: blue-collar wages rose beyond the earnings of white-collar workers, whose salaries are not linked to productivity.[30]

The off-farm incomes of farm families were only 5 percent of on-farm incomes in 1980 but grew to 33 percent in 1985, even though farm incomes increased substantially, from 182 yuan per family to 264 yuan. The impact of off-farm work on industrial product per worker was large because most of the labor of farm family members in industrial activities is not included in the labor force of industry, since it is largely part-time work. China has a long way to go in raising the share of off-farm incomes, which is low compared to over 100 percent for Taiwan and 55 percent for Thailand. The rise in China's service sector productivity may have been due to the increased demand for services occasioned by the rise in family incomes in the 1980s. Workers in service firms tend to be less than fully engaged under normal circumstances, but with quickly rising economic activities and family incomes they become busier per hour and work longer hours. World Bank figures show that service output rose 9.4 percent, while official sources indicate that the service labor force grew 7.2 percent between 1980 and 1986.[31]

The prospects for China are promising for the years to come. Further liberalization in industry may strengthen market forces enough to overcome the inefficiencies of the planning mechanism, and privatization may enable technicians to have a greater voice in management. If peasants are given longer leaseholds on their farms, they may be more willing to invest in irrigation, drainage, and other land improvements. With greater opportunities to earn off-farm incomes, they may invest the proceeds of such incomes in labor-saving equipment so that more time for off-farm work will be available. With more off-farm work, underemployment will be reduced, and the higher purchasing power of peasants can wipe out the 2 percent or so of open unemployment. With these developments, disguised unemployment in public enterprise can eventually be reduced.

But with the return to power of the old guard, liberalization trends appear to have stopped or even been reversed. Nevertheless, whatever the thinking of the old guard may be, it will have to face the consequences of returning to the pre-1978 period of low growth of productivity and per capita GDP. Total factor productivity declined by 13 percent in agriculture during the 1952–77 period, including a decline in value added per agricultural worker in 1957–77.[32] In a monsoon economy such as China's, agricultural productivity has to be improved if the economy as a whole is to prosper. This means that per hectare yields must rise, which means crop diversification. Farm family incomes must rise, too, which means off-farm employment. In other words, China's development strategy must be like those of Japan, Taiwan, and South Korea in the early stages of their economic development. The Marxian strategy of development with capital accumulation is not sufficient, and it may even be harmful if it stresses heavy industrialization.

# CHAPTER 3

# Capital Formation and Technological Change

The previous chapter focused on the increase of GDP as a result of productivity gains and posited that the larger part of this increase is not the result of increased output per worker. This and the next chapter examines total investment, savings, and consumption, not just the increment: capital formation is one of the two most important proximate factors in productivity growth, the other being labor, or employment.[1] Technology is included in the qualitative aspect of capital in the same way that education is subsumed in the quality of labor.

## DEFINITIONS AND CONCEPTS

Gross domestic capital formation (GDCF) is the purchase of machines and other equipment, housing and other structures, and inventory additions without adjustment for wear and tear of capital used in the course of the year's production and irrespective of their ownership within the confines of a country. The GDCF level is many times higher in East Asia than in South and Southeast Asia (see table 3.1). This indicates that during the transition from an agricultural to an industrial economy, a great deal of physical infrastructure must be put in place to convert traditional agriculture into a modern, commercialized agriculture and to transform handicrafts into output produced in factories and plants. After the first transition, the physical infrastructures needed will taper off because, in the transition from an industrial to a service economy, the service sector is less demanding of physical infrastructure. As to equipment expenditures, agriculture and services during the first transition use relatively small amounts, and the demand of the industrial sector is the most conspicuous. In the latter portion of the agroindustrial transition, equipment expenditures rise to the level of construction expenditures (see table 3.2). Since the growth of product per worker underlies most of the growth of product per capita, it seems more convenient to go first into the analysis of product per worker than to product per capita as in the Solow and Harrod income growth equation, which links income growth to the contribution of labor, capital, and technology.[2]

TABLE 3.1

Per Capita Gross Domestic Capital Formation, 1970 to 1985 (constant prices)

| Country | Gross Domestic Capital Formation (billions of currency) | Population (millions) | Gross Domestic Capital Formation per Capita (thousands of currency) |
|---|---|---|---|
| Japan (1980 yen) | | | 4,045.00 |
| 1970 | 53,902 | 103.72 | 519.7 |
| 1975 | 62,191 | 111.94 | 555.6 |
| 1980 | 75,876 | 117.06 | 648.2 |
| 1985 | 87,163 | 121.05 | 720.1 |
| South Korea (1980 won) | | | 337.60 |
| 1970 | 4,228 | 31.44 | 134.5 |
| 1975 | 6,818 | 35.28 | 193.3 |
| 1980 | 11,789 | 38.12 | 309.3 |
| 1985 | 17,769 | 41.06 | 432.8 |
| Taiwan (1981 NT$) | | | 716.28 |
| 1970 | 163.3 | 14.51 | 11.3 |
| 1975 | 292.2 | 16.00 | 18.3 |
| 1980 | 528.7 | 17.64 | 30.0 |
| 1985 | 424.7 | 19.11 | 22.2 |
| Hong Kong (1980 HK$) | | | 866.06 |
| 1970 | 13.8 | 3.96 | 3.5 |
| 1975 | 21.9 | 4.40 | 5.0 |
| 1980 | 49.3 | 5.06 | 9.7 |
| 1985 | 47.6 | 5.46 | 8.7 |
| Singapore (1985 S$) | | | 2,201.65 |
| 1970 | 5.1 | 2.07 | 2.5 |
| 1975 | 7.7 | 2.26 | 3.4 |
| 1980 | 12.6 | 2.41 | 5.2 |
| 1985 | 16.6 | 2.56 | 6.5 |
| Philippines (1972 pesos) | | | 17.67 |
| 1970 | 10.8 | 36.68 | 0.29 |
| 1975 | 18.3 | 42.07 | 0.43 |
| 1980 | 26.6 | 48.32 | 0.55 |
| 1985 | 11.1 | 54.67 | 0.20 |
| Thailand (1972 bahts) | | | 53.15 |
| 1970 | 43.1 | 36.37 | 1.2 |
| 1975 | 50.1 | 41.39 | 1.2 |
| 1980 | 74.3 | 46.72 | 1.6 |
| 1985 | 77.8 | 51.68 | 1.5 |
| Malaysia (1970 M$) | | | 155.45 |
| 1970 | 2.0 | 10.40 | 0.19 |
| 1975 | 3.7 | 11.92 | 0.31 |

(*continued*)

TABLE 3.1 (*Continued*)

| Country | Gross Domestic Capital Formation (billions of currency) | Population (millions) | Gross Domestic Capital Formation per Capita (thousands of currency) |
|---|---|---|---|
| 1980 | 7.0 | 13.75 | 0.51 |
| 1985 | 8.5 | 15.68 | 0.54 |
| India (1980–81 rupees) | | | 43.88 |
| 1970 | 264.6 | 539.08 | 0.49 |
| 1975 | 338.1 | 603.46 | 0.56 |
| 1980 | 429.3 | 675.16 | 0.64 |
| 1985 | 426.6 | 750.86 | 0.57 |
| Sri Lanka (1975 rupees) | | | 11.87 |
| 1970 | 3.9 | 12.51 | 0.31 |
| 1975 | 4.0 | 13.50 | 0.30 |
| 1980 | 7.0 | 14.75 | 0.47 |
| 1985 | 6.0 | 15.84 | 0.38 |

*Source:* Asian Development Bank, *Key Indicators; Japan Statistical Yearbook.*

Productivity and capital may be linked in an equation where the increase in labor productivity is the product of the incremental capital productivity (capital efficiency) and the increase in capital per worker (capital intensity). That is,

$$\Delta O/L = (\Delta O/\Delta K)\ (\Delta K/L),$$

where $O$ is output, $L$ is labor, and $K$ is capital; $\Delta K$ is $I,$ thus canceling itself and leaving an identity. The more capital the worker labors with and the higher the efficiency of capital, the greater labor productivity is. The marginal productivity of capital is the reciprocal of the marginal capital-output ratio. The latter was widely discussed in the 1960s in connection with the growth equation, which assumed that the capital-output ratio was stable. Most economists argued at that time that it fell in the course of development because the productivity of capital rose.

At the beginning of the agroindustrial transition, the average capital-output ratio was around 2, which implies that the productivity of capital was one-half; as development proceeded, the capital-output ratio rose, implying that the productivity of capital falls.[3] The reason is that the agroindustrial transition entails the construction of physical infrastructure such as schools, roads, railways, harbors, public utilities, public buildings, sanitation systems, factories, dwellings, and, in rural areas, irrigation and drainage systems. All of these are long-duration constructions, with low rates of return per unit of time.

Although the returns on these costly infrastructures are low, capital intensity

TABLE 3.2

Construction, Equipment, and Stock Increase as Percentage of Gross Domestic Product, 1950s to 1980s

| Country | Construction | Equipment | Increase in Stock | Construction ÷ Equipment |
|---|---|---|---|---|
| Taiwan (annual average) | 9.3 (40.8) | 10.9 (47.8) | 2.6 (11.4) | 0.85 |
| 1950s | 6.8 (43.0) | 6.3 (39.9) | 2.7 (17.1) | 1.08 |
| 1960s | 8.7 (40.6) | 9.2 (43.0) | 3.5 (16.4) | 0.94 |
| 1970s | 11.2 (37.5) | 15.1 (50.5) | 3.6 (12.0) | 0.74 |
| 1980s | 10.7 (45.5) | 12.8 (54.5) | 0.0 (00.0) | 0.84 |
| South Korea (annual average) | 12.4 (56.1) | 8.2 (37.1) | 1.5 (6.8) | 1.51 |
| 1950s | 6.9 (54.3) | 3.1 (24.4) | 2.7 (21.3) | 2.23 |
| 1960s | 10.3 (56.0) | 6.7 (36.4) | 1.4 (7.6) | 1.54 |
| 1970s | 14.6 (53.5) | 10.9 (39.9) | 1.8 (6.6) | 1.34 |
| 1980s | 17.8 (60.3) | 11.9 (40.3) | (0.2) (0.6) | 1.50 |
| Japan (annual average) | 5.7 (17.6) | 24.3 (75.0) | 2.4 (7.4) | 0.23 |
| 1950s | 3.5 (12.8) | 19.8 (72.5) | 4.0 (14.7) | 0.18 |
| 1960s | 5.6 (15.6) | 26.7 (74.6) | 3.5 (9.8) | 0.21 |
| 1970s | 7.6 (22.0) | 25.7 (74.3) | 1.3 (3.7) | 0.30 |
| 1980s | 5.7 (19.1) | 23.7 (79.3) | 0.5 (1.6) | 0.24 |
| Philippines (annual average) | 9.6 (46.2) | 7.8 (37.5) | 3.4 (16.3) | 1.23 |
| 1950s | 9.0 (58.4) | 4.1 (26.6) | 2.3 (14.9) | 2.20 |
| 1960s | 8.5 (43.6) | 7.7 (39.5) | 3.3 (16.9) | 1.10 |
| 1970s | 9.2 (35.4) | 11.0 (42.3) | 5.8 (22.3) | 0.84 |
| 1980s | 12.4 (54.1) | 8.7 (38.0) | 1.8 (7.9) | 1.42 |
| Thailand (annual average) | 11.0 (47.6) | 10.5 (45.5) | 1.6 (6.9) | 1.05 |
| 1960s | 10.6 (50.9) | 8.5 (40.9) | 1.7 (8.2) | 1.25 |
| 1970s | 10.7 (42.8) | 12.3 (49.2) | 2.0 (8.0) | 0.87 |
| 1980s | 12.1 (51.5) | 10.7 (45.5) | 0.7 (3.0) | 1.13 |
| Singapore (annual average) | 30.6 | 15.1 (49.3) | 15.5 (50.7) | 0.97 |
| 1960s | 18.2 | 9.6 (52.7) | 8.6 (47.3) | 1.12 |
| 1970s | 35.2 | 15.1 (42.9) | 20.1 (57.1) | 0.75 |
| 1980s | 43.8 | 24.4 (55.7) | 19.4 (44.3) | 1.26 |
| Hong Kong (annual average) | 24.9 | 15.6 (62.7) | 9.3 (37.3) | 1.68 |
| 1960s | 23.7 | 14.3 (60.3) | 9.4 (39.7) | 1.52 |
| 1970s | 24.5 | 15.5 (63.3) | 9.0 (36.7) | 1.72 |
| 1980s | 27.7 | 18.1 (65.3) | 9.6 (34.7) | 1.88 |
| Sri Lanka (annual average) | 20.6 | 12.1 (58.7) | 8.5 (41.3) | 1.42 |
| 1970s | 16.9 | 10.1 (59.8) | 6.8 (40.2) | 1.48 |
| 1980s | 27.9 | 16.0 (57.3) | 11.9 (42.7) | 1.34 |

*Source:* Official national accounts.

*Note:* Figures in parentheses are the percentage of each of the components in gross domestic capital formation.

($K/L$) rises faster than labor productivity, offsetting the decline in capital productivity. One reason that capital intensity rises so rapidly is that irrigation and other rural infrastructure are used during the dry season for diversified agriculture by the same workers who grow rice during the wet months. Hence, these workers do not increase labor in the denominator of the capital intensity ratio. The fuller employment in the rural areas reduces underemployment in the urban areas through higher rural purchasing power. The reduction in underemployment offsets the decline of productivity with a rise in capital intensity. This holds true too for marginal capital intensity and marginal labor productivity, since the rising average quantities imply rising marginal quantities.

Japan's early agroindustrial transition took place between 1887 and 1938. Marginal capital output ratios in these decades rose higher than the upswing of the long swing periods, from 2.9 in 1887–97 to 3.8 in 1904–19 to 4.6 in 1930–38. Part of the increase comprised military structures and equipment. In the postwar period, 1953–69, the ratio was 2.6 with no military expenditures. More important was the full utilization of capacity with rapid growth, as Japan exported such labor-intensive manufactures as garments, textiles, and toys. The meager savings were applied to modernizing export industries with import of the latest technologies and to mechanizing agriculture when farm workers moved to the cities. There was little left for the financing of construction. In the 1970s and 1980s, the capital-output ratio rose from 1.6 in the 1970s to 2.3 in the 1980s.[4] More could not be spent on infrastructure, as income levels rose. These were very low average capital-output ratios in the history of economic growth, implying that the productivity of capital was extremely high, and were due mainly to the lack of land, the high costs of which limited construction of dwellings.

The incremental capital-output ratio of Taiwan rose from 1.6 in the 1950s to 2.2 in the 1960s and to 2.7 in the 1970s; it fell to 2.3 in the 1980s. These ratios were also low and attested to the labor intensity of Taiwan's industrial growth compared to South Korea's, whose ratios were 2.9, 3.0, 3.4, and 4.4 for these years. South Korean ratios were also higher than those of Taiwan because of the need for reconstruction after the North Korean invasion in the early 1950s; this and South Korea's emphasis on heavy industries required not only large equipment but also extensive infrastructures.[5]

These findings disagree not only with the views of those who believe that the capital-output ratio falls in the course of growth but with the views of those who, looking at the prewar and early postwar decades, thought there was no trend. The rise in the ratios for postwar Japan, Taiwan, and South Korea may be related to the exceptional speed with which these countries grew. To grow rapidly there must be a concentration of savings on the most productive type of capital, namely equipment, in the early postwar period. Later, with the rise of income, more can be spent on construction, especially residential and public construction, whose rates of return are relatively low. The rise in the capital-output ratios was due to the large amounts of savings available as growth sped up and to the use of increasing amounts for investments with low productivity.

This shift to construction tends to dampen labor productivity, but the shift was moderate—not much went to dwellings in East Asia. The shifts to investments in equipment were larger (table 3.2), which kept 1970 labor productivity high in Japan, Taiwan, and South Korea (see Table 3.3).

Nevertheless, without the protection from the elements that factories and plants give to the machines on the factory floor, their lifespan would be shortened and their efficiency impaired. It is, therefore, somewhat arbitrary to separate the productivity of construction from that of equipment, as they are cooperating factors of production. Nor is it right to think of construction in agriculture as less directly productive than equipment. Without irrigation, water to increase yields per hectare in the wet season and to grow additional crops in the drier months would not be available. Both rural and urban roads are needed to transport agricultural products to the city and manufactures from the city. Inventories are necessary for the smooth operation and full utilization of

TABLE 3.3

Investment and Productivity per Worker, 1950s to 1980s

| Country | 1950s | 1960s | 1970s | 1980s |
|---|---|---|---|---|
| Japan (thousand yen, 1980) | | | | |
| Investment per worker | 196.9 | 608.7 | 1270.4 | 1464.2 |
| Incremental GDP per investment | 0.33 | 0.31 | 0.14 | 0.12 |
| Incremental GDP per worker | 65.0 | 188.7 | 177.9 | 175.7 |
| Taiwan (thousand NT$, 1981) | | | | |
| Investment per worker | 7.11 | 19.15 | 53.95 | 68.42 |
| Incremental GDP per investment | 0.64 | 0.46 | 0.17 | 0.23 |
| Incremental GDP per worker | 4.55 | 8.81 | 9.17 | 15.74 |
| South Korea (thousand won, 1980) | | | | |
| Investment per worker | . | 245.3 | 639.4 | 1044.4 |
| Incremental GDP per investment | | 0.53 | 0.32 | 0.22 |
| Incremental GDP per worker | | 130.00 | 204.6 | 229.8 |
| Thailand (thousand baht, 1972) | | | | |
| Investment per worker | | | 2.69 | 2.87 |
| Incremental GDP per investment | | | 0.32 | 0.22 |
| Incremental GDP per worker | | | 0.86 | 0.63 |
| Philippines (pesos, 1972) | | | | |
| Investment per worker | 617.35 | 789.84 | 1200.62 | 1109.73 |
| Incremental GDP per investment | 0.30 | 0.23 | 0.24 | −0.04 |
| Incremental GDP per worker | 185.21 | 181.66 | 288.15 | −44.39 |

*Source:* Official national accounts and yearbooks; International Labor Organization, *Yearbook of Labor Statistics.*

*Note:* Investment per worker ($\Delta GCF/L$) $\times$ incremental GDP per investment ($\Delta GDP/I$) = Incremental GDP per worker ($\Delta GDP/L$).

equipment. Also, output in the capital productive ratio should not be attributed entirely to capital, as it may be due to longer hours of work, improved skills, and harder work by workers.

There is a need to single out equipment. Much of the increase in the productivity of capital in the twentieth century in the West may be traceable to the immense increase in the variety, speed, power, and versatility of machines and other equipment. In Taiwan and South Korea, horsepower per worker for industrial machines tripled between 1960 and 1980; it quadrupled in Japan in the same period. The difference this rise makes in labor productivity gains can be seen when such increases are compared with the rise in U.S. horsepower per worker of only 20 percent.[6] When full employment was approached in East Asia, the accelerated substitution of equipment for labor sped the growth of per worker product. This rise in efficiency enabled East Asia to increase its exports to the West and, hence, to import more efficient machines. The shortage of labor induced East Asia to replace aging machines with new machines, which employed less labor than the old machines. In the West, the replacement was slower, since labor was more abundant.

In the productivity growth equation, the growth of capital per worker, especially in the form of equipment investment, offsets the negative impact of construction investment on labor productivity. When labor markets became tighter with labor scarcity, East Asia substituted more powerful and speedier equipment for existing equipment. Without the faster rise in capital intensity over the decline in capital productivity ($\Delta K/L > \Delta O/\Delta K$), the growth of labor productivity would have been negative.

In Taiwan and South Korea, the rapid rise of incremental GDP per worker vis-à-vis the decline of capital productivity accelerated the rise of labor productivity (table 3.3). But note that capital productivity rose in the 1980s over the 1970s for both countries; this was due to the greater rise of equipment expenditures over construction and inventories in the 1980s, as petrodollars from the Middle East dried up and made the financing of construction difficult. Per worker productivity rose rapidly in the 1960s over the 1950s in Japan mainly because incremental capital per worker went up substantially, owing to the full mechanization of agriculture, the shift to heavy industrialization, and labor scarcity. Worker productivity growth slowed somewhat in the 1970s and virtually stagnated in the 1980s with the slow growth of GDP in the 1970s and the slowdown of incremental capital intensity.

In contrast, the fall in the growth of product per worker in the Philippines in the 1960s was due to the decrease in investment per worker, as capital-intensive industries built in the 1950s operated with excess capacity. Investment per worker rose sharply in the 1970s with the availability of petrodollars from the Middle East, but these investments were poorly made, and product per worker dropped in the 1980s as it did in the 1970s. Thus the entire postwar period was a tragedy of incredibly inept mismanagement of investment, a legacy the Philippines must live with today. The only way its economy can become viable is to open up to foreign entrepreneurs and let them develop the country. Although data for Thailand exist only for the 1970s and 1980s, they show why the Thais have caught up with the Philippines, surging ahead to become one of the newly industrializing economies.

The sustained and rapid rise of per capita income in East Asia was accompanied by increasing real wages, which shifted comparative advantage to higher levels of industrialization and induced these countries to graduate to more sophisticated industries. In Japan, the share of manufacturing value added contributed by heavy industry increased from 59 percent in 1965 to 66 percent in 1980. In South Korea the heavy industry share rose from 29 percent in 1960 to 60 percent in 1980. The value of machinery and equipment used per worker was four to six times greater in heavy industries than in light industries (food, textile, and wood products). Monthly earnings were generally higher in heavy industries, with basic metalworkers averaging about 50 percent more than textile workers. In Taiwan, the share of heavy industry rose from 57 percent in 1961 to 72 percent in 1981. Labor productivity rose much more in heavy industries, whose 1987 earnings were higher than those in light industries.[7]

Unfortunately, India's employment data are inadequate for the analysis of capital intensity. In China, the weighting of components of national products and investment affects the growth of these magnitudes substantially. Nevertheless, the failure of both countries' capital-intensive industries built in the 1950s (as in the Philippines) caused capital per worker and capital productivity to grow very slowly.

Annual average marginal capital output ratios are among the highest in India and the Philippines, even though they are the slowest growing countries in South and Southeast Asia. Their economies reflect the capital-intensive pattern of industrial growth, and unlike Japan, whose ratios are also among the highest, their entrepreneurs were not ready for complex industries: they did not have the experience to operate the facilities efficiently, capacity was substantially underutilized. In contrast, East Asia grew rapidly, with low marginal capital-output ratios (with the exception of Singapore, which invested heavily in public housing and permitted foreigners to invest and operate their industries). China went in massively for heavy industries during the Mao decades and, like India, experienced a slowing of growth.[8]

CONSTRUCTION

The role of construction in major, long-run fluctuations has been widely discussed in the literature, starting with Simon Kuznets's discovery of long swings in the nineteenth century and the delineation by Moses Abramovitz of a model of long swings in which construction plays the major role.[9] Despite major changes in the nature of the long swings since World War I, Abramovitz has held that construction influences wages, employment, capital formation, and aggregate demand, and through the lagged adjustment in capital stock brought about by the long gestation period, construction expenditures continue to produce imbalances between capacity to produce and aggregate demand.[10] The significance of construction in the growth of GDP lies in the fact that general business cycles (the Kitchens) are too short for the forces of secular growth to act themselves out, while the fluctuations of five to ten years (the Juglars) and those of half a century (the Kondratieffs) have not been theoretically established.[11] This leaves the swings as the main vehicle for observing secular growth, which are not easily observable without considerable manipulation of the raw data—aggregating, deflating, averaging, and so on.

In table 3.4 are shown the shares of construction in GDP in various Asian countries. For many of these countries, 1970s construction shares more than doubled those of the latter 1950s. This acceleration was made possible by the availability of foreign loans, largely petrodollars from Middle Eastern countries, which colluded to hike oil prices. With these loans, most Asian countries were able to raise the growth rate of total investment and GNP in the 1970s and into the early 1980s, even though there was a slowdown in growth in Western countries. The exceptions were Thailand, India, and Japan. When growth accelerated in Thailand during the latter half of the 1980s, there was a severe

TABLE 3.4

Construction Expenditures in Gross Domestic Product, 1955 to 1985 (constant values, percent)

| Country | 1955–1959 | 1960–1964 | 1965–1969 | 1970–1974 | 1975–1979 | 1980–1985 |
|---|---|---|---|---|---|---|
| Japan[a] | 4.0 | 4.9 | 6.6 | 7.7 | 7.5 | 5.3 |
| Taiwan[b] | 6.4 | 8.6 | 9.8 | 9.9 | 13.6 | 11.8 |
| South Korea[c] | 4.6 | 5.9 | 10.6 | 12.4 | 13.5 | 17.1 |
| Philippines[d] | 7.4 | 7.7 | 8.4 | 6.1 | 11.0 | 11.2 |
| Thailand[d] | 6.8 | 9.1 | 11.4 | 9.6 | 9.7 | 10.2 |
| Hong Kong[c] | | | 11.2 | 9.4 | 11.6 | 11.7 |
| Singapore[e] | | 8.1 | 11.4 | 11.9 | 10.9 | 17.2 |
| Malaysia[f] | | 9.9 | 9.5 | 11.3 | 16.0 | 18.7 |
| India[g] | 8.4 | 9.1 | 11.3 | 10.9 | 9.5 | 8.4 |
| Sri Lanka[f] | 2.8 | 8.5 | 8.8 | 4.3 | 7.6 | 12.1 |

*Source:* Official national accounts; United Nations, *Yearbook of National Accounts.*
[a] 1975 prices.
[b] 1981 prices.
[c] 1980 prices.
[d] 1972 prices.
[e] 1968 prices.
[f] Before 1972, current prices
[g] Data are from 1955–56, 1960–61, 1965–66, 1970–71, 1980–83.

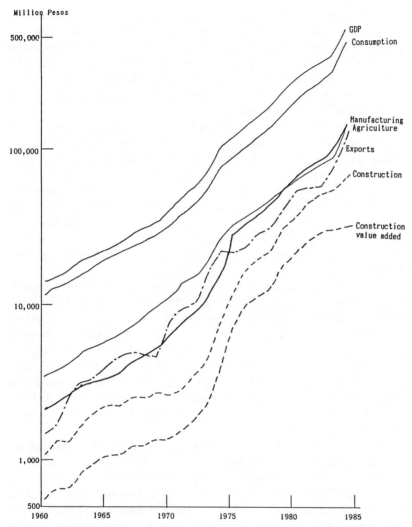

FIG. 3.1. The Philippines: gross domestic product and sector expenditures, 1960 to 1984 (in current prices). *Source:* Official national accounts.

shortage of infrastructures, which became a bottleneck in the expansion of the economy.

Construction expenditures on the expenditure side of the GDP account are transformed into (1) value added in the construction industry on the product side of the GDP account and (2) intermediate inputs produced in other industries. Thus, in the Philippines (figure 3.1) a total of P7,500 million in construction expenditures is converted into P3,100 million of value added in the construction industry and P4,400 million intermediate inputs purchased from other industries, chiefly lumber (P322 million), cement (P459 million), chemicals (P44 million), metals (P700 million), and trade (P357 million). These industries in turn add value to intermediate inputs purchased from other manufacturing industries, mining, and services. The multiplier mechanism and the accelerator work through the P4,400 million of intermediate inputs in other industries and the P3,100 million of value added.

The value added in construction is paid out in the form of employee compensation (76 percent of P3,100 million), property and proprietor's income (18 percent), taxes (4 percent), and depreciation allowances (4 percent). These are spent for consumption and investment goods, and the rest is saved. To the extent of the spending, the sales in the relevant industries are increased. These sales are divisible into value added and intermediate inputs. Similarly, the P4,400 million of intermediate inputs, decomposed into sales for the various industries, are decomposed into value added and intermediate input in the next round, and these are spent for consumption and other goods and the remainder saved.

In this chain of transactions, simple multiplier theory holds that eventually construction expenditures (less leakages abroad) will amplify incomes into multiples equal to the reciprocal of the marginal propensity to save. The final multiplied incomes are larger for construction expenditures than others because of the small leakages out of the country in the initial multiplicand (only P28 million in 1974). Moreover, the marginal propensity to save is likely to be very small for the construction industry and the industries selling to it, since most employee compensation is paid to manual workers. These workers do heavy work at low pay, so their Engel coefficient (the share of income spent on food) is among the highest in the economy.

In the Philippines in 1971 the propensity of the families of construction and manual workers to save was negative; even if we allow for understatement of income, the marginal propensity to save was still likely to be close to zero. For the average Filipino family, the ratio of savings to personal income was about one-tenth (8 percent of national income) during the second half of the 1970s, according to official national accounts. By including corporate and government savings (about 10 percent), the savings ratio to national income was 20 percent. Thus the multiplier for the nationwide average multiplicand may be five, but for construction expenditures it may be larger than five, since the bulk of the first rounds of value added from initial construction expenditures is paid to manual workers in the construction and construction material industries. The first and second rounds of the multiplier are overwhelmingly important in the dwindling series of rounds, but the later rounds are not unimportant if construction expenditures rise for several years.

The accelerator may also be larger for construction expenditures than for others. National accounting data show that value added in industries selling to

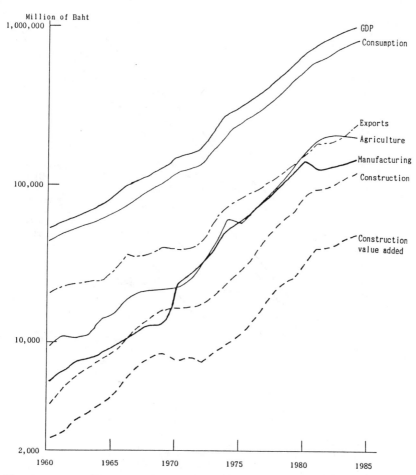

FIG. 3.2. Thailand: gross domestic product and sector expenditures, 1960 to 1984 (in current prices). *Source:* Official national accounts.

construction grew faster than in other manufacturing industries in the latter 1970s, when construction expenditures spurted. The growth in these industries was slower in the 1980s, when construction tapered off and then fell. The larger multiplier and accelerating effects imply that in the upswing the impact on GDP growth is likely to be strong but that when construction expenditures slow down, the downward impact is also likely to be large, worsening the imbalance between the capacity to produce and the capacity to consume in the downswing. During the upswing, construction expenditures pressure prices to rise, because the demand for food of the manual workers is large but the contribution to food production is meager. Hence, consumer prices, in which food prices loom large, are sensitive to construction expenditures.

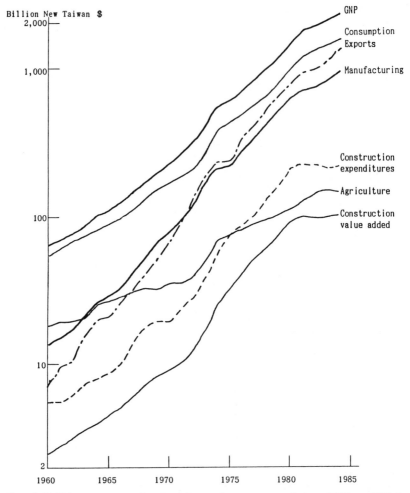

FIG. 3.3. Taiwan: gross national product and sector expenditures, 1960 to 1984 (in current prices). *Source:* Official national accounts.

Moreover, the sensitivity of GDP to construction in Asia (except in Japan) is due to the larger portions of GDP originating in sectors—particularly small enterprises (small peasant farms, the informal service sector, and most small and medium industries)—producing mainly for subsistence. Except for good or bad harvests, the growth of these sectors is fairly steady and slow. Thus the volatile sectors are construction and export, which fluctuate with changes in external conditions (pertaining to matters of finance or demand). Figures 3.1 through 3.8 show the relations between changes in construction, exports, and GDP, especially changes in the slopes of construction expenditures relative to exports and consumption expenditures and changes in the slopes of construc-

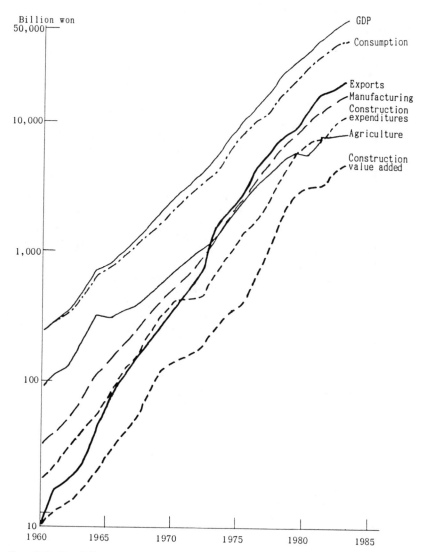

FIG. 3.4. South Korea: gross domestic product and sector expenditures, 1960 to 1984 (in current prices). *Source:* Official national accounts and yearbooks.

tion value added and of exports relative to agriculture and manufacturing for eight Asian countries.

In the Philippines, construction expenditures grew more slowly than exports and agriculture in the 1960s; in the 1970s these expenditures accelerated. Both construction expenditures and value added came closer to the GDP in the 1970s, contributing to the acceleration of consumption expenditures and GDP.

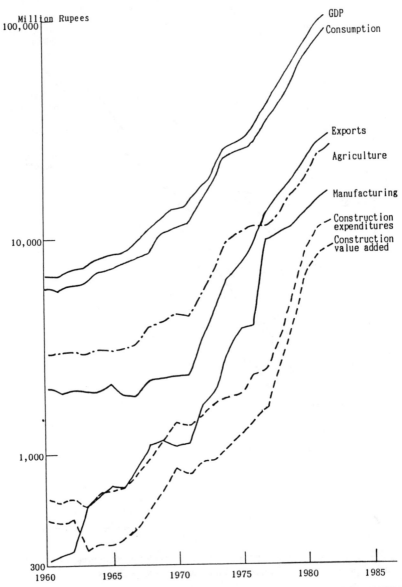

FIG. 3.5. Sri Lanka: gross domestic product and sector expenditures, 1960 to 1982 (in current prices). *Source:* Official national accounts.

Since agriculture was not growing as fast and manufacturing would have grown even slower if it were not for the multiplier, acceleration effect of construction, GDP would have grown slower than shown for the 1970s. The acceleration of both construction series led the acceleration of other series in the 1970s, but in

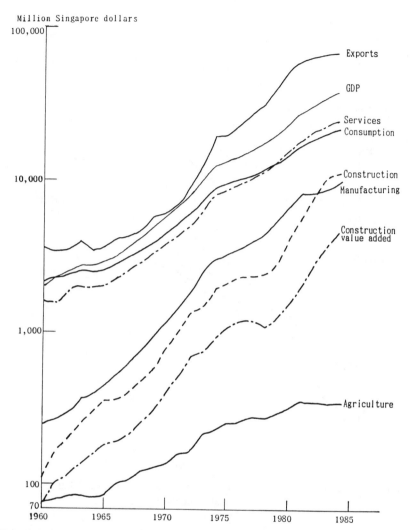

FIG. 3.6. Singapore: gross domestic product and sector expenditures, 1960 to 1984 (in current prices). *Source:* Official national accounts and yearbooks.

the early 1980s, when construction and exports tapered off, there was a slow-down in the other series. The constant-price GDP fell absolutely in 1984 and 1985, as construction and exports fell sharply.

In Thailand, construction expenditures rose faster than other expenditures in the 1960s and led the acceleration of GDP in the later years of the same period, despite the slow growth of exports, agriculture, and manufacturing. In the early 1970s, construction slowed considerably, and despite the acceleration of exports and manufacturing, GDP rose more slowly than in the 1960s. In the later

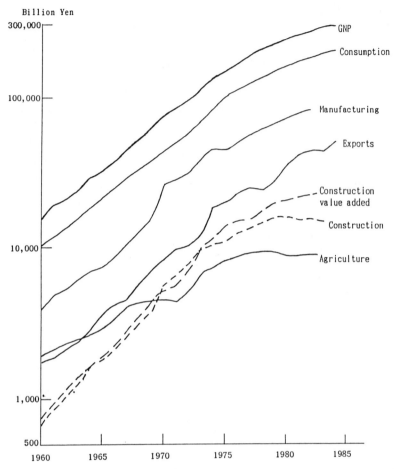

Fig. 3.7. Japan: gross national product and sector expenditures, 1960 to 1984 (in current prices). *Source:* Official national accounts and yearbooks.

1970s, the acceleration of construction and exports again pushed the GDP upward. In the 1980s construction slowed, retarding manufacturing and GDP.

In Taiwan, exports and construction grew rapidly in the 1960s and 1970s, more than offsetting the sluggish growth of agriculture. If it were not for the growth of exports and construction, industry and GDP would have grown more slowly than shown. In the 1980s construction tapered off, slowing GNP, although exports grew sufficiently to keep GNP rising—but at a slower pace than previously. Similarly, South Korean GDP growth was kept high by the rapid rise in exports and construction, despite the slower movement of agriculture in the 1960s and 1970s. Manufacturing would have grown slower than shown if it were not for exports and construction.

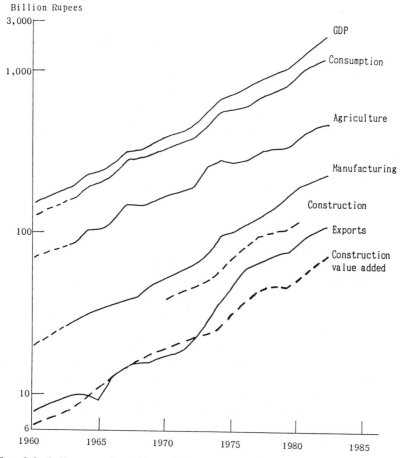

FIG. 3.8. India: gross domestic product and sector expenditures, 1960 to 1982 (in current prices). *Source:* United Nations, *Yearbook of National Accounts.*

In Sri Lanka, the growth of GDP was mainly due to the rise of construction in the 1960s, which also influenced manufacturing. In the early 1970s, the rapid growth of exports, manufacturing, and agriculture sustained GDP growth. In the latter 1970s, construction led the way to rapid GDP growth. In Singapore, throughout the 1960s construction spearheaded growth, pulling manufacturing up with it via the multiplier effect, despite slower increases in exports and services. This trend continued into the early 1970s. From the mid-1970s, construction growth sagged, slowing down GDP, but in the latter part of the 1970s and into the 1980s construction picked up and sustained GDP growth despite the slowing of exports and the other sectors. For countries not shown, data for the 1960s are not available.

In the 1970s, Hong Kong's construction expenditures in current prices rose twice as fast as GDP, sustaining it at a rate higher than the growth of exports and other sectors. The rapid growth of construction value added in Malaysia contributed to a faster rise of GDP than in Thailand, the Philippines, and Indonesia, where the growth of construction accelerated substantially in the 1970s. In countries where construction did not significantly accelerate, GDP did not accelerate but moved along at about the pace of the other sectors.

In Japan and India, the growth of construction was approximately the same as in the 1960s. There was little or no acceleration of GDP in these countries in the 1970s. In Japan, construction expenditures in the 1960s and 1970s moved roughly parallel to exports, manufacturing, and GNP, though it moved faster than the sagging agriculture sector. But in the 1980s, when construction slowed, exports rose, keeping GDP from slowing down. In India, exports moved more rapidly in the 1970s, offsetting the slowdown in agriculture. The U.S. data from its national accounts also show construction moving parallel with GNP, the ups and downs of construction being offset by exports, which grew faster than construction. In large economies, the impact of externally induced sectors play a lesser role in the economy. In Japan and the United States, with long industrial experience, physical infrastructures were largely built in the prewar decades, making unnecessary sharply rising construction in the postwar period.

Table 3.5 shows the growth rates in several Asian countries of GDP and construction expenditures (or construction value added) and exports. In all the countries except Hong Kong, the combined growth rates of construction and exports were highest in the 1970s.

It is often said that East Asian growth was export led, but the discussion above shows that it was not only export led but construction led, particularly in the 1970s, when exports tended to weaken with the slowdown in U.S. growth. To get high overall growth rates, it is not enough to generate high growth in manufacturing alone. If agriculture is not growing rapidly, construction growth must supplement exports if GDP growth is to come close to double digit.

Without increased construction expenditures and high export growth, a slowdown in GDP would have occurred by the early 1980s, perhaps along the lines of Japan's slowdown in the 1970s. Asian governments, sensing the adverse impact of OECD slowdown on their exports and investments in the latter 1970s, raised their borrowing from abroad for construction and resorted to deficit financing for countercyclical measures. But in doing so, they may have aggravated the situation and made more difficult the later adjustments, as events in the 1980s show. Unlike the Keynesian situation, excessive borrowing, public spending, and deficits preceded the difficulties in the 1980s, and to resort to them would rekindle the inflationary fires. Nor did the difficulties originate in excessive savings, as in Keynesian contractions.

In South Korea, Hong Kong, and the ASEAN Four, huge construction

TABLE 3.5

Growth of Gross Domestic Product and Construction and Exports, 1950s to 1980s (percent)

| Country | 1950s | 1960s | 1970s | 1980s |
|---|---|---|---|---|
| Taiwan | | | | |
|   Gross domestic product | 8.8$^a$ | 8.9 | 9.7 | 6.7 |
|   Construction and exports | 10.0$^a$ | 18.0 | 15.7 | 9.0 |
| Korea | | | | |
|   Gross domestic product | 3.7$^b$ | 8.4 | 8.0 | 7.0$^c$ |
|   Construction and exports | 7.5$^b$ | 23.0 | 15.9 | 12.1$^c$ |
| Philippines | | | | |
|   Gross domestic product | 6.5 | 5.1 | 6.2 | 0.7 |
|   Construction and exports | 3.8 | 5.1 | 9.5 | 0.5 |
| Thailand (current prices) | | | | |
|   Gross domestic product | 8.3 | 11.3 | 15.9 | 10.5 |
|   Construction and exports | 9.5 | 11.0 | 21.0 | 8.9 |
| Hong Kong | | | | |
|   Gross domestic product | | 8.9$^d$ | 9.4 | 5.4$^c$ |
|   Construction and exports | | 10.3$^e$ | 9.9 | 11.5$^f$ |
| Singapore | | | | |
|   Gross domestic product | | 9.2 | 9.1 | 8.1 |
|   Construction and exports | | 6.2 | 23.0 | 6.8 |
| Malaysia | | | | |
|   Gross domestic product | | 6.1$^g$ | 5.1$^h$ | 6.6 |
|   Construction and exports | | 4.1$^g$ | 6.1$^h$ | 9.0 |

*Source:* Official national accounts and yearbooks.

$^a$ 1951–60.
$^b$ 1953–60.
$^c$ 1980–83.
$^d$ 1961–70.
$^e$ 1966–70.
$^f$ 1980.
$^g$ Current prices.
$^h$ 1973–80.

expenditures, together with high oil prices, accelerated money supply and consumer prices in the latter 1970s and in the 1980s, as the multiplier, acceleration effects raised aggregate demand and overheated the economies. Most of these countries were forced to devalue their currencies as the deficits in their balance of payments mounted.[12] When export growth slowed in 1985, the second prop underlying high growth was removed, and to the financial difficulties was added a sharp fall in aggregate demand.

What may have happened is somewhat along the lines of past retardation in long swings. The slowdown or decline in construction and exports prior to 1985 produced a minus multiplier, acceleration effect on incomes and aggregate demand that canceled out the increase of the previous years as the economies

TABLE 3.6

Debt Service in Central Government Revenues, 1973 to 1983 (percent)

| Country | 1973 | 1976 | 1980 | 1983 |
|---|---|---|---|---|
| South Korea | 38.1 | 19.2 | 24.2 | 25.5 |
| Taiwan | 8.7 | 7.8 | 16.6 | — |
| Singapore | 3.6 | 5.5 | 9.6 | 9.4 |
| Malaysia | 6.4 | 11.0 | 5.8 | 11.9 |
| Thailand | 4.0 | 3.9 | 9.1 | 15.1 |
| Indonesia | 8.7 | 10.9 | 10.8 | 16.0 |
| Philippines | 15.2 | 9.6 | 12.9 | 30.0 |

Source: World Bank, World Tables; International Monetary Fund, Government Finance Statistics Yearbook.

settled down to lower equilibrium levels of aggregate activities. The process manifested itself in various forms. In nonagriculture, full-time and part-time unemployment increased while the hours of work per week of full-time employees shrank, thereby reducing aggregate hours worked per year. Real earnings per hour fell as wages were frozen or increased at rates lower than the rise in consumer prices. To varying degrees, this has happened in the first half of the 1980s in South Korea, Taiwan, Hong Kong, and the ASEAN Four, with adverse impact on the distribution of family incomes in most of these countries. Even in Taiwan, where inequality has been extremely low throughout the decades, there was a slight rise after 1980, in large part due to the decline in the share of employee compensation in total personal income. In Southeast Asia, the lowest inequality was in Thailand, but it rose in the 1980s, a situation associated with increasing idleness of the labor force.[13]

In addition to the pronounced negative multiplier, acceleration effect, construction booms are followed by large debt repayment flows (besides interest payments), which dampen household, government, and business spending. Singapore and Hong Kong illustrate the problem of household repayments on mortgages and the like: their residential construction booms were accompanied by an upsurge of home ownership based on loans extended by private banks and public institutions. In 1983 these amounted to about one-tenth of total personal income (estimated from official GNP data). To the extent of the annual repayments out of personal incomes of households, consumption expenditures must be reduced. The share of debt servicing (debt repayments and interest on loans outstanding) as a percentage of central government revenues are shown in table 3.6. The debt servicing of households, governments, and businesses, taken together, composes a substantial chunk of national income and has a major constraining effect on consumption and on governments' ability to create jobs.[14]

TECHNOLOGY AND EQUIPMENT

*Technology Transfer*

Since much of purchased capital incorporates new technology, the productivity gains from capital formation must be largely attributed to technological progress. Robert Solow and others have found that more than half of per worker productivity gain in the United States may be attributed to technological change and the other half to increases in labor and capital.[15] For developing countries, however, contributions from technological change are smaller than in developed countries, partly attributable to the predominance of agriculture and services, in which technological change is slower than in the industrial sector.[16] In developing countries, especially during the agroindustrial transition, most manufacturing enterprises are not mechanized, or if mechanized, only a few operations are mechanized, oftentimes with simple, old, and primitive equipment. Developing countries must also spend more on building modern physical infrastructure (bridges, harbors, highways, postal and communication systems, public health, sanitation, public utilities, etc.), which are by nature less directly productive than machines.

Countries not yet at the frontier of technology import most of their technologies instead of developing them. If their demand for technology is high and sustained, these countries can grow more rapidly by importing technology than those at the frontier, since it takes much longer to generate new technologies. Despite little difference in R and D investments between the United States and Japan in the 1970s, Japanese productivity grew faster with reductions in employees, while U.S. firms were adding employees.[17] This was probably because Japan imported a lot of technology throughout the 1970s. The number of agreements for technological imports rose from 1,157 in 1970 to 1,700 in 1979, averaging 1,569 in the late 1970s. One reason for this was that only in 1968 was the import of technology liberalized as government controls were relaxed. Expenditures for R and D increased from 1.1 billion yen in 1970 to 4.6 billion yen in 1980 to 8.9 billion yen in 1986, while registered patents rose from 31,000 in 1970 to 46,000 in 1980 and to 60,000 in 1986. Direct foreign investments from the United States to Japan rose in the 1970s, contributing more to the rise of Japan's GNP than to that of the United States.[18] The United States was the main supplier of technology to Japan. While the United States paid $218 million in royalties for technology imports in 1971, it received $2,465 million for technology exports, compared to Japan's $488 million and $60 million, respectively. Japan's policies for selecting, adapting, and diffusing imported technologies were more effective in raising productivity than those of the United States. Then, too, more of U.S. R and D was directed toward creating new (not more) products (47 percent) than in Japan (17 percent).[19]

Most of the industries in East Asia before the 1980s were not fully mechanized, and the process of substituting machines for people yielded large increases in productivity. But once production processes are fully mechanized, productivity increases slow down, because they depend on replacing old machines with new ones, which takes time. It is not economically feasible to junk a machine that operates well even though an improved type is available. Just as Japan's iron and steel industry produced more cheaply than that of the United States in the 1970s and 1980s, since its plant and equipment was newer, so in the early 1990s the younger Korean steel industry is able to make headway against the Japanese steel industry not only in Southeast Asia but in Japan itself. This is true especially for heavy and chemical industries, where plant and other structural investments are very large and where it is very costly to discard obsolete equipment—particularly in poor countries like India and China, which have invested extensively in heavy and chemical industries.

### Technology Supplies

A quick way to obtain a technology is through the import of a machine embodying the technology. Often this requires that the importing firm send its technical experts abroad to learn about the use of the machine and master its reproduction. If the machine is not too complex, it can be imported and taken apart to learn how to operate and reproduce it. For most of the less sophisticated technologies in light industry, skilled workers can master them by working with the machines and then setting up their own enterprises. This happened in the early postwar decades in Hong Kong's textile industry.

Figure 3.9 shows the course of machinery importation to Japan, Taiwan, South Korea, Hong Kong, and Singapore. Of course, not all of the imported machinery necessarily embodied the newest technologies. Some older machinery has to be imported because the capability to reproduce them is not available, particularly machinery produced on a mass scale, such as automobiles. For Japan, South Korea, and Taiwan, machinery imports may be a rough proxy for machines embodying new technologies. Japan's imports tapered off after the mid-1960s in part due to its slowdown in growth but also to its growing technological capabilities in reproducing machines with its expanded R and D. The slowdown in the 1970s and 1980s was mild in Taiwan and South Korea, showing that they were still not at the technological frontier. They will likely approach that frontier in the 1990s and find themselves relying on their own R and D for new technologies.

Another way in which technology can be imported is through direct foreign investment. Foreign firms bring in equipment embodying technologies that are usually not available to local firms. But if foreigners refuse to transfer the technologies by keeping them secret from local workers, by not using local supplies, or because of language barriers or the inability of locals to absorb the new technology, their contribution to overall growth will be limited.[20] Ma-

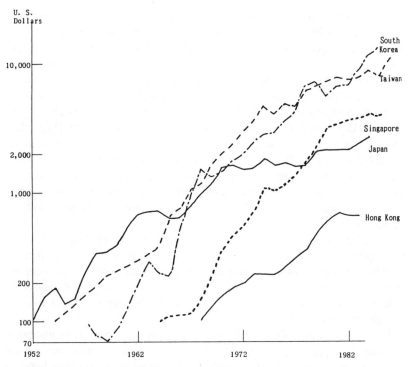

FIG. 3.9. Dollar value of imports and equipment, 1952 to 1986. *Source:* Official national accounts and yearbooks. *Note:* In constant prices except for Singapore.

laysia, Hong Kong, Singapore, and Taiwan grew rapidly by allowing foreign investors to come in in considerable numbers. Japan and South Korea, however, restricted the entry of foreign firms. Mainland China opened up in the 1980s. The Philippines and the South Asian countries were very restrictive. Taiwan's direct foreign investment was 4 percent of GNP in 1986; foreign investment was less than 0.05 percent in South Korea, Indonesia, the Philippines, Sri Lanka, and Pakistan.[21] Japan and South Korea, with well-developed entrepreneurial classes, brought technologies from abroad through royalties and other payments and did not have to depend on foreign investors.

An increasingly important source of technology, especially during the second transition, is through the purchase of patents and payment of royalties, although sometimes these technologies are pirated, and payments are not made. Japan made technological progress through royalties. Taiwan's payments were large, about $5 million per capita in 1983, followed by South Korea's $3.7 million and Thailand's $1.4 million. Bangladesh had the lowest, with $3 thousand per capita.[22]

Fearful of the boomerang effect, developed countries withhold their newest technologies from developing countries. The latter then have no other choice but to develop them through their own R and D. This happened to Japan in the 1980s, and now Japan is doing the same to Taiwan and South Korea with respect to certain electronic technologies. Japan developed R and D capabilities before World War II. During the two centuries of Tokugawa isolation, technological capabilities had to be developed, since outside information was not available. Japan's high level of education made this development possible. After the Meiji Restoration, the family conglomerates (Zaibutsu) were large enough to spend on R and D to develop new technologies.[23] In 1983 Japan's R and D spending was the highest in Asia, at 2.3 percent of GNP; Korea was second, with 1.3 percent; India followed, with 0.9 percent; then came Taiwan with 0.7 percent; and the Philippines, with 0.2 percent.[24] India's high share for a poor country is due to the need for its big industries to keep abreast (although without much success) of rapid technological developments in the heavy chemical and machinery industries.

In the Philippines, the highly protected capital-intensive industries were not under pressure to conduct R and D, since they had monopolies in the domestic market and had no need to meet foreign competitors, since they were too inefficient to export. An example of the former is the cement industry, and of the latter the consumer appliance industry, both of which operate with technologies brought in in the 1970s.

In sum, the supply of new technologies in East Asia appears to be enough to upgrade the capital used for raising productivity, while for most other Asian countries, this is not the case. Thailand and Malaysia fall midway between these two groups. But it is demand for technologies that is more relevant to the pace at which technological change takes place, especially in developing countries. (I should note that foreign investors often import to these countries secondhand machines that have become obsolete in their own countries.) Without the need to incorporate new technologies, firms do not do so.

But more than competition is involved in rapid technical change; this discussion has been confined to industrial technology, but a word needs to be said on plantation crops. British plantations in Malaysia have improved rubber and palm oil crops through extensive R and D, but this cannot be said of Indonesia and Philippine plantations growing coconut and sugar crops. This contrast accounts in large part for the better performance of Malaysian agriculture over agriculture in Indonesia and the Philippines, especially in the 1960s and 1970s.[25]

*Technology Demand*

The experience of East Asia suggests that, when an economy begins to approach full employment, its diminishing pool of unemployed workers is the most important factor in the pace at which technologies are absorbed into the economy. When surplus labor begins to disappear and it becomes difficult to hire workers, especially skilled ones, the entrepreneur must resort to substituting machinery and other labor-saving devices for workers and must use more powerful and efficient equipment under conditions of highly competitive markets.[26] Electric-powered (in contrast to steam-powered) technologies were introduced into the United States at a slow pace around the turn of the twentieth century until there was labor scarcity in the 1920s. This was the experience of the textile industry in Japan and Hong Kong in the 1950s and in Taiwan and South Korea in the late 1960s, of the iron and steel industry in Japan in the 1960s, and of the electronics industry in the 1980s in all of East Asia.

Moreover, with rising per capita incomes under full employment, the demand for higher quality products accelerates: many technologies are designed not to save labor but to improve the quality of existing products or to make new products. The diffusion process is also relevant on the demand side: diffusion of new technologies will depend on the technical capabilities to absorb them. This capability depends on the supply of skilled workers and technicians, especially scientists and engineers, which in turn depends on the educational system.

The best index of the pace of technological introduction is number of technologies imported. Unfortunately, data going back to the 1950s exist only for Japan. These show that in the 1950s technological imports were around 250, and growth was slow in most of the 1950s. There was a speeding up from the end of the 1950s, when full employment was reached, and into the 1960s and 1970s, when labor shortages became severe. From 250 in 1958, the number of technology imports rose to 600 in 1960, doubled to 1,200 in 1963, rose to 1,700 in 1968, and to 2,500 just before the oil price hike in 1973. Taiwan's machinery imports accelerated in the mid-1960s, when full employment was being reached; imports tapered off in the latter 1970s. In South Korea, even though there was some unemployment, acceleration began in the 1970s, in part to meet the competition from the other NIEs, especially Taiwan. Singapore's acceleration also began in the late 1960s, when the economy began to grow rapidly— but was, like South Korea, not yet at full employment. Thus the pace at which new technologies are demanded quickens even before full employment is reached, because firms are forced to incorporate the latest technologies in order to compete in domestic and foreign markets. There is an interplay between competition and labor scarcity in the demand for technologies: where there is limited rivalry in highly protected industrial markets, as in the Philippines, Indonesia, India, and other South Asian countries, and where labor surplus is large and capital is scarce, technological progress is likely to be slow.

This points to the greater importance of technology demand in the growth of GDP in the first transition. Technology can readily be imported from abroad, since industries at this point are largely low technology. When economies move into the second transition, they need more sophisticated technologies, which are difficult to import, making R and D capabilities essential. Thus in the first transition, the demand side governs the pace of technological progress. In the second transition, the supply side comes to the fore.[27]

### Technology Policies

Japan's technology policies in the 1950s and 1960s were essential to the rapid growth of its economy. The government directed imported technologies to industries strategic to economic growth[28] and to firms capable of adopting and using them effectively.[29] These policies helped to keep the price of technological imports low by reducing the rivalries of Japanese firms bidding to buy the technologies; they also promoted their widespread diffusion and adaptation by private industry. After industrial development made considerable headway by the end of the 1960s and exports rose, government restrictions on technology imports virtually disappeared. In the 1950s, the government was concerned with the use of scarce foreign exchange earnings to pay for imported technologies to speed the renovation of the iron and steel and chemical industries (which were given top priority in industrial policies). In the first half of the 1960s, imported technology was channeled to consumer goods industries, which were targeted to earn foreign exchange through exports.

Unlike Japan, Taiwan and South Korea did not promote technology imports, but the need to meet internal and external competition spurred entrepreneurs to bring in foreign technology. As long as the export industries were low tech, light industries, as they were in the 1950s, 1960s and 1970s, there was little need for government intervention except to promote the training of technology manpower through appropriate educational and training policies. But in the 1980s, as these countries moved into higher technology industries, they saw the need for policies to generate, import, adapt, and disseminate technologies. Their R and D expenditures rose rapidly to levels comparable to those of industrialized countries, their policies to attract direct foreign investment were expanded, their policies on foreign technology imports were liberalized, and they collected information on foreign technologies.[30]

The following lessons may be drawn from the experience of East Asia. It is important to build technological capabilities for the assimilation, adaptation, and modification of imported technology. Most Asian countries are in the first transition, when import of foreign technologies, not their generation, is the cheapest and the most expeditious road to technological progress. But one gets the impression that countries in South and Southeast Asia are spending more for generating than importing technologies. In Bangladesh and Sri Lanka, royalties for imports are less than 10 percent of their R and D budgets, while in Pakistan and Thailand, royalties are lower than R and D spending.[31] Not enough is spent on the modification and adaptation of imported technologies, perhaps due to pressure from academic scientists interested in developing science and basic technologies. But benefits from basic research are likely to be slim in developing countries, where the funding, equipment, and personnel for research are meager.

It would be better if these scientists went abroad to work in good laboratories with well-trained colleagues. The experience they would get would be valuable when they returned home to train students and conduct basic research. This is happening in South Korea and Taiwan, whose scientists get basic research experience in the United States and return home to meet the research needs of their countries—which increase as these countries approach the technology frontier. In the past, Japan emphasized adaptive and applied research in comparison to the West, whose scientists opted for pure research, which gains them prestige but has little impact on GNP.[32] And finally, more should be spent on collecting and disseminating information and on improving and modifying foreign technologies, especially those of interest to export-oriented small and medium industries. The best way to learn how to generate new technologies may be through improving and modifying imported technologies.[33]

Above all, the experience of East Asia indicates that the spread of technological progress in the first transition is associated with the demand for, and not the supply of, technologies. This implies that macropolicies to generate employment and reach full employment are crucial in raising the demand for labor-saving technologies and, together with policies to maintain vigorous competition in the domestic and foreign markets, will force entrepreneurs to junk old machines and buy new ones based on better technology. An open foreign investment policy will attract foreigners to bring in investments with advanced technologies. Educational programs, emphasizing math and science together with good engineering colleges are required to generate improved technologies. Not to be neglected is vocational training to increase the supply of skilled workers. In these and other ways, the productivity of capital can be raised and maintained so that productivity per worker rises even without rising capital per worker. More than anything else, the full utilization of capital capacity and its efficient operation by well-trained workers underlie the productivity of capital.

# CHAPTER 4

# Personal Savings and Consumption

The importance of savings is that, in the transition from agriculture to industry, it is the shortage of savings that constrains investment. Current savings not only finance current business and public investment but accumulate funds for children's education, for down payments on houses and consumer durables, and for old age and emergencies. These savings are in the meantime loaned to businesses for investment to expand current production. The greater the need for households to save for the future, the higher may be the propensity of householders to work, since the harder they work, the less need there is to minimize consumption to meet savings needs. Accordingly, the decline in the need for saving may have an unfavorable impact on productivity in at least three areas: lower investments for businesses, weaker propensities to work, and smaller amounts saved for children's education.

In the developed countries of the West, the urgency to save has declined, since most of the physical infrastructure (plants and equipment and dwellings) have been built and the needs for old age are being met by social security systems. Not only the supply of savings but also the demand for capital has slowed. But this is not the case in Asia—not even in Japan, where many more physical infrastructures and homes must be built and where the costs of higher education are relatively high.

One of the concerns of this chapter is to see how Japan and Taiwan have reached a stage of development where gross national savings exceed their huge gross domestic capital formation.

The data on savings and investment is of better quality than the data on consumption but not as good as government expenditure data. Equipment expenditures are mainly taken from import statistics and industrial censuses, and construction estimates are based on building permits, but these sources usually do not cover the smallest firms, which employ fewer than a dozen workers. Inventory estimates are poor for farms and small firms. Corporate and government savings are far better than personal savings, which are obtained as residuals in the saving and investment account and checked against the difference between personal income and consumption.

Table 4.1 shows the sources of financing of gross domestic capital formation for five countries. (The other countries were unable to estimate personal savings and depreciation, although many were able to estimate national and domestic savings based on gross capital formation data.) Table 4.1 shows that the total of finances of gross capital formation (or gross domestic savings) in current prices increased most rapidly in South Korea and least rapidly in the Philippines. In real terms, Thailand's savings rose even faster than those of Japan and Taiwan, whose GDP growth rates were much higher. But in relation to GDP (see table 4.2), Japan, Taiwan, Singapore, and Hong Kong registered the largest percentage of savings to GDP; if the 1950s had been included, Japan and Hong Kong probably performed best, as Singapore, South Korea, and Taiwan started the 1950s much more slowly. In the 1960s in Singapore, forced savings through high social security contributions—by both employers and employees—raised savings. For comparison, trends in the Western industrialized countries are shown in table 4.2. Savings rates fell sharply in the West after the 1960s. By the 1980s, except for Japan and France, savings fell to 10 percent or lower in the other countries. The fall was due to declines in the business, household, and government sectors.

In all countries except the Philippines, personal savings contributed the largest amount to the financing of gross domestic capital formation. Even in the Philippines, personal income in constant prices fell in the 1980s, and most households had to spend all their incomes on consumption. Normally, under conditions of growing real GDP per capita, personal savings are the largest contributor to the financing of gross domestic capital formation in monsoon Asia, where corporations play a far less important role in the private sector than unincorporated family enterprises, where savings are included in personal savings. The latter do not generally practice depreciation accounting, so that depreciation allowances contribute far less to the financing of gross capital formation than in the industrialized West.[1] This is one reason that depreciation estimates are poor, leading to the use of gross data instead of net data.

South Korea financed its capital formation through borrowing abroad, piling up the highest external indebtedness per capita in Asia by the mid-1980s. Taiwan began to lend abroad in the latter 1970s, since its personal savings rate was much higher than South Korea's, and Taiwan refrained from investing huge sums in heavy industry, as South Korea did in the 1970s. The Philippines had the next highest per capita foreign borrowing, but it was much worse off than South Korea because the borrowed funds were wasted on bad investments and were funneled into the pockets of Marcos and his cronies.

Depreciation allowances and corporate savings are mainly a function of the stage of development. In the early stage, corporations are not extensively developed, and business is conducted by family enterprises, most of them small. Only in the latter stages do capital needs for large industries and businesses become extensive. Government savings can be especially important in

TABLE 4.1

Sources of Financing of Gross Domestic Capital Formation, 1950s to 1980s
(billions of local currency)

| Source of Financing | Taiwan | Japan | Thailand | Philippines | South Korea |
|---|---|---|---|---|---|
| Households and nonprofit industries (simple average) | 110.7 | 15,535.2 | 44.2 | 6.4 | 1,403.5 |
| 1950s | 0.9 | 900.2 | | 0.8 | 3.8 |
| 1960s | 9.6 | 4,107.7 | 9.1 | 1.9 | 29.6 |
| 1970s | 78.6 | 22,444.7 | 36.5 | 10.1 | 975.5 |
| 1980s | 353.7 | 34,688.0 | 87.0 | 12.9 | 4,605.0 |
| General government (simple average) | 44.8 | 3,750.9 | 2.8 | 5.3 | 978.0 |
| 1950s | 1.2 | 528.0 | | 0.2 | 0.6 |
| 1960s | 3.3 | 2,233.2 | 3.0 | 0.3 | 3.0 |
| 1970s | 46.7 | 5,186.8 | 5.8 | 4.7 | 31.5 |
| 1980s | 127.8 | 7,055.7 | −0.5 | 15.8 | 3,876.9 |
| Public and private corporations (simple average) | 32.2 | 1,932.4 | 6.9 | 3.3 | 1,576.4 |
| 1950s | 0.7 | 329.9 | | 0.1 | 6.2 |
| 1960s | 4.0 | 1,666.5 | 1.4 | 0.3 | 48.6 |
| 1970s | 24.3 | 3,180.3 | 6.6 | 5.0 | 828.8 |
| 1980s | 99.9 | 2,552.7 | 12.6 | 7.8 | 5,422.1 |
| Net external borrowing (simple average) | −71.2 | −805.3 | 17.4 | 4.4 | 399.4 |
| 1950s | 0.5 | 7.6 | | | −0.1 |
| 1960s | 1.2 | 108.4 | 1.0 | −0.1 | 38.3 |
| 1970s | −9.7 | 858.4 | 12.0 | 5.2 | 516.9 |
| 1980s | −276.8 | −4,195.5 | 39.3 | 8.0 | 1,042.4 |
| Depreciation provision (simple average) | 59.0 | 14,822.4 | 33.3 | 19.9 | 1,275.8 |
| 1950s | 1.7 | 860.9 | | | 7.1 |
| 1960s | 7.3 | 4,146.7 | 4.5 | 1.3 | 53.3 |
| 1970s | 44.5 | 19,588.8 | 21.7 | 12.3 | 863.2 |
| 1980s[a] | 182.4 | 34,693.3 | 73.8 | 46.0 | 4,179.4 |
| Total (simple average) | 175.5 | 35,235.6 | 132.4 | 29.9 | 4,832.7 |
| 1950s | 5.0 | 2,626.6 | | 1.2 | 17.6 |
| 1960s | 25.4 | 12,262.5 | 5.3 | 3.7 | 172.8 |
| 1970s | 184.4 | 51,259.0 | 100.7 | 32.2 | 3,215.9 |
| 1980s | 487.0 | 74,794.2 | 291.1 | 82.4 | 15,924.3 |

Source: Asian Development Bank, *Key Indicators;* Asian Development Bank, Asian Development Outlook; World Bank, *World Tables.*

Note: Gross national savings is equal to gross domestic savings plus net factor income from abroad. Gross domestic investment is equal to gross national savings plus net transfer abroad and net borrowing from abroad. For the other countries in Asia for which data were available, gross domestic investment exceeded gross national savings in most years, except in a few years for Indonesia, the Philippines, and Malaysia, which was due to their need to pay off their debts. This was not the case in East Asia.

[a] 1980–86.

TABLE 4.2

National Savings as Share of Gross Domestic Product, 1960s to 1980s

| Country | 1960s | 1970s | 1980s |
|---|---|---|---|
| Gross national savings | | | |
| Japan | 23.2 | 32.8 | 30.8 |
| Taiwan | 21.2 | 32.2 | 37.0 |
| Korea | 17.5 | 25.1 | 27.2 |
| Singapore | 14.1 | 23.7 | 42.4 |
| Hong Kong | 11.3 | 34.4 | 30.2 |
| Malaysia | 19.8 | 26.6 | 26.4 |
| Philippines | 19.4 | 24.9 | 18.1 |
| Thailand | 20.6 | 20.6 | 16.3 |
| Indonesia | 2.6 | 18.6 | 22.1 |
| Pakistan | 10.8 | 10.7 | 15.3 |
| Bangladesh | 8.9 | 2.5 | 5.6 |
| India | — | 19.2[a] | 20.4 |
| Sri Lanka | — | 15.4 | 10.0 |
| Nepal | — | — | 11.9 |
| United States | 18.6 | 19.1 | 17.7 |
| Net national savings[b] | | | |
| United States | 10.6 | 8.9 | 3.9 |
| Japan | 25.6 | 24.6 | 20.2 |
| West Germany | 19.9 | 14.3 | 10.7 |
| France | 26.3 | 25.4 | 19.6 |
| United Kingdom | 11.2 | 8.2 | 6.2 |
| Italy | 15.0 | 12.1 | 7.5 |
| Canada | 11.3 | 13.3 | 9.4 |

*Source:* Asian Development Bank, *Key Indicators;* United States, *Statistical Abstract;* Organization for Economic Cooperation and Development, Working Paper 67.

*Note:* As there are conceptual differences, the figures are not strictly comparable, especially with respect to the U.S. and the Japanese data. See Fumio Hayashi, "Is Japan's Saving Rate High?" Federal Reserve Bank of Minneapolis, *Quarterly Review* (Spring, 1989).

[a] 1975–79.

[b] 1980s are 1981–87.

this early stage, when corporate activities are minimal and personal incomes are too low to generate much savings. The Meiji government in Japan transformed its traditional feudal economy in the latter decades of the nineteenth century through high land taxes. Forced savings were extracted from the peasantry through high land taxes to finance the modernization of transportation, communication, education, and the mechanization of the textile industry and others. Through policies such as taxes, subsidies, and price controls public savings can substitute for private savings. But they can be excessive and have undesirable social and political repercussions, as they did in Meiji Japan.[2] It may be that farm families were excessively taxed in Taiwan and South Korea in the 1950s and 1960s.

Personal savings become an increasingly important component of gross national savings as household incomes of the majority rise beyond subsistence levels—but it is not necessarily the central problem in economic development.[3] This is an overly simplified view of economic development, despite the great importance of personal savings, since in the early stages of growth nations can borrow from abroad, and forced savings can be generated by government. Personal savings were minimal in Japan before World War II and in Taiwan and South Korea in the 1950s and 1960s. Only after the early stages, when incomes begin to grow rapidly, do personal incomes rise to high levels. Hence, savings are partly a function of economic growth in the later stages of the transition from agriculture to industry. They are a function of growth, because families with higher incomes begin to save for the future: to educate their children for work in a growing economy with a changing technology and to provide for their own old age, as average life expectancy lengthens beyond retirement age.

When incomes are growing rapidly, it is easier to save large amounts from the incremental incomes flowing out of productivity gains, because consumption needs may be satisfied by income earned before productivity gains. Since the amount of savings responds much more to the future needs of savers instead of to the current needs of investment (because interest rates may not be so important to the amount of savings), savings can be lower than investment needs in the early stages and higher than investment needs in the later stages of the agroindustrial transition. Nevertheless, savings are always in great demand by small firms with little access to organized credit markets.

Several theories focus on the growth of personal income as the determinant of savings. For Keynes, the determinant is the absolute level of income; for Duesenberry, it is relative incomes; for Friedman, it is the increase of transitory income over permanent income; and for others, it is the life cycle.[4] But incomes (whether absolute, relative, or changing) do not sufficiently explain changes in personal savings.[5] This was especially true for 1980 personal savings in the West and in East Asia. In Europe, West Germany, with higher income growth than France, had lower savings rates; and in the United States, savings rates (defined to include public pensions) slowly fell despite positive GNP growth rates. Japan's share of savings in personal incomes has been one of the highest among the industrialized countries, even though real incomes are much lower in Japan than in the United States and Germany. Taiwan, with very much lower incomes than Japan or the West, has registered the highest personal (and total) savings rate in the world.

Savings and income levels in the distant past are just as important in explaining 1990 levels. Japan and Taiwan became affluent only in the 1980s, and they have a long way to go before they will accumulate enough consumer wealth (such as homes and cars), stocks and bonds, education, physical infrastructure, old age pensions, and so on to catch up with the wealth of Westerners, whose affluence has been high for about a century (with the exception of Italy, a latecomer, which in the 1980s had a personal savings rate of 21.7 percent, the highest in Europe and higher than Japan's 20.2 percent).[6] In the early 1960s, capital formation by U.S. business firms had reached levels high enough to transfer some of their savings to finance household purchases of homes and consumer durables, while consumer incomes were high enough to repay the debts incurred.[7] But East Asian businesses have only in the 1980s become affluent and are not able to generate excess savings to lend to consumers, who must save enough to buy homes and durables. Consumer credit cards, for example, are of limited use in East Asia.

In Japan in 1986, 79 percent of consumers saved for emergencies, 50 percent saved for children's education, and 44 percent saved for retirement. Other goals were less important: homes and durables, leisure, children's marriages, bequests, cars. In Taiwan in 1984, the most frequent purpose cited by savers was children's education, followed by emergencies, house and durables purchases, old age, and marriage. In South Korea in 1986, the most important was children's education, followed by house purchase, old age, emergencies, and weddings, with leisure the lowest.[8]

With not much worry about accumulating consumer assets, the United States became in the 1980s a more leisure-oriented nation, compared to its work orientation of the 1950s and 1960s. In Western countries, higher education is relatively cheap because the high incomes of the past half century have enabled their public institutions to acquire buildings and campuses, while private colleges and universities have inherited wealth from many generations of alumni. Loans and scholarships are also plentiful.

If aspirations for home and durable goods ownership, security in old age, and advanced education for children are universal, then with income growth, people in Southeast and South Asia will also begin to save more of their incomes. But there is something peculiarly Confucian in survey responses by East Asians: they appear to be less attracted to leisure and entertainment, to cars and other durables, and to have a higher regard for their children's education and marriages, for bequests, and for debt repayments. These responses are in line with Confucian teachings on paying homage to ancestors by improving family status and continuing the family lineage. Similarly, no system of ethics puts as great an emphasis on the importance of education as Confucianism, which teaches that the ills of the world can be corrected only by educated men and that the well-being of the family can be best promoted by the education of descendants.[9]

Taiwan's strong propensity to save may be due to traditional (as against neo-) Confucianism, which emphasizes the need to provide all male descendants not only with education but with a home and a start on their careers.[10] The situation is different in Japan and South Korea, where under primogeniture only the eldest son is provided with a home and helped to start his career. Japan's savings rates—despite much higher incomes—have not reached the level in Taiwan.

But the higher personal savings rate for Taiwan in the 1970s and 1980s may also be due to low savings rates in the 1950s and 1960s. It may be that Taiwan was trying to catch up to Japan, just as Japan was trying to catch up to the United States. South Korea's rate may rise to higher levels but not perhaps as high as Taiwan's.

In Japan, where the costs of education are higher than in other countries, older families dissave to pay for the current education of their teenagers, offsetting the savings of younger families for the future education of their young children; this equation reduces personal savings, with net dissaving. Then, too, the proportion of Japanese families with retired persons to families with workers is larger than in other Asian countries, so that there are more families dissaving. Dissaving is also large for families spending for weddings.[11] Japan's fertility fell much earlier than in other Asian countries.

In both Japan and Taiwan, the proportions of personal savings rose sharply when full employment was approached—in Japan from around the mid-1950s and in Taiwan from the mid-1960s. The reason for this is that disposable incomes rise as full employment is reached. Unincorporated businesses find loans difficult to obtain from the organized banking system, and they must rely on their own savings or loans from relatives, friends, or the curb markets, where interest rates are high because risks are high. Also with full employment, there is a saving on food consumption. In the rural sector, full employment came about as peasants found more to do off the farm, and the additional incomes thus earned enabled even the smallest farms to save much of their off-farm incomes.[12]

Thus the forces influencing the savings rates in East Asia are many—not simply personal income or interest rates. Increases in income raise disposable and discretionary income, but how much of this discretionary income is saved or consumed depends on what future needs are. And how much is provided for future needs depends on the social values and beliefs of the family. Hence, income can be said to be just one of three components determining savings, future needs and social values being the others. In East Asia, the desire to save for the future is strong. Their unsatisfied needs must be taken into account by Western countries, which look with suspicion on the East for saving too much. Note also that East Asia has moved toward consumption-led growth and away from export-led growth. Nevertheless, some time will have to elapse before its savings rates will be substantially reduced.

It is not easy to see how much other countries in Asia will save as their incomes rise. Thailand's personal savings ratio rose to nearly 20 percent in the expansion of the 1970s, and Malaysia's national savings share of GDP also rose in the 1970s. It is likely that with full employment these countries will begin to save as much as East Asia did, but the work ethic appears to be stronger in East Asia than in the rest of Asia. It may take a longer time before savings rise to a very high level in these other countries, all of which, except Thailand, are troubled by high unemployment and underemployment. On the other hand, the personal savings ratio is low in these other countries because of low personal incomes, which force lower income groups to borrow (or dissave) in order to consume. With higher incomes, these lower income groups may begin to save, as in East Asia, raising net savings.

It is tempting to conclude that East Asian countries should save less and shift the task of providing for the future to the state, as the West has done. But if the assumption is true that an intense desire to save is an important factor underlying a strong work ethic, the issue arises whether it is desirable to shift the provision for future needs entirely to the state. Most of East Asia will need a strong work ethic to catch up with Western real incomes, and this may take a decade or so. Until one can assess how well the welfare state in the West can cope with the changes in the coming decades, it may be well for Asia to use the family as the main savings institution. If a large part of the drop in U.S. savings is related to the welfare state (social security, medicare, unemployment, insurance, etc.), the impact on the propensity to work and invest will not be desirable for most of Asia.[13]

EXCESS SAVINGS AND THEIR IMPLICATIONS

After several decades of rapid economic growth, East Asian countries appear to have transformed themselves into creditor nations, with their economies generating a chronic excess of gross national savings over gross domestic investment. Because the excess savings are sent abroad to the United States, mainly in the form of excess exports over imports, the United States has called not only for a reduction in import restrictions but also for a decrease in savings and an increase in construction in these countries. While it is highly desirable that East Asian countries open up their economies to imports, it is not necessarily desirable that East Asia reduce excess savings. Savings are increasingly in short supply globally, because highly developed countries with high incomes consume too much and do not save enough to supply lower income countries with savings to speed their growth. Excess savings is an excess of gross national savings over gross domestic investment. Gross national savings is equal to gross domestic savings plus net factor income from abroad. A chronic excess is a sustained or persistent accumulation of excess savings over several years.

When gross national savings exceed the purchase of investment goods (i.e., private purchase of houses, buildings, plant equipment and inventory, and government purchase of capital goods and inventories), the unused savings has nowhere to be invested domestically and hence must go abroad. Thus the yearly output of a nation consists of current and capital goods or consumption and investment goods. If the total savings generated exceed the purchase of consumption and capital goods (which already include imported foreign goods), the excess must be invested abroad. When the excess over a period of years persists, the country becomes a creditor nation. All this is shown in the capital finance account (or the savings and investment account) in the system of national accounts. Debt repayment is part of the savings going abroad. In the case of South Korea, it was part of excess savings and net foreign investment in the 1980s. Excess savings spent on existing assets such as purchase of land and stocks previously issued merely transfers the ownership of excess savings from one person to another, so that eventually excess savings end up as net foreign investment in the rest-of-the-world account in a flow-account chart.

Since excess savings are converted to net foreign investment, they are related to the excess of trade (or the excess of exports over imports of goods and services), as may be seen from the rest-of-the-world account. If GDP is defined to be equal to gross domestic income (as in a flow-account chart), then GDP is equal to income spent on consumption and investment. But if savings exceed investment, then GDP is equal to income spent on consumption, plus investment, plus income saved. (Only under the Keynesian identity of savings and investment does GDP = $C + I$.) Since there is always a product counterpart to the income saved, the product counterpart shows up in the excess of goods and services exported over imports. Thus excess savings translate into an excess of exports over imports, or net foreign investment.

Table 4.3 shows the excess savings for East Asia, and figure 4.1 depicts the differential pace at which its savings and investment grew. In Japan, GNS and GDI grew fairly closely up to the early 1980s. In Taiwan by the 1970s, GNS tended to outpace GDI by small amounts. In Singapore, GDI exceeded GNS by a wide margin in the 1970s and into the early 1980s. In South Korea for most of the decades, GDI exceeded GNS. But in all cases, toward the latter half of the 1980s savings began to exceed investment needs. This tendency toward excess savings was due to the slowing of GDI, not to the growth of GNS except in South Korea, where GDI continued to grow robustly.

Japan generated excess savings early in the 1970s, largely because much of its basic construction expenditures were made during the prewar and war years, and rehabilitation of the infrastructure took less time than new construction did in Taiwan and South Korea. Taiwan began to generate excess savings in the 1970s, especially the mid-1970s, much earlier than South Korea, which suffered considerable infrastructural damage during the Korean War, in the early 1950s. Moreover, South Korea spent large sums for the establishment of costly heavy industries throughout the 1970s, diverting public funds from infrastructure construction. And in the latter 1980s, South Korea constructed infrastructure in preparation for the Olympic Games; but even so, the growth of GNS was somewhat steeper than that of GDI. Both Hong Kong and Singapore undertook massive construction of housing and other urban structures to replace the dilapidated structures inherited from the prewar period.

For other Asian countries, GNS was generally less than GDI for all the countries where data are available, although for a few years of high growth

TABLE 4.3
Excess of Gross National Savings over Gross Domestic Investment, 1960 to 1989

| Year | Japan | | Taiwan | | South Korea | | Hong Kong | | Singapore | |
|---|---|---|---|---|---|---|---|---|---|---|
| | Bn Yen | % of GNS | Bn NT$ | % of GNS | Bn Won | % of GNS | Mn HK$ | % of GNS | Mn S$ | % of GNS |
| 1960–64 | −139 | −1.8 | −3 | −25.0 | −40 | −190.5 | −1,214 | −448.0 | −12 | −4.5 |
| 1965–69 | 425 | 2.5 | −3 | −8.8 | −151 | −82.1 | −542 | −27.5 | 235 | 27.1 |
| 1970–74 | 763 | 2.0 | 1 | 0.9 | −340 | −39.2 | −53 | −0.9 | −1,474 | −69.8 |
| 1975–79 | 1,045 | 1.7 | 18 | 6.5 | −1,194 | −24.9 | 24 | 0.1 | −1,372 | −26.2 |
| 1980–84 | 2,731 | 3.3 | 110 | 18.3 | −3,565 | −29.2 | −3,210 | −6.0 | −1,957 | −14.4 |
| 1985–89 | 14,048 | 12.4 | 478 | 42.9 | 2,518 | 7.3 | 20,836 | 17.9 | 2,195 | 11.3 |
| Total | 18,873 | | 601 | | −2,772 | | 15,841 | | −2,385 | |

Source: Asian Development Bank, Key Indicators; Asian Development Bank, Asian Development Outlook; World Bank, World Tables.

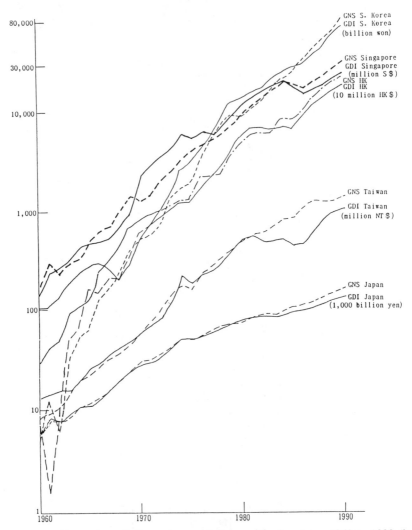

FIG. 4.1. Gross domestic investment and gross national savings, 1960 to 1990 (in current prices). *Source:* Asian Development Bank, *Key Indicators;* Asian Development Bank, *Asian Development Outlook;* World Bank, *World Tables.*

starting in the 1980s, Indonesia, the Philippines, and Malaysia showed occasional excess savings.[14] But the excess was small and appeared transitory, due more to low GDI than high GNS. But Malaysia may be an exception: it has high per capita incomes and savings rates, and it has completed an extensive network of physical infrastructure—and may become another creditor country. Despite high growth rates, Thailand's need for physical infrastructures is enormous since, unlike Malaysia, Hong Kong, and Singapore, it was not occupied by a colonial power that built infrastructure for doing business in the colonies; and in the 1970s Thailand did not take advantage of Middle Eastern loans for infrastructure construction as other countries did. It may therefore continue to be a debtor nation as it tries to make up for the 1970s, despite very high growth rates in the 1980s.

Table 4.4 shows that the slowdown in gross fixed domestic investment was due to construction rather than equipment. In all the countries in the table, the fall in growth rates was larger for construction than for equipment. In Japan, the fall started from the 1970s, when excess savings began to be substantial. Construction growth is shown in current prices, but construction in constant prices fell even more.

In East Asia, the high growth rates of GNP and incomes in the earlier decades of the postwar era raised both the demand for construction and the incomes to pay for the costs of construction. Huge waves of migrants from the rural areas needed urban housing and infrastructure. In rural areas, roads, irrigation, and electrification were constructed, but it was mainly the growth of urbanization that raised the demand for houses, buildings, streets, and utilities. City population trebled between 1950 and 1980 in Japan, Taiwan, and South Korea. By the 1980s, the agricultural labor force had fallen to low levels, and movements out of the rural sector had slowed to a trickle. In Japan, only 11 percent of the labor force in the 1980 census was in agriculture, and in Taiwan 19 percent; these fell even lower in 1985. Birth rates dropped to levels below replacement, as total fertility rates were reduced below 2.0 by the mid-1980s in most of East Asia (in South Korea it was 2.2).

Much of the basic network of infrastructure for a modernized agriculture (rural roads, irrigation, marketing facilities) and for industrialization (urban roads, homes, factories, offices, stores, and public utilities) must be completed if an economy is to make the transition from a predominantly agricultural to a predominantly industrial society. Once these are completed, the demand for

TABLE 4.4

Growth of Construction and Equipment, 1960s to 1980s (current prices, percent)

| Country | Construction | | | Equipment | | |
|---|---|---|---|---|---|---|
| | 1960s | 1970s | 1980s | 1960s | 1970s | 1980s |
| Taiwan | 13.1 | 27.0 | 7.9 | 20.0 | 23.0 | 6.2 |
| Japan | 21.0 | 12.3 | 0.4 | 17.2 | 9.8 | 4.6[a] |
| Korea | 39.0 | 31.0 | 13.3 | 38.0 | 37.0 | 15.4[a] |
| Singapore | 22.0 | 18.7 | 5.1 | 28.0 | 18.2 | 7.8[b] |
| Hong Kong | | 29.0 | 7.0 | | 21.0 | 15.6[c] |

*Source:* Official national accounts.

[a] 1980–86.

[b] 1980–88.

[c] 1980–87.

additional construction may not be large, comprising mainly maintenance and replacement, extensions of the basic network, and some expansion. There is a tendency for infrastructural construction to overshoot current needs, since the gestation periods of most construction projects are very long, as the theory of long swings points out.[15] In most of the East and Southeast Asian countries, this overshooting may have occurred in the late 1970s and early 1980s, when loans for construction from the Middle East became available. The share of construction expenditures in GDP in constant prices in Taiwan rose from 10 percent in 1965–74 to 13.1 percent in 1975–83, in South Korea from 12.4 percent to 17.8 percent, in Hong Kong from 10.2 percent to 11.8 percent, in Singapore from 11.6 percent to 12.9 percent, and in Malaysia from 10.4 percent to 17.2 percent. In Japan and India, which did not borrow from the Middle East, there were declines, since construction reached higher levels than the previous decades, which averaged much less than 10 percent.[16]

Of course, in the long run, an almost unlimited amount of infrastructure needs to be constructed, and excess savings could be used for this. But excess savings are in the private sector, especially in households, and there is a limit to the amount that can be taxed or borrowed by governments, which do not want interest payments for bonds and other debts to rise to a disproportionate share of the budget. And of course, there is a limit to the amounts that households and businesses may want to invest in government debt.

Moreover, the labor force in East Asia will move increasingly away from the industrial to the service sector, especially to personal, financial, and business services. (I include transport and communications in the industrial sector.) In Japan in 1987, 50 percent of the labor force was in the service sector, while in Taiwan it was 39 percent and in South Korea it was 38 percent (and of course, much larger in Hong Kong and Singapore, where the agriculture sector is very small).[17] The shift to the service sector, in the long run, will substantially dampen the demand for fixed capital (both construction and equipment), because the service sector's use of fixed capital is much smaller than the industrial sector's.[18]

Although it is unlikely that excess savings in East Asia will be wiped out in the coming years, they may be reduced. Population is rapidly aging in East Asia, where birth rates have fallen sharply. The aging of the population will raise consumption propensities, since the retired population tends to consume more than their incomes. The shortage of labor may compel firms to invest more in equipment to substitute for workers. This is in part because excess savings going abroad tend to increase the growth rate of the countries they are invested in while detracting from their own, since factor incomes from abroad will be only partly offsetting. Also, wages in East Asia have risen rapidly, especially in Taiwan and South Korea, and this together with the appreciation of the currency has slowed the growth of exports. The exodus of labor-intensive industries to other countries will reduce the exports of textiles, shoes, toys, and so on, and structural change as a source of growth will slow as agriculture shrinks.

Historically, excess savings played an important role in the development of the West. The Netherlands, which led the mercantilist world in the eighteenth century, began toward the latter portion of that century to invest overseas large amounts of the excess savings accumulated in the earlier decades. It has been estimated that Dutch foreign investment in the eighteenth century amounted to more than three times the Dutch national product.[19] Leadership in the world economy in the nineteenth century passed from the Dutch to the British, who, with the aid of the powerful technologies generated by the industrial revolution (in the textile, iron, and coal industries) and of the trading monopolies overseas, amassed huge savings, some of which were invested abroad. Around the turn of the century, foreign investment amounted to as much as domestic investment.[20] British capital financed railroads and other infrastructure and contributed to the shift of world leadership across the Atlantic to the United States in the early decades of the twentieth century. The United States became rich by taking advantage of the electric- and gas-powered technologies of the second industrial revolution. Excess savings were first used to repay the British, after which, in the 1950s and 1960s, they were invested abroad.

In all three cases, savings going abroad tended to slow domestic productivity growth, because they represented capital going into foreign, not domestic, industries. British total factor productivity growth fell from 1.5 percent per year in 1856–73 to 0.6 percent in 1873–1937.[21] U.S. labor productivity growth fell from around 2.0 percent in the 1950s and 1960s to around 0.35 percent in 1973–86.[22] Although many other factors contributed to the loss of productivity leadership in these countries, the leakage of savings abroad was a factor, since foreign investment abroad transfers not only capital but also entrepreneurship, management, and technology.

A major cost to the recipients of foreign investment is interest, dividends, and other factor incomes as payment for the investment. But this is likely to be no more than 10 percent or so of the value of the foreign investment, much smaller than the total income created by that investment in the form of wages and salaries and other incomes. Factor income from abroad (without netting out income from abroad) as a percentage of total foreign assets was 3 percent for Japan in 1986, which is slow relative to other countries because of the greater amounts invested by Japan in low-yielding securities and government bonds (605,000 billion yen) compared to stocks (152,800 billion yen).[23] In Taiwan gross returns from foreign investment were relatively larger, about 9 percent of foreign assets, because of the smaller share invested in bonds. In South Korea it was 4 percent.[24]

If, instead of going abroad, gross national savings stay in the country of origin and are invested locally (whether in private housing, buildings, factories, stores and equipment, or public physical infrastructures and equipment), the impact is likely to be a faster growth of GDP than returns to foreign investment bring. The jobs created and the incomes generated in constructing the facilities and then operating them are likely to add more to GDP than the returns to investing abroad.

Employee compensation is about double the size of the operating surplus in national income accounts. In Japan employee compensation in 1985 was 173 trillion yen, compared to 77 trillion in 1988. In Taiwan it was NT$1.2 trillion and NT$0.7 trillion.[25] But only a part of the operating surplus is normally paid out as returns to investments, most of which are reinvested or paid to governments as taxes, to landowners as rents, and to others, all of which remain in the foreign country and not in the country where the excess savings originated. This may be part of the reason for the slowdown in growth experienced by the Japanese economy in the early 1970s, when excess savings became substantial. A slowdown in the other East Asian countries may begin in the 1990s as savings going abroad become substantial and productivity begins to sag. In Taiwan, this may have started at the close of the 1980s.

A major benefit from the excess savings of East Asia that is not explicitly credited to them is their contribution to the continued expansion of the U.S. economy. It is surprising that despite the difficulties of the U.S. economy it did not fall into a recession after 1982. This may be related to the large federal budget deficits of almost $200 billion per year since 1983, but if this excess spending had been financed by the savings of American consumers, the expansion of the economy could not have continued so long, because excess federal spending would have been offset by a reduction in consumer spending. Instead, the excess savings from East Asia financed most of the budget deficits, thereby permitting American consumers to continue expanding their consumption despite the slow growth of personal incomes. U.S. consumer savings fell from about 6 percent in 1983–84 to 3 percent in the late 1980s.[26] Indeed, U.S. consumers, business, and government were spending so much that, without imports from East Asia, there would have been inflationary tendencies. From 1984 to 1987, total spending in the United States exceeded GNP by $3,350 billion, which had to be made up by imports, most of which came from East Asia. In turn, these goods contributed to the high growth in East Asian economies in the latter 1980s. East Asian savings took long hours of diligent work plus restrained consumption at a time when the developed countries were turning increasingly away from work toward leisure.

Some voices in the West are urging East Asian households not to save so much and to consume more. They pressure East Asian governments to reduce excess savings by greater spending on public works. But it is better for East Asian consumers to stick to their desire to save in order to accumulate funds instead of buying things not urgently needed. Fortunately, the tendency of the West toward antisaving changed as a result of the liberalization of Eastern Europe and the U.S.S.R. and the realization that enormous amounts of capital would be needed to pull these countries out of poverty. All of the savings of the top excess saver in Europe—Germany—will probably be needed to develop the former East Germany alone.

Even greater is the need for foreign investment to speed growth in Asian developing countries. In the late 1980s, excess savings began to flow to Thailand, Malaysia, and Indonesia, raising their exports and accelerating GNP growth rates. Thailand has been the major recipient of foreign investment, and its growth averaged 10 percent per year between 1986 and 1988, making it the fastest growing economy in the world. Political instability and poor economic management have discouraged investments in the Philippines; huge amounts of official development assistance from Japan are flowing in, but even more will be needed to keep the Philippines from becoming the basket case of Asia. In the future, East Asian savings will be called upon to pull out of poverty and stagnation the economies of Vietnam, Cambodia, Laos, mainland China, and the countries of South Asia.

The world needs all the savings East Asia can generate. Japan's savings rate as a percentage of personal income fell in the late 1980s, as more people retired, as more children entered college and got married, and as more houses and durables were bought. Similarly, those of the other East Asian countries will begin to fall in the 1990s. Savings rates have been falling in the main industrialized countries since the mid-1980s. By 1988, households in Sweden, Norway, and Finland were dissaving, with personal savings a negative 3.9 percent, 1.2 percent, and 1.4 percent, respectively, while the United States, the United Kingdom, and the Netherlands were saving only 2–4 percent of personal income. Moreover, the savings of government and corporations also fell in most countries and were barely able to cover domestic investment.

Consumers in the affluent countries in the West will not soon be able to substantially cut down on consumption: there is in the modern economy a dazzling array of goods and services to spend incomes on. Consumer credit outstanding in the United States rose from 1 percent of personal income in 1950 to 22 percent in 1987. And because of entitlements such as health insurance, old age pensions, and loans for education, the desire to save weakened. Accordingly, saving as a social value changed since the 1950s and 1960s, when personal savings were 15 percent and 16 percent, respectively.[27]

Interest rates began to rise in the early 1990s, reflecting a shortage of savings globally. It may be a sign of the times that the heavily militarized nations of the West began (even before the recent decline of communism) to set aside ideologies and reduce military spending as a step toward balancing their budgets. Western countries may need to take other steps to dethrone spending and enthrone saving among households. The West is no longer living in a Keynesian world, with excessive consumption and benefits from welfare funds. Instead of Mandeville's *Fable of the Bees,* which Keynes quoted at length with approval, we may have to turn to the Confucian *Analects,* where saving is extolled.

CONSUMPTION

The accumulation of so much personal savings in East Asia was made possible by the slower growth of consumption than of personal income (table 4.5). Many Asian countries have not constructed personal accounts due to lack of data; for countries with the data, personal income figures are much more reliable than consumption estimates, since most components of personal income are derived from production data. These products pass through numerous channels, such as processors, middlemen, transporters, wholesalers, and retailers, before they are purchased by consumers, and the data on value added at each point are difficult to get. Countries often use data from household income and expenditure surveys to supplement estimates of commodity flows, but these surveys tend to understate household purchases.

The faster rise of personal income in East Asia over personal income in other Asian countries is, of course, related to the faster rise of GNP and national income. Aggregate employee compensation and proprietors' incomes tend to rise together, with the former rising faster than the latter. (This is also true in real terms, as prices tend to rise more slowly in East Asia than in other countries.) The size of the wage-earning class grows faster than the number of proprietors, as proprietors become transformed into wage and salary earners— a normal tendency in the economic transition during which agriculture and the number of peasant proprietors is reduced and the number of corporate enterprises in the urban sector rises with increasing economies of scale. Per capita personal income rose faster than per capita consumption (table 4.6) for Japan and Taiwan, indicating that personal savings were going up. In Thailand and the Philippines in the 1980s, the growth rate of per capita consumption was higher than that of per capita income.

Kuznets points out that "the low level of consumption may be as important in explaining the low level of productivity in the underdeveloped countries as the level of material capital stock or material capital formation."[28] Though savings are essential to finance investment, consumption also has a strategic role to play in development. If there are insufficient consumer goods, workers will not have the motivation to work very hard, nor can they labor hard if they do not consume enough calories to work energetically. Medical services are required to keep them in good health and to reduce absenteeism. Recreation and entertainment are also essential to sustain the zeal for work. The impact of these consumption goods is similar to that of fertilizer and animal feed on agricultural productivity. Hence, the ability to consume enough can be an incentive to work hard, especially for the working class. Soviet experience points to excessive investment, which reduced the share of consumption to such low levels that the propensity to work was blunted. The share of consumption in GNP of 56 percent in the 1950s was one of the lowest in the West, which averaged 66.6 percent.[29] Consumption should be optimized rather than maximized or minimized. The advantage of rapidly rising incomes is that both consumption and savings can be increased rapidly.

The growth rate of personal income is equal to the growth rate of consumption weighted by the average propensity to consume and the growth rate of savings weighted by the average propensity to save.[30] The average growth of consumption ($\Delta C/C$) over the postwar decades was much higher in the East Asian countries, even though the average growth of savings ($\Delta S/S$) was higher because of the faster growth of GNP, which makes it possible to have your cake and eat it too. This was also made possible by the tendency of family incomes to be distributed less unequally.

The consumption function in Keynes's general theory spawned an extensive discussion of the relation between consumption (and savings) and income. But the concepts and hypotheses generated by the discussion pertained to the relation of consumption to income in the various phases of the business cycles and not to growth through economic transition. Less developed countries are interested in growth analysis, since they are not much bothered by business cycles; it is the trend that dominates the movement of GNP. Also, consumption is a very large aggregate in the national accounts of any nation, and the components composing the total are numerous and heterogeneous. Hence there is a need to disaggregate the aggregate into manageable groupings. In the following discussion, consumption is broken down into food, clothing, housing, and others. Each is analyzed with some attention given to subgroups (see table 4.7).

As income rises beyond a certain threshold, food expenditures as a percentage of personal income tend to fall (see figure 4.2). This Engel effect is said to be due to the limited size of the human stomach, which can hold only a certain amount of food at a time.[31] This may be so, but the limit is not rigidly set if we think about the higher priced foods that could be afforded as income rises, even though some cannot be consumed excessively. Nevertheless, it is possible to spend almost unlimited amounts on expensive foods and drinks, especially in high-priced restaurants. Thus it must be for other reasons as well that, when incomes rise, consumers limit their food expenses and spend on other things.

One reason is that, in order for labor productivity (and hence income) to grow, more machines and other technologies must be used in the workplace. The substitution of machine power for muscle power implies the substitution of electric power for carbohydrates, so that there is less need to consume cereals and other sources of calories.[32] But this does not mean that the increased incomes are spent on more expensive and less caloric food. Much of the rising incomes are earned in settings where work requires more skills and where the cost of living is higher. More education is needed for higher skills; there are costs of commuting to the workplace; clothing in white collar occupations is more varied and expensive than clothing needed in rural settings; housing in cities, including furniture, kitchen utensils, and electrical appliances, are much more expensive; and the more sophisticated urban entertainment and recreation

TABLE 4.5
Sources of Personal Income, 1960s to 1980s (current prices)

| Country | Source of Income (percent) | | | | Personal Income (bn. currency) | Population (mn.) | Per Capita Income (1,000 currency) | Implicit Deflators |
|---|---|---|---|---|---|---|---|---|
| | Employee Compensation | Operating Surplus | Property Income | Transfers | | | | |
| Japan | | | | | | | | |
| 1960s | 57.2 | 25.6 | 11.8 | 5.4 | 24,967.0 | 97.8 | 255.3 | 32.8 |
| 1970s | 60.4 | 19.1 | 7.4 | 13.1 | 123,269.0 | 110.7 | 1,113.5 | 68.5 |
| 1980s | 60.6 | 13.9 | 7.0 | 18.5 | 251,494.0 | 119.1 | 2,111.6 | 107.5 |
| Taiwan | | | | | | | | |
| 1960s | 53.7 | 23.6 | 21.4 | 1.3 | 83.4 | 12.5 | 6.7 | 26.2 |
| 1970s | 63.4 | 10.4 | 25.5 | 0.7 | 419.8 | 16.0 | 26.2 | 50.7 |
| 1980s | 68.3 | 6.0 | 24.8 | 0.9 | 1,582.0 | 18.7 | 84.6 | 101.3 |
| South Korea | | | | | | | | |
| 1960s | 35.2 | 61.5[a] | | 3.3 | 763.0 | 28.3 | 27.0 | 7.9 |
| 1970s | 42.3 | 54.5[a] | | 3.2 | 8,934.0 | 34.9 | 256.0 | 39.9 |
| 1980s | 53.7 | 35.8 | 3.4 | 7.1 | 40,467.0 | 39.5 | 1,024.5 | 125.5 |

| | | | | | | | | |
|---|---|---|---|---|---|---|---|---|
| **Thailand** | | | | | | | | |
| 1960s | 28.6 | 60.6 | 10.1 | 0.6 | 70.8 | 30.4 | 2.3 | 91.8 |
| 1970s | 26.2 | 65.0 | 8.0 | 0.8 | 237.9 | 40.9 | 5.8 | 139.2 |
| 1980s | 35.0 | 53.8 | 10.8 | 0.4 | 710.0 | 49.6 | 14.3 | 264.9 |
| **Philippines** | | | | | | | | |
| 1960s | | 97.3 | | 2.7 | 19.5 | 31.4 | 0.6 | 57.1 |
| 1970s | | 96.4 | | 3.6 | 87.2 | 41.9 | 2.1 | 156.6 |
| 1980s | | 95.6 | | 4.4 | 367.3 | 52.1 | 7.0 | 468.0 |
| **Sri Lanka** | | | | | | | | |
| 1970s | 53.5 | 31.3 | 2.9 | 12.3 | 21.3 | 13.5 | 1.6 | 135.6 |
| 1980s | 52.1 | 41.9$^a$ | | 6.0 | 88.9 | 15.2 | 5.8 | 274.9 |

*Source:* Official national accounts; Asian Development Bank, *Key Indicators.*

*Note:* Employee compensation includes wages and salaries and employers' contributions to social security; operating surplus includes income from farms, professions, and other unincorporated enterprises less interest on consumers' debt; transfers include transfers from general government.

$^a$Operating surplus plus property income.

TABLE 4.6
Personal Disbursements as Percentage of Total, 1960s to 1980s

| Country | Private Consumption Expenditures[a] | Direct Taxes[b] | Other Transfers to Government | Transfers to Rest of World | Savings | Private Consumer Expenditures per Capita (1,000) | Growth Rate in Decade |
|---|---|---|---|---|---|---|---|
| Japan | | | | | | | |
| 1960s | 73.1 | 8.9 | 1.4 | 0.1 | 16.4 | 185.5 | |
| 1970s | 64.8 | 12.4 | 5.6 | 0.0 | 17.1 | 712.2 | 14.4 |
| 1980s | 64.0 | 16.2 | 6.9 | | 13.0 | 1,351.2 | 6.6 |
| Taiwan | | | | | | | |
| 1960s | 85.8 | 1.2 | 2.0 | 0.1 | 19.0 | 5.7 | |
| 1970s | 75.3 | 3.1 | 2.6 | 0.2 | 18.7 | 19.6 | 13.1 |
| 1980s | 69.9 | 5.0 | 2.9 | 0.7 | 21.4 | 58.3 | 11.5 |

| | | | | | | | |
|---|---|---|---|---|---|---|---|
| **South Korea** | | | | | | | |
| 1960s | 93.5 | 2.7 | 1.3 | 0.2 | 2.3 | 24.7 | 24.0 |
| 1970s | 85.8 | 3.5 | 1.4 | 0.4 | 8.8 | 214.0 | 14.8 |
| 1980s | 83.0 | 3.9 | 1.3 | 0.3 | 11.5 | 847.3 | |
| **Thailand** | | | | | | | |
| 1960s | 85.3 | 1.4 | 0.3 | 0.1 | 12.8 | 1.99 | 9.2 |
| 1970s | 82.7 | 1.9 | 0.3 | 0.1 | 15.0 | 4.78 | 9.6 |
| 1980s | 83.7 | 3.3 | 0.3 | 0.1 | 12.6 | 12.01 | |
| **Philippines** | | | | | | | |
| 1960s | 90.0 | 2.5 | -3.1 | 0.0 | 10.5 | 0.56 | 12.4 |
| 1970s | 86.2 | 3.2 | 0.0 | 0.0 | 10.5 | 1.80 | 13.8 |
| 1980s | 92.6 | 3.0 | 0.4 | 0.0 | 4.0 | 6.58 | |
| **Sri Lanka** | | | | | | | |
| 1970s | 92.4 | 3.7 | -0.8 | 0.4 | 3.5 | 1.47 | 13.5 |
| 1980s | 89.5 | 3.0 | | 0.5 | 7.8 | 5.21 | |

*Source:* Official national accounts.

[a]Includes households and nonprofit institutions.

[b]Includes social insurance contributions.

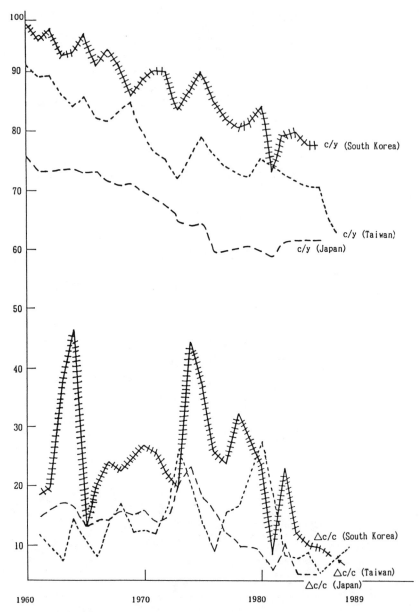

FIG. 4.2. Personal consumption expenditure as a percentage of personal income, 1960 to 1987 (in current prices). *Source:* Official national accounts; United Nations, *Yearbook of National Accounts*.

TABLE 4.7

Consumption in Gross National Product, 1950 to 1985 (constant prices, percent)

| Country | 1950–1955 | 1956–1960 | 1961–1965 | 1966–1970 | 1971–1975 | 1976–1980 | 1981–1985 |
|---|---|---|---|---|---|---|---|
| **Japan** | | | | | | | |
| Food | 31.2 | 29.2 | 23.0 | 19.3 | 16.7 | 15.3 | 13.3 |
| Clothing | 6.8 | 7.1 | 7.0 | 5.7 | 4.9 | 4.5 | 3.7 |
| Housing | 12.1 | 11.7 | 11.9 | 12.1 | 12.7 | 13.1 | 12.6 |
| Other | 11.8 | 13.7 | 15.6 | 16.4 | 17.5 | 19.2 | 19.5 |
| Total | 61.9 | 61.7 | 57.5 | 53.6 | 51.9 | 52.1 | 49.1 |
| **Taiwan** | | | | | | | |
| Food | 48.7 | 43.8 | 38.3 | 33.2 | 28.3 | 23.8 | 20.8 |
| Clothing | 2.2 | 2.3 | 2.3 | 2.4 | 2.5 | 2.6 | 2.7 |
| Housing | 11.6 | 11.3 | 12.4 | 13.0 | 14.0 | 14.2 | 14.9 |
| Other | 9.6 | 10.1 | 12.1 | 13.1 | 13.1 | 13.4 | 13.0 |
| Total | 72.1 | 67.5 | 65.2 | 61.7 | 57.9 | 54.1 | 51.3 |
| **Korea** | | | | | | | |
| Food | 55.7 | 57.9 | 52.9 | 46.2 | 41.7 | 35.1 | 32.1 |
| Clothing | 8.0 | 10.2 | 10.2 | 9.5 | 11.5 | 10.8 | 9.2 |
| Housing | 11.4 | 12.7 | 13.8 | 13.5 | 13.9 | 14.7 | 14.5 |
| Other | 5.0 | 6.2 | 5.2 | 6.1 | 5.8 | 5.2 | 6.2 |
| Total | 80.1 | 87.0 | 82.2 | 75.4 | 72.9 | 65.8 | 62.1 |
| **Thailand** | | | | | | | |
| Food | | 46.4 | 41.8 | 37.5 | 35.6 | 33.8 | 31.3 |
| Clothing | | 9.6 | 9.4 | 9.7 | 10.7 | 11.2 | 11.8 |
| Housing | | 14.3 | 14.3 | 14.5 | 13.9 | 13.9 | 15.0 |
| Other | | 6.4 | 6.3 | 6.6 | 6.1 | 6.9 | 6.1 |
| Total | | 76.8 | 72.5 | 68.3 | 66.3 | 65.8 | 64.1 |
| **Singapore** | | | | | | | |
| Food | | 34.8 | 28.0 | 21.5 | 17.9 | 14.6 | |
| Clothing | | 8.7 | 7.9 | 6.5 | 6.0 | 5.9 | |
| Housing | | 27.3 | 23.8 | 21.9 | 21.4 | 19.5 | |
| Other | | 13.4 | 12.0 | 16.0 | 14.9 | 13.1 | |
| Total | | 84.2 | 71.6 | 66.0 | 60.1 | 53.1 | |

*Source:* Official national accounts; Asian Development Bank, *Ken Indicators.*

*Note:* Food includes beverages and tobacco; clothing includes footwear and personal care; housing includes water, rent, fuel, light, transportation, and communication; other includes recreation, entertainment, education, health, net spending of residents abroad.

cost more than in rural areas. A minimum of expenditures for housing, clothing, transportation, education, and recreation becomes a necessity—as urgent as food.[33] Hence it is not mainly the size of the human stomach that is responsible for the Engel effect. Long before the limits of the stomach are reached and the consumption of higher valued food is exhausted, spending must be shifted to nonfood consumption goods, which are necessary for incomes to rise.

Japanese per capita intake of calories, which reached a peak of 2,300 in 1970, fell to 2,100 in 1985.[34] In part, the fall may have been due to the rise in the retired population—which, however, is offset by fewer preschool children—both of which groups are assumed to consume fewer calories. But the fall in calories may also be due to the lesser need for calories with greater mechanization. In the 1970s, electric power used per worker in manufacturing reached close to Western usage, and the agricultural labor force (a large consumer of calories) fell to 10 percent and lower.[35] Hence, despite their much higher incomes than in other East Asian countries, the Japanese were consuming fewer calories, as the economy moved into a stage where required human exertion was much lower than in traditional economies.

Other Asian countries do not have periodic food consumption and nutrition surveys, and we must resort to food balance sheets, which are regularly worked out by the Food and Agriculture Organization. Food production statistics from agricultural surveys are used as the starting point of the computation; exports are deducted, imports are added, and deductions are made for industrial uses, for wastage, for feed to animals, and so on, as food products pass from producers to final consumers. A number of assumptions must be made in these various steps, so it is difficult to tell how adequately food consumption is represented by these data. Experience in various countries shows that the food balance sheet estimates give levels higher than those from available food consumption and nutrition surveys. Food balance sheet data represent supplies rather than consumption. It would be better, then, to analyze the changes over time rather than concentrate on levels.

In Taiwan and Thailand, there were rapid increases in caloric supplies up to the 1970s, but since then satiation was reached—and stability was reached in the 1980s. Per capita calorie intake declined since the mid-1970s in Singapore and since the early 1980s in Hong Kong. In South Korea and Malaysia, with the same level of per capita income, there were rapid increases up to 1980 and stability in the 1980s. Calorie levels are higher in Taiwan and South Korea than in Singapore and Hong Kong, despite higher incomes in the latter; this may be due in part to the predominance of the service sector and the minor role of agriculture in the latter. The lower levels of Malaysia than in South Korea are difficult to explain except that paddy agriculture is much more important in South Korea, and there is greater unemployment in Malaysia. More of a puzzle is Thailand, where calorie intake has not risen since the 1970s. With low per capita incomes in Thailand, one would expect its calorie consumption to have risen into the 1980s, as in the Philippines and Indonesia. It may be that data from food balance sheets are not adequate for cross-section comparisons, since the quality of food production data and the estimated deductions are of varied reliability across countries.[36]

With full employment, there is economy in the utilization of calories, since a large part of the daily calorie intake of an average Asian adult (about 3,000 for a person doing work of moderate intensity) can be compared to the overhead costs of a business enterprise. This is the portion needed for the basic, metabolic, physiological functions of the body, such as the production of protoplasm or the circulation of blood, and does not vary with the amount of work done. For these functions, the body requires a certain number of calories whether at rest or in motion; this amount is estimated by nutritionists to be one calorie per minute, for an average Asian adult, or about 1,500 per day. Hence, about one-half of the 3,000 calories consumed per day is needed to keep the body alive—a cost that must be borne whether work is performed or not. Therefore, when an unemployed person begins to work, the calorie intake needs to increase by only 50 percent, while his income goes up 100 percent. Since East Asia had full employment during most of the postwar era, they were able to optimize the use of calories.

Calorie intake is too low in India, Bangladesh, and Nepal; they may have risen during the 1980s, especially with a decline in underemployment. With such low levels of calorie intake, many in the population do not have enough to eat, even though they are unemployed and underemployed some months of the year. In Bangladesh in 1985–86, food expenditures as a percentage of household income was 66.3 percent in the lowest income bracket and 70.2 percent in the middle bracket, which together comprise about half of total households.[37] This can be interpreted to mean that incomes in this range of households are so low that not enough is earned to buy food. More is spent on food as incomes rise (contrary to Engels' law) and is true even for the upper half of households, where the food share of income was 44.5 percent. The food curves in India and Nepal are rising, with per capita incomes about those of Bangladesh; if the data on households were grouped less broadly—say by percentiles rather than deciles—many other countries might show rising food share curves, especially among the poor.

Table 4.7 shows expenditures for major categories of consumption—food, clothing (which included footwear and personal care), housing (including water charges, rent, fuel, light, furniture, transport, and communication), and other (recreation, health, education, and all other services)—as a percentage of GNP in the postwar decades in East Asia. In the United States, where data since 1929 are available, food and clothing peaks were simultaneously attained in the 1940s, 33 percent and 15 percent, respectively, and dropped until 1985, when they were 19.3 percent and 9 percent. Housing shares were highest in the early 1930s. Services rose slowly to 24 percent in 1970, falling to 20 percent in 1985.[38] It is interesting that there was a rising Engels' curve in the United States between 1933 and 1943, even though incomes were rising. This may be the result of the large number of unemployed or of the workers employed in public works who got such low incomes that their food consumption was large relative to their incomes. Also, it is surprising that the housing peak was reached earlier relative to food expenditures, unlike East Asia. Considering the low income-demand elasticities of food, one would expect the trends to be more in line with Asian trends.

It may be that after an economy reaches a level of development as advanced as that of the United States, the shifts of population to urban areas and to higher income occupations slow so much that other changes—demography, share of personal consumption in GNP, income distribution, new consumer goods, and many others—dominate consumption patterns. Apparently, Engels' law does not hold beyond certain levels.

CONCLUDING REMARKS

The examination of consumption patterns indicates that the large personal savings that contributed much to the financing of East Asian investments and productivity gains were made possible by the sharp decline in Engels' coeffi-cient. Without substantial reductions in food shares as incomes rose, the growth not only of savings but also of expenditures essential for structural changes in production, occupations, and industry would have been slower, constraining the growth of income and product. The strategy of export-led growth was clearly a great success, propelling East Asia to high per capita incomes and large increases in exports in a few decades. Savings do not appear to have been residually determined by East Asian consumers but were targeted to increase rapidly through the slower growth of consumption. Social values dictated that savings be maximized for the future well-being of the family, as children grow up to enroll in higher levels of education and parents retire. That part of production not consumed domestically but sold abroad was maximized.

There are lessons for other countries from the successes of East Asia. Com-prehensive land reform wiped out landlord-dominated agriculture, giving peas-ants an opportunity to improve their productivity and earning power. The consumption-oriented landlord class was replaced by peasants who grasped the chance to improve their lot by working hard and saving for their future needs. The Philippines and India, where landlord agriculture is prevalent, should reform their land tenure systems. Policies to reduce birth rates and slow the growth of population (and mouths to feed) would help reduce future consump-tion.

Japan, Taiwan, and South Korea promoted savings through tax exemptions of interest earned from savings deposits. They made it convenient for bits of savings to be deposited in the postal offices of the villages, thereby promoting thrift among peasants and laborers. Education that glorified thrift as a virtue paid off not only in greater savings in the home but also in a greater propensity to work. All these affected productivity in the workplace. Thus an important lesson from the East Asian experience is the virtual circle between productivity and savings during the earlier stages of the agroindustrial transition, when incomes are low and efforts need to be made to foster savings in order to overcome the strong urge to consume.

# PART II

## Distal Processes

# CHAPTER 5

# Underemployment and Unemployment

If one had to single out the foremost problem of monsoon Asia, it would be the problem of idleness, especially underemployment—the lack of enough work in the dry season of the year (see table 5.1). This may be the major factor in low productivity in the rural sector of monsoon Asia, with farms too small to furnish enough work in the wet season and with insufficient water for agricultural production in the long dry season. Without full employment, substitution of machines for labor is slow to occur, and productivity growth is sluggish.

## EMPLOYMENT AND ECONOMIC GROWTH

In the growth theories of Arthur Lewis, Gustav Ranis, and John Fei, densely populated countries grow rapidly with unlimited supply of labor and constant real wages. But postwar experience in Asia shows otherwise. East Asia had the highest growth rates of GNP per capita, the ASEAN Four grew slowly, and South Asia grew the slowest.

There are several reasons for the positive association between employment and growth. The hiring of unemployed workers expands output, not only because more workers are producing but because unused capital facilities are more fully utilized. And after full employment, with the rise in the elasticity of capital-labor substitution, full employment causes wages to rise faster than capital returns and induce firms to use more capital to buy better technologies to replace unskilled workers. Moreover, by working with more sophisticated technologies, workers' skills improve rapidly—since the main source of skill formation in developing countries is learning by working. With rising wages, labor is economized and the factory floor layout is rationalized, with improvements in auxiliary operations (such as storing, packing, and transporting) and the introduction of disembodied technologies. Better pay motivates people to work harder. Labor productivity rises, enabling the production structure to shift quickly from lower paying sectors like agriculture to higher paying non-agricultural sectors.

TABLE 5.1

Unemployment and Underemployment, 1955 to 1987 (percent)

| Year | Japan Unemployment | Taiwan Unemployment | Underemployment | South Korea Unemployment | Underemployment | Singapore Unemployment | Hong Kong Unemployment |
|---|---|---|---|---|---|---|---|
| 1955 | 2.5 | | | | | | |
| 1956 | | | | | | | |
| 1957 | | | | | | 4.9 | |
| 1958 | | | | | | | |
| 1959 | | | | | | 13.2 | |
| 1960 | 1.7 | | | | | | |
| 1961 | | | | | | | 1.7 |
| 1962 | | | | 8.4 | | | |
| 1963 | | | | 8.1 | | | |
| 1964 | | 4.3 | | 7.7 | | | |
| 1965 | 1.2 | 3.3 | 3.1 | 7.3 | | | |
| 1966 | 1.2 | 3.0 | 2.4 | 7.1 | 25.5 | 9.0 | 3.6 |
| 1967 | 1.3 | 2.3 | 2.0 | 6.1 | 22.7 | 8.1 | |
| 1968 | 1.2 | 1.7 | 1.2 | 5.0 | 21.1 | 7.3 | |
| 1969 | 1.1 | 1.9 | 2.2 | 4.7 | 16.6 | 6.7 | |
| 1970 | 1.2 | 1.7 | 1.5 | 4.4 | 18.4 | 6.0 | |
| 1971 | 1.2 | 1.7 | 1.1 | 4.4 | 17.6 | 4.8 | 4.8 |
| 1972 | 1.3 | 1.5 | 1.1 | 4.5 | 17.8 | 4.7 | |
| 1973 | 1.2 | 1.3 | 0.8 | 3.9 | 15.8 | 4.5 | |
| 1974 | 1.3 | 1.5 | 0.8 | 4.0 | 12.5 | 3.9 | |
| 1975 | 1.9 | 2.4 | 1.1 | 4.1 | 12.1 | 4.6 | 9.1 |
| 1976 | 2.0 | 1.8 | 0.6 | 3.9 | 11.4 | 4.5 | 5.6 |
| 1977 | 2.0 | 1.7 | 0.4 | 3.8 | 13.0 | 3.9 | 4.5 |
| 1978 | 2.2 | 1.7 | | 3.2 | 10.6 | 3.6 | 3.0 |
| 1979 | 2.1 | 1.3 | | 3.8 | 10.9 | 3.4 | 2.9 |
| 1980 | 2.0 | 1.2 | | 5.2 | 9.7 | 3.5 | 3.8 |
| 1981 | 2.2 | 1.4 | | 4.5 | 9.3 | 2.9 | 4.0 |
| 1982 | 2.4 | 2.1 | | 4.4 | 8.0 | 2.6 | 3.6 |
| 1983 | 2.6 | 2.7 | | 4.1 | 8.7 | 3.3 | 4.5 |
| 1984 | 2.7 | 2.4 | | 3.8 | 8.3 | 2.7 | 3.9 |
| 1985 | 2.6 | 2.9 | | 4.0 | 7.1 | 4.2 | 3.0 |
| 1986 | 2.8 | 2.7 | | 3.8 | 10.4 | 6.5 | 2.8 |
| 1987 | 2.8 | 2.0 | 0.6 | 3.1 | | | |

*Source:* Official national accounts and yearbooks; Asian Development Bank, *Key Indicators;* Edna Reyes, "The Philippine Labor Market, 1956–1986," paper prepared for the APDC conference, Kuala Lumpur, December 1988; Lamduan Pawakarammd and Kosit Panpiemras, "Employment Strategy for Accelerated Growth: Thailand," paper prepared for the APDC conference; Abu Bakar Karim and Tham

| Philippines | | Thailand | Malaysia | | Indonesia | |
|---|---|---|---|---|---|---|
| Unemployment | Underemployment | Unemployment | Unemployment | Underemployment | Unemployment | Underemployment |
| 6.3 | | | | | | |
| 6.4 | | | | | | |
| 6.5 | | | | | 0.3 | |
| 4.6 | | | | | 0.3 | |
| 6.4 | | | | | 0.3 | |
| 6.2 | | | | | 0.2 | |
| 7.0 | | | | | 0.2 | |
| 7.7 | | | | | 0.1 | |
| 7.9 | | | | | 0.1 | |
| 6.7 | | | | | | |
| 7.6 | | | 7.5 | | | |
| 5.3 | 15.0 | 0.2 | 6.8 | | | |
| 9.6 | 13.3 | 0.5 | 6.3 | | | |
| 1.6 | 12.1 | 0.4 | 5.7 | | | |
| 4.8 | 10.1 | 0.6 | 5.2 | | | |
| 4.2 | 13.3 | 0.4 | 6.9 | 2.0 | | |
| 5.0 | 10.6 | 0.8 | 6.1 | | 2.3 | 45.0 |
| 4.5 | 17.4 | 0.9 | 6.1 | | 2.3 | |
| 4.2 | 19.6 | 0.8 | 5.4 | | 2.5 | |
| 4.2 | | 1.0 | 5.4 | | 3.3 | |
| 5.0 | 20.9 | 0.9 | 5.6 | 2.4 | 1.7 | 38.0 |
| 5.3 | 23.9 | 1.1 | 4.7 | | 2.7 | |
| 6.0 | 25.5 | 1.3 | 4.6 | | 3.0 | |
| 5.4 | 29.8 | 3.0 | 5.2 | | 2.0 | |
| 7.3 | 36.4 | 2.9 | 5.8 | | 2.0 | |
| 12.1 | 22.2 | 3.6 | 6.9 | 3.2 | 2.1 | |
| 11.5 | 28.4 | 3.5 | 8.3 | | 2.2 | 12.7 |
| 9.1 | | | 8.2 | | 2.2 | |

Ah Fun, "Trends in Employment, Unemployment, and Underemployment in Malaysia," paper prepared for APDC conference; S. Hasibuan, "Labor Force Growth, Structural Change, and Labor Absorption in the Indonesian Economy," paper prepared for the APDC conference.

Full employment means more complete utilization of food, clothing, consumer durables such as cars, and material and human capital. In food consumption, food for the basal metabolic rate of the human body can be economized. Income distribution also improves with full employment, and purchasing power for industrial products increases. As long as new technologies (and capital) can be imported from abroad, full employment is favorable to economic growth. When importation is no longer possible, the economy reaches its technological frontier and graduates into a fully developed economy, as was the case for Japan in the 1970s. Growth might then slow, but this is not because surplus labor is exhausted but because technological and other changes (e.g., structure and population) take more time to evolve, and further development becomes sluggish. We can say, therefore, that the reduction of unemployment and underemployment is desirable not only for welfare reasons (the eradication of poverty, higher living standards, and improved income distribution) but also for the shift into a higher growth path.

Full employment is attained when unemployment and underemployment fall to levels where the wages of unskilled workers rise as fast as those of skilled workers. This assumes that the latter are fully employed earlier than the former. The East Asian experience indicates that 3 percent unemployment corresponds to full employment. After full employment is approached, rising wages attracts housewives, students, retired workers, and rural workers into the labor market. When these sources of labor are exhausted, full employment may give way to a labor shortage. (Labor shortages began to occur in Japan and Hong Kong in the mid-1960s and in Taiwan in the early 1970s.) From this point on, there is a further acceleration of technological progress, as firms find it difficult to hire workers to expand output, and the substitution of existing machines for labor may be exhausted. In sum, if the Southeast Asian GNP growth rates of 4–5 percent are raised to 8–9 percent as in East Asia, full employment would be soon attained.

THE CONCEPTS OF UNDEREMPLOYMENT AND UNEMPLOYMENT

Underemployment in Asia was identified early in the postwar decades by Western economists, who were struck by the widespread idleness they found in Asia.[1] But their understanding of underemployment was flawed, as they thought of underemployment as disguised unemployment, that is, people who were working and being paid but not being productive, so that their marginal product was zero. A mountain of controversy on the concept of disguised unemployment ensued, and the resulting consensus was that underemployment did not exist, at least not sufficiently to constitute a problem. In my research, I found that underemployment in Asia was the product of the dry half of the year, when the monsoon rains virtually disappear and leave rural Asians with little to do for many months.[2] Subsequently, labor force surveys began to be conducted; questions on hours of work showed that large numbers were employed, but there was insufficient work during the slack months of rice production.

Unemployment and underemployment are variously defined in labor force surveys, but the fundamental definitions are (1) those who are willing and able to work but cannot find work are *unemployed* and (2) among those employed, those who are working less than full time and want more hours of work are *underemployed*. Some part-time workers among housewives, students, and the retired do not want or cannot work full time. For some countries, underemployment is taken simply as all those who are working part-time, since the question as to whether they want more work was not asked.

The concepts of full employment, labor shortages, unemployment, and underemployment should be taken in a broad sense, because the concepts from which they are derived—such as labor force and employment—are themselves imprecise. Moreover, markets operate sluggishly because of distortions and frictions. For example, in peninsular Malaysia, unemployment rates appeared to fall to around 3 percent in 1984, but in 1981 through 1983 the consumer price index indicated full employment, with prices for services by unskilled workers (domestic servants, laundry workers, restaurant workers) rising sharply.

The concepts of unemployment and underemployment derive from labor force surveys, which originated in the United States.[3] The difficulties with these data stem from the differences in the structure and behavior of Asian labor markets and those of the United States, for which the concepts and surveys were devised. In Asia, most workers are hired on a short-term basis (daily and weekly), unlike in the United States. Most labor force surveys in South and Southeast Asia are taken once a quarter, which may not be frequent enough to represent that quarter. (East Asian surveys, as in the United States, are monthly.) And when workers change jobs, they frequently switch from one industry to another, one occupation to another, and one region to another. Also, the South and Southeast Asian economies are dominated by very small units of production, most of which are operated by the family and without accounting records. To get past some of these difficulties, the concepts and surveys were changed from time to time, impairing the continuity of the time series. And there are differences in the survey designs used by the various countries, so that small differences in the data between countries cannot be taken seriously.

## THE RECORD OF UNEMPLOYMENT AND UNDEREMPLOYMENT

Figures 5.1 and 5.2 show that idleness (the percentage of unemployment and underemployment in the labor force) rose in most countries of South and Southeast Asia during the 1980s, although it declined in Southeast Asia in the late 1980s, when the 1987 currency appreciation and increased wages in East

FIG. 5.1. Underemployment as a percentage of the labor force, 1965 to 1987. *Source:* Official national accounts; World Bank, *World Development Report;* Harry T. Oshima and Ismael Getubig, Jr., eds., *Towards a Full Employment Strategy for Accelerated Economic Growth* (Kuala Lumpur: Asian and Pacific Development Centre, 1991). *Note:* Scale for Thailand is 0 to 5 percent instead of 0 to 10 percent. Comparable data are not available for Nepal, Malaysia, and India.

Asia drove Japanese and Taiwanese enterprises to these countries. In some countries, notably the Philippines, Malaysia, and Sri Lanka, unemployment is alarmingly high. In the larger, predominantly agricultural countries of Indonesia, India, and Bangladesh, underemployment is no less alarming. In these larger countries, unemployment is small because the urban population is relatively small—and it is in urban areas that most unemployment is found. (In 1985, the shares of urban population to total population in Bangladesh, India, and Indonesia were 18, 25, and 25 percent, respectively.)[4] In rural areas, it is much easier to find part-time work, even though it may only be for a few hours a day. Such work is more difficult to find in cities and large towns.[5]

Underemployment in Japan and South Korea is much higher than in Taiwan, due to the cold winters of the former countries. Underemployment in the

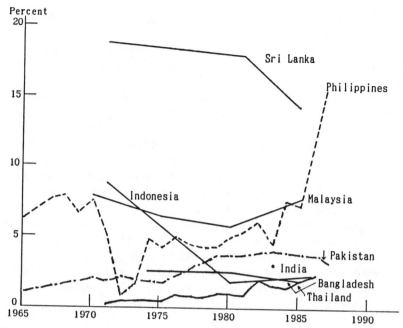

FIG. 5.2. Unemployment as a percentage of the labor force, 1965 to 1987. *Source:* See figure 5.1.

tropical countries of the Philippines, Indonesia, Bangladesh, Pakistan, and Sri Lanka is too high. Unlike the others, Indonesia's definition includes all those working fewer than thirty-five hours, not just those desiring more hours. Even if we assume that half of these are housewives and students who do not want more work, underemployment is still very high. The seriousness of underemployment in these countries is underscored by the fact that those working part-time are doing menial work of low productivity and at low compensation. This may be the reason the Indonesian labor force survey calls underemployment "hidden" unemployment. The Philippines and Sri Lanka have the most serious problem of unemployment and underemployment in Southeast and South Asia, respectively.

As can be seen in table 5.1, the underemployment rate is low for Malaysia. Malaysia is unique in that in other countries of Asia insufficient rains during the first half of the year make for difficulties in crop growing unless there is irrigation, but in Malaysia there is a minimonsoon, which brings rain for several months in the first half of the year, keeping Malaysia green throughout the year. Hence, tree crops such as rubber and palm oil, which need rain throughout the year, can be grown in Malaysia—which has evolved into the largest tree-crop economy in Asia. Work is available throughout the year on plantations and peasant farms, which are among the largest in Asia, second only to Thai farms.[6]

This chapter does not include the socialist economies of China, Vietnam, Cambodia, and Laos, nor the economies of Burma and Nepal. Burma's rate of unemployment is reported to be 5 percent of the labor force, but data on underemployment are not reported. Data are not available for Nepal, Laos, and Vietnam. For China unemployment in 1985 was 0.47 percent.[7] Communist countries are not supposed to have unemployment, as jobs are guaranteed to all. Because of this, the government keeps large numbers of unwanted workers in their enterprises, even though they are not productive. This disguised unemployment may be many times the open unemployment (such as the 0.47 percent reported for China). And since all these countries are monsoon economies, rural underemployment may be chronic. Lately, the Chinese government has been encouraging peasants to start private enterprises to supplement farm incomes, and much of the high growth in the past decades of the Chinese economy has been attributed to the increases in off-farm employment. Nepal—with its great densities, long dry season, high population growth, and limited land—may have unemployment problems as severe as those in Bangladesh.

FACTORS CONTRIBUTING TO IDLENESS

I dwell on the demand side, since on the supply side the labor force in the 1980s in Taiwan, South Korea, and Hong Kong has grown just as rapidly as it has among the ASEAN Four, India, and Sri Lanka. The reason is that population growth in the 1960s (which are relevant for labor force growth in the early 1980s) was not very much different in East Asia (with the exception of Japan) from those in the other countries of Asia. To the extent that these figures were somewhat lower in East Asia, higher life expectancies (and in-migration to Hong Kong) offset the impact on labor force growth. The major exception was Japan, with its exceptionally low population growth, participation rates, and in-migration in the 1960s, which combined to produce the lowest labor force growth.

Hence it is not so much labor supply as labor demand (the absorptive power of the economy vis-à-vis labor) that explains South Asian and ASEAN unemployment and underemployment. The most important factor is, of course, the growth rate of real GNP per capita, which is higher in East Asia than among the ASEAN Four and substantially higher than in South Asia (table 5.1). To understand the differences in growth rates of GNP per capita, we examine the pre-1980 period, since most of the causes of idleness originated before the 1980s.[8]

Most countries in South and Southeast Asia started their development late in the postwar decades because of various political reasons. The exceptions were

India, Sri Lanka, and the Philippines, which gained independence early in the postwar era. East Asia began development when Taiwan and South Korea gained independence with the surrender of the Japanese army in 1945. More important, they—together with Hong Kong and Japan—were in a position to take advantage of the opening of U.S. markets with large exports of labor-intensive products, especially textiles. The reason for this early start was that many experienced entrepreneurs from Shanghai and Canton escaped to Hong Kong as the Red Army marched into their cities. South Korea and Taiwan gained experience in manufacturing beginning in the late 1930s, when Japan was preoccupied with military production and depended on its colonies for textiles and other manufactures. The migration of experienced entrepreneurs from the north to the south as a result of the Korean War in the early 1950s and of Chinese entrepreneurs from the mainland to Taiwan also boosted industrialization.[9]

Malaysia started late because of civil war, Indonesia was bogged down with fighting for independence from the Dutch and then with the loquacious Sukarno, while Bangladesh was under Pakistani rule until the late 1960s. Thailand and Nepal were ancient kingdoms with very little physical infrastructure and modern social institutions. For various reasons, India, the Philippines, and Sri Lanka grew slowly, even though they had a head start. Singapore started late because of tensions and political instability in the 1950s.

The Philippines' poor economic performance and high population and labor force growth originated in the early decades of the postwar era. Instead of starting out with an agricultural development strategy, as all low-income countries with a large farm sector should, it plunged into capital-intensive industrialization. Because they were heavily protected for long periods, its industries continue to be inefficient right up to the present. They were unable to expand, since the domestic market was limited by the failure to develop the large agricultural sector; and they were unable to export. Thus these industries stagnated and could not absorb the rapidly growing labor force. In the late 1970s, loans from the Middle East were used to construct new industries, which, however, were capital-intensive and underutilized and thus did not hire many new workers.

In the Philippines' neglected agricultural sector, landlord-dominated farming kept incomes low for tenants, and landless workers and productivity increased very slowly. Landlords may not favor full employment since it would raise rural wages, thereby reducing their rents. The Philippines once had the most efficient sugar and coconut plantations, but they were poorly managed, and productivity grew very slowly.[10] Poverty among the peasant and working population breeds insecurity and uncertainty about the future, which must be insured for by a large number of children; low incomes must be augmented with income from the labor of grown children. Thus despite the large exodus of populations to foreign countries, population growth has been rapid. Per capita

GNP and aggregate GNP grew slowly, and the population multiplied.[11]

Sri Lanka perhaps has the most serious problem in South Asia, as the Philippines does in Southeast Asia, but the reasons are different. Unlike landlord-dominated Philippines, a leftist regime came into power in Sri Lanka in the early part of the postwar period and harassed the British-owned plantations, which had been highly efficient enterprises. High taxes were levied, and eventually the plantations were taken over by the government. As with most nationalized industries, they were inefficiently run, and production and employment stagnated. The same thing happened to nationalized industries and to new industries built and operated by the government.

What went wrong was the adoption of a welfare strategy that grew to be the most comprehensive in Asia—with free education; subsidized food, health care, and housing; and social security pensions. The welfare state was spending 6 percent of GNP on welfare (or 35 percent of the national budget). In a poor, low-income, and low-saving country like Sri Lanka, such spending took badly needed funds away from physical infrastructure and crowded out private use of capital. Taxes on productive British enterprises had to be high to pay for all these expenditures. With so many basic needs guaranteed by the state, the propensity to work to meet such needs was weakened. Also blunted was the urge to save for the future, with little to worry about the needs of old age, health care, and children's education. The welfare state did reduce insecurity and lower total fertility rates, but the final outcome was slow economic growth, slow employment growth, and slow productivity growth.[12]

In the Philippines and Sri Lanka, spending (both private and public) on education was exceptionally high; perhaps too much was spent on higher education and not enough on vocational training. But the slow progress of technology was not conducive to the employment of educated manpower, and the unemployment of the educated became a major issue in both countries. New administrations came into power in the 1980s, but the dismantling of welfare programs was slow in Sri Lanka, while in the Philippines the power of the landlords and import-substitution industrialists does not appear to be shaken.

The Indian experience is not unlike that of the Philippines, and if adequate data were available, underemployment may prove to be as serious. Heavy industries were inefficient and stagnant; downstream industries were forced to purchase their equipment and materials from these heavy industries and thus also became inefficient. Slow growth in industry was matched by stagnation in agriculture, which was unable to get sufficient funding for irrigation. In most parts of India, as in the Philippines, landlord power was pervasive.

The situation was also different in Bangladesh: with a small urban sector, its unemployment rate was low, but rural underemployment was extensive. Farmland per worker was the smallest in Asia (0.4 hectare in 1980—too small to furnish enough work even during the wet months) and was subject to flooding. Population and labor force growth was one of the highest in Asia, and GNP growth the lowest, all of which translated into the lowest growth of GNP per capita and per worker in Asia. With the highest population densities in Asia, the solution to the problem of rural underemployment was difficult to find.

Southeast Asian countries other than the Philippines fared better in employment generation than South Asia did. Indonesia improved its rice-growing capacity in the 1970s, becoming self-sufficient. It also enhanced the efficiency of its nationalized plantations. But in the late 1970s and early 1980s, when loans from the Middle East became available, the government constructed capital-intensive industries (iron and steel, aluminum, machinery) and paid insufficient attention to agroindustries and to the development of diversified agriculture in the uplands of Java and the outer islands. Since capital-intensive industries did not generate much off-farm employment, peasant families were unable to find jobs in the dry seasons. Since the farms in Java were tiny, almost as small as in Bangladesh and Nepal, young people coming into the labor force were unable to find jobs in the rural sectors and had no choice but to migrate to the cities. Moreover, beginning in 1985, prices for sugar, palm oils, rubber, and other plantation crops fell. Though Indonesia's unemployment rate of 2.2 percent was as low as Thailand's, disguised unemployment (such as women selling tiny quantities of produce at low prices and *becak* boys waiting the whole day long for a few passengers) was 17 percent of the labor force.[13]

Malaysia did well in the 1960s and 1970s after putting down the rebellion in the 1950s. Its rubber and palm oil plantations expanded, becoming the most efficient in Asia. From the 1960s, irrigation projects were built, and double cropping of rice lands expanded. Peninsular Malaysia's unemployment began to fall in the 1970s, when large tracts of land were distributed to smallholders; underemployment fell to only 2–3 percent with the work generated by double cropping in the drier seasons. As the purchasing power of the farm population rose, urban industry began to grow. This growth together with the rapid growth of the electronic industries induced rural to urban migration in the early 1980s. In 1984 full employment appeared to have been attained, but only momentarily—the world markets for rubber, palm oil, lumber, tin, petroleum, and electronics fell in 1985. The Malaysian leadership turned to heavy industries (cars, iron and steel, cement), but as in Indonesia, these turned out to be inefficient, and capacities were substantially underutilized. Malaysia also adopted a number of welfare policies and enlarged its bureaucracies, which proved to be costly.[14]

Thailand performed better than its Southeast Asian neighbors, in part due to its more diversified agricultural exports (cassava, soybeans, rice, corn, vegetables, fruits, pork, chicken, rubber, sugar, and coconut), most of which were exported to Asia and not to the West and thus were less affected by the drop in Western markets. But it was also due to the cautious fiscal policies of the political leadership, which refrained from borrowing from the Middle East to finance capital-intensive industries, as Indonesia, Malaysia, and the Philippines did.[15] Hence, Thailand is not being drained by the huge debt payments and deficits of big industries. With good management from a fairly efficient bureaucracy, its economic growth has been remarkably stable, and assistance to the peasantry has reduced urban unemployment and rural underemployment, even though the dry season of the monsoon is one of the longest and driest in Asia. Thailand has had a postwar average labor productivity growth of 4.8 percent. In the later 1980s, the Thais reached full employment and increased the growth rate of GDP to double-digit levels. (Malaysia's unemployment also began to fall, reaching 6.5 percent in 1990, as both countries receive large amounts of investments from East Asia.)

In sum, idleness represents a serious waste and misallocation of human resources. The hardest hit are people in their twenties who are most anxious to work, to save, and to start families. In the streets of Manila there are youths who jump onto jeepneys at red-light stops to shine the shoes of surprised passengers, and who hang around parking lots and rush to help drivers park their cars and then look after the cars while the drivers are away—for whatever the traffic will bear. They work also as jeepney barkers, sidewalk vendors, and rag hawkers, which adds little if any to per capita or per worker product, as they simply take sales away from the stores or create new work of low value. On the campus of the University of the Philippines are growing numbers of young people selling cigarettes and candies from tiny stalls. These manifestations of unemployment are harbingers of social unrest and political instability.

The experiences of these countries contrast with the greater stability of East Asia, despite transitory problems in Singapore and the change from authoritarian to democratic rule in Taiwan and South Korea. At this point, we will examine the experience of East Asia to see what can be learned that might be useful to monsoon Asia in the coming years.

EAST ASIA AND FULL EMPLOYMENT

Over the four postwar decades, Japan, Taiwan, South Korea, Hong Kong, and Singapore were the only countries in monsoon Asia where full employment was attained and sustained. (Mainland China appears to be fully employed, with 0.5 percent unemployed, according to official figures, but China has disguised unemployment in the form of overstaffing and underemployment.) Below, I analyze for each of the East Asian countries how full employment was attained and sustained, with emphasis on their policies and strategies.

*Japan*

Japan was the first country in Asia to achieve full employment. Agriculture was the largest sector in terms of employment throughout the 1940s and 1950s;

thereafter, the largest sectors were industrial and service. The Supreme Command of the Allied Powers (SCAP), which occupied Japan between 1945 and 1952, undertook drastic land reform in 1947, seeing that this was the only way in which Japan could be made into a peaceful society. SCAP felt that the sickness of the Japanese society, which had led to its militarization, was due to the misery of the peasantry, whose meager incomes fell from 1,600 yen in the mid-1920s to 900 yen in 1937, with tenant-landlord disputes rising from a few hundred in the pre–World War I decades to 4,000 in the 1930s.[16] Land reform wiped out the power of the landlords not only in the ownership of farmland but in the control of such institutions as rural cooperatives and government agricultural extension services, which were democratized. Labor productivity rose by 5 percent per year in the 1950s, after the reform. Another source of social tension and unrest was insufficient employment, especially underemployment in the drier periods, when the monsoon rains stopped.

In the latter half of the 1950s, unemployment and underemployment rates averaged about 1 percent and 15 percent, respectively. By the usual standards, these rates were low, but it should be kept in mind that Japanese social values forbid idleness among adults. Because of Japan's dire poverty due to the damage caused by Allied bombing of its factories, many urban people resorted to such menial work as collecting used paper, cans, and pieces of wood. Those with relatives in rural areas went to the farms to help in any way they could. This may be a kind of disguised unemployment, in which people work but produce little. It is in keeping with the Japanese dictum, Don't stand or sit down, doing nothing; look busy. Thus the percentage of self-employed workers rose to one-fourth of the employed population and by 1955 was greater than the percentage of regular laborers. By 1960 self-employed workers were only one-half of regular workers, and by 1965 only one-third.[17]

Nevertheless, Japan's labor surplus fell substantially from the early 1950s, partly due to its sale of goods to the U.S. military forces for its efforts in the Korean War. Also, the West bought large quantities of Japanese textiles, and U.S. department stores and chains went to Japan to purchase garments, toys, radios, and so on. Hence, Japan did not have a large pool of surplus labor in the early 1950s, except in rural areas, where underemployment may have been substantial; in the 1950s, a program of diversified agriculture succeeded in solving this problem.

Thus throughout the 1950s, Japan was well on the road to full employment. Unemployment fell to 0.6 percent in the early 1960s. Underemployment fell to 12 percent in the early 1960s, to 10 percent in the second half of the 1960s, and to 9 percent in the first half of the 1970s. (These rates include working housewives not wanting full-time work.)

Full employment was accompanied by a rise in real wages, which rose on the average by 5.9 percent per year in the 1960s, compared to 4.5 percent in the 1950s. The consumer price index rose by 5 percent per year between 1959 and

1966, compared to 2 percent between 1952 and 1959. Before 1963 new applications for jobs exceeded new job openings, but in 1963, openings began to be greater than applications. The number employed in agriculture began to fall absolutely in 1950, and rural to urban migration began to accelerate. This was accompanied by the speeding up of farm mechanization, from simple equipment such as sprayers to cultivators, transplanters, and reapers.[18] Urban workers who could not find jobs in the the cities in the late 1940s—and who moved to rural areas—came back to the cities. Japan completed the agroindustrial transition by 1960, when the industrial labor force began to exceed the agricultural labor force.[19]

How did Japan attain full employment? The first step was comprehensive land reform, which motivated the new landowning peasants to put in more labor on their farms to maximize yields. Average man-days for rice (in five-year averages) increased by 20 percent, from 95 days before land reform to 115 days after 1950; for barley and wheat, man-days rose from 130 days to 164 days; for vegetables, from 108 to 113; for fruits, from 93 to 99; for industrial crops, from 77 to 110; for livestock, from 93 to 107. For all crops, average man-days per crop rose from 91 in 1945–50 to 103 in 1950–55 and to 104 in 1955–60.[20] In 1961 the smallest sized farm used 26 man-days; as farm size rose, labor input fell to 18 man-days for the largest farms.[21]

Most income elastic products were more labor intensive than rice cultivation, which in 1960 required 106 man-days. In comparison, average man-days for vegetables were 129, fruits 172, industrial crops 469, and livestock 130.[22] The increased labor input represented by agricultural diversification in the 1950s is consistent with data showing that the labor force engaged in agriculture fell steadily, from 15.7 million in 1951 to 13.4 million in 1960.[23] The reason is that the diversified crops were produced in the drier months of the off season, using workers who produced the main rice crops. Despite the lower labor requirements of the main grain crops, yields rose between 1950 and 1960 from 316 to 398 kilograms per one-tenth of a hectare.

These changes were accompanied by various government policies: land reform, the democratization of cooperatives, farm credit and subsidies, land improvement schemes such as irrigation works, agricultural education in secondary schools, and extension services. Research centers and experiment stations were decentralized to meet the varied needs of local farms. These services were made available to all farmers and did not favor the landlord class.[24]

Off-farm (or nonagricultural) incomes of farm families rose from 28 percent of on-farm incomes in 1950, to 73 percent in 1960, to 167 percent in 1970, and to 393 percent in 1981. Off-farm jobs in 1959 were in manufacturing (21 percent), services (21 percent), transport and communication (14 percent), construction (11 percent), and commerce (4 percent).[25] In the 1950s most of these jobs were agriculture based and were in nearby towns; later, they were not agriculture based and were found in the cities, to which the male adults com-muted, leaving to the women and the elderly the operations of the farms, which could be carried out with mechanized equipment.

In the 1950s, Japanese industries grew rapidly not only with the rise of rural purchasing power but with exports. Promoting these exports was the under-valued yen, which was 360 to the U.S. dollar. These were labor-intensive industries, generating more jobs than could be filled by the urban labor force. With the rise of urban real wages, wives came out of homes and participation rates rose to a peak of 56 percent in the latter 1950s. Young workers migrated to the cities to take advantage of the higher wages. When the pool of surplus labor was exhausted, small industries began to move to rural towns to hire male farm workers.

The consequences and implications of full employment to the subsequent growth of the Japanese economy were unusually favorable. Real GNP per capita accelerated from 6.6 percent per year in the 1950s to 10.1 percent in the 1960s. Real annual wages in agriculture and industry also rose, the latter from 4 percent per year in the 1950s to 6.3 percent in the 1960s. With labor surplus gone, entrepreneurs turned to machines instead of labor. By the end of the 1970s nearly all operations in rice farming were mechanized for the first time in the long history of monsoon paddy agriculture. What was particularly notable was the introduction of reapers and transplanters, which mechanized the most labor-intensive operations in paddy farming. In manufacturing, horsepower per worker rose from 1.4 in 1950 to 6.8 by the end of the 1970s. Labor productivity, which grew at 6 percent per year in the 1950s, rose to nearly 8 percent in the 1960s. This was due not only to the rise in capital per worker but to increased utilization of production capacity and the improvement of manpower skills with more sophisticated technologies and in-service training.

Japan completed its demographic transition in the early 1960s, when fertility rates fell to 2 and below, declining from 4.5 in 1947. Contributing to this decline was the sharp fall in infant mortality, from 200,000 deaths in 1947 to 43,000 in 1961. Also important was the increase in secondary school enroll-ment, which doubled between 1947 and 1961.[26] With higher incomes, families in the lower income brackets could save to send their children to high school and college. With technology in the workplace progressing so quickly, parents found that advanced schooling would be necessary for their offsprings' future, and they opted to have small families to assure that maximal education could be given, especially since housewives had to work outside the home to increase family incomes. Family planning surveys by the Mainchi newspapers during the 1960s found that the major reason parents practiced contraception was their desire to restrict the number of children in order to give them good educations. After their children began to attend school, mothers went to work.[27]

*Taiwan*

Taiwan's experience is the most pertinent among East Asian countries for countries in other regions of monsoon Asia. Taiwan is not as industrially advanced as Japan, its agriculture is more tropical than that of South Korea, and it is much larger than Hong Kong and Singapore.

Taiwan reached full employment around 1968. Double-digit unemployment rates (as a share of the labor force) in the early 1950s steadily fell to around 6–7 percent in the early 1960s and to 1.8 percent in the late 1960s. Underemployment (those working less than thirty-five hours per week) fell to about 1 percent in the late 1960s. These low levels were sustained throughout the 1970s and into the early 1980s; they rose slightly to around 2 percent on the average up to 1987.[28]

The usual symptoms that accompany full employment were discernible in Taiwan, such as the wages of the less skilled rising as fast or faster than those of the more skilled workers. Although Taiwan wage statistics are not broken down by skill, proxies can be arrived at using wages in industries (food, tobacco, textiles) using unskilled workers; these wages rose 9 percent between 1960–62 and 1970–72, compared to wages in printing, ceramics, metals, and transport, which grew 8 percent. Real wages grew at an annual rate of 4.3 percent between 1952 and 1960 and at 4.7 percent between 1960 and 1970. The consumer price index (100 = 1981) rose four points in the seven-year period 1960–67 (from 22.9 to 27.2) and twenty-seven points in the next seven-year period (to 53.9 by 1974).[29] This was due not only to oil price hikes but to wage increases.

In 1968 for the first time job openings outnumbered job seekers. This situation continued throughout the rest of the 1970s and into the 1980s. Labor turnover rose as jobs became more plentiful relative to demand.[30] Labor force participation rates of females fifteen years old and older began to escalate in 1967, reaching a peak in 1974 (rising from 33.4 to 41.5 percent), indicating that, in response to rising wage rates, women left their homes to enter the labor market. In contrast, male participation rates declined to 77.1 percent in 1973 from 83.7 percent in 1964, as prosperity enabled young males to remain in school. And as urban wages rose, migration from rural areas accelerated, from 1 percent between 1955 and 1965 to 2 percent between 1965 and 1974, and in 1967, for the first time, employment in agriculture declined absolutely—and has continued to do so since. Thus the transition from a predominantly agricultural economy to an industrial economy began in Taiwan with the secular shrinking of the agricultural sector.[31]

How was full employment attained? Agricultural development was strategic, with land reform leading the way to greater labor absorption. The number engaged in agriculture rose from 1.5 to 1.9 million between 1952 and 1958, with virtually no increase in farmland.[32] This represents not only higher labor inputs per hectare but more crops cultivated per hectare (multiple cropping).

Land reform provided incentives for owner-cultivators to produce, since more of the remainder after expenses and taxes become entirely theirs. It was worthwhile for them to work hard, putting more labor into cultivating, fertilizing, watering, spraying, and so on. Moreover, land reform—by removing control of cooperatives, extension services, local governments, and other rural institutions from the landlords—made these institutions more responsive to the needs of the small farmers.[33]

All these changes enabled farmers to cultivate more than one or two crops per year, and the multiple-cropping index rose from 1.7 in the early 1950s to an all-time peak of 1.9 in the mid-1960s, the highest recorded in the history of Asia. Multiple cropping enabled peasant families to work in the drier months, which was especially helpful to smaller farmers, whose families tended to be large and therefore to have more surplus labor in the drier months.

As self-sufficiency in rice production was reached in the early 1950s, and with rising per capita income, food consumption patterns began to shift away from rice. The share of output other than rice (fruits, vegetables, pulses, poultry, livestock) began to mount, reaching two-thirds of total output by 1968 (compared to one-half in 1950). Since diversified crops were generally labor-intensive, the labor required per hectare was large (averaging 185 days per hectare per crop between 1961 and 1965). This ratio was larger for smaller farms than for larger farms.

Most diversified crops are process-intensive; that is, they require work after harvesting for drying, pickling, preserving, canning, freezing, or dehydrating. Employment in food processing industries rose from 11,000 in 1954 to 144,000 in 1968, and the wage bill rose from NT$57 million to NT$1.9 billion. The multiplier effect of wages from additional employment is estimated at 3.3–4 times, based on 70–75 percent propensity to consume. Thus the processing of diversified crops provided farm families with jobs even after harvest. In addition, jobs were generated in the transporting, financing, and marketing of the processed goods. The higher purchasing power of farmers attracted small labor-intensive industries to small rural towns.[34] Incomes derived from off-farm jobs rose to 83 percent of on-farm incomes by 1970 and rose to 186 percent in 1980. In the 1970s, most of the sources of off-farm incomes were not crop processing but industries related to agriculture, suggesting that it was the processing of diversified crops that triggered rising off-farm employment. The efficiency with which crops were grown enabled Taiwan to export a larger share of these crops. The proceeds financed half of imports throughout the 1950s and until the mid-1960s. These imports were mostly machines used for the mechanization of industry. Without the large markets abroad, agricultural diversification could not have proceeded so rapidly.

In the 1950s, import-substitute industrialization was promoted, but toward the end of the decade, the domestic market became saturated. Because heavy industrialization does not contribute to the solution of foreign trade deficits and unemployment, the government chose to promote labor-intensive industrialization for export. This strategy called for substantial devaluation of the currency, extensive financial and fiscal reforms, and the promotion of competition and other market forces. In 1965, exports accelerated in textiles, garments, footwear, plastics, and simple electric machinery; in part, this acceleration was due to the rapid rise in real wages in Japan and Hong Kong, which were experiencing labor shortages and loss of competitiveness in labor-intensive exports. Taiwan's share of industrial exports rose sharply, from 55 percent in 1965 to 85 percent by 1970.[35]

Labor was also absorbed by the construction of extensive networks of roads, railways, harbors, airports, and telecommunication, which were used to market the output of commercial agriculture and of labor-intensive, decentralized industrialization. U.S. aid was large, averaging US$100 million a year in the 1950s and the first half of the 1960s, but sharply declining thereafter. Large as it was, it mainly compensated for the enormous military effort required to fend off possible attacks from mainland China. The size of the army was 600,000 in the early 1950s. The upkeep and equipment for such an army was too large for such a small country and could be maintained only by large foreign aid.

Full employment was sustained after the late 1960s, with only slight fluctuations in the percentage of joblessness. This was partly due to the growth of GNP per capita, from 6.3 percent per year in the 1960s to 6.7 percent in the 1970s. Also, it was due to the further growth of the domestic and export markets for diversified agricultural output. Labor-intensive industrialization ensured that employment growth kept up with GNP growth, with the result that jobs increased at a rate of 4.7 percent in the 1970s, compared with 4.2 percent in the 1960s, both rates exceeding the growth of the labor force.[36] The consequences and implications of full employment were extensive and highly favorable to the rapid growth and improved distribution of income. Per capita GNP accelerated after full employment, and the Gini coefficient in Taiwan fell from .36 in the years before 1970, to .32 in 1970, and to an unprecedented low of .30 in 1980.

Before full employment was reached, the main source of growth was surplus labor; afterward, the sources were several. The rise in wages of unskilled workers raised product per worker (from 5.3 percent in 1960–69 to 6.2 percent in 1969–80), because wage increases speeded the substitution of technology for workers. Manpower skills improved as rising wages motivated the labor force to learn more skills to get better pay. High wages and more family members employed meant more food and better nutrition and health services; in turn, child mortality fell. The latter, together with the rise in the opportunity cost of raising children due to the employment of housewives, reduced birth rates sharply.

*South Korea*

Among East Asian countries, South Korea attained full employment most recently—in the latter 1970s. Its unemployment rates are about 1–2 percent higher than those of Taiwan and Japan. The winter in South Korea, which is long and severe, reduces economic activities much more than winter in Japan, where the Pacific Ocean keeps winters milder. (Taiwan's winter is like South Korea's spring.) Temperatures in most parts of South Korea are close to minus centigrade from December through February and most of March, with meager precipitation in the dry months. Rainfall is more evenly distributed in Japan between the wet and dry months of the monsoon than it is in South Korea. Hence, unemployment rates are usually 2 percent higher in the first and last quarters of the year and largely account for the higher unemployment in South Korea than in Japan and other East Asian countries. A 2 percent unemployment rate in Japan and Taiwan thus corresponds to a 3–3.5 percent rate in South Korea.[37]

South Korea's all-time low unemployment rate of 3.6 percent was reached in 1976–79. Its high unemployment rates in the 1950s were probably due to the slow growth of the economy and a large influx of people from the north during the Korean War. In 1963, the first year of the regular labor force survey, 8.1 percent of the labor force was unemployed. This rate fell to 7 percent in the next few years, to a 5 percent average in 1966–69, to 4.5 percent in the early 1970s, and to 4 percent in 1983–86. The underemployment rate also fell steadily. The level and trend of these rates are similar to those of Japan in the 1950s. The lower levels of Japanese unemployment in the 1950s compared to those of South Korea in the 1970s and Taiwan in the 1960s and 1970s may be accounted for by their definitions of employment. Underemployment of 10 percent or less indicates full employment, since most of the underemployed do not want more work. In 1985, 80 percent of the underemployed did not want additional work.[38]

Wages of workers in industries where unskilled operations are dominant (textiles, leather, wood, and food) rose faster than wages in skilled industries (basic metals, printing, transport, industrial chemicals, and petroleum): wages in the former industries rose by 11.5 percent per year between 1973 and 1985, compared to 11 percent in the latter industries. Consumer prices doubled between 1977 and 1981, compared to a 63 percent rise in the previous four-year period, 1974–77. Female labor force participation rates went up from 37 percent in the mid-1960s to 43 percent in the latter 1970s. Migration to the cities accelerated to 18 percent per year between 1978 and 1983, compared to 14 percent in the previous five years.[39] South Korea completed its agroindustrial transition in 1979, with employment in industry exceeding agricultural employment.[40] The demographic transition was completed around the mid-1980s, with the fertility rate falling to 2.1 in 1985, a drop from 6 in 1961.[41] Both transitions were about half a decade later than those of Taiwan and two decades later than those of Japan.

The delay in the completion of the two transitions was in part due to the Korean War and also to the pattern of economic development in South Korea, which was different from those of Japan and Taiwan. Land reform was as comprehensively carried out in South Korea as in Japan and Taiwan, with tenancy reduced from 49 percent of households to only 6 percent. Landlords were minimally compensated, as the price of land amounted to only 1.25 times annual yields. Labor per hectare rose each year by 2.7 percent male-equivalent hours between 1952 and 1954 after the reform and even more per year (4.7 percent) between 1954 and 1960. The increase in labor input in 1952–54 was mainly for spraying and fertilizing, but in the late 1950s, it was also for feeding livestock. Output rose much faster than labor input in 1952–54, in part due to the recovery from low production levels during the Koran War. But in 1954–60, output rose 2.75 percent, 2 percent less than labor input growth. Labor input per hectare increased only 1.3 percent per year between 1960 and 1965 and decreased 3.2 percent between 1965 and 1973.[42]

Agricultural employment began to decline in 1976, long before self-sufficiency was approached. Overall net food imports were large throughout the 1960s and 1970s, with rice and other grains composing the bulk of imports.[43] Despite this, South Korean agriculture in 1980 required 36 percent of the labor force, compared to 20 percent in Taiwan and 11 percent in Japan.[44] The poorer performance of South Korean agriculture was the result of autocratic controls by the central government, which was intent on industrialization during most of the postwar era and did not provide enough agricultural support after land reform. Even though the share of spending in the central government budget was about that of Taiwan (both much lower than Japan's), the South Korean government monolithically controlled agricultural and rural institutions, with little leeway for grassroots participation and initiatives.[45] In the latter 1970s the government increased its spending for public works (rural roads, irrigation, electrification), extension services, agricultural education and research, storage and marketing services, buildings for the production of fertilizer and pesticides, and loans for mechanization, after more than two decades of neglect following land reform in the early 1950s. Farm prices were maintained at higher levels in the 1970s through higher government procurement prices.[46]

Agricultural diversification lagged behind that of Taiwan during the 1960s and 1970s, with fruits, vegetables, and livestock composing only one-half of Taiwan's production. But the government began to step up diversification in the late 1970s and early 1980s by increasing spending for rural infrastructure (irrigation, roads, and electrification). This enabled the peasants to use their land for the production of fruits, vegetables, livestock, and pulses between rice crops, thereby increasing employment and reducing underemployment. The share of diversified crops relative to grain rose to an average of 107 percent in the 1980s, higher than those of Taiwan and Japan. However, the reason for this was that South Korea did not reach rice self-sufficiency as the others did, continuing to import rice throughout the first half of the 1980s.[47]

Off-farm employment of farm workers was much lower in South Korea than in Japan or Taiwan (and even Thailand), despite the increase in diversification. In the latter 1960s, South Korean off-farm income shares increased slightly, from 18 percent in the first half of the 1960s to 20 percent, rose to 34 percent in the latter 1970s, and then to 51 percent in the first half of the 1980s. (Taiwan's off-farm share was 200 percent in the 1980s; Japan's share was 400 percent.) One reason for the rapid increase in the 1980s in South Korea was diversified crops, whose output requires more processing and servicing (transporting, marketing, and financing); another reason was the rapid growth of labor-intensive industries, all of which were operating at peak capacity in 1978, when full employment was reached.[48]

A reason for the lower off-farm incomes in South Korea compared to Japan and Taiwan was that South Korean industrialization was concentrated near Seoul and Pusan. Thus agricultural regions were isolated, and industrial jobs during slack growing periods were difficult to reach, a major reason for the departure of young workers from the farms to the cities. Also, South Korean industrialization was much more capital-intensive and was centralized in a handful of large firms. Moreover, financial marketing and transport services were highly concentrated either in the manufacturing firms themselves or in large transporters and banks.

Despite shortcomings in agricultural policies, which delayed full employment by half a decade at least, South Korea made up for them through rapid industrialization. This was partly due to its industrial experience during the colonial period, when in the early 1930s the Japanese developed industries in North Korea to prepare for the invasion of Manchuria and, later, Kwantung.[49] Industrial growth in the 1960s and 1970s was one of the highest in the world, unmatched by other East Asian countries, with real product originating in industries averaging 16 percent per year. This growth partly compensated for the delays occasioned by the northern invasion, but it was due to the concentrated effort by military authorities to secure the south against another thrust from the north. For this, the south could not depend solely on labor-intensive industry, which tended to slow down when the domestic market was limited by insufficient purchasing power of farm families. When credit from petrodollars from the Middle East became available in the 1970s, South Korea shifted gears to high capital intensity.

The consequences and implications of South Korea's manner of reaching full employment differed from other East Asian countries, but there were similarities. Per capita GNP in the 1970s accelerated over that in the 1960s. The rapid rise of real wages included capital-labor substitution, as in Japan and Taiwan. Labor productivity grew faster after 1978 than before, but total factor productivity growth was slower because of the huge increases in the capital stock. Consumer prices shot up by more than 8 percent per year in the latter 1970s and into the early 1980s (in part because agriculture was insufficiently developed), and the currency was devalued from 484 won to US$1 in the 1970s to 890 won by 1985, unlike the Japanese and Taiwanese experience. Capacity utilization reached a peak in the late 1970s as far as the labor-intensive industries were concerned, but there was underutilization in some of the heavy industries (petroleum, rubber, paper, copper, and shipbuilding). But South Korea began to improve the efficiency of its heavy industries in the 1980s.

Gini coefficients for South Korean family income have been estimated at .34 for 1965, .33 for 1970, and .38 for 1976.[50] These coefficients are low when compared with those of Southeast and South Asian countries but higher than Taiwan's, which averaged .31 between 1976 and 1985. Apparently, the equalizing effects of more earners per family in the lower income groups as full employment was approached were offset by the slow rise in real wages and farm family incomes and the faster rise of entrepreneurial property incomes and salaries. The low wages of urban workers and low farm incomes limited the size of the domestic market, forcing industries to seek markets abroad.

*Hong Kong and Singapore*

The two city-states, Hong Kong and Singapore, reached full employment at different times (Hong Kong about the same time as Japan, in the late 1950s, and Singapore in the early 1970s) and in ways different from each other and different, too, from Japan, Taiwan, and South Korea. The reason for these differences is that the city-states did not have an agricultural sector large enough to have an impact on the labor market; hence it was the service sector that released workers for industrialization. The city-states inherited a large service sector (relative to the labor force) from the prewar decades. Services were built by the British rulers into highly efficient businesses as centers of trade of the British Empire. Services encompassed a formal sector and an informal sector, with sharp wage differences. It was from the informal sector that labor was released for the industries. But the labor from this sector was much smaller than labor that came from the rural areas of other countries, so that full employment was quickly reached in both city-states.

Labor force statistics are not available for Hong Kong for the latter 1940s and 1950s, but it is likely that unemployment was extensive in the 1940s and in the early 1950s, when the United Nations clamped an embargo on trading with the Chinese mainland, as the Communist armies swept through China.[51] In the early 1950s, Hong Kong began to develop a highly efficient textile industry, which penetrated Western markets about the same time Japan's did. So extensive was this penetration that Western countries imposed a restriction through "voluntary" quotas for Hong Kong and Japan by the end of the 1950s. Real wages rose rapidly in Hong Kong during the latter 1950s, as full employment was approached, even though migrants from mainland China were moving in. The population census of 1961 shows that only 1.7 percent of the labor force was unemployed. Underemployment in Hong Kong and Singapore was negligible, since agriculture was of minor importance.

During the early 1960s, many Hong Kong textile manufacturers moved their operations to nearby Taiwan, where wages were lower and where textile exports were not subject to Western quotas. Fortunately, in the mid-1960s, U.S. mass distributors (Sears, Penney's, Montgomery Ward, and others, to be followed by European department stores) came to Hong Kong (and Japan) to purchase radios, television sets, garments, toys, watches, clocks, wigs, and other labor-intensive products for marketing in the United States and Europe. They came with their managers and engineers to teach Hong Kong and Japanese entrepreneurs how to make these products. Exports grew in the 1960s. Even though the labor force grew at an annual rate of 3.2 percent, Hong Kong sustained full employment throughout the 1960s, since the economy and employment grew faster—10 percent and 4.2 percent, respectively. The doubling of real wages in manufacturing attracted workers from the informal service and primary sectors. Full employment was sustained into the 1970s and 1980s with the exception of the years immediately following the oil price hike.

The impact of full employment was generally similar in Hong Kong to that in Japan, Taiwan, and South Korea. GNP accelerated in the 1950s, and real wages rose rapidly. There was a restructuring upward to more mechanized and skill-intensive operations in the organized firms. The distribution of income improved (from a Gini coefficient of .48 in 1957 to .40 in 1979). Children in secondary schools rose from 20 percent of children in 1957 to 69 percent in 1984.[52] To cope with the rising costs of child rearing, the number of offspring was restricted. Also important was the shift in employment status from own-account, proprietary, and family help status (which decreased from 14.8 percent in 1961 to 7.8 percent in 1981) to the employer-employee group, which increased from 85.2 percent to 92.2 percent. Own-account and proprietary enterprises needed large families as a source of cheap and assured labor.

The rise in female participation in Hong Kong was due not only to the tight labor market but also to the spread of small machines, which increased light jobs suitable for females, unlike the cumbersome machines of the steam-powered technologies of the nineteenth century. Also, the electric-powered technologies of the twentieth century brought about labor-saving household appliances, enabling housewives to go to work. This raised the opportunity cost of staying home and rearing children, which together with the need for house-wives to go to work to save for children's education, rapidly lowered the fertility rates of lower income families, thereby completing the demographic transition.[53] All these were in addition to the sharp decline in infant mortality, which fell from twenty-eight to nine per thousand from 1965 to 1985, as nutrition and medical services improved.[54]

In Singapore full employment was reached about a decade later than in Hong Kong, as Singapore struggled with political difficulties in the 1950s. With the coming into power of the present regime, a program to speed up the development of Singapore was launched, first with the reorganization of the bureaucracy and other official agencies to make them more efficient and effective. When a 1966 labor force survey showed that full-time equivalent unemployment was high (about 11 percent of the labor force), the decision to industrialize was made, as Singapore's small land size precluded the development of agriculture, and the tertiary sector was limited by the entrepôt trade, which declined with the decision of Indonesia and Malaysia to conduct most of their trade directly instead of through Singapore.[55] And when Singapore was left out of the Malayan Union and became a full-fledged city-state, there was no need to retain the tariffs and protection to nurture domestic industries, which were growing too slowly.

Singapore did not have a large industrial entrepreneurial class, unlike Hong Kong, which was fortunate to get the influx of Chinese entrepreneurs in the late 1940s. Singapore's leadership opened its doors to foreign enterprises, which responded quickly, attracted by the excellent physical infrastructure (built by the British in the prewar era for their own shipping, trading, and financial activities) and by the diligent, well-educated labor force. Despite the capital intensity of most industries established by the multinational firms, the employment generated was sufficient to reach full employment in 1974, when the unemployment rate fell to 3.9 percent. It increased to 4.5 percent in 1975 with the oil price hike but dropped to 3.5 percent thereafter, up until 1981. In 1981–84, the rate averaged about 2.7 percent; it rose to 6.5 percent in 1986.[56]

One unique aspect of the city-state economies is their compelling need to achieve efficiency in order to export. Without foreign exchange from exports, the city-states cannot survive, as they must import most of their food and raw materials. In order to export, they must buy food and raw materials from the cheapest sources. There is no need to protect a meager domestic market, even though in the short run employment declines with free trade. In the long-run, their all-out efforts to raise efficiency generated enough jobs to reach full employment.

In both Hong Kong and Singapore, GNP accelerated after full employment was reached, as the wages of unskilled workers began to escalate, especially those of housewives who joined the labor market. However, in the 1970s, Hong Kong's female participation rate was higher than that of Singapore (43.5 and 37.0, respectively). This has been attributed to the more labor-intensive industrialization of Hong Kong, which permitted women to work at home through a putting-out system.[57] One important job-creation measure in Singapore was the massive construction of high-rise apartment buildings, which in the early 1970s housed two-thirds of its population. Hong Kong also undertook such a program, but on a smaller scale.

The size distribution of personal (or individual) incomes declined in Singapore from a Gini coefficient of .49 in 1966 to .44 in 1975. There are no surveys dealing with family incomes in Singapore, and the 1966 and 1975 surveys excluded property incomes. Hence these are not comparable to the data for other East Asian countries. Within-sector disparities declined in agriculture, manufacturing, commerce, transport, and personal services between 1966 and 1975.[58] This must have been due to the fact that full employment drew workers from low-income agriculture, manufacturing, and services (i.e., smaller farms, informal home industries, stall keeping, peddling, and domestic services). This is shown by the increase in the share of employees over other classes of workers in manufacturing, commerce, transport, and other services. This shift was also seen in Hong Kong.

All these changes contributed to the decline in birth rates in Singapore, which completed the demographic transition in 1977, earlier than Hong Kong. In that year, the fertility rate fell to 1.8 per thousand females. It dropped to 1.6 in 1983.[59] Fertility had started to fall in the 1950s (from 6.5) but accelerated after full employment for reasons similar to those in Hong Kong. Singapore's early demographic transition may be due to several factors. First, it does not have a farming sector. Second, Singapore restricted the immigration of blue-collar workers during the 1950s, 1960s, and early 1970s because of unemployment, and migrants tend to have higher birth rates (although they eventually are affected by constraints on large families in urban settings). Third, a large share of Singapore's population was housed in high-rise apartment buildings, where space was severely limited and costs were higher than in the older Hong Kong houses. Only those with few children could get an apartment in Singapore. These apartments promoted nuclear families, which made arrangements for the care of children difficult. Fourth, the Singapore government conducted a vigorous family planning program in the early 1970s, during which 20 percent of the population visited family planning clinics. Singapore also has one of the most complete social security systems in Asia.

CONCLUDING REMARKS

What emerges from the examination of the employment experience of East Asia is the important role played by employment in the sustained and rapid growth of their economies throughout the postwar era. A major source of increased growth before full employment was the employment of the unemployed and the fuller utilization of the underemployed. After full employment, the major sources of accelerated growth were the rising labor force participation of women and the growth of labor productivity through capital-labor and technology-capital substitutions and structural shifts to firms and industries paying higher incomes.

In the approach to and maintenance of full employment, these economies utilized marginal labor power (housewives, teenagers, women postponing marriages, and older persons). Full employment attracted workers away from low productivity sectors such as small farms, self-employment, own-account enterprises, and menial service occupations. Hours of work increased for most workers. What this meant was that the economy shifted to a long-run growth path, above the underemployed growth path. Once the economy was moving along this higher plane, it was difficult to dislodge it, as it moved with exceptionally high macroefficiency, with full utilization of physical capacity and manpower, and with rapid structural changes, all of which improved productivity and promoted exports. In short, it was now easy to sustain full employment over long periods, even though shocks and short-run contractions might temporarily throw many out of work. With the higher incomes of farmers and blue-collar workers, the domestic market was enlarged. Lower fertility rates imply slower growth of the future labor force. Both contributed to a rising savings rate and lower dependency ratios. Thus the rapid growth of East Asian economies was due not only to the diversity in export growth but to falling income disparities and sharp declines in birth rates.

Countries in South and Southeast Asia have relied too much on the indirect effects of an industrialization strategy, hoping that employment creation as a spillover effect would be large enough to promote full employment. Measures such as tourist promotion and afforestation (in Thailand), resettlement (in Malaysia), transmigration (in Indonesia), and international migration (in the Philippines) are helpful but are easily offset by negative policies, such as minimum wages, overprotected markets, monopolies, landlordism, government ownership of enterprises and so on. As full employment is approached, the opportunity will come for these countries to raise the labor force participation of women. It is a waste of human resources to keep so large a share of the population from participating in the production of GNP. It will be almost impossible to achieve high economic growth and low population growth if women are kept from economic production to stay home to produce babies.

# CHAPTER 6

# Agricultural Diversification and Structural Change

Self-sufficiency in rice production was reached by several countries in monsoon Asia with the high-yielding varieties (HYVs) from Japan and the International Rice Research Institute (IRRI). But even after such self-sufficiency is attained, agriculture still has a crucial role to play in employing the farm labor force in the long dry season and in supplying the calories, protein, vitamins, and minerals not supplied by rice. Rice production uses nearly all farmland during the wet season. Thus the additional output during the dry months represents an increase in overall productivity for the economy.

Hence it is misleading to say that, with rice self-sufficiency, agriculture cannot generate more employment and that these Asian countries must industrialize. This chapter is in part a reaction to this widely held view and deals in the first part with relations between agricultural and nonagricultural development in a monsoon setting. In the second part, the impact of diversification on overall structural changes is analyzed. And in the last part, the impact of structural changes on rural densities is discussed.[1]

## AGRICULTURAL AND NONAGRICULTURAL DEVELOPMENT

### The Concept and Significance of Diversification

In the literature, agricultural diversification is contrasted with specialization, from a one-crop economy as the most specialized to an infinite-crop economy as the most diversified. Diversification is the shifting from a monoculture or a few crops to a larger assortment of crops and to animal, fishery, and forestry products. (A simpler concept leaves out the last three and restricts diversification to crops only.) Diversification is measured in various ways; one method is to take the reciprocal of the sum of squared shares of the value of each crop to the total value of crops in a country. This reciprocal rises from a value of 1 for one crop and is equal to the number of crops, assuming equal value for each crop.

It is often useful to have another concept of diversification, such as the share of nonfood grains in the total value of agricultural production. (Nonstaple foods can be substituted for nonfood grains.) This shows the extent of diversification—away from grains as a source of energy and toward protective foods, for example. Or if value figures are not available, as is often the case, harvested quantities in metric tons or harvested areas in hectares can be used.

A closely related index is the multiple-cropping index computed as the proportion of area harvested to area planted. In Asia, where land is severely limited, the main way of diversifying is to plant a second crop after the rice is harvested. And since the dry season is long, the second (or third) crop can be grown only with irrigation. U.S. agriculture is highly diversified but in a different way from monsoon diversification. Because of plentiful land in the United States, many crops other than cereals are planted during the main cropping season.

In the traditional monsoon economy, when rice productivity was very low, most dry season crops had to be root crops, such as sweet potatoes and cassava, to supplement the calories from cereal crops. With rising rice yields, especially in East Asia before World War II with HYVs from Japan and in South and Southeast Asia in the postwar decades with HYVs from the IRRI, self-sufficiency was attained or approached, and the substitution of rice (the preferred grain in Asia) for other grains and root crops made possible the expansion to more nutritive crops. By the mid-1980s, rice yields per hectare reached a peak of about five metric tons in Japan, Taiwan, and South Korea.

Nonrice crops are grown on both large and small farms. My interest is diversification on small farms, as I am mainly concerned with the use of labor during the dry months. Large farms, especially estates, mainly grow perennial crops, often with the use of machinery. The significance of agricultural diversification on small farms is that full employment is difficult, if not impossible, without it.

Also important is the impact of diversification on food consumption patterns of Asians, most of whom, outside of East Asia and West Malaysia, do not consume enough calories and nutrients. China's calorie level per person is lower than that of the other East Asian countries, but its 2,500 calories per person per day may be sufficient because of its low income disparity and large food subsidies—with the exception of villages in parts of China with poor soil and little water (see table 6.1) The per capita consumption of 2,400 calories in Southeast Asia (even fewer in South Asia) indicates insufficient consumption in the lower classes, especially among the lowest income groups: peasants, landless workers, and urban laborers. This is so even though most of these countries have reached rice self-sufficiency. But nutrition surveys show large numbers of the lower classes with insufficient intake of not only calories but nutrients such as ascorbic acid, riboflavin, thiamine, iron, calcium, and protein.[2] The data in table 6.1 represents available food supplies, not actual intake. Nutrition surveys

TABLE 6.1
Supply of Calories and Nutrients, 1969 to 1985 (per capita)

| Country | Calories | | | | Proteins (mg.) | | | | Fat (mg.) | | | Calcium and Iron (mg.) | | |
|---|---|---|---|---|---|---|---|---|---|---|---|---|---|---|
| | 1969–1971 | 1974–1976 | 1980–1982 | 1985 | 1969–1971 | 1974–1976 | 1980–1982 | 1985 | 1969–1971 | 1974–1976 | 1980–1982 | 1969–1971 | 1974–1976 | 1980–1982 |
| Japan | 2,758 | 2,789 | 2,869 | 2,804 | 82.5 | 84.9 | 90.8 | | 59.7 | 69.5 | 82.6 | 536.3 | 556.2 | 592.0 |
| Taiwan | 2,658 | 2,758 | 2,763 | 2,880 | | 75.0[a] | 77.5 | 80 | | | | | | |
| South Korea | 2,456 | 2,610 | 2,938 | 2,910 | 64.5 | 73.4 | 82.1 | 78 | 23.0 | 29.1 | 40.5 | 344.0 | 410.0 | 482.3 |
| Singapore | 2,682 | 2,801 | 2,937 | 2,700 | 68.9 | 75.3 | 76.0 | 68 | 52.0 | 62.1 | 72.8 | 506.7 | 568.7 | 532.3 |
| Hong Kong | 2,690 | 2,685 | 2,768 | 2,690 | 76.7 | 78.6 | 82.0 | 84[b] | 98.6 | 101.5 | 112.2 | 405.6 | 421.0 | 450.9 |
| China[c] | 2,110 | 2,210 | 2,290 | 2,560 | 50.0 | 52.0 | 55.0 | 59 | | | | | | |
| Malaysia | 2,417 | 2,500 | 2,636 | 2,600 | 49.9 | 54.5 | 61.5 | 60[b] | 46.6 | 49.8 | 55.3 | 291.2 | 296.4 | 344.6 |
| Philippines | 2,026 | 2,116 | 2,405 | 2,390[b] | 48.1 | 50.4 | 54.3 | 53[b] | 31.1 | 31.1 | 32.3 | 243.3 | 247.1 | 293.3 |
| Thailand | 2,160 | 2,211 | 2,312 | 2,320[b] | 46.8 | 45.8 | 46.4 | 45[b] | 25.9 | 24.7 | 27.0 | 251.8 | 246.8 | 272.1 |
| Indonesia | 1,872 | 2,048 | 2,363 | 2,480 | 38.5 | 42.1 | 50.5 | 49 | 25.3 | 30.0 | 34.0 | 215.7 | 236.8 | 265.8 |
| Sri Lanka | 2,308 | 2,040 | 2,331 | 2,310[b] | 46.0 | 41.2 | 44.5 | 47[b] | 51.7 | 46.1 | 57.6 | 296.3 | 261.0 | 307.1 |
| India | 1,992 | 1,921 | 2,030 | 2,180[b] | 49.5 | 47.7 | 49.2 | 53[b] | 28.8 | 28.9 | 33.4 | 378.1 | 379.3 | 389.7 |
| Nepal | 2,020 | 2,010 | 2,005 | 2,000 | 48.9 | 48.7 | 48.2 | 51 | 27.2 | 27.5 | 27.2 | 324.9 | 327.8 | 321.7 |
| Pakistan | 2,018 | 2,084 | 2,232 | 2,180 | 53.6 | 56.3 | 57.3 | 56 | 35.0 | 37.0 | 45.9 | 483.0 | 479.4 | 472.4 |

Source: Food and Agriculture Organization, Production Yearbook; Taiwan Statistical Yearbook, Asian Development Bank, Key Indicators.

[a] 1975.

[b] 1984.

[c] 1970, 1975, 1980.

attempt to collect data on actual intake. In the Philippines in 1982, when 2,400 calories were available, nutrition surveys showed actual intake levels of 1,808. Even if we assume that intake levels are about 2,100 or 2,200 calories, which nutritionists regard as adequate for the size of Asian bodies, it is not likely that laborers and peasants are consuming that much.

First, peasants and laborers are not only the lowest income groups but do the heaviest work. For most countries with nutrition surveys, food expenditures rise from the lowest to the highest income groups, absolutely though not relatively to income (due to the Engel effect).[3] The physical amounts of food consumed (in grams per capita) rise from the lower to the higher income groups. In South Korea, Taiwan, Hong Kong, and Singapore, this rise was only in the most income elastic foods (meat, fish, poultry, vegetables, and fruits), but in the Philippines, Malaysia, Thailand, and Indonesia all categories of foods tend to be purchased more by higher income families (on a per capita expenditure basis). The cross-section Engel coefficient from family income and expenditure surveys rose in the lower income groups in India, Nepal, and Bangladesh. Thus energy needs (expressed in calories) of workers and peasants should be supplemented by calories from noncarbohydrates among the diversified crops.

In all countries of Asia, children up to ten years old as a share of the population will decline. They need only about half the calories and proteins of adult males doing moderate activity. Teenagers (ten to nineteen years old) and adult women eat, on the average, about 85 percent of adult male consumption. The population will age as birth rates fall and life expectancies rise. The share of children (up to ten years old) will decline from 23 percent in 1985 to 20 percent in the year 2000. The teenage group is expected to decline from 23 percent to 18 percent during the same period. The fall in the share of children and teenagers from 43 to 38 percent should raise the demand for calories, proteins, and other nutrients, which will be offset only slightly by the increase in the share of the aged (sixty years old and older), a group expected to rise from 7 to 9 percent between 1985 and 2000. This decline in the share of children and teenagers will be greater in South and Southeast Asia than in East Asia.[4] Instead of demand for calories, the demand for proteins, vitamins, and minerals will be greatest in the coming decade. There will be a relative shift of the labor force toward white-collar occupations and urbanization. Between 1980 and 2000, the share of urban population will double in Bangladesh and Nepal, rise by 50 percent in India, Sri Lanka, the ASEAN Four, and mainland China, and rise by 5–10 percent in East Asia. Food consumption will rise with urbanization (which implies rising per capita incomes).[5]

The export potential for diversified agriculture in Southeast Asia should not be overlooked. At current rates of per capita income growth in the NIEs, consumer incomes should double by 2000, and the shift toward diversified dietary patterns should accelerate, as it has in Japan. The protection of agricultural products in Japan, Taiwan, and South Korea cannot be maintained forever, and sooner or later it will end. The demand for diversified crops is mainly determined by per capita income and its purchasing power, together with the export demand for such crops. On the supply side, the availability of land with water and labor in the dry months are the main constraints. A few regions in monsoon Asia have enough rainfall in the dry season for fruit crops and vegetables, which require much less water than rice. (These are parts of Malaysia, Sri Lanka, Sumatra, Kalimantan in Indonesia, and Mindanao and Bicol in the Philippines.) Elsewhere, irrigation is needed. The high crop diversity in Japan and Taiwan are the outcome of an extensive irrigation system built before and after World War II, making multiple cropping possible. The supply of labor is a constraining factor in East Asian countries, where industrialization has drained labor away from the farms. Multiple cropping has declined in Japan since the 1960s and in Taiwan since the latter 1970s.

A potential for diversified agriculture in South and Southeast Asia probably exists, although data are not available for most of these countries. In the Philippines, 10.6 million hectares of 30 million are suitable for a variety of cropping patterns, of which the three major diversified crops for import substitution (corn, soybeans, and cotton) were suited to 3.7 million hectares.[6] Private profitability (private net profit as a percentage of gross revenues) was high for these crops. For other exportable crops (mungbeans and cassava) the private profit rate was lower but still positive. It was high for goats, caraboas, and cattle and lower for hogs, broiler chickens, and laying hens.

From a social point of view, based on domestic resource cost analysis and social profitability measures, L. A. Gonzales found that, under conditions of foreign exchange constraints, "a strong economic argument of efficiency exists in the domestic production of current imported commodities (cotton, corn, and soybeans), and potential export crops (rice, white potato, cassava, sorghum, garlic and peanuts)."[7] Gonzales also found that, except for broiling chickens, the Philippines had a comparative advantage in livestock production and that the improvement in domestic corn, soybean, and cassava production could result in comparative advantage. These results were obtained even though many of the crops were rain fed and only a small part (1 percent) of the diversified crops was grown with irrigation, despite many potentially irrigable areas in the Philippines (58 percent). With rice self-sufficiency, investment funds for irrigation construction could be shifted to more water and drainage for diversified crops. Moreover, as rice yields per hectare continue to rise, some irrigated rice lands could be shifted to the production of diversified crops.[8]

In Indonesia, the Centre for Agribusiness Development investigated thirty-six crops and eleven agroindustries; it recommended the planting of diversified crops on 250,000 hectares in the uplands of Java in 1988, followed by an additional 250,000 hectares each year for the following five years. The program is expected to create about a million jobs. If there is such potential in densely populated Java, diversification should be possible in all of South and Southeast Asia—even in Bangladesh, with irrigation.[9]

Further, if the multiplier effect of spending for infrastructure investments and for increased production is taken into account, a major impact on job creation can be expected. For the Philippines, a 10 percent increase in spending on diversified production (with 30 percent leakage) would generate enough jobs to absorb nearly all the country's unemployed workers.[10] There seems to be no reason why such results cannot be translated to Indonesia, where the propensity to consume is higher and the leakages abroad even lower.

### Trends and Patterns in Diversification

One difficulty in a study of diversification is measurement. Since our interest is mainly employment creation, production value is the best measure. But since most crops are consumed by farmers, the issue of what price to use comes up. Measuring production in metric tons gives undue weight to heavy crops, such as sugarcane, cassava, and other root crops, and not enough weight to labor-intensive vegetables, tobacco, and other leafy crops. Area harvested gives undue weight to tree crops like coconut, rubber, and palm oil, which are less labor-using than grains and vegetables. Actually, we have no choice but to use production data, because value data are available for only a few countries, and area data are not available for vegetables and tree crops in several countries. Hence, table 6.2 gives the ratio of vegetables, fruits, and tree crops to cereals

TABLE 6.2

Ratio of Vegetable, Fruit, and Tree Crops to Cereal and Root Crops, Based on Metric Tons, 1961 to 1986

| Country | 1961–1965 | 1969–1971 | 1974–1976 | 1979–1981 | 1984–1986 |
|---|---|---|---|---|---|
| Japan | 53.3 | 84.2 | 97.4 | 110.5 | 96.8 |
| South Korea | 31.8 | 43.4 | 61.5 | 104.6 | 104.8 |
| Taiwan | | | | | 42.4 |
| Malaysia | 21.0 | 57.9 | 50.1 | 56.5 | 62.5 |
| Indonesia | 39.5 | 15.4 | 13.6 | 13.8 | 16.4 |
| Philippines | 20.6 | 37.5 | 43.6 | 47.2 | 46.5 |
| Thailand | | 20.8 | 21.2 | 23.1 | 20.7 |
| Bangladesh | 15.4 | 16.4 | 13.0 | 11.5 | 10.7 |
| Burma | 30.3 | 33.0 | 32.0 | 24.9 | 23.3 |
| India | 51.2 | 44.7 | 45.4 | 46.5 | 45.5 |
| Nepal | 10.1 | 8.7 | 9.3 | 12.4 | 11.7 |
| Pakistan | 35.2 | 32.5 | 36.3 | 28.6 | 31.0 |
| Sri Lanka | 49.2 | 34.5 | 51.2 | 80.6 | 55.2 |

*Source:* Food and Agriculture Organization Production Yearbook. *Taiwan Agricultural Yearbook.*

*Note:* The table excludes livestock, fishery, and forestry production.

TABLE 6.3

Ratio of Vegetables, Fruit, and Livestock to Cereal and Root Crops, Based on Value, 1955 to 1985

| Country | Percentage of Fruit, Vegetables, and Livestock | Detailed Diversity Index |
|---|---|---|
| Taiwan | | |
| 1955–60 | 10.1 | 3.73 |
| 1965–70 | 30.3 | 4.36 |
| 1971–75 | 51.4 | 4.25 |
| 1976–80 | 60.0 | 3.97 |
| 1981–84 | 82.8 | 3.95 |
| South Korea | | |
| 1961–66 | 12.1 | 3.40 |
| 1971–76 | 24.5 | 3.96 |
| 1977–81 | 67.9 | 3.67 |
| 1982–85 | 66.1 | 3.76 |
| Japan | | |
| 1947–52 | 14.2 | 2.84 |
| 1957–62 | 19.6 | 3.45 |
| 1965–1970 | 47.9 | 3.76 |
| 1975–1980 | 61.5 | 3.91 |
| 1982–84 | 65.2 | 4.04 |
| Philippines | | |
| 1970 | 46.9 | |
| 1975 | 46.8 | |
| 1980 | 48.5 | |
| 1985 | 36.1 | |
| Thailand | | |
| 1970 | 49.6 | |
| 1975 | 28.2 | |
| 1980 | 44.2 | |
| 1985 | 61.7 | |

*Source:* V. Ruttan, Y. Hayami, and H. M. Southworth, eds., *Agricultural Growth in Japan, Taiwan, South Korea, and the Philippines* (Honolulu: University Press of Hawaii for the East-West Center, 1979); official national accounts and yearbooks.

*Note:* The diversity index is computed using the formula $1 \Big/ \sum_{i=1} \left( \frac{Y_i}{Y} \right)$, that is, the increase of the ratio of the sum of shares of each crop in total value of agricultural production in current prices.

and root crops based on metric tons. Table 6.3 gives the percentage based on value figures for Japan, Taiwan, South Korea, the Philippines, and Thailand, the only countries that have value data.

The association of the diversity index with per capita income is taken cross sectionally for the three regions. This association is erratic due to weather changes and is trendless except in Japan and South Korea. Other forces, such as the difference between tonnage and the value of exported crops, together with the divergence between the different indexes, give a complex picture. Per capita income is important because, with higher incomes, relatively less is spent on cereals and more is spent on fruits and vegetables. But production and exporting patterns must be considered in a country like Taiwan, which exports more types of crops than do Japan and South Korea. In Southeast Asia, Thailand exports more types of crops than do the Philippines and Malaysia, which concentrate on a few plantation crops. The low per capita income countries of South Asia must use all their land for rice and other staples. The index is high for India because of large amounts of pulses and beans consumed, while Malaysia produces large amounts of plantation crops, which are exported. The detailed diversity index is clearly the best measuring method, as it takes into account each crop in detail. An index based on the value of each root and cereal crop, and not on the weight of these crops is also workable: the value of a crop is much more closely related to employment than the quantity of the crop is.

In East Asia, in the 1980s Japan had the highest diversity index, closely followed by Taiwan. But Taiwan's value index was far larger than Japan's, perhaps due to its relatively larger production of high-cost fruits, vegetables, and meats, a large part of which are exported to Japan, Hong Kong, and Singapore. Moreover, the Japanese eat much less rice and other cereals per capita than the Taiwanese. In Southeast Asia, a diversity index was not available. The value index showed Thailand's index in the 1980s to be much higher than that of the Philippines, but the weight index showed the reverse. The latter was high in the Philippines because of large estate crops such as sugar and coconuts, which are heavier than poultry, vegetables, and fruits and which Thailand exports to many Asian countries. Pound by pound, the latter are of greater value than sugar and copra. Malaysia scores highest in the weight index because of its large exports of rubber and palm oil.

Over time, the diversity index has been rising throughout most of the postwar decades in Japan, due to the shift in demand away from rice to fruits, vegetables, and meat and the market protection accorded to these crops. But in Taiwan, the diversity index has been falling since the latter 1960s and the weight index rising. This is due to the decline in the production of sugarcane, tobacco, cotton, and other industrial crops.[11] Unlike tropical Taiwan, Japan's share of such crops has always been negligible. In contrast, South Korea's diversity index has not changed much, partly a reflection of its neglect of agricultural development. This is also the case for the Philippines, where the value index was stable up to the 1980s. In contrast, Thailand rapidly diversified its production, exporting all types of agricultural crops to its neighbors, especially the expanding city-states and west Malaysia. While the diversity index has been rising in East and Southeast Asia, it has fallen or remained stagnant in South Asia, where GNP growth has been slow. The exception is the welfare state of Sri Lanka, whose growth may be slow but—through social welfare measures—consumption by low-income groups has been kept up.

In sum, the disparate results obtained from cross sections and trends over time are due to the weights used in the indexes—value or weight. But it may also lie in the shortcomings of cross-section data to represent changes over time.[12] Institutions, technologies, social values, and so on change relatively slowly within a country, much slower than the differences between countries at a point of time. Some of the problems in the data could be reached if we could get data on the average prices at which agricultural products were sold for countries other than those shown in the tables. If time and resources permitted, and with the use of unpublished data from the files of the national agricultural ministries, computation of the detailed diversity indexes would have been possible. This computation would advance the study of comparative diversification in Asia.

### The Impact of Diversification

The most strategic impact of diversification in East Asia was the attainment of full employment—directly through more farm employment in the dry months and indirectly through the processing of the diversified products.[13] Most diversified crops are process-intensive, requiring factories for the cleaning, cooking, bottling, canning, packaging, and storing of fruits and vegetables. In addition, commercial crops such as rubber, sugarcane, and palm and coconut oils require machines for crushing, boiling, drying, and other treatments. Various processes are needed to convert feed crops, such as cassava, corn, and soybeans, into pellets.

Diversification requires the construction of irrigation, drainage, roads, electrification, and other rural infrastructure, which increases employment for farm families. Japan reached full employment in the late 1950s, when its diversification index rose from 2.84 in 1947–52 to 3.45 in 1957–62. Taiwan reached full employment in the late 1960s, when its diversification index rose from 3.73 in the late 1950s to 4.36 in the late 1960s. In both cases, diversification was widely dispersed regionally, enabling these economies to take advantage of underemployed labor. South Korea's diversification was delayed by the haste with which the government turned to industrialization. The impact of full employment on wages and farm employment was considerable in East Asia. As it became more difficult to hire labor, wages rose; this together with more family members employed meant an increase in family incomes and savings. Diversified agriculture is much more varied and complex; it extends the skills of peasants beyond rice culture. Work in the industries processing diversified crops enables these workers to acquire experience in industrial occupations, which is valuable to those who eventually migrate to the cities. The financing, marketing, and transporting involved in diversified production prepares them for service occupations. Finally, income from diversified agriculture and processing lowers rural income disparities.

The most important policy to promote diversification is the provision of irrigation for the dry season. Land reform is also needed in landlord-dominated areas, and credit must be supplied to peasants for the purchase of seeds, fertilizer, and other inputs. Rural roads, transportation and communication, assistance in marketing, and extension agents to teach methods of cultivation and experiment stations to improve the seeds are also necessary.[14]

### DIVERSIFICATION AND STRUCTURAL CHANGE

Diversified agriculture and processing had a major impact on structural change. The shift away from cereals to a variety of crops was the initial major structural change in the agricultural sector in modern times. It also initiated between-sector structural change, that is, from agriculture to industries and services and from rural to urban areas. Productivity increases originate from structural changes that occur as the population moves from low-income sectors to high-income sectors. This usually involves shifts from agriculture to nonagriculture. Changes in occupations, labor force status, rural-urban structure, female participation, and family structure are associated with structural changes.[15] One other impact, most important for monsoon Asia, is that on rural densities.

### The Agricultural Sector

The agricultural sector tends to generate low incomes in part because of the low income elasticities of its products as a whole compared to those of other sectors; as costs of producing farm products fall with technological progress, prices tend to fall. Moreover, the skills for agricultural production are low and do not require extensive education. For the prewar period of modern economic growth, the share of agriculture in gross domestic product fell for all Western countries.[16] Moreover, in England without the increase in agricultural production and productivity in the seventeenth and eighteenth centuries, the shift of the labor force to the industrial sector would not have been possible, and the rise of industrial capitalism would have been inhibited. In fact, it was the stagnation of agricultural productivity that prevented Asia from taking advantage of the technology of the first industrial revolution, since agriculture could not release workers or supply food for the industrial sectors.[17] But even if agriculture could have released them, the workers would not have had other sectors to go to if agricultural productivity was not high. Thus for sustained structural changes, differences in productivity are crucial.

There is a symbiotic relation between agriculture and industry in the early stages of the agroindustrial transition. To initiate industrialization in the early stages, a mass market for industrial products must exist over and beyond the markets in the urban sector. This must be supplied by the farm sector. The food, textile, and wood industries need raw material for their operations, ample supplies of cheap food to feed their workforce, and food exports to earn foreign exchange (as in Taiwan). If food and materials are not available (as in the city-states), industries have to import them, which reduces the foreign exchange needed for the import of machinery for the emerging industries. Increases in labor productivity in agriculture releases young, educated workers into industry. Savings from rising agricultural productivity contributes to the financing of capital formation in the urban areas. Finally, without agricultural development, the regions beyond the large cities cannot be developed and regional industrialization cannot make much headway. Mass markets for industries, raw materials for labor-intensive industries, food for urban workers, agricultural exports, migrants, and so on—all are required for initiating structural changes.

Illustrative of the difficulties encountered when agricultural development is insufficient is South Korea's effort to industrialize in the 1970s. It had to import rice, using up the foreign exchange needed to import industrial machinery. There was tension and unrest among peasants in underdeveloped provinces. With insufficient purchasing power among the peasants, South Korea subsidized its industries, borrowing enormous sums to do it, as domestic savings were inadequate. Similar difficulties were encountered in India during the 1960s and 1970s and in Japan in the Meiji and Taisho eras.

The rural sectors in monsoon economies are densely populated, and so it is essential that population be shifted from the agricultural sector to the industrial sector. But this shift must not be carried out prematurely—before the agricultural sector is well-developed. Otherwise, the purchasing power of the rural population will not be sufficient to buy industrial products, nor will there be sufficient supplies of cheap food to feed the urban workers and of raw materials for the textile and wood industries. A major mistake made in several countries of Asia was the haste with which they moved into industrialization in the early postwar decade.[18]

### The Industrial Sector in Structural Changes

The agricultural sector comprises cropping, fishery, forestry, and animal husbandry; the industrial sector includes manufacturing, mining, construction, public utilities, transport, and communication; the service sector includes finance and commerce.[19] The rapid shifts of employment away from the agricultural sector to industry in Japan, South Korea, and Taiwan were unprecedented; what took centuries in the Western countries was completed in these countries in decades. The drop in the agricultural share in South Korea was slower than in Japan and Taiwan, because it paid less attention to agricultural development. The decline in agriculture in the city-states was also rapid, with the employment share falling from 7.5 percent in 1961 to 2.6 percent in 1976 in Hong Kong, and 8.6 percent in 1957 to 2.3 percent in 1976 in Singapore. This was largely due to the shortage of land for urban use, which forced land prices to rise to levels too high for farming.

The transformation was slower in Thailand, Malaysia, the Philippines, and Indonesia. All four countries were largely agricultural economies during most of the postwar era, dependent on agricultural exports for foreign exchange earnings to import machinery and materials for industrialization. Structural changes in South Asian countries were minimal. The pace at which structural changes occurred in all three regions was related to the speed of the growth of the economy.

The agricultural labor force moved to the industrial and service sectors in East and Southeast Asia, although in the city-states it went entirely to the industrial sector. In Singapore, with the largest service sector, there was a small shift from service to industry in the postwar era. Singapore was developed by the British as the center of trading, financing, and shipping for countries like Indonesia and Malaysia before World War II. But with independence these countries began to develop their own exporting centers, reducing the use of Singapore as an entrepôt. Confronted with unemployment in the service sector, Singapore was compelled to industrialize, particularly after it was thrown out of the Malayan Union.

Japan, Hong Kong, and Singapore may be reaching a point where the agricultural sector's decline may taper off as they move into the second transition, when the labor force shifts from the industrial sector to the service sector (as has happened in Western countries). Even in the city-states, some minimal number of workers will remain in the agricultural sector to fish for fresh seafood and to raise orchids. Once diversification is completed, the agricultural sector should begin to raise its productivity by mechanizing, thus releasing workers to the other sectors.

Japan began mechanization in the 1950s and completed it in the 1980s. But its mechanization used small-scale machines appropriate for one- or two-hectare farms. The process should have gone on to enlarge farm size and to shift to large-scale mechanization, along the lines of U.S. farms. But politically it was difficult to consolidate small farms, and productivity stopped far short of U.S. levels. This means that food prices are extremely high in Japan. This together with high prices of services and housing has brought Japan the highest cost of living in the world, despite low prices of manufactures. Politically, it was also difficult to convert small retail stores to larger units, because the ruling party needed the votes of peasants and small retailers. The same thing appears to be happening in South Korea and Taiwan.

In terms of shares of value added, manufacturing is the largest subsector of industry, which includes transport-communication, construction, mining, and public utilities. Transport-communication is the second largest sector, partly because taxi, bus, and railways must be used when consumers do not own cars. Construction is next and tends to be large in the early stages of the first transition in monsoon Asia because of the cost of agricultural infrastructures, especially for irrigation and drainage. The smallest is the public utility sector, which has a small labor force and is the most capital-intensive sector. Mining varies with the importance of the mineral deposits of the country. Conceivably, in a small country such as Vanuatu in the Pacific, with its huge copper deposits, mining may be the most important subsector of industry. There is not much regularity in the time trends of the shares of construction, transport-communication, and mining—nor among countries.[20]

As the economy completes the agroindustrial transition, the share of heavy and chemical industries in total manufacturing value added rises. In Japan, the food industry's share of value added was 22 percent in 1950 and 14 percent in 1960.[21] The reason for the high food share is that consumers were too poor to buy houses, cars, and other durables in the early stages, and industries were not developed to the stage where demand for machines and chemicals was high. And on the supply side, the skills of workers and technicians for the more complex operations of the heavy and chemical industries were not developed. If countries begin as India and China did in the 1950s, with capital-intensive industries (iron and steel), the productivity growth in these industries would be low and even negative.[22] Even in the case of low-stream heavy industries, such as cement and fabricated steel in the Philippines, efficiency went down throughout the 1960s and 1970s, in large part because workers and technicians were unable to operate them efficiently.[23]

In the 1980s, Malaysia began building sponge iron, methanol, paper and pulp, and car manufacturing plants, while Indonesia went in for iron and steel, chemical fertilizer, glass, cement, and other capital-intensive complexes. Most of these were unable to operate at full capacity, so costs were high and quality was poor.[24] Structural changes were even slower in mainland China and India, which started out with industrialization as their development strategy. Vast sums were invested in the whole range of heavy industries (iron and steel complexes, chemical and petrochemical plants, aluminum smelting, paper and pulp, heavy machinery, cement, and so on). Unfortunately for these capital-poor countries, nearly one-half to one-third of capacity of these capital-intensive manufacturing facilities went unused most of the time. And since their R and D capabilities were limited, the facilities soon became obsolete and had to be rehabilitated and renovated with foreign expertise and technology.

In contrast, Japan concentrated on improving its light industries in the 1950s, especially textiles, in order to export, earn foreign exchange, and begin the development of heavy industries. Taiwan's growth was mainly due to its light industries in the 1950s, 1960s, and most of the 1970s. By the 1980s it had accumulated enough foreign exchange and experience in industrialization to move into the more capital-intensive industries. South Korea's light industries also grew in the 1950s and 1960s. It turned to heavy industries early in the 1970s, but this premature effort proved costly. Huge losses were incurred in iron and steel, petrochemicals, paper and pulp, copper and aluminum smelters, and heavy engineering—which partly accounts for the substantially lower per capita incomes of the South Koreans compared to the Taiwanese, even though their GNP per capita growth rates were the same. But the South Koreans, like the Taiwanese, had sufficient industrial experience to efficiently operate the heavy industries by the mid-1980s. The Chinese and Indian economies would have been better off today had they concentrated on light industries and confined their efforts to a small number of heavy industries, for which they may have had sufficient skilled technicians and workers, and gradually enlarged them as their ability to absorb foreign technologies and expertise improved.

The food industry's share in Southeast Asia is unexpectedly higher than in South Asia, with its lower incomes. The high shares of food and agricultural industries in the Philippines, Thailand, and Indonesia are due to their large exports of agricultural products that must be processed: pineapple canning and sugar mills in the Philippines and cassava, sugar, pineapple, and vegetable processing in Thailand. But it is puzzling that Malaysia's share is smaller. It may be that much of the processing of palm oil and rubber on the estates is highly integrated with their growing and is treated as part of agriculture and not manufacturing. Off-estate processing is relatively small. Nepal's highest share of food and agriculture reflects its low level of industrialization, perhaps the lowest in Asia; it does not as yet have a modern textile industry. Hand spinning and weaving are not designated as industries in Nepal, nor separated from agriculture.

### The Service Sector in Structural Change

Although early economists considered services an unproductive sector, this is not the case with modern services. The service sector found markets abroad for manufactures, provided financing, and educated technicians and skilled workers, as the experience of Hong Kong and Singapore shows. Another part of the service sector caters to consumers directly: restaurants, hotels, entertainment, and other consumer services are important not only for local customers but to attract tourists, whose spending generates much needed foreign exchange. The heterogeneous service sector may be divided into two subsectors, one requiring the highest level of education (banking, real estate, business, and public services) and the other minimal education (retail trade, restaurants, and domestic and other personal services). The latter subsector supplies workers for the lower paying jobs in the former sectors and for factories.

This diversity underlies the disparities in service incomes, the highest being in finance, commerce, and public services, and the lowest being in domestic service, retail sales, restaurants, and street stalls, some of whose workers are partially and marginally employed. Service workers in the middle range are relatively few, comprising lower level civil servants and technical and skilled workers.[25]

On the small, labor-intensive farms of the densely settled lowlands of monsoon Asia, villages are large groupings of farm families, which can support many small workshops and stores. This contrasts with the West, where large farms make for long distances between families, and farmers have to travel far to town to market their produce and purchase supplies. This distance was originally possible because horses for transportation could be raised, since there was enough grazing land. In Asia, land is too scarce for growing feed for animals. Hence numerous small neighborhood stores to which the consumer can walk were needed: the traditional cities of monsoon Asia are thus clusters of towns with numerous market centers.

In the United States in 1880, when its per capita dollar income was about the same as in South Korea in 1970, 20 percent of the labor force was in the service sector, compared to South Korea's 25 percent. In 1900, with U.S. per capita dollar income about that of Taiwan in 1970, it was 25 percent, compared to Taiwan's 30 percent. And in 1920 with U.S. per capita dollar income about that of Japan in 1960, it was 28 percent as against Japan's 33 percent.[26] All this despite the fact that in East Asia the service sector had been trimmed down and was relatively lean compared to other Asian countries.

There is another reason for the large size of the service sector in Asia, besides its labor intensity. Those who could not find work in the commodity-producing sectors (agriculture and industry) sought work in the service sector's petty trades—stall keeping and peddling and in retail stores, restaurants, barber shops, domestic services, and so on. These were operated mainly by families that accommodated their neighbors and friends by using their unemployed family members at low wages. Hence the labor not needed in the goods-producing sectors gravitated to the service sector, which became a depository of surplus labor in the densely populated urban sector. The bunching of low-income countries on the left of figure 6.1 is indicative of the piling up of surplus labor in the service sector, a form of disguised unemployment. East Asia, after reaching full employment, wiped out excess labor in most of the menial and marginal sectors, but small family-operated stores, restaurants, and shops continue to exist to this day. Like the tiny farms of monsoon agriculture, the sheer number of families depending for their livelihood on these stores makes their phasing out politically difficult, particularly in democratic countries like Japan, which from an economic point of view should eliminate them. The high cost of living in Japanese cities is caused not only by the agriculture sector but also by the service sector. In these small units, workers are not fully utilized, as they wait for customers, who come at long intervals. With full employment, the slack disappears, with more customers per clerk. Furthermore, as wages are

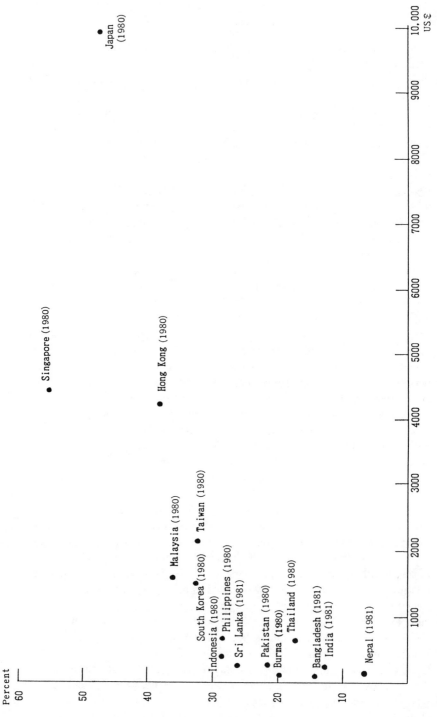

FIG. 6.1. Employment in the service sector and per capita income, 1980 or 1981. *Source:* International Labor Organization, *Yearbook of Labor Statistics;* World Bank, *World Development Report.*

lower in this sector than in the others, clerks are difficult to hire. This is another benefit of full employment—the fuller utilization of existing capacity. This is shown by the flatness of the curve in figure 6.1.

Figure 6.1 shows per capita dollar incomes and the size of the service sector, measured in terms of employment. The latter is approximately correlated with income, with some exceptions. For Singapore (and to a lesser extent, Hong Kong), the importance of urbanization, tourism, and business services is responsible for the very high service sector. Also, the government's role is greater in Singapore than in laissez-faire Hong Kong, with larger military and social welfare expenditures. Singapore's traditional entrepôt trade was still intact in 1970, while Hong Kong's was dismantled with the complete closing of trade with China in the 1950s. There has been a revival of this trade but not on the former scale.

Another major deviant is Thailand, with its service share much lower than would be expected by its income level. The major reason is the extraordinarily high female participation rate in agriculture (about twice that of other Asian countries), which increases the share of employment in agriculture and depresses that in services. If we assume that the Thai definition of female participation in agricultural activities is too broad and make appropriate adjustments, its service sector share comes up to that of the Philippines but is probably still somewhat lower because of the Philippines' greater urbanization.

Burma's service sector share is three times that of Nepal, which has the same per capita dollar income. Nepal has smaller military expenditures and a smaller nondefense public sector, but what is more important is the extremely small urban sector: only 4 percent of the total population is in the urban sector, compared to 17 percent in Indonesia, 19 percent in Burma, 20 percent in India, and 22 percent in Sri Lanka. This suggests that, in the lowest income nations, urbanization may not be correlated with income. The reason is that, in the earliest stage of development, many services are still in the homes and not separated out as specialized occupations.

Sri Lanka's service sector share is also higher than expected by its low income level, six times higher than Nepal's, with income only 25 percent higher. Sri Lanka is one of the major welfare states of the world, including developed countries. To dispense half the rice ration free to all families, manage free medical and hospital facilities, and allocate subsidies for housing and transportation requires a vast bureaucracy. Sri Lanka's share of government expenditure in GNP is one of the highest in Asia (21 percent in 1971), compared to Nepal's 5 percent.

Table 6.4 shows the changes in the employment share of the service sector and subsectors for the postwar decades. One group of countries shows an increasing share of service employment (Japan, Taiwan, South Korea, west Malaysia, the Philippines, Thailand, Indonesia, and Pakistan). These countries have high (5–6 percent) or moderately high (2–4 percent) GNP per capita

TABLE 6.4
Service Employment, 1950s to 1980s (percent)

| Country | Total Service Employment | A Wholesale and Retail Trade, Restaurants, Hotels | B Financing, Insurance, Real Estate, Business Services | A and B | Community, Social, and Personal Services | Growth rate of Gross Domestic Product (per capita) | | |
|---|---|---|---|---|---|---|---|---|
| | | | | | | 1950–1960 | 1960–1970 | 1970–1980 |
| Japan | | | | | | | | |
| 1950 | 25.0 | | | 11.8 | 13.1 | 7.3 | 10.2 | 3.5 |
| 1960 | 32.4 | | | 17.5 | 14.9 | | | |
| 1970 | 40.0 | 20.2 | 4.1 | | 15.6 | | | |
| 1974 | 43.7 | 21.0 | 3.1 | | 19.0 | | | |
| 1980 | 47.9 | 22.5 | 5.7 | | 19.6 | | | |
| 1987 | 52.0 | 23.1 | 7.4 | | 21.5 | | | |
| Taiwan | | | | | | | | |
| 1956 | 23.3 | | | 7.5 | 15.8 | 4.8 | 6.3 | |
| 1965 | 27.9 | | | 11.1 | 14.3 | | | |
| 1970 | 29.5 | | | 14.6 | 14.6 | | | |
| 1976 | 28.6 | 13.3 | 1.9 | | 13.44 | | | |
| 1980 | 32.2 | 16.0 | 2.1 | | 14.1 | | | |
| 1987 | 36.6 | 17.9 | 2.8 | | 15.9 | | | |
| South Korea | | | | | | | | |
| 1966 | 24.8 | | | 10.5 | 14.3 | 2.6 | 6.5 | 6.2 |
| 1970 | 25.6 | 12.6 | 1.0 | | 12.0 | | | |
| 1974 | 26.7 | 15.2 | 1.3 | | 10.2 | | | |
| 1980 | 32.5 | 19.2 | 2.4 | | 10.9 | | | |
| 1987 | 39.4 | 22.1 | 4.1 | | 13.2 | | | |

| Country / Year | | | | | | | | |
|---|---|---|---|---|---|---|---|---|
| **West Malaysia** | | | | | | | | |
| 1947 | 18.6 | 8.5 | | | 10.1 | 0.8 | 2.9 | |
| 1957 | 24.4 | 9.3 | | | 15.2 | | | |
| 1970 | 30.4 | 11.3 | | | 19.2 | | | |
| **Philippines** | | | | | | | | |
| 1948 | 16.8 | 5.0 | 2.5 | 9.0 | 9.2 | 3.2 | 2.4 | 3.1 |
| 1960 | 19.8 | | | 7.4 | 11.0 | | | |
| 1970 | 24.0 | | | 11.2 | 16.6 | | | |
| 1974 | 25.6 | | | | 14.4 | | | |
| 1981 | 30.2 | 11.3 | 1.9 | | 17.0 | | | |
| 1987 | 33.0 | 13.7 | 1.9 | | 17.4 | | | |
| **Thailand** | | | | | | | | |
| 1937 | 8.4 | | | 5.2 | 3.1 | 2.6 | 4.8 | 4.7 |
| 1947 | 11.0 | | | 8.0 | 3.1 | | | |
| 1960 | 10.6 | | | 5.8 | 4.8 | | | |
| 1970 | 12.5 | | | 5.3 | 7.3 | | | |
| 1973 | 16.2 | | | 8.2 | 8.1 | | | |
| 1980 | 16.9 | | | 8.5 | 8.4 | | | |
| 1982 | 18.8 | | | 9.2 | 9.6 | | | |
| **India** | | | | | | | | |
| 1951 | 16.4 | | | 5.8 | 10.6 | 2.3 | 2.0 | 1.0 |
| 1961 | 13.0 | | | 4.1 | 8.9 | | | |
| 1971 | 13.4 | 4.9 | 0.7 | | 7.8 | | | |
| **Sri Lanka** | | | | | | | | |
| 1953 | 26.0 | | | 8.8 | 17.2 | 1.3 | 2.5 | 2.2 |
| 1963 | 26.0 | | | 9.6 | 16.4 | | | |
| 1971 | 25.9 | 10.4 | 0.8 | | 14.7 | | | |
| 1981 | 35.2 | 10.6 | 1.4 | | 23.2 | | | |

*(continued)*

TABLE 6.4 (Continued)

| Country | Total Service Employment | A Wholesale and Retail Trade, Restaurants, Hotels | B Financing, Insurance, Real Estate, Business Services | A and B | Community, Social, and Personal Services | Growth rate of Gross Domestic Product (per capita) | | |
|---|---|---|---|---|---|---|---|---|
| | | | | | | 1950–1960 | 1960–1970 | 1970–1980 |
| **Pakistan and Bangladesh** | | | | | | | | |
| 1951 | 11.5 | | | 5.3 | 6.1 | | | |
| 1961 | 13.1 | | | 5.0 | 8.2 | | 4.0 | |
| 1968 | 14.3 | | | 7.9 | 6.4 | | | |
| 1980 | 21.9 | 11.1 | 0.7 | | 10.1 | | | |
| 1985 | 24.1 | 11.5 | 0.9 | | 11.7 | | | |
| **Hong Kong** | | | | | | | | |
| 1961 | 33.8 | | | 11.2 | 22.6 | 3.6 | | |
| 1971 | 33.9 | 16.3 | 2.6 | | 15.0 | | 6.6 | |
| 1980 | 45.1 | 23.0 | 6.7 | | 15.4 | | | 6.9 |
| 1987 | 47.0 | 23.3 | 6.4 | | 17.3 | | | |
| **Singapore** | | | | | | | | |
| 1947 | 56.5 | 24.0 | 3.0+ | | 30.3 | | | |
| 1957 | 59.8 | | | 25.9 | 33.9 | | 6.6 | |
| 1970 | 54.3 | 23.5 | 3.6 | | 27.2 | | | |
| 1974 | 50.4 | 21.0 | 5.7 | | 23.7 | | | 7.5 |
| 1980 | 51.5 | 23.0 | 7.4 | | 21.1 | | | |
| 1987 | 53.9 | 23.4 | 8.9 | | 21.6 | | | |

growth rates. Exceptions are Singapore and Hong Kong, which grew very rapidly in the 1960s but whose service share did not increase, even though the number employed in this sector increased in Hong Kong from 297,000 in 1961 to 537,000 in 1971 and in Singapore from 281,000 in 1957 to 353,000 in 1970. The rapid growth of industrialization and foreign trade and the slow growth of urbanization reached nearly 90–100 percent during the early 1970s. In India and Sri Lanka, the slow growth of per capita income was associated with the slow growth of industrialization and urbanization. The decline in the share of agricultural employment was negligible, and industries absorbed most of the workers coming from agriculture. Since the commodity sectors remained static, there was no need for additional services.

For countries with clearly rising service sector growth and GNP per capita, the latter's impact on the former varied with the type of structural change. Thailand started modernization the latest, Japan the earliest. The variations may be explained by the commercialization of agriculture, the industrialization of secondary industries, urbanization, and income disparities in the service sector. In a completely self-sufficient village economy (with each household self-sufficient), the need for the service sector may be minimal: perhaps it needs a village chief, a priest, a teacher, and few others. (Nepal with 95 percent in the agriculture sector even in 1970 comes close to this model.) As agricultural productivity rises, trading emerges, requiring the services of merchants and moneylenders. Agriculture becomes commercialized. Thailand's service sector was considerably larger than its secondary sector; it was dominated by wholesale and retail sales, restaurants, and hotels, employing 75 percent of the service labor force.[27]

A substantial rise in productivity and per capita income occurs with industrialization, even though it may be predominantly small scale and labor-intensive. This generally occurs after the commercialization of agriculture has made some headway. Commercialization and industrialization are accompanied by urbanization, as enlargement of enterprises, division of labor, and specialization require some degree of agglomeration. Large concentrations of population also necessitate public services for sanitation, security, education, welfare, and so on. In Thailand, after two decades of rapid commercialization, industrialization, and urbanization, the number employed in public and personal services in 1970 exceeded those in the commercial services.

These structural changes entail rising disparities in the distribution of family income in both urban and rural sectors, since only a small group in the higher income brackets will benefit. These families begin to purchase personal services with high income elasticities—medical and dental services, recreational, cultural, and educational services, domestic services, and so on. Most of the changes take place during the earlier stages of the transition, when the agricultural and rural sectors are fairly large and the absolute number of those engaged in agriculture may still be rising. Employment in the commerce and finance subsectors tends to grow more slowly than employment in the public and personal subsector (an exception is Indonesia). This disparity may be due to the replacement of the traditional commerce and finance units with modern units and to the increase of public employment and personal services as urbanization speeds up.

The relative trends in the shares of the two subsectors in Japan, Taiwan, and South Korea (and Australia and New Zealand) reversed as their economies moved into the middle and later stages of growth. Commercial and financial service grew more rapidly than public and personal service. The absolute decline of agricultural employment indicates that industrialization had accelerated, along with a demand for new types of stores and retailers (gasoline stations, automobile and appliance dealers, department stores, and supermarkets), new financial institutions (savings banks, personal credit institutions, security dealers, foreign exchange banks, brokers, insurance firms, and real estate companies), and business services (accounting and legal services, data processing, engineering, architectural and other technical services, advertising, management and consulting, detective and protective services). The increase in tourism made possible by modern travel facilities promoted the growth of restaurants and hotels, which are included in these subsectors. Moreover, with income inequalities no longer widening, the middle and lower brackets utilized commercial and financial facilities, such as banking.

On the other hand, the growth of public services may have slowed because basic community services were provided. These were countries with very high GNP per capita growth in the 1960s, growth exceeding that of the labor force, which resulted in full employment. In this situation, the wages of unskilled service workers rose rapidly as the labor market tightened, especially for those in the lowest wage groups, such as domestic service. In Japan, Taiwan, and South Korea, maids, cooks, and gardeners became difficult to hire, not only because of labor shortages but also because of higher incomes, resulting in the increased use of modern household appliances (washing machines, refrigerators, and stoves). Other durables (televisions, radios, and stereos) tended to substitute for amusement, recreational, and cultural services.[28]

The rapid structural change in East Asia was accompanied by a substantial upward shift in the occupational structure of the labor force. In Japan, 41 percent in 1975 and 46 percent in 1984 were in white-collar categories (professional, administrative, clerical, and sales). In Taiwan, the shares were 28 percent in 1975 and 34 percent in 1984; and in South Korea, 23 percent and 33 percent, respectively. But in the slow-growing Philippines (the only other country where occupational data are available), the changes were slight, from 21 to 23 percent.[29] The economic structure of East Asia is approaching that of the most advanced Western countries, despite the constraints imposed by their great population densities. In the late 1980s they moved into a diversity of service industries, many of which are highly technology-intensive, requiring complex skills and paying high incomes.

## STRUCTURAL CHANGE AND RURAL POPULATION DENSITIES

The concept of density relates population to total land, but agricultural population is related to arable land.[30] For predominantly agricultural economies, the amount of arable land to the agricultural labor force is a major factor in productivity per worker, which is the product of yields per hectare and arable land per worker. If productivity is low because of population density, the low incomes thus generated spill over to the urban sector through the migration of workers willing to accept low wages in urban industries and services. The large pool of workers available contributed to the labor intensity of small workshops, stalls, and small stores.

Arable land in hectares fails to take into account land quality, which varies. Java's volcanic soil and plentiful rainfall permit the land to support much larger populations per hectare than the soils of Mongolia and Manchuria, which the monsoons do not reach, or the northeast of Thailand, which gets light rains. The rivers of Bangladesh bring plenty of water for the rice paddies. The year-round rains of Malaysia and Sri Lanka make these countries suitable for plantation crops; Malaysia, with a lot of land and year-round rains, can devote large tracts of land to plantation crops, yielding high per capita income. High density Java and Bangladesh have the lowest per capita incomes in Southeast and South Asia, respectively.

Asian poverty has been traced to the great population densities generated by monsoon agriculture—which over the past millennia became increasingly labor-intensive. Deep plowing, terracing, manuring, ratooning, irrigating, and draining appeared centuries before the birth of Christ. Intensive preparation of seedling beds, transplanting, water management, and reaping with knives came in the early centuries A.D. Then, in the first century of this millennium, multiple cropping of rice was introduced, raising further the labor intensity of land preparation, transplanting, reaping, threshing, and water management. This contrasted with Western agricultural development, where plentiful farmland made possible capitalistic farming, with broadcasting of seed, crop rotation and fallowing, multiple-horse plowing, and harvesting with scythes and cradles in fifteenth- and sixteenth-century England. In monsoon Asia, population rose to meet the demand for labor on small farms; these densities continued to rise in the rural and urban areas.

Colonial rulers did little to improve public health facilities, and in the countries where some effort was made (Sri Lanka, the Philippines, Malaysia, Taiwan, and the city-states), the use of health facilities was limited to a small fraction of the population, with the possible exception of innoculation against infectious diseases. In the post–World War II period, the newly independent governments were compelled to establish nationwide systems.

With the coming of colonialism, agriculture population densities rose further—for an additional reason. The agricultural production that the colonialist extracted for export used labor needed for producing the sustenance of the peasant families during the wet season. And machine-produced textiles and other industrial products brought in by the colonialists took away the urban markets of the peasants, who produced handmade goods during the dry months of the year. Hence, more children had to be raised to provide the manpower to produce the sustenance needed by the peasant family.[31]

This process of intensification is best illustrated in Bangladesh and Java, the most densely settled rural areas in the world. The British took rice away from the Bengal peasants in the form of land taxes. To make up for this, the peasants had to cultivate more intensively in order to survive. The Dutch forced Javanese peasants to produce cash crops for export to Europe—the time lost being made up with more manpower producing on less rice land for their own sustenance. In the Philippines, too, the Spanish forced the peasants to supply free labor; an indigenous landlord class then arose, which exploited the peasants even more than the Spanish had. In India the British collected land revenues through the Zamindars, part of which the latter kept. In Taiwan and Korea, the Japanese levied taxes in the form of rice, which was sent to Japan for its armies. Similarly, the gentry in China levied taxes. In all these cases, peasants raised large families in order to provide workers for the rice farms, which had to produce for their exploiters and for their own sustenance.

It was somewhat different in Sri Lanka and Malaysia. The British brought in Tamils from India to work on the plantations. Population increased with the influx of foreign laborers. In Thailand, the freeing of serfs and slaves in the midnineteenth century opened opportunities to carve out new lands from the forests. Because of this new land, Thai peasants had many children, most of whom established new farms. Thus population densities in monsoon Asia accelerated from the colonial period because of colonial and indigenous exploiters, who had to be supported by the peasantry with intense cultivation.

In the early postwar years, East Asian countries had the highest agricultural population densities in Asia, with the exception of Java and Bangladesh, but by the 1980s, densities in East Asian had fallen. Densities were lower in Southeast Asia, except for Malaysia and Thailand. In South Asia, density is still rising. Japan's density lowered the most, as a result of shifts of population away from agriculture in the early 1960s. The prospect for the future is a continuation of present trends, with East Asia leading the way to lower densities. Annual population growth rates by the year 2000 will be less than 1 percent in East Asia; around 1.5 percent in China, Sri Lanka, and Thailand; nearly 2 percent in Indonesia, Malaysia, and India; and over 2 percent in the Philippines, Burma,

Nepal, and Bangladesh. Despite the great densities in some of the latter countries, the poor need children to help with rice growing.

Structural change in the urban sector will speed up in the future, especially in East Asia. Capital intensity in industries is rising rapidly, as wages rise, capital-labor substitution speeds up, and urban infrastructures become more capital-intensive. In the 1980s, structural change in East Asia slowed because of the protection given to small farms whose production had lost comparative advantage. Japan has taken steps to dismantle this structure of protection. Taiwan and South Korea will have to do the same if the shift of the labor force away from agriculture is to continue.

The last constraint on Asia's development—the monsoon—is being compensated for, which should be of great advantage in the journey toward the Pacific century. In the next chapter, we shall see how diversification has generated jobs, both directly and indirectly through the development of off-farm employment, which has led to full employment, greater productivity, and the higher purchasing power of farm families.

# CHAPTER 7

# Off-Farm Employment
# and Macroproductivity

It was once thought that industrial development would wipe out underemployment in South and Southeast Asia. However, with the economic slowdown in the industrialized countries, the prospects of industrial labor absorption were no longer promising. Others thought that intensification of rice growing could solve underemployment, citing the fact that rice farms in Japan and Taiwan used about three times more labor per hectare than rice farms in South and Southeast Asia. But this view did not take into account the fact that rice farms in Japan and in subtropical Taiwan were almost entirely irrigated, substantially more than in tropical Asia, where rain-fed paddies required much less labor. Moreover, rice lands, especially rain fed, were more plentiful in most of tropical Asia, so that rice self-sufficiency (with the help of high-yielding varieties) was reached long before there was need for extensive and costly irrigation, which Japan and Taiwan needed to reach self-sufficiency in rice. Finally, absorbing more labor in intensified rice farming in the wet season and diversified agriculture in the dry season were not sufficient to absorb the larger work force in the dry season.

These dilemmas compelled economists to look in other directions for labor absorption. Findings from Japan, Taiwan, and South Korea showed substantial increases in the shares of off-farm incomes as these countries moved to higher development, contrary to the conclusions of the Hymer-Resnick model. When on-farm incomes began to slow in the mid-1970s, the acceleration of off-farm incomes prevented total farm family incomes and productivity from falling. In this chapter, the available data and studies of other countries in Asia are brought together with those of Japan, Taiwan, and South Korea, and forces underlying the levels and trends are examined.[1]

In the West, after the decline of feudalism and the manorial economy came the revolution in agriculture, and in England large-scale capitalistic estates emerged, which paved the way for the industrial revolution: the unity of manorial agriculture and industry was dissolved, and agriculture became specialized into a combination of farming and animal husbandry. But the separation of rice farming from industry was not possible in Asian rice farming, as there was not enough land to grow crops to feed work animals. The integration of agriculture and industry prevails everywhere in Asia, even in Japan and Taiwan, where rice growing is most advanced. Japan, right after the Meiji Restoration, attempted to bring in Western agriculture, but after a decade of experimentation it gave up and went back to small-size family farming. In China, Mao established large-scale, communal farming but without much success, and family farming has been brought back, with off-farm activities spreading rapidly.

## CONCEPTS AND FRAMEWORK

Following Hymer and Resnick, it has been customary to think of rural non-agricultural activities as producing $Z$ goods; these activities are carried out in rural households and in rural or village service and artisan establishments.[2] This definition, however, unduly restricts the concept and leads to mistaken conclusions, such as that nonagricultural activities for farm workers decline with the growth of the economy. However, in a growing monsoon economy, there is an upsurge of employment opportunities for farm workers in nearby cities and towns to which they can commute daily or seasonally. The narrower concept emphasizes the substitution effects between $Z$ goods and idleness and urban manufactures, which may not come to grips with the essential elements in the analysis.

In place of $Z$ *activities,* I use the term *off-farm activities.* But this raises the question whether marine fishing, forestry, and work on plantations and other farm activities are included. The term *nonagricultural activities of farm families* may be a less ambiguous concept, defining agriculture as cropping, animal husbandry, fishing, hunting, and forestry, as in the International Standard Industrial Classification (ISIC) system of the United Nations. These nonagricultural activities comprise all activities in the industrial sector (mining, manufacturing, construction, public utilities, transportation, and communication) and the service sectors (both personal and public). But because of the widespread use of the term *off-farm activities* (or *off-farm income*), I use these terms interchangeably with *nonagricultural activities* (or *nonagricultural income*), as defined above.

The term *farm families* includes landless farm families and those employed on estates but excludes nonfarm families in rural areas. The difficulty with the concept of rural nonfarm employment is that the definition of *rural* varies widely from country to country, from localities with a population of less than 2,000 in the Philippines to localities with less than 20,000 in Taiwan; many countries do not provide any definitions of *rural* in terms of size. It is crucial that *rural* and *urban* be uniformly defined so that rural nonfarm families can be standardized for comparisons among countries and over time. Otherwise, families of rural public officials, teachers, professionals, merchants, crafts people, construction and transport workers, and others will be included for countries with broad definitions of *rural* and will be excluded for countries with narrow definitions. Thus it is best to dispense with the rural-urban distinction and confine the discussion to farm families, which are taken to be synonymous with agricultural families in the ISIC sense, even though the definition of *farm families* is not without ambiguity.[3]

Analytically, the focus is agricultural families in monsoon economies and their low annual incomes. Historically, these low incomes have held Asia back, and the transition from agriculture to industry is not possible without a substantial and sustained rise in these incomes. In monsoon Asia, where farms are very small, annual farm family incomes must grow not only with rising yields per hectare but with multiple cropping and with off-farm employment—if the agroindustrial transition is to be rapid.

Statistically, the data are more plentiful for the nonagricultural income of farm families than for employment, and this is all to the good, as employment is too blunt a measure for my purpose. I use data from family income and expenditure surveys supplemented and checked by data from national accounts. Income or product originating in agriculture from the national accounts is compared with total farm family income (from family income and expenditure surveys) to arrive at the nonagricultural income of farm families. This is a procedure that cannot be applied to rural nonfarm activity and $Z$ concepts.

SHARES OF OFF-FARM INCOMES

In table 7.1 are assembled estimates of the share of the nonagricultural income of farm families for as many countries in Asia as data are available. These shares are sufficiently comparable for a rough comparison of income levels and of time trends across countries. In the note to the table are estimates for the United States, Ireland, and Yugoslavia. It would have been desirable to compute for a much larger number of Western and other countries, including those of Latin America and Africa, if their household surveys had been available in Southeast Asian libraries. If the figures for the three non-Asian countries are representative, they indicate that, despite their higher per capita incomes, their nonfarm shares are low compared to Taiwan and Japan.[4] This is to be expected, considering the longer period of dry weather in monsoon Asia.

The data are better for Japan, Taiwan, and South Korea than for other Asian countries. Farm household surveys are conducted annually in East Asian countries, largely on a record-keeping basis, and extend over several decades. As the note to table 7.1 points out, agricultural income data from Japan and Taiwan come fairly close to the estimates of income originating in the official national accounts. There are slight variations in income concepts from country to country; those of the Philippines and China, for example, exclude transfer receipts

TABLE 7.1

Annual Farm Family Income, Agricultural and Nonagricultural, Various Years

| Country | Agricultural Income | Nonagricultural Income | Ratio of Nonagricultural Income to Agricultural (percent) |
|---|---|---|---|
| China (RMB) | | | |
| 1978 | 130 | 3.44 | 2.6 |
| 1979 | 154 | 5.81 | 3.8 |
| 1980 | 182 | 9.11 | 5.0 |
| 1981 | 207 | 16.50 | 8.0 |
| 1985 | 264 | 86.26 | 32.7 |
| South Korea (1,000 won) | | | |
| 1970 | 195 | 33 | 16.9 |
| 1975 | 700 | 97 | 13.9 |
| 1980 | 1700 | 550 | 32.4 |
| 1985 | 3699 | 2,037 | 55.1 |
| Taiwan (1,000 NT$) | | | |
| 1970 | 17 | 18 | 105.9 |
| 1975 | 40 | 48 | 120.0 |
| 1980 | 54 | 165 | 305.6 |
| 1984 | 75 | 227 | 302.7 |
| 1988 | 97 | 303 | 312.4 |
| Japan (1,000 yen) | | | |
| 1950 | 145 | 41 | 28.3 |
| 1960 | 225 | 165 | 73.3 |
| 1970 | 510 | 850 | 166.7 |
| 1981 | 968 | 3,805 | 393.0 |
| 1984 | 1,065 | 4,296 | 403.4 |
| Philippines (pesos) | | | |
| 1965 | 3,046 | 357 | 11.7 |
| 1971 | 3,790 | 776 | 20.5 |
| 1975 | 2,522 | 488 | 19.3 |
| Malaysia (mn. M$) | | | |
| 1973 | 233 | 36 | 15.5 |
| 1979 | 424 | 166 | 39.2 |
| Thailand (baht) | | | |
| 1971 | 10,000 | 6,000 | 60.0 |
| 1978–79 | 11,049 | 6,758 | 61.2 |
| Indonesia (1,000 rupiah) | | | |
| 1985 | 420 | 139 | 33.0 |
| Bangladesh (rupees) | | | |
| 1963–64 | 720 | 156 | 21.7 |

*(continued)*

TABLE 7.1 (*Continued*)

| Country | Agricultural Income | Nonagricultural Income | Ratio of Nonagricultural Income to Agricultural (percent) |
|---|---|---|---|
| 1973–74 | 812 | 229 | 28.2 |
| 1976–77 | 672 | 144 | 21.4 |
| Sri Lanka (rupees) | | | |
| 1963 | 1,788 | 660 | 36.9 |
| 1978–79 | 5,640 | 2,208 | 39.2 |
| Nepal (rupees) | | | |
| 1977 | 3,588 | 1,981 | 35.6 |

*Source:* Official national accounts and yearbooks; S. R. Osman and A. Rahman, *Study of Income Distribution in Bangladesh* (1981); World Bank, *Growth and Employment in Rural Thailand.*

*Note:* Ratio was around 65% in U.S., (1951–70), 55% in Ireland (1973), and 81% in Yugoslavia (1976).

and property incomes in nonagricultural incomes. Most of the estimates exclude the imputed rent of owner-occupied houses, but they all include the imputed value of home-consumed food.

With the exception of the Philippines in 1975 and Bangladesh in 1976–77, the absolute values and shares of nonagricultural incomes rose over time in each country. This is also true for the United States, where the share doubled from the prewar years to the early 1970s. The rise in shares in Japan, Taiwan, China, and Malaysia in the 1980s was much faster than in the rest of Asia and the United States. The Philippine survey for 1975 is not strictly comparable with the 1965 and 1971 surveys, as the 1975 survey comprised nearly 400,000 households, compared to about 20,000 in the earlier surveys. The larger sample covered a variety of communities—very rich districts and very poor ones. But because of the extensiveness of the coverage, the time spent by interviewers for each sampled household was brief, and incomes were understated since insufficient questioning made for omissions. Hence the decline in average farm household incomes, both agricultural and nonagricultural. The figures for Bangladesh are low for 1976–77 because of a harvest about 10 percent lower than in the previous year. The figures for nonagricultural incomes for all years understate the contribution by women, whose production is often overlooked. In Moslem countries, women tend to be confined to the house, but they do a great deal of work in the house other than customary home chores.

Despite these caveats, the results show a rough association between nonfarm shares in income and the country's economic development stage: the highest shares are in Japan and Taiwan, and the lowest are in China and Bangladesh. Generally, shares rise with growing incomes, the exception being the Philippines and Bangladesh. Nepal, with the lowest per capita income, has higher shares than China, the Philippines, South Korea, and Sri Lanka; but Nepal's survey, not being a random, probability survey, may not be representative nationwide. South Korea has lower shares than Thailand, Malaysia, Sri Lanka, and Indonesia. The loose positive relationship may be related to greater opportunities for off-farm work in an economy where agriculture has become more diversified and industry has spread to the big cities. In the next section, forces other than development are noted in the cross-section results, followed by a discussion on the forces underlying the differential paces of the upward trend in the shares of the countries.

DIFFERENCES IN OFF-FARM INCOME

As in all cross-section results, a variety of factors intervene to blur the relationship between stages (or per capita incomes) and shares. The amount of labor farm families can supply to the nonagricultural labor market is determined mainly by the length of the dry season minus how much of the dry season is spent on farm work.

The monsoon rainfall pattern varies among world regions (figure 7.1). Three major patterns may be singled out: the first is shown in figure 7.2: Bangladesh, Burma, India, the Philippines, and Indonesia, show a pronounced rainfall peak, higher than the average pattern in figure 7.1. The second pattern is shown in figure 7.3: in Thailand, China, South Korea, Vietnam, Japan, Taiwan, Sri Lanka, and Malaysia the peak is less pronounced and is lower than in the average pattern. There is no conspicuous mode in the third pattern, though rainfall is heavy enough in the summer months for paddy rice; but there is a minimonsoon in the winter months, which enables perennial crops (which need all-year rainfall) such as rubber, tea, palm oil, and coconuts to thrive.[5]

With even rainfall, farm employment during the drier months can be found in the harvesting of perennials, reducing the labor supply for the nonagricultural labor market. Besides monthly patterns, the annual average rainfall is also of some consequence. In Thailand and Nepal, where the rainfall is half of the average in the Philippines, the raising of livestock and the growing of vegetables and fruits after the main harvest are more difficult; thus more labor is available for nonagricultural activities. And with heavier rainfall throughout the year, small irrigation works are easier to construct.

On the demand side of the nonagricultural labor market, the main forces are the extent of labor-intensive, decentralized manufacturing and the stock of transport, communication, and other infrastructure that can be used by farm families to reach the labor markets. In the postwar decades, institutional forces were also important. In the beginning of development in the postwar era, the forces on the demand side are a historical given. Data on nonagricultural incomes for the early 1950s are not available for most countries. In Japan and

Rainfall in inches

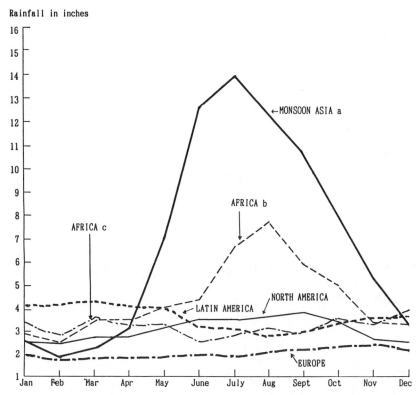

FIG. 7.1. Rainfall patterns, major world regions, by month. *Source:* Harry T. Oshima. *The Transition to an Industrial Economy in Monsoon Asia* (Manila: Asian Development Bank, 1983).
a. Includes the densely populated countries of East, Southeast and South Asia and excludes Hokkaido and Manchuria in the northeast, the Mongolias in the north, western China, Afghanistan and Pakistan in the west, the southeastern islands of Indonesia, and India west and south of Delhi.
b. Excludes Africa north of the Sahara.
c. Excludes, besides countries north of the Sahara, the small west African countries of Sierra Leone, Cameroon, and Gambia. Because the above are simple averages, heavy rains in the little corner of west Africa make the big difference in the rainfall patterns of the two African curves.

Taiwan, this share was around one-third, a level similar to later levels in Nepal and Sri Lanka, countries with relatively low rainfall. Sri Lanka's 1963 level and Nepal's 1977 level may represent the 1950s, since these countries developed slowly in the postwar decades. The low levels in China in 1978 are due to Maoist policies that severely restricted peasant movement and activities in the informal sectors, which are the major sources of nonagricultural activities in the

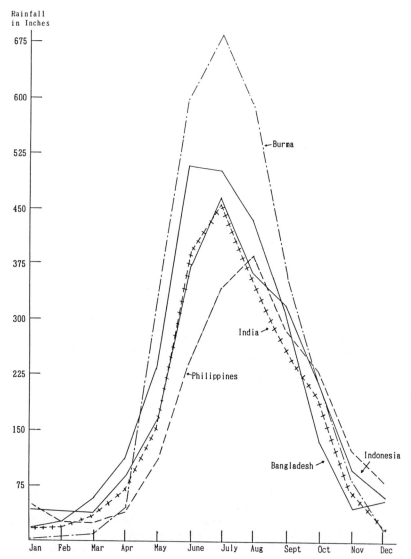

FIG. 7.2. Countries with high peaks of rainfall, by month, 1970s. *Source:* Official national accounts and yearbooks.

early stages of the transition. With the relaxation of these policies under Deng in 1978, this share rose rapidly, as peasant families opened small rural enterprises, such as eating places, trading, handicrafts, and diversified agriculture.

The low share in the Philippines in the 1960s may be due to the sugar and coconut industries, which provided jobs during the dry months; to marine

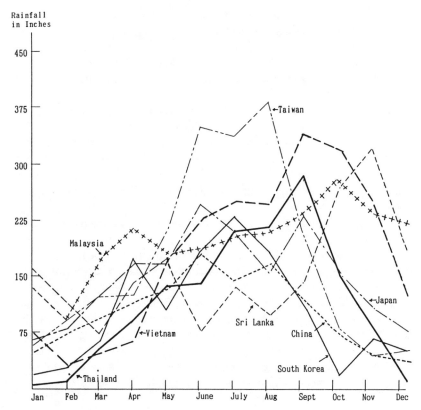

FIG. 7.3. Countries with low peaks of rainfall, by month, 1970s. *Source:* Official national accounts and yearbooks.

fishery along the coastal areas of thousands of islands; and even more to rainfall in Mindanao, Bicol, and other regions on the Pacific Ocean. The share is low in high-income Malaysia because of its vast plantation sector and extensive irrigation. The low levels in Bangladesh may be attributed to the almost complete loss of handicraft skills and the insufficient development of modern industries under long periods of exploitive British rule, which converted Bangladesh into the rice basket of South Asia. Shares may turn out to be low for Burma and India, which went through a similar experience under the British. In Nepal, the rugged mountains were such an obstacle to British traders that village crafts were better preserved. Thai levels are high partly because average rainfall is low (especially in the northeast) and irrigation is limited.

Several forces account for the differences in the trends of the shares. In China the slow rise in the share before the 1980s (the entire Mao period) may be due not only to the virtual ban on informal activities and movement to the cities but also to Mao's heavy industrialization strategies of the early 1950s, which reduced work for the peasants in the formal sector. Capital-intensive industrialization meant that seasonal work for peasants was minimal, since the big factories had to be operated by full-time, regular workers, while the large demands made by heavy industries on existing resources left little for the development of labor-intensive industrialization, which uses the bits of part-time labor of the peasantry.[6]

Similar statements may be made for South Korea, which in the 1970s began an accelerated capital-intensive strategy, focusing resources on fifty or so big firms, known as *chaebols*. As in China, these large enterprises were concentrated in a few places, either near the sources of raw materials for upstream industries or near large cities for the externalities required by big industries. The Philippines opted for capital-intensive industrialization heavily concentrated in or near Manila.

In contrast, industrialization in Thailand and Malaysia was labor-intensive and decentralized, although Malaysia turned to heavy industries in the 1980s. This meant that construction of roads and other infrastructure and services, all of which are supportive of manufacturing, was more dispersed, opening up job opportunities for farm families. The sharp increases in off-farm employment in Japan and Taiwan had their origin in the agricultural-based and regionally dispersed labor-intensive industrialization strategy of the earlier postwar decades. The early attainment of full employment and labor scarcity forced small firms to move out of the main cities, since they were unable to obtain labor in these cities. Rising farm wages led to extensive mechanization of farm operations, freeing members of farm families to take on full-time as well as part-time jobs in nearby towns and cities.[7]

Although in the United States off-farm income was low relative to per capita income both before and after World War II, the share rose steadily between 1936 and 1982. The reason for this throws some light on the experience of Japan and Taiwan in the 1970s. In a highly developed economy like the United States, agriculture becomes predominantly commercialized and diversified, and activities in agriculture become increasingly process-intensive, requiring a great deal of milling, packing, preserving, hauling, and servicing. After harvest, as much as a third of the army of field laborers on large U.S. farms move from the fields into mills, canneries, and factories. Wages and salaries in 1976 in the manufacture of food, tobacco, paper and pulp, and lumber products were five times wages and salaries in agriculture; in 1938 they were three times these wages.[8]

Three types of off-farm industrial employment may be identified: (1) full-time, regular work in fairly knowledge-intensive, mechanized factories and offices in nearby towns, best exemplified in Japan during the 1970s; (2) year-round but irregular work in nearby towns in less capital-intensive factories employing young workers without modern skills, best exemplified in the industrial estates of Taiwan, South Korea, and west Malaysia in the 1970s; and (3) seasonal and intermittent work in construction, handicrafts, and handwork in or near villages, in very labor-intensive units (often in homes to eliminate rent), and employing all types of workers from young to old; this work is best exemplified by handicrafts in Chiang-mai and Java and food processing in Taiwan in the 1960s.

The Japanese pattern may be less relevant to Southeast Asia than the Taiwanese pattern. Japan's primogeniture system of inheritance contrasts with the Chinese system, in which the land is divided and distributed to all sons. Younger sons in Japan migrate permanently to cities. This was the basis of the unprecedented wave of migration in Japan during the 1960s. In contrast, there is a tendency for younger sons in Taiwan to remain on the farm within the extended family, helping with the farm work. Since inheritance patterns in Southeast Asia are closer to the Taiwanese pattern, commuting rather than migration may be more likely, which favors off-farm employment rather than the establishment of new urban households. A major reason for the rapid rise in Japan's share of off-farm income is also the slow growth of its agricultural income compared to Taiwan.

STAGES IN OFF-FARM EMPLOYMENT

The growth of nonagricultural shares and their composition go through three stages. Although data are scarce, trends in these shares and in overall development can be discerned and may provide a framework for identifying gaps that could be filled by research.[9]

In general, in the early stage of the agroindustrial transition, the nonagricultural employment of farm families is largely traditional, whether in manufacturing, construction, transporting, or services; it is mainly handwork and uses little modern equipment. On the supply side, labor is mainly seasonal, since farm work demands a lot of time during the wet season. In the middle stage, nonagricultural employment using semimechanized equipment begins to spread, replacing traditional employment and paying better as productivity increases. The increasing use of cultivators and threshers speeds up farm work, releasing labor for off-farm activities. In the later stage, the use of fully mechanized equipment in manufacturing, transport, and construction opens up nonagricultural employment further away from the villages, while the supply of labor rises with the use of mechanized equipment for transplanting and reaping. This year-round availability of labor opens up opportunities to work in factories, which pay higher wages than agriculture. The emphasis here is on the demand side of the labor market, as it is more important than the supply side in determining the incomes earned in nonagricultural activities.

*Stage One*

In the early stage of the transition, the products of agriculture are carbohy-drates and require relatively little processing, the most important being rice milling. For economies with tree and shrub crops, such as rubber, palm oil, cocoa, coconut, sugar, tobacco, and lumber, there is more processing. In this stage most types of nonagricultural activities are carried out in the homes and in the shops of neighboring villages and towns, where foods, handicrafts, and artisan products are made using only a few workers, most of them fully active only during the seasonal slack months. Raw materials are obtained from farms, forests, and rivers, and the technology is composed of hand tools, which often require dexterity and know-how passed on from one generation to the next through apprenticeship systems. Capital requirements are minimal, and mar-keting is local, confined to nearby villages or towns. Hence transport and communication needs are limited, and commuting to work is infrequent. In these traditional industries dominated by handwork, productivity and remu-neration are low, with wages tending to fall below those in agriculture.[10]

In Nepal, Bangladesh, and India, handicrafts, artisan work, and food pro-cessing predominate in the industrial sector. In India and Bangladesh, these include grain milling, seed crushing for oil, fruit and fish drying, the processing of dairy products, weaving, knitting, sewing, silk reeling, blacksmithing, brick and tile making, papermaking, leather processing, potting, mat making, bas-ketry, woodworking, carpentry, tying fishnets, rope making, and brush mak-ing.[11] Very little powered equipment is used; electric power is not available in the villages or even in the towns, while diesel engines for power generation are beyond the means of most families. Where perennial crops are grown, seasonal work is available in the processing of coconuts, tea, sugar, rubber, banana, jute, and lumber.[12]

In this stage, transport, construction, and services are important sources of nonagricultural employment, although earnings are low. The carriages and carts are pushed by hand or pulled by animals, and construction is entirely muscle work. Peddling, vending, hawking, and other forms of petty trading are important because the limitations of transportation lead to numerous, small, localized markets and marketing. With large pools of poor peasants and domes-tic servants, the richer peasants and the more educated families have plenty of time to do salaried white-collar work, such as in government and schools. Thus the volume of off-farm activities in the early stage is large in employment terms but low in value because of low productivity and earnings, which on a per day basis are lower than in agriculture.[13]

*Stage Two*

In the middle stage of the transition, semimodern off-farm activities are superimposed on traditional off-farm activities. As per capita farm incomes rise with the shift away from agriculture, the demand for nonagricultural production increases, expanding the market for processed foods, clothing, household articles, kitchen utensils, services, and farming inputs. By this time, import-substitute industries have been established in the cities and are able to supply these needs, making inroads into the markets of traditional handicrafts, but this loss is more than offset by a rise in off-farm activities in other areas. To transport urban products to rural areas, modern roads and other infrastructure are built, connecting the city to the hinterland and supplying jobs for rural families. Commerce spreads into the towns and villages. Handicraft work may then be replaced by better paying work in construction, transportation, and services. With the increase in population and in per capita income, demand for rice expands, and so the need for more irrigation, drainage, extension, and other public services in agriculture becomes another source of off-farm activities. The infrastructure connecting villages to urban centers or to railways and trunk roads opens up opportunities for farm families to commute or to migrate seasonally to urban work paying better wages.

With the rise in per capita income and urbanization, food purchases shift from inferior grains and root crops to rice, and there emerges the demand for diversified crops, especially fruits, vegetables, pulses, and animal and fish products, most of which are more process-intensive than cheaper crops. There is an expansion of agroindustries: cleaning, preserving, canning, refining, packing, hauling, warehousing, and so on. Generally speaking, semimodern industrial products are more highly valued than handicrafts made in the home, as the former use more modern technologies, some of them semiautomatic and power-driven and are produced on a larger scale.[14] This is particularly true in labor-intensive urban factories, to which farm workers commute to work longer than a season. Construction and transportation begin to use more equipment, some diesel powered. Services become more sophisticated, requiring higher levels of education and equipment. Accordingly, in the middle stage, there may be a trade-off between diminishing man-days in traditional off-farm activities and increasing man-days in higher valued, semimodern off-farm activities, the latter more than offsetting the decline, so the share of nonagricultural income rises.

In Thailand in 1975–76, only one-fourth of nonagricultural income came from manufacturing, mainly from food processing and textiles; half came from services; the other one-fourth came from construction, transport, and mining. The large amounts from construction are due to the haste with which Thailand's inadequate physical infrastructure was built, as it tried to catch up with neighboring countries, where colonial regimes in prewar decades had started infrastructure construction. In the Philippines, rural manufacturing is also dominated by food, textiles, and wood products. Services also dominate off-farm income in west Malaysia, and food, textiles, and wood products loom large in Malaysian manufacturing. In Java, services such as trading and transport dominate off-farm activities, with construction and small industries (food, textiles, and cottage) being less important. In Taiwan in 1966, about half of non-agricultural income was from services, the other half being from industry, of which manufacturing comprised only one-fifth.[15] Thus in the middle stage, perhaps because of the decline of handicrafts, services dominate, followed by construction.

*Stage Three*

In the last stage, off-farm work increases faster in manufacturing than in construction and services, each contributing about one-third of off-farm incomes. Cottage and handicraft industries continue to decline but are more than offset by the expansion of factory industries and large workshops, using semi-automatic and fully automatic equipment. As import-substitute, labor-intensive industries mature, they begin to export abroad. Commuting and temporary migration to these industries become cheaper and more convenient as an expanded infrastructure and motorized transports, such as buses and railways, become widely available. Earnings from work obtained by commuting and by seasonal migration begin to loom large, offsetting reductions from traditional handicrafts.

There is an expansion of crop diversification, which begins to rival rice production, and commercialized agriculture supplants subsistence farming. Processing industries become a major source of off-farm income in rural areas, as fruit, vegetables, and animal products are prepared for marketing. Where plantation crops are extensive, their increased exports expand job opportunities in processing plants. Construction tapers off as major infrastructures—trunk roads, irrigation, and electrification—and the systems of schools and local administrations near completion. Trading by large commercial and industrial units reduces the need for petty commerce.

The 1962 data for Japan indicate that more than a third of agriculturists worked in construction, another third in manufacturing, mining, and transport, and a fourth in services. Since earnings from services are higher than in construction, service incomes comprised a third of total income. In Taiwan in 1975, service employment seemed somewhat more important than construction and manufacturing, with handicraft declining to 4 percent. In South Korea in 1960, two-thirds of rural, nonfarm employment was in services. The rest was in industry, with manufacturing accounting for 18 percent; this rose to 30 percent in 1980, while services fell to 50 percent.[16]

## The Japanese and Taiwanese Experience

In the second stage of the agroindustrial transition, a major acceleration in nonagricultural income occurs. Not until the mid-1960s in Japan and the mid-1970s in Taiwan did nonagricultural incomes equal farm income. In these years, both countries moved into the second, industry-to-service, stage. In addition, signs of labor scarcity began to appear after a decade of full employment, beginning around 1960 in Japan and 1970 in Taiwan. During the years immediately after full employment, labor scarcity was not felt in the cities, because the migration of young workers from the farms and the entry of urban housewives into the labor market satisfied the needs for expansion in urban industries and services. But after a period of rising migration and increases in the female labor force in response to rising wages, the flow of workers from these sources slowed, particularly migration to the largest cities. In Japan the acceleration in nonagricultural income coincided with the slowdown in migration around the mid-1960s. Migration to Japan's two largest cities, Tokyo and Osaka, reached a peak in 1965, although for other large cities the peak was reached between 1965 and 1970.[17] Hence, with the diminished migration to large cities, small industries moved to small cities, generating job opportunities for those residing nearby.

As the larger cities began to be congested and as costs rose, the advantages of locating in these cities declined for smaller firms, especially those not needing such externalities as efficient communication and transportation and experienced, specialized workers, which only big cities offer. These were the firms that could use the cheaper, less experienced labor obtainable in agricultural districts. The spread of secondary educational facilities to these areas provided a pool of young workers with the requisite education for mechanized production. Wages were lower than in the big cities, since food and dwelling costs were lower; commuting costs were minor because of good roads and shorter distances.[18] With this migration, nonagricultural incomes rose substantially and rapidly.

In 1981, a third of Japan's employment in manufacturing establishments outside Japan's major cities was in food, textiles, garments, wood products, and ceramics; another third was in the production of fabricated metals, machinery, transport equipment, and instruments.[19] The latter grew faster than the former in the postwar decades and required more male than female workers. The men commuted to work by train and bus, leaving the farm work to women and older men. In turn, this meant that farming had to be mechanized with small, light equipment (without economies of scale) that women and the elderly could handle. Without the release of large numbers of workers through mechanized rice farming, the increases in off-farm incomes could not have occurred, as they did after full employment was reached, since full employment meant that the supply side became more important than the demand side in the nonagricultural labor market. In Taiwan there were more females than males among off-farm workers, which was related to the greater proportion of light work in the production of textiles, processed foods, drugs, plastic, and handicrafts than in the production of metal products.

The time it takes to complete stage two is far less than for stage one—a matter of one decade if growth is rapid. The reason is that demand elasticity for services is higher than for industrial products, while the potentials for the use of labor-saving mechanization are much lower in services.

Despite the rise of Japanese manufacturing as a source of employment (from 25 percent in 1962 to 31 percent in 1979), there was no decline in services, which rose slightly (from 29 to 30 percent). Construction fell from 38 to 31 percent.[20] The service sector held its own as Japan completed the second stage and moved into an economy dominated by modern services. Construction for the needs of agriculture and industry was losing the importance it had in the first stage, when the basic physical infrastructure for modern agriculture and industry had to be established. Trade declined and was replaced by personal services as the dominant activity in the service sector. Among personal services, it was not in domestic services but in the higher valued services—education, health, recreation, and culture—where the increases occurred. Domestic services declined drastically as consumer appliances replaced the services of maids, cooks, and gardeners, whose wages rose with full employment. Because industrial workers using powered equipment needed less energy—and service workers even less—agriculture began to produce fewer carbohydrate foods and more diversified foods. The latter require more processing than energy foods, thereby opening more off-farm jobs to farm families.

ECONOMIC GROWTH AND OFF-FARM EMPLOYMENT

Additional off-farm employment contributed to better utilization of the labor force in monsoon economies. Workers who were idle or underemployed during the dry months and during the slack months between transplanting and reaping shifted to off-farm work. Instead of time-consuming handicrafts (spinning, weaving, and sewing) and leisurely work doing farm irrigation and drainage, weeding, marginal multiple cropping, low-value farming, and so on, more remunerative and interesting work in nearby factories, shops, stores, and offices was found. Off-farm workers were able to help out with plowing and planting and with the reaping and threshing in the peak season. The higher incomes enabled farm families to purchase machine-made clothing, housewares, and other products, which they formerly had made by hand.

Perhaps more important, higher incomes enabled the purchase of farm inputs (machines, equipment, fertilizer, insecticides) and more education for children. Although spinning and weaving skills were lost, more modern skills were learned, and commuting from their villages opened up to the villagers new ways of living and thinking. This learning experience and the additional education prepared off-farm workers for permanent migration later on, as opportunities for permanent jobs or better jobs opened in towns and cities. It may be that the predominantly peasant background of Asian migrants make for their great efficiency in industry and services, unlike those in Latin America and Europe. People living on family farms must make managerial decisions, they must learn to economize and to maximize earnings, and so they learn skills and work ethics—unlike farm laborers on the capitalistically managed farms of Europe and Latin America.

The use of existing rural roads, buses, rails, and postal services for commuting and for freight makes for fuller utilization of these infrastructures. Their joint use for farming and for nonfarming makes for stronger justification of new infrastructure, particularly because commuting from farm to city reduces the need for additional urban housing, which permanent migrants require. The low wages that off-farm workers would work for enabled small- and medium-sized urban enterprises to prosper: off-farm workers can afford to work for low wages if they don't live in the city, with its higher living costs. In addition, with off-farm workers living on the farm, they are on hand to help during the busy seasons. Data on most of these are difficult to find. The actuality will depend on the country, the region within the country, and the type of off-farm employment.

Gini coefficients of farm family income in Japan were extremely low and stable throughout the postwar decades (between .23 and .25), because the rapid increase in off-farm family income offset the relative decline in on-farm incomes. The share of off-farm income going to small and medium farms rose and then tapered off beginning in the late 1960s, as surplus labor was exhausted. And throughout the postwar decade, the rapid rise of off-farm employment contributed to the small difference between agricultural and nonagricultural households income. Similar data and analysis seem to hold for Taiwan, where the farm income Gini was stable and only slightly higher than in Japan, varying between .28 in 1970 and .29 in 1974. South Korea's Gini was also low but was unstable, rising .24 in 1964 to .39 in 1975, with a rising trend in the 1970s (see figures 7.4, 7.5, and 7.6). South Korea's neglect of agricultural development produced regional inequalities in farm income, and off-farm income failed to rise fast enough to offset the retardation in the growth of on-farm income. In Japan by 1980, the income of large, medium, and small farms was almost equal (figure 7.6), largely because of off-farm incomes.

Farm income Ginis for Southeast Asia were in the .3–.4 range. The historic importance of capitalist plantations, the small share of off-farm employment, the large number of landless farm workers, the slower adoption of multiple

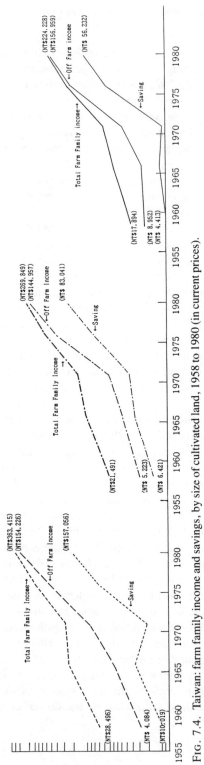

FIG. 7.4. Taiwan: farm family income and savings, by size of cultivated land, 1958 to 1980 (in current prices). *Source: Report of Farm Record-Keeping Families in Republic of China* (Taipei: Directorate-General of Budget, Accounting, and Statistics). *Note:* NT$ is new Taiwan $.

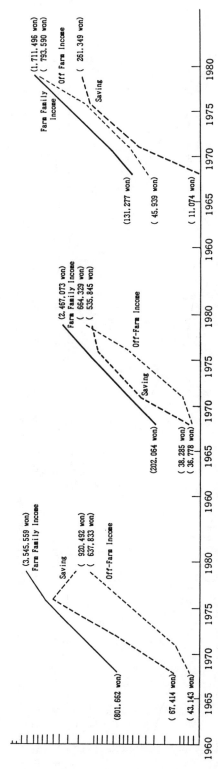

FIG. 7.5. South Korea: farm family income and savings, by size of cultivated land, 1968 to 1980 (in current prices). *Source: Report on the Results of Farm Household Economy Survey* (Seoul: National Bureau of Statistics).

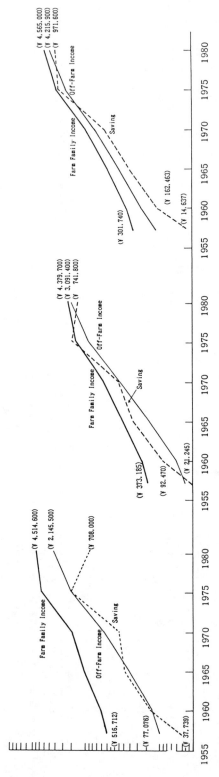

Fig. 7.6. Japan: farm family income and savings, by size of cultivated land, 1957 to 1980 (in current prices).

*Source: Farm Household Economy Survey* (Tokyo: Japan Statistical Bureau).

cropping and high-yield crops, the lack of mechanization on farms, and the uneven development of regional physical infrastructure all contributed to low farm income.

With larger incomes, peasant families were able to save. These large incomes contributed to Japan's high propensity to save throughout the postwar decades, to Taiwan's saving in the 1960s, and to South Korea's in the 1970s. Also, the thriftiness of these people is the product of many centuries of Confucian teachings—but it was not until farm incomes rose in the postwar decades beyond meager subsistence levels that Confucian ideals could be realized. The rise of peasant income beyond subsistence meant that they did not have to borrow to meet subsistence needs, which in the past had converted the positive savings of the families on large farms into negative overall net savings. Important to the change was the contribution of income from off-farm work; the savings it made possible went toward the purchase of machinery and transport equipment, which in turn made more off-farm employment possible. And as peasants began to realize that more education was needed to get better off-farm jobs, they began to save for the future education of their children. Appropriate data for these processes are impossible to get, since decisions to save or spend are made on the basis of total income, which is the sum of many activities other than off-farm work. In Taiwan, the rise of off-farm income and savings relative to on-farm income was greater for medium-sized farms than for large farms, and greater for small farms than for medium-sized farms, implying that part of the savings must be coming from off-farm income (figure 7.4). Similar trends are true for Japan (figure 7.6). In South Korea, off-farm income relative to on-farm income was larger for small farms (figure 7.5).

When unemployment and underemployment are extensive, off-farm jobs are often low paying, menial, and irregular. In these cases, such employment may not contribute to income equalization, as in Java and Kelantan, Malaysia.[21] There are also demographic implications. Outside employment of housewives raises the cost of child rearing, but more jobs also means that the demand for children goes up. This might raise birth rates if there is no parallel acceleration in farm mechanization. Mechanization is probably a quicker and surer way of meeting the increased demand for off-farm workers. There is thus a substitution of machines for children. Furthermore, the opportunity cost of child rearing rises as the future labor force requires education beyond the primary grades in order to work in either farm work or nonfarm work. Most important, the ownership of a piece of land whose values are rising gives the parents enough security for the future without a large family. These factors—together with the modernizing impact of working away from villages on traditional ways of thinking and living—contribute to falling birth rates in the farm sector, which was a major factor in the swift completion of the demographic transition in Japan in the 1960s and in Taiwan and South Korea in the 1980s.

## POLICY IMPLICATIONS

Off-farm employment—by raising farm productivity, income, and savings—plays a strategic role in the growth of a monsoon economy by enabling farm families to raise their incomes beyond the limitations of their farm size. Wealthier farm families enlarge the market for urban industries, and their savings finance urban industries. Jobs provided by crop diversification and off-farm employment raise overall productivity by increasing output without raising employment in the denominator of the productivity ratio. Thus off-farm employment enables agriculture to grow out of the poverty imposed by the labor intensity of monsoon paddy cultivation.

Development strategies for countries in the first stage of the agroindustrial transition should thus promote off-farm, nonagricultural activities. This entails a labor-intensive strategy for multiple cropping, a strategy for the regionalization of industry, and a strategy for constructing physical infrastructure. Strategies then should gradually shift to become more capital-intensive, with less emphasis on agriculture and more on industry. The Taiwan experience supports the view that direct strategies, such as locating industry in certain places and undertaking entrepreneurial training, are not necessary if the basic developmental strategy is an appropriate one; in some cases, such policies may even be wasteful. This is not to say that a small industry institute providing marketing information, industrial extension on management, technological know-how, and selective credit cannot be valuable, especially if administered efficiently.

There is one caveat: the experience of Japan shows that too much of a good thing is not good. From the later stage of the second transition and beyond, expansion of nonagricultural rural activities may not be desirable. Japan's small farms, with their low productivity per worker, are major contributors to the high cost of food and to political pressure to maintain protective tariffs and subsidies. So there is a need to convert to large-scale farming, using large-scale technologies (bulldozers, airplanes, and combines, as in the West). Small farms prosper only because adult males earn large incomes by commuting to cities in subsidized trains, leaving their wives and others to grow rice on small plots, thus propping up the whole system of petty farming. Without the large earnings from commuting to work, family income from farming would be only one-fifth of the present level.

Japanese farm families have come to enjoy this combination of farming and nonfarm activities. They can live in large houses free from the congestion, pollution, and noise of the city, while enjoying most of the amenities of urban living (television sets, cars, electrical appliances). The commuting men receive high urban incomes, and the wives earn incomes probably higher than in urban jobs, while living costs are lower—surely the best of two worlds. If so, nonagricultural incomes may contribute not only to the perpetuation of monsoon petty farming and its high costs but perhaps to the unduly small scale of some industries and services in nearby towns and small cities. Since large industrial and service enterprises require mostly full-time, year-round workers, small enterprises are the main source of the off-farm work of farm families.

All this makes it politically difficult to adopt policies to liberalize the importation of farm produce. The historic mission of nonfarm activities in monsoon Asia was to supply work in the slack season to supplement farm income, not the other way around. The present situation simply prolongs the life of petty agriculture and industry and retards the removal of an obstacle to faster productivity growth and the eradication of poverty.

# PART III

## Ultimate Processes

# CHAPTER 8

# Human Resource Development

If we think of capital as being created by human resources acting on natural resources, the two basic economic inputs are natural and human resources. Human resources are more important than natural resources, because natural resources can be imported. But without human resources, natural resources cannot be developed. In the postwar decade East Asia developed a strong competitiveness despite its meager natural resources.

The productivity of human resources is due not only to education (which includes in-service training) and health but to other dimensions—attitudes toward such social values as work, saving, learning, and cooperation. These values were strategic to East Asia's remarkable performance.

## THE INDUSTRIAL AND DEMOGRAPHIC TRANSITIONS

In a study of human resources, it is necessary to begin with population growth, because it affects future demand not only for jobs but also for educational and health services, housing, and, above all, arable land. Most countries in Asia have reached the land-use frontier, and further expansion is likely to be very costly. While rapid population growth may not be a serious problem elsewhere in the world, it is serious in resource-poor Asia, which has nearly half the world's population.[1]

The decline in fertility in East Asia in the 1980s was exceptionally rapid, due in large part to a sharp fall in rural fertility. In other Asian countries, despite a rapid fall in urban fertility, rural fertility remained high. For example, in Thailand in 1985–86, urban fertility was 1.8, but rural fertility remained at 3. In Japan by 1980, urban and rural fertility rates were about the same, 1.8 and 1.9, respectively. By the end of the 1980s, fertility in all East Asian countries was below replacement levels of 2, and population growth fell below 1.5 percent per year.

The population growth of 2.4 percent in South and Southeast Asia is too high, particularly because it implies a growing labor force, which will make full employment difficult to reach and will require expenditures for developing these human resources. For South Asia, there is another compelling reason for bringing down growth: the per capita supply of calories of about 2,000 or so is too low for the health and vigor to do heavy manual work, which is still needed in the predominantly nonmechanized South Asian economies. The too slow rise in food production in India and its fall in Nepal and Bangladesh under conditions of high population growth indicate that these countries must import food with their scarce foreign exchange, which could be better used to import equipment and other raw materials.

Another disadvantage of high population growth (and low life expectancy) is the smaller percentage of the population of working age (fifteen to sixty-four years), which means a larger share of dependent population. The share of working-age population is highest in East Asia, averaging 67 percent, which contrasts with 57 percent in Southeast Asia and 55 percent in South Asia.[2] Per capita product tends to grow faster where the share of working-age population is larger. If we deduct from the working age population housewives, students, the disabled, and the retired, we are left with the available supply of labor.

The growth of the labor force has fallen in East Asia despite its large working-age population because of the large percentage of this group attending secondary and tertiary schools. Southeast Asia's labor force is growing more rapidly than that of South Asia because of its much higher share of working females. The exceptionally low rate in South Asia is partly cultural and partly a statistical artifact. In Moslem countries women are not permitted to be seen working in the field. Although they do work at home threshing rice, weaving cloth, and making garments (using hand looms and hand spindles), their work is less productive than that of East Asian and Southeast Asian women. Because Moslem women work at home, they can care for their babies better than if they worked outside the home; thus this type of work is not a deterrent to having children.

In Thailand, women are busy in the house only on crafts, but on the farm they plow, weed, and plant. This high labor force participation was an important factor in the rapid fall of fertility in both rural and urban Thailand. But if female participation is low and child labor is used extensively, as in India, Bangladesh, and Nepal, birth rates will be high, because the value of children is high and the value of the housewife's time is low.

The large and complex topic of population policies is beyond the scope of this chapter, which is concerned with population growth only as it affects the development of human resources. The consensus among demographers is that economic and social development is the underlying cause of fertility decline but that population policies, such as family planning, can speed its pace.

The lowest total fertility rates in Asia are in Japan and Singapore, both of which adopted effective family planning and other population policies early in the postwar era. In addition, they have the highest per capita income in Asia. Southeast Asia's 1986 fertility rate was 3.7, with the lowest in Thailand (3) and the highest in the Philippines (4.6). Per capita income was roughly the same in the two countries, but family planning was much better implemented in Thailand than in the Philippines, and there was a much higher female work participation rate in the former. Malaysia had the highest per capita income in Southeast Asia, four times that of Indonesia, which had the lowest. But the 1986 fertility rates of the two countries were about the same (3.5 and 3.6, respectively). Malaysia's high fertility may be due to its pronatal policies and its low population densities.

South Asia, with lower socioeconomic development and per capita income and less extensive population policies than Southeast Asia, had higher fertility rates (4.9). But low-density Pakistan reported higher fertility rates than India, Bangladesh, and Nepal, which had lower incomes.[3] (In fact, high mortality in these countries is also a major factor in their fertility rates.)

Population per cropped land is also a factor in Asian fertility levels and trends. (Densities of total land areas, including mountains and deserts, are not relevant to this discussion.) India's densities are half those of China, and its total fertility rates are nearly double: 2.3 for China and 4.4 for India. Pakistan, with higher fertility, has densities much lower than those of Bangladesh, Nepal, and Sri Lanka. Java's great densities may have played a role in its rapid fertility decline compared to Malaysia. Generally speaking, the larger the farm size per worker (or the lower the density), the greater the need for additional workers, especially if cultivation cannot be mechanized, as in the tree-crop farms of Malaysia and Sri Lanka. (Or stated differently, the larger the farm, the more children that are needed to help with cultivation.) Countries with extensive employment of children in factories should ban such child labor, which will reduce the monetary value of children. Lowering the birthrate, will raise the employment of wives.

There is a concern in Western industrialized countries that their fertility rates have fallen below replacement levels (2.1 children per family), and there has been discussion as to the need for pronatal policies. This concern has also been expressed in Japan, Singapore, Malaysia, and the Philippines. But this worry may be premature for Asian countries. East Asian countries have had a labor shortage for some time and have imported labor from neighboring countries with excess labor, such as the Philippines. Even in Western countries, it is not certain that fertility levels will persist or that sometime in the future a reversal may not occur. Moreover, policies could be adopted to raise fertility.[4] Although opposition to immigration is strong in below-replacement-level countries, this may change with the persistence of low fertility.

Where population densities are too high, below-replacement fertility would be welcome. This is true even for countries already below replacement level— for example, East Asia, where labor shortages have induced the rural population to migrate to the cities. This is the only way farm size will be increased, which would make large-scale mechanization feasible and would upgrade industrialization, which would in turn cause labor-intensive industries to move to the populous countries in South and Southeast Asia.

Social values comprise beliefs, ideals, views, and attitudes that directly influence our reproduction, work, saving, and learning behaviors and also our behavior in such institutions as the family, business enterprises, religious organizations, and government.[5] Attitudes toward work and learning versus leisure and entertainment, attitudes toward saving versus consumption, and attitudes toward community interests versus individual interests all directly affect productivity and income. Social values are *attitudes* and are distinguished from *activities*—such as work, saving, and learning. Thus even though one's attitude toward saving is favorable, the amount saved may be nil if one's income is low. One's work ethic may be strong, but if one is unemployed, productivity will be zero. The same is true of learning. Social values are "systems of views that dominate and govern the behavior of men—views on the relation of man to man and of man to the universe."[6] We are interested here in social values as they pertain to economic productivity. Since social values in this narrow sense influence important processes underlying the growth of productivity, the differences in social values among countries should not be neglected in the study of comparative growth of productivity and per capita incomes.

People's work values affect the speed at which they perform, their willingness to work overtime, the extent of female participation in the labor force, the quality of their work, and the diligence of entrepreneurs. People's learning values influence their own knowledge and skills and also their willingness to save for their children's education and to oversee their homework. These values also affect teachers' diligence and dedication. People's money-saving values affect their consumption patterns and their drive to maximize profits, make loans, and receive interest payments. People's values regarding government and governance influence political stability and cooperation—their ability to work together to solve social problems. These social values permeate the behavior of the entire work force: entrepreneurs, managers, professionals, skilled workers, farmers, and laborers.

In the early stages of the agroindustrial transition, when the economy is steeped in traditionalism, the quality of entrepreneurship is especially important. If growth is to begin, individuals must be willing to risk their savings in businesses with uncertain prospects, to work long hours and forgo leisure, and to learn new trades and skills. Savings are scarce in the early stages of the transition, and it is up to entrepreneurs, most of whom cannot depend on banks for loans, to save for the operation of the enterprise. Important also is the behavior of governments, which must take the initiative to build infrastructures and institutions.

A knowledge of the history of ancient Asia is essential to the understanding of the origins of social values that prevailed in the postwar decades. These social values were formed in various ways over the centuries. Some were fostered by the rules and laws of ancient monarchs, others were taught by religious leaders and priests, and others were the product of the natural surroundings. The meagerness of nature under monsoon conditions was an important source of the thrift and diligence of Asians.

Of the various sources of social values, the most important may be religious and ethical systems (such as Confucianism) inherited from the past. Most of society's social values are enshrined in religious scriptures and elaborated in the writings of priests. These were examined by Max Weber and his followers in their effort to account for the origin and development of capitalism. There was the revolutionary European Weltanschauung (world view) brought about by the Renaissance and the Reformation, after the fall of the Roman Empire and before the agroindustrial revolution. In particular, Weber pointed to the importance of Protestant teachings, which modernized the work ethic. Working hard and maximizing profits were doing God's will and were not to be regarded as greedy, selfish acts.

In Asia, there was no Reformation; attitudes toward economic activities varied with the different religions of each country. Weber thought that, of all Asian religions, Confucianism was most conducive to the development of capitalism—although Protestantism was more suited to bring about capitalism. Confucianism teaches that people should work to please their ancestors by contributing to the well-being of their families and, through them, to the state. To do this, family members must work hard, be thrifty, enlarge their knowledge, improve their skills, and educate their children. Wealth should be accumulated and used to live a healthy, moral, virtuous, and dignified life and, above all, to give descendants a start in their life work and career. People should strive for peace and harmony through compromise and moderation and obey rulers, who should govern benevolently and wisely to earn the loyalty of their subjects.[7]

While Confucius teaches people to worship their ancestors, other Asian religions have a divine being to worship and obey. Unlike the Confucian, whose heaven is neither godly nor divine, one's loyalty is to a divinity over and above the family and state; behavior is governed by rules, norms, and goals relating to the divine. Loyalty to the state and nation is secondary to obedience to God, Allah, or the caste, and little effort is made to promote a strong work or saving ethic. Since wealth cannot be taken into the Islamic heaven, the desire to accumulate is blunted, and the desire to work and save is weakened. To the peasant and laborer of India, Nepal, and Sri Lanka, most of whom are in the lower castes, the belief that they cannot improve their lot because their fate has been determined by their behavior in their previous lives contributes to passivism and weakens the desire to work and save. In contrast, the Confucian is exhorted to work and save to please his ancestors, whom he must meet after death, and is compelled to work to promote the future well-being of the family through the children's education. If fighting to vindicate the ways of Allah is extolled by the Muslim, peace, harmony, and stability are difficult to achieve, and wars and internal fighting make it difficult to sustain the effort needed for economic growth and drain the resources needed for capital formation. In contrast, Confucian values promote harmonious relations among classes and nations.

In Islamic countries such as Pakistan and Bangladesh, females are extensively discriminated against. Men are thought to be the earners and women to be servers of men. They are kept away from the workplace and confined to the homestead. Women are also discriminated against in Hinduism, although to a lesser extent than in Islamic countries. Only 20 percent of South Asian women fifteen years of age and older are in the labor force; the figures are 37 percent for East Asia and 33 percent for the ASEAN Four.[8] The rates for East Asia would be higher if large numbers of young women were not attending senior high school and college. The working population as a share of total population in 1986 was 26 percent in Bangladesh, 35 percent in Malaysia, 37 percent in the Philippines, 40 percent in Indonesia, and 51 percent in Thailand.[9] Even if account is taken of a large share of dependents in the total population of Bangladesh, the level of GNP per capita is unfavorably affected.

Because receiving and paying interest are regarded as sinful in Islam, savings in Muslim countries have grown slowly and few loans are made to Muslim businesses. To get past the Islamic taboo on interest, there are proposals in Indonesia to open Islamic banks that will make loans on an equity basis to businesses and will receive dividends. The dividends will be distributed to the depositors of the banks as profit sharing. This is acceptable to modern Muslims, who feel that the taboo on interests has held back the economic development of Islamic countries, but traditional Muslims are yet to be convinced.[10] The slow growth of Islamic countries, especially Pakistan and Bangladesh, may thus be due to social values that discourage female employment and the accumulation of savings.

In East Asia, religious rituals and worship intrude minimally into the normal routines of work and living. Most people go about their daily schedules of eating, working, resting, and leisure without bothering about prayers and homage. The priests of Mahayana Buddhism (a less ritualistic form of Buddhism than the Theravada Buddhism of Sri Lanka, Burma, Laos, Cambodia, and Thailand) are called upon mainly for the rites of birth, marriage, and death. In contrast, other religions require frequent prayers and attendance (Muslims have to pray five times a day), and many aspects of daily life are regulated by Islamic law, such as what food to consume and what types of clothing to wear. Theravada Buddhism's emphasis on earning merit by giving gifts to the priests furnishes the rationale for an extensive welfare state in Sri Lanka and Burma; as a result, a great deal is spent on welfare and little on capital formation. Peasants in Theravada countries are content to produce only enough for their own subsistence and gifts to their priests. In Thailand, moral education courses are patterned after those of the Japanese.

The Hispanic Catholic priests in the Spanish period taught the Filipinos that their lot was determined by fate and that nothing could be done to improve their present life except to pray in church for the hereafter. Their harsh treatment at the hands of Spanish rulers and their exploitation under Spanish institutions over the centuries have made Filipinos suspicious of the government and other institutions, forcing them to trust and rely on only their kin. The family became the all-important institution, and loyalty to it became the overriding social value. This loyalty to family weakened loyalty to business enterprises, unlike in Japan, where a looser loyalty to the family made it easier to be loyal to public and private enterprises and other institutions, thereby strengthening them.[11]

Hinduism, like Islam, is not favorable to modern economic growth. The belief that one's present status is the result of what one did in the previous life makes for fatalism and passivism. Most peasants and workers are forever condemned to the lower castes, such as the untouchables, weakening the incentives to work hard and save. The segmentation, barriers, and hierarchy of the caste system militate against the free flow of resources and social mobility and promote ill feeling and conflicts.

Social values probably play a more important role in the early stage of development, when traditionalism prevails. But with the passage of time and the introduction of modern modes of production and livelihood, the influence of religious teachings tends to erode. This may be seen in South Korea, where affluence has weakened the strong Confucian ethic and its president had to urge the citizenry to "halt sumptuous consumption and encourage a renewed work ethic."[12] In contrast, Buddhist Thailand and predominantly Muslim Indonesia and Malaysia have made steady postwar progress in modernization and have begun to display the hustle and bustle seen in East Asia. And even in some states in Hindu India (the Punjab, Haryana, and the United Provinces), rapid progress has begun. In brief, traditional religions need not constitute a barrier to economic progress, particularly because social values can be modified by institutions other than religion.

Countries in Southeast Asia have taken steps to overcome some of the deficiencies in their social values. Thailand has instituted moral education courses, and the Philippines has introduced the teaching of better work behavior. Indonesia adopted in its Pancasila a set of political and social codes; and to get past the mysticism prevailing in Java, logic and scientific attitudes were emphasized. Singapore invited leading Confucian scholars from the United States to rewrite textbooks for secondary schools. Little, however, has been done in Southeast Asia along these lines.

In sum, human beings require guidelines on attitudes and beliefs, especially if they are to move into the era of modern economic growth, with its high demands for efficiency and diligence. But the processes by which social values affect economic progress are very complex, and more studies are needed to improve educational practices that modify social values. Whatever the prevailing religion, social values can be changed, as the experience of the Japanese colonialists in prewar Taiwan and Korea shows.

## THE ACQUISITION OF KNOWLEDGE AND SKILLS

The sources of knowledge and skills are not only schools and training centers but also the home, the workplace, and mass media, and these sources are closely connected. Preschool children must be motivated in the home on the importance of learning if they are to do well in schools, and general knowledge must be well taught in the classroom if basic vocational skills are to be properly transmitted. Specific skills can be best learned in the workplace, where the appropriate machines and instructors are. And the mass media can be important conduits in the flow of knowledge and skills to all age groups. Through all these institutions, work ethics and work propensities can be strengthened in the process of transmitting knowledge and dexterity.

### The Prewar Era

Japan began compulsory primary education in the last quarter of the nineteenth century. When the census of 1950 was taken, its labor force averaged seven years of schooling and was almost completely literate. Japanese colonial rulers introduced extensive primary and vocational education in Taiwan and Korea in the early twentieth century to establish modern agriculture. They wanted to increase rice production in those countries so that the surplus could be imported to feed Japan's industrial workers. Thousands of Japanese agricultural and industrial extension agents were sent to Taiwan and Korea to give training in agriculture and industrial skills.

By the mid-1940s over half of the children of primary school age in Korea and Taiwan were attending public schools, far greater than in the Asian colonies of the Dutch, the British, and the French.[13] The education was of good quality, far better than the Theravada Buddhist temple education in Sri Lanka, Burma, Thailand, and Cambodia. Thus Korea and Taiwan started the postwar era with literacy levels higher than other Asian countries, with the exception of Japan, the Philippines, and Sri Lanka. In some instances, the education provided by religious sects, including Islam and Hinduism, did not teach writing but only the reading of the scriptures and was limited to religious subjects, with few or no secular subjects such as mathematics, science, and vocations. A notable feature was the inclusion of Confucian moral and work education, which contributed to a strong work ethic in Taiwan and Korea, as in Japan. With fairly well-developed human resources, East Asia got a quick start when the postwar era began.

In prewar Southeast Asia, the Philippines' literacy rate was high, due to the emphasis the United States put on education. A boat load of approximately 600 American teachers was brought to the Philippines during the early twentieth century. By the beginning of World War II, Philippine literacy (at 60 percent) was probably the highest in Asia after Japan.[14] Not far behind was Malaysia, with 53 percent literate. This was not due to British policies but to the efforts of each ethnic group, which established its own private schools. Chinese immigrants in Malaysia put a high priority on education, supporting a large network of schools, which went beyond the primary level. Thailand's literacy stood at about the same level as Malaysia's (58 percent) in 1960, the work of the Theravadan priests, who before World War II taught boys to read, to write, and to do simple arithmetic. Thai girls were taught in their homes. From the 1880s, the Thai government extended schooling to a larger number of people through public schools. And in the 1930s, the Japanese system of moral and vocational education was brought in to inculcate the duties and responsibilities of citizenship—patriotism and national solidarity.[15]

The Dutch in Indonesia did even less for public education than the British did in Malaysia—establishing schools only to train candidates for the bureaucracy. Indonesians started the postwar era with only 20 percent adult literacy, and in 1971, the average years of schooling completed were the lowest among Southeast Asian nations (2.9 years, compared to 5.3 in Thailand and 5.6 in the Philippines).[16] This low stock of educated manpower was to be a major constraint in the growth of postwar Indonesia, where mysticism still prevails among the Javanese. Burma's adult literacy rate was relatively high, 58 percent, an outcome of learning in Theravada Buddhist temple schools and British-supported private schools.

The country with the highest prewar adult literacy rate in South Asia was Sri Lanka. In Sri Lanka, as in Thailand, Theravadan priests taught the children in the temples of the towns and villages. The Dutch from the latter seventeenth century and the British from the early nineteenth century established schools in order to convert Buddhists to Protestantism, similar to the efforts of the United States in the Philippines to convert Catholics to Protestantism.

Educational levels of the giants of Asia—India and China—were among the lowest at the beginning of the postwar era. The 1951 Indian census found that only 17 percent of the population had any education, compared with 40 percent for Ceylon in 1950. No such data are available for China, but in 1950 the number of students enrolled in primary and secondary schools was only twenty-nine million, about the same per capita as India's twenty-four million, since the Chinese population was about one-fourth larger. Since the capacity of the educational system depends largely on the number of educated adults, especially teachers, this low enrollment may reflect China's low educational attainment. The low level in India was primarily due to the British policy of providing education only for the elites, especially for employment in the civil service. For the others, Hindu education was given mainly to the sons of Brahmanic families and Muslim education only to boys. In both cases, the main purpose was to read read the Hindu scriptures or the Koran. In traditional China, Confucianism was also concerned with the preparation of the elites for civil service examinations, although toward the late 1930s the Kuomintang established schools for 20 percent of school age children.

Prewar education patterns in Pakistan and Bangladesh were similar to that of India, and both started the postwar era with levels of literacy about the same as in India. Nepal's extremely low levels may be attributable to the opposition of the Rana dynasty (1846–1950) to any form of schooling for the public except for the ruling elites.

*The Postwar Era*

With the end of World War II, most of the newly independent countries of Asia quickly built schools, even though income per capita was low and their budgets were small.[17] Most of the East and Southeast Asian countries consistently spent about one-fifth of their budgets for education in the 1970s and 1980s; only 10 percent or less was spent in South Asia, the Philippines, and Indonesia.[18] Literacy was very high in East Asia by 1960, probably approaching Western levels, and by 1980 Japan's literacy surpassed that of the United States (see table 8.1). Southeast Asia nearly caught up with East Asia by 1980. In contrast, South Asia's literacy was only about half that of East Asia in 1980, as low as East Asia's 1960 rate. Not only literacy but average years of schooling rose substantially in East Asia (except in China), and by the late 1980s average years of schooling in Japan nearly caught up with those of the United States, which has the highest in the world.

Although U.S. secondary education was one of the best in the world during the first half of this century, it deteriorated by the 1980s. Dropout rates were high in contrast to an almost zero rate in Japan. The poor quality of American preuniversity education is mainly due to insufficient financial support from the federal government to local governments, in contrast to the large support given by the Japanese national government (about half of total expenses). Also, in contrast to Japanese mothers, American mothers are too busy with work outside home to pay much attention to the homework of the children. More important perhaps, American students are in school only 180 days a year, compared to

TABLE 8.1
Educational Measures, 1960s to 1980s

| Country | Adult Literacy (percent)[a] | | Years of Schooling | | Ratio by Schooling Level (percent) | | | Percentage of Vocational Students to Total (latest year) | Dropout Rate 1970s, 1980s |
|---|---|---|---|---|---|---|---|---|---|
| | 1960s | 1980s | 1960s, 1970s | 1980s | Primary | Secondary | Tertiary | | |
| East Asia | 67.2 | 86.2 | 6.4 | 7.9 | 107 | 77 | 13 | 12.3 | 6 |
| Hong Kong | 74.5 | 90.0 | 6.8 | 8.8 | 105 | 69 | 13 | 7.1 | 3 |
| South Korea | 68.1 | 88.0 | 3.9 | 8.0 | 96 | 94 | 32 | 16.7 | |
| Singapore | 68.9 | 82.9 | 5.3 | 6.0 | 115 | 71 | 12 | 4.8 | 10 |
| Taiwan | 71.8 | 90.8 | | 8.6 | 100 | 92 | 14 | 25.9 | |
| Japan | | 99.7 | 9.7 | 11.7 | 102 | 96 | 30 | 12.8 | |
| China | 52.8 | 65.5 | | 4.5 | 124 | 39 | 2 | 6.5 | |
| Southeast Asia | 57.8 | 79.1 | 4.0 | 5.8 | 105 | 47 | 18 | 9.5 | 31 |
| Indonesia | 39.0 | 72.0 | 2.9 | 4.9 | 118 | 39 | 7 | 10.4 | 32 |
| Malaysia | 52.8 | 73.0 | 5.0 | 6.5 | 99 | 53 | 6 | 1.6 | 3 |
| Philippines | 71.9 | 83.3 | 4.6 | 7.0 | 106 | 65 | 38 | | 33 |
| Thailand | 67.7 | 88.0 | 3.3 | 4.6 | 97 | 30 | 20 | 16.6 | 57 |
| South Asia | 30.7 | 42.2 | 2.9 | 3.1 | 81 | 30 | 5 | 1.3 | 54 |
| Afghanistan | 6.4 | 20.0 | | 2.1 | 60 | 18 | 5 | 0.6 | 80 |
| Bangladesh | 21.6 | 29.2 | | 2.4 | 102 | 24 | | 1.4 | 68 |
| Burma | 59.7 | 71.0 | | | 92 | 35 | | 1.3 | 59 |
| India | 27.8 | 40.8 | 0.5 | 0.9 | 79 | 25 | 5 | | |
| Nepal | 8.8 | 20.6 | | | 47 | 17 | 5 | | |
| Pakistan | 15.4 | 26.7 | | 2.5 | 103 | 63 | 5 | 1.7 | |
| Sri Lanka | 75.1 | 86.8 | 5.3 | 7.5 | | | | | 9 |

Sources: Ernesto Pernia, "Human Resources and Economic Development in Asian Developing Countries: Patterns and Differential Performance," August 1988; UNESCO, Statistical Yearbook; Asian Development Bank, Key Indicators.
[a]Fifteen years and older.

220 days in West Germany and 240 days in Japan.[19] Summer vacation in the United States is too long, and schools close on Saturdays.

In the Philippine educational system, which is based on the U.S. system, teachers are poorly paid, because the financing of most of the secondary schools has been turned over to the local communities, which are too poor to pay teachers adequately. Students spend only four or five hours per day in school, five days per week. Summer vacations are as long as in the United States, and only ten years of pretertiary education are provided, compared to the standard twelve years. The Department of Education of the Philippines found that secondary school graduates attained an educational level equivalent to only seven years of schooling, while science achievement tests showed fourteen-year-old Filipino students scored the lowest among students from the Philippines, Singapore, Hong Kong, Thailand, and South Korea.[20] The educational system was the major contribution of the U.S. occupation to the Philippines, and in the 1950s it was one of the best in Asia. But over the postwar decades it gradually degenerated into one of the worst in Southeast Asia.

Taiwan and South Korea follow Japanese practices and keep their students in school for seven or eight hours, with a half day on Saturdays and only one month of summer vacation. Elsewhere in Asia, the British influence has been extensive, with standards midway between those in Japan and the United States. The main support for primary and secondary schools in these countries comes from the national government. The lesson from the U.S. and Philippine experience is that the costs of primary and secondary education should be borne largely by the central government, which is the only institution with the resources to support education adequately. Central governments should improve tax collections instead of passing on educational financing to the local governments, as the Aquino administration did in the Philippines, where the share of central government revenue to GDP is one of the lowest in all of Asia.

Despite good progress, the goal of education for all is likely to be very difficult for some Asian countries, especially in South Asia, with rapid population growth, slow economic growth, and meager resources. The great dilemma is that resources are also needed to speed economic growth from the low rates of 1–2 percent per capita GNP during the 1980s. Spending on physical infrastructure, agricultural and industrial development to create jobs and reduce poverty, and on food, clothing, shelter, and other subsistence needs competes with spending to educate children for future production. Furthermore, children are needed to help on family farms and in cottage industries. Against these urgencies, parents may not view the education of their children as of high priority, particularly because the ability to read and write may not be of much value in traditional farm work and handicrafts. To peasants in the largely self-sufficient villages of most parts of India, Bangladesh, and even some Southeast Asian countries, public expenditures for irrigation, roads, extension agents, and loans for fertilizers are more desirable.

In Japan during the early Meiji period, angry peasants refused to comply with universal compulsory education, shouting to the teachers that children were needed on the farms and in the homes. There was a relapse into illiteracy when, after primary education, people went on working on traditional farms and in cottage industries, where literacy and numeracy were not needed. The high dropout rates in South Asia and parts of Southeast Asia (table 8.1) may reflect the need of poor farmers, especially tenants, for all the help children can give on the farm and in handicrafts.[21] According to the ESCAP Survey,

The drop-out rate is higher among pupils from poor homes and rural areas than from rich homes and urban areas. The poverty of households compels parents to withdraw children from schools and to use their labor for augmenting the family's meager resources. . . . Furthermore, ill-fed children from poor homes tend to become sick more frequently causing them to give up school as they fall behind. Other causes include inappropriate and irrelevant curricula, poorly trained teachers, lack of textbooks and other relevant materials, and poor physical facilities in schools. The lack of even small amounts of resources to buy clothing, transport to schools and outside meals also prevents children from continuing in schools.[22]

If the goal of education for all is to be retained in South Asia, innovative methods that cost much less than classroom teaching will have to be tried. Classroom size may be increased above forty pupils, even if quality falls— although some studies suggest that larger classrooms do not affect quality.[23] It may be better to economize on the construction of schools by having two school shifts, as in the Philippines now and in the newly industrialized countries of East Asia in the early postwar decades.[24]

Distant nonclassroom teaching methods may be needed for poor countries to pursue the goal of education for all, although this may mean the sacrifice of quality for quantity. In villages without schools, radios may be installed and lessons broadcast from nearby cities during the dry season. India has installed television sets in villages to broadcast general education and vocational courses. Similarly, for adult education in the towns and cities, greater use should be made of radio and television programs. Academic credit and diplomas could be granted for completion of courses. For those unable to attend adult education classes in the daytime or to own a radio or a television set, public facilities should be made available in the evening for education programs. Correspondence courses are also inexpensive ways of acquiring education.

For the poor, slow-growing countries of South Asia, education for all may be elusive unless quality is sacrificed for quantity. This may not be so serious if these countries can maintain quality in the schools of cities where modern industry is beginning to grow and where the demand for manpower with good literacy and numeracy is high. In the hinterland, where traditional crafts and farm work still prevail—and are likely to for some time to come—the sacrifice of quality for quantity may be less serious, as long as the education is enough to enable children to improve their education in later years through adult education courses—which implies that these countries should have an adult education program.

In the past, countries of Southeast Asia sacrificed quality for quantity when there was an upsurge of enrollment in primary and secondary schools. But they are now in a position to improve quality without sacrificing quantity and should do so in order to begin higher technological development. The children in schools today must be prepared when they grow up to deal with sophisticated technologies (electrical and electronic machines and biotechnologies), which have already made their appearance in the West and East Asia. Countries attract these industries precisely because they possess a workforce trained to handle these technologies.[25]

Although adequate measures of educational quality are lacking in Asian countries, complaints about quality of graduates are numerous. Most urgent is better training of teachers, especially in math, science, and guidance.[26] Not to be neglected are steps to improve the motivation of teachers: sufficient pay and good working conditions. Even more important is the parents' interest in their children's schoolwork.

Moral education courses that include work ethics teach children, parents, and teachers diligence in work and living. The decentralization of school management allows the curriculum to be adjusted to the needs of the locality and enhances teacher participation in the selection of textbooks, courses, and teaching methods, thereby motivating them to do a good job. In less affluent countries, budget deficiencies prevent a sufficient supply of textbooks and other teaching materials. In the Philippines, there is not only a shortage of textbooks but of desks and chairs in many parts of the country.[27] And of course, insufficient school buildings, forcing two shifts of classes, cut short the time that teachers can work with students. In East Asia the improvements called for are the development of creative analytical thinking to foster independent problem solving, since these countries, having approached or reached the technology frontier, must create their own technologies.

As to tertiary education, there may have been too much emphasis on expanding public colleges in predominantly agricultural countries. The level of industrialization is too low to absorb large numbers of college-trained graduates. Traditional services, in contrast to modern services, require simple vocational skills. Under these circumstances, college graduates are likely to be unemployed or to settle for jobs requiring no more than secondary education. It may be better to emphasize vocational education and technical training. In the Philippines, the large number of students in private colleges is partly due to the insufficient training received in the truncated public secondary schools, not only in general education but also in vocational education.[28]

There is a tendency for students to enroll in the humanities and the social sciences and not in engineering or technological and scientific fields, including agricultural sciences. Singapore has the highest proportion of enrollment in these "hard" disciplines, but this involved a drastic restructuring of education at the secondary and tertiary levels in the 1960s, which reduced classes in the "soft" disciplines, forcing students to shift to the "hard" ones. A government campaign also educated parents and students on job prospects.

No Asian country has as many good tertiary institutions as the United States. Entrance examinations must be taken by all who want to get into these better schools, but "complaints are quite common that examinations are inefficient in that they encourage rote learning and fail to measure skills, knowledge, and ability, and to indicate potential for future achievement. The examination systems may even distort the motive for education, as both teachers and students tend to become obsessed with performance in examination and lose sight of the broader objectives of the cultivation of the mind and the acquisition of skills."[29]

Fortunately for East Asian countries, their affluence permits them to expand public colleges. Japan has established a number of new universities; its problem is not financing but the availability of qualified instructors. One way to overcome this is to invite foreign universities to assist with instruction. This serves also to inject an element of internationalization, using teachers accustomed to teaching analytical methods rather than facts. The expansion in Taiwan and South Korea of tertiary education is even greater than in Japan. In South Korea there was a tenfold increase in enrollment between 1965 and 1987; in Taiwan, it was fourfold, compared to Japan's doubling. A third of this age group is enrolled in college, which is about the fraction in Western Europe but lower than the 60 percent in the United States.[30] While the educational systems in East Asia met the needs of industrialization, they now face the challenge of a postindustrial society, which requires a labor force capable of solving problems in innovative ways.[31]

### Vocational Skills

East Asia has met the demand for skills in its rapidly industrializing economies through large enrollments in secondary schools, vocational and technical schools, and on-the-job training systems. Rapid mechanization calls for more and higher skills in industry, services, and also in farming, where the repair of cultivators, pumps, threshers, reapers, and dryers requires capabilities beyond those called for in the traditional villages. Many other Asian countries have overemphasized general education at the secondary level at the expense of vocational education, which has had inadequate teachers, curricula, and teaching material. Such training should impart skills for employment in small firms, which are not in a position to invest in in-service training. Basic skill training is an introduction to higher skill training in institutes and on the job.

In many countries of South and Southeast Asia before World War II, educational facilities were limited. During the early postwar years, the number of illiterate and barely literate workers among middle-aged and older people was very large. These people need to be taught work skills as well as how to read and write. Adult literacy programs and public training can raise the productivity of these workers. Most important is in-service training, since work skills are more cheaply and better transmitted on the job. Private enterprises can supply the best teachers and the most up-to-date equipment and are the most interested in teaching their workers how to raise production and reduce waste. Moreover, because in-service training is highly specific to the job and to the firm, it enables secondary schools and training centers to concentrate on general and basic skills.[32]

In-service training is the main source of skills among Japanese workers. Employers prefer to train their workers themselves, thereby ensuring workers' loyalty and long-term employment. But the tradition of the free mobility of labor is strong in other Asian countries, where Western industrial relations have prevailed.[33] In this situation, the problem is how to induce firms to invest in on-the-job training if workers might leave to take higher paying jobs in other firms before the full costs of training are recouped. The problem is a difficult one, since the free mobility of labor cannot easily be regulated by legislation. The newly industrialized countries of East Asia had to face this problem in the mid-1960s, when they began to establish a system of vocational training. Singapore set up a number of vocational training programs under its Vocational Training and Industrial Training Board. When it found that these programs did not meet the demand for skilled workers, the board encouraged private enterprises to establish their own programs. Singapore required workers to contribute 4 percent of their monthly wages to a fund, from which employers would be reimbursed for training. There are similar programs in South Korea and Taiwan.

When industry demanded skills that could not be obtained through on-the-job training, East Asian governments established public training centers to upgrade the skills of the work force. In Singapore employers are charged 1 percent of their payrolls to finance these training centers. The National Manpower and Youth Council of the Philippines signed training contracts with private companies in which 70 percent of training costs are reimbursed by the government. But the coverage is small, not more than 8,500 in 1983, so that skill shortages are still severe.[34] Limited programs of in-service training are also found in other low-income countries, where wages are too low to be taxed for reimbursement. For these countries, there should be a law requiring workers to stay for a specified number of years in the firms that provided their training (of a quality approved by the government). If workers quit before the period, there would be a deduction from their terminal pay to cover the cost of their training. This may induce firms to undertake more in-service training. Such training benefits workers, so they should pay for it. The government should subsidize training that is to the national benefit, in the same way that agricultural extension services are paid for by the government.

As part of the system of vocational training, most countries have an apprenticeship program in which apprentices receive a certain fraction of a regular workers' pay (usually from a third to a half). This fraction rises with increased training until it is on par with regular pay. In some countries, especially in South Asia, there are off-the-job training programs to teach workers to start enterprises for their own employment, but it is not clear how effective the programs are. Nor do we know how useful training programs to improve the bureaucracy are. About a decade ago, major efforts were made by the Development Academy of the Philippines, but there are no signs that bureaucratic behavior has improved, and there are indications that it has degenerated.

In sum, after starting with a heavy emphasis on general education, countries in South and Southeast Asia began to shift to greater emphasis on vocational and technical training. It takes time to develop such training, because qualified teachers cannot be developed overnight, and the institutional arrangements required to meet the needs of diverse groups of students, workers, and employers are not easy. In most countries, training is available at lower and upper secondary schools, specialized trade and industry schools, fishery and agricultural colleges, and polytechnics where short-, medium-, and long-term courses are given. In industries, apprenticeship, in-service, and off-the-job schemes are found. With the increasing complexity of technologies, this is clearly the right direction to take in the future. Nevertheless, this rather bewildering array of institutional arrangements has brought about difficulties in cooperation and coordination.

Islamic and Hindu countries have programs to develop entrepreneurs: apparently these countries are experiencing a shortage of industrial entrepreneurs. There was no shortage of entrepreneurs in East Asia, although Singaporeans hesitated at first to move into manufacturing. If entrepreneurs have to know how to purchase inputs, to manage industrial relations, public relations, finances, production, and to transport and market, these can be learned in business schools. But the other attributes of successful entrepreneurs—such as the ability to take risks, to work long hours, to save and accumulate, and to innovate—are not easily learned in a few years at business school. They are rooted in social values developed over a long period in moral education courses, such as those found in the primary and secondary schools of East Asia, and in working for many years under successful entrepreneurs. South Korean entrepreneurs attribute their success to training in Confucian teachings.[35]

It is said that Indonesian entrepreneurs do not like to compete and regard the competitive Chinese as greedy. Philippine businesses, with decades of protection and monopolization, fear liberalization, as it will force them to compete. In Malaysia, the Chinese have established enterprises in the numerous industrial and export zones and have built up the manufacturing sector. Thai entrepreneurs appear to be doing well, but the Thais originally came from western

China and, besides, studied moral education in the schools. Clearly, more needs to be done to strengthen social values in the primary and secondary schools of Indonesia and the Philippines.[36] The same may be said for improving the bureaucracy, whose technical competence, but not its integrity and efficiency, can be raised by training programs.

As to the rural sector, farmers' cooperatives and associations are well developed in Taiwan and Japan and have become the institutional vehicle through which extension agents meet with farmers to instruct them on modern farming practices and to train them to repair and maintain their equipment. Elsewhere, the task of mobilizing and bringing farmers together is a problem. Extension agents find it difficult to visit each far-flung farm and village, especially in the mountains. In Japan and Taiwan, where farm families can afford television sets and radios, the mass media can be used to teach basic skills. South Korea's rural development movement (Saemul Undong) has substituted for the insufficient development of farmers' organizations. Elsewhere, various schemes have been established, but their coverage is limited.

## NUTRITION AND HEALTH

Nutrition is probably the most important component in human health in densely populated, land-scarce monsoon Asia, where food is not abundant. Poor nutrition may account for much of the child mortality, adult morbidity, and low life expectancies in South and Southeast Asia. While much progress has been made against communicable diseases like malaria, poor nutrition predisposes the population to infectious diseases such as tuberculosis, pneumonia, and diarrhea, and is the cause of kwashiorkor and marasmus. The core of the problem lies in food intake levels which among low-income families are insufficient for vigorous and efficient work.

In 1985 there were 200–300 million undernourished people in Asia, or about three-fifths of the world's undernourished people.[37] Appropriate calories per capita for Asians under full-employment conditions can be estimated by looking at East Asian countries at the time their economies reached full employment. For Japan in the early 1960s, Taiwan in the late 1960s, and South Korea in the 1970s, per capita calorie intake was around 2,600. On this basis, one can say that all the countries in South and Southeast Asia (except Malaysia) are not consuming enough for vigorous work in a fully employed economy, since their per capita intake ranges from 1,910 in Bangladesh to 2,550 in Indonesia.[38] From the point of view of health, Southeast Asians may consume enough, since they are not fully employed, although there may be protein and calorie deficiencies among the children of low-income groups. The main problem in Southeast Asia is malnutrition due to insufficient intake of proteins, vitamins, and chemicals. This can be overcome with agricultural diversification during the dry season—which would also bring up protein and calorie levels to those needed for full employment. The major nutritional problem from the work and health point of view is in South Asia. Available caloric supplies of 2,000–2,100 in all South Asian countries except Burma and Sri Lanka imply an intake of about 1,700 to 1,900 calories, which is clearly too low—and underlies the high infant mortality and low life expectancies of South Asia.

In addition to nutrition, insufficient water supplies and facilities for waste disposal contribute to low life expectancies through diarrheal diseases. Poor sanitation and housing in the urban areas are the result of large migrations to the cities, as rice self-sufficiency in rural areas reduced employment opportunities in agriculture.

An indicator of nutrition and health is life expectancy. Short life expectancies such as in South Asia mean that members of the work force do not work long enough to make their full economic contribution. But if they live too long, as in Japan and the West, the retired population becomes dependent on the work force. If we assume that the average person retires at around sixty-five years of age, the optimal life expectancy for the national economy is sixty-five years. In this respect, Southeast Asian countries are most favorably situated, together with South Korea and China, if we give male life expectancy greater weight.

Japan's life expectancy at birth (seventy-eight years) is the highest not only in Asia but in the world. The average life expectancy of the newly industrializing countries is moving close to that of the Western industrialized countries, whose average is about seventy-six years—even though per capita incomes in the former are only half those in the West. The reason may be found in dietary patterns: Asians consume less fatty meals and more fish and vegetables. The higher incomes of Westerners enable them to buy more meat, milk, and other rich foods, thereby incurring heart diseases. In 1985 the Japanese consumed only about a fifth the amounts of meat, dairy, oil, and fats of that consumed in Western industrialized countries.[39] But with rising affluence, richer Asian families are beginning to consume foods with high cholesteral content, and heart disease is on the rise.

In the countries where nutrition is inadequate and health is poor, medical services are least available. A good indicator of available medical services is number of physicians, which is closely correlated with number of nurses and hospital beds. The number of patients per physician is highest in Nepal and Bangladesh. It is also high in Indonesia, the Philippines, Thailand, and Sri Lanka. More important is the distribution of medical services. Access to these services is limited mainly to the urban populace. In India, China, and Bangladesh, perhaps half the population is not served. In part, this is the problem of inability of the lower income groups to afford the services of doctors and hospitals, but it is also due to the reluctance of medical personnel to locate in the hinterland, where working and living conditions are unattractive.

Some countries have committed themselves to meet the minimal needs of the urban poor and rural communities by providing immunization against communicable diseases, programs to control infectious diseases, health and nutrition education, food fortification, and improved sanitation and water supply. But several countries, especially in South Asia, are unable to provide the finances, manpower, and other resources to meet everyone's primary health care needs. Resource scarcity is compounded by the tendency for medical personnel to be expensively trained in order to meet the needs of those who can pay for the best services and to use the most highly sophisticated medical technologies. Also, there is inefficient utilization of hospitals and equipment and insufficient community participation.[40]

## SUMMARY

Most Asian governments began to adopt family planning programs in the 1970s, when they saw that population growth was getting out of hand. The most extensive programs were in East Asia. Those in Southeast Asia were smaller, as resources were limited. Thailand achieved the greatest drop in fertility, with voluntary use of contraceptives. Malaysia in the 1980s began to pursue pronatalist policies, contending that its population was too small to create mass markets for industrial goods and that its farmland was large enough to accommodate more people. Seeing that its educated families were not having as many children as its less educated families, Singapore's leaders worried about the quality of its future population and reversed its antinatal policies for educated families. The Philippines made good headway in the 1970s but later succumbed to the pressure of the pronatal Catholic church and began to weaken its family planning programs. South Asia's family planning services were limited by insufficient resources and the lack of a strong demand for limiting family size. There was strong opposition to the attempt by Indian authorities to force compulsory sterilization on wives; furthermore, the poor in India needed children for farm work. In Japan, on the other hand, women made great use of abortion clinics, even illegally.

Educational policies at first aimed at education for all, but South Asian governments found that resources were not sufficient to provide schools all over their countries, especially in the hinterland. Parents in rural areas also found that they needed their children to help on the farm—whose traditional operations did not require literacy and numeracy. Resources were also needed for improving the quality of schools, especially teachers. To educate the illiterate and semiliterate adult population, various education programs were started, but these too were found to be too costly on the scale needed to educate and train substantial numbers. Too strong an emphasis on general instead of vocational education at the secondary level tended to cause a mismatch between the supply of graduates and the demands of the labor market. But vocational education was found to be much more expensive than general education.

Too much was spent on universities, in part to fill the demand of the new governments for civil servants. After this demand was met, the problem of the unemployment of the educated emerged, particularly for those trained in the humanities and the social sciences, since the need in private industry was for engineers and other technicians. To meet the need for skills not taught in schools, governments established vocational and technical institutes. To encourage firms to give more in-service training, a policy was adopted of charging workers or giving government subsidies to these firms. In agriculture, governments in South and Southeast Asia could not afford to employ enough agricultural extension agents to meet with farmers, especially those with small farms.

Immunization programs wiped out the major communicable diseases such as malaria, but a substantial reduction in infectious diseases and improved nutrition were more than the poor countries of South Asia could finance. Even primary health care was beyond their means. Nutrition policy was directed at education and at the fortification of foods. In Sri Lanka, large subsidies underwrote increased rice consumption.

Sri Lanka's strategy to improve human resources by spending heavily on free education and health care for all and by subsidizing medicine, rice, and housing was at the expense of capital formation in the form of the physical infrastructure needed for agricultural and industrial development. More important, entitlements and benefits from welfare programs weakened people's desire to raise their income and to save for their children's educations, emergencies, and old age. This was also the case with socialist regimes in China, Vietnam, and North Korea. Philippine work values were weakened by a long occupation by rapacious colonialists.

I emphasize the importance of strengthening social values through moral education courses in primary and secondary schools. To meet the needs of the adult population who are no longer in school, the mass media, adult education, agricultural and industrial extension, and vocational and in-service training can improve social values. They are most meaningfully taught on the job.

It is desirable to distribute facilities for developing human resources regionally by establishing branches of top universities and hospitals outside the metropolis. Concentrating school and medical facilities in the metropolises encourages both the young and the old to congest the cities. By locating these facilities in smaller cities, business enterprises will be encouraged to locate in these smaller cities, too.

# CHAPTER 9

# Family Income Distribution and the Alleviation of Poverty

The distribution of personal income is strategically located between production and consumption and hence can play an important role in the growth of productivity. When more of personal income is received by low-income groups, these groups—which compose most of the laboring class—are motivated to work more diligently, and their purchasing power increases. They can save for the education of their children, thereby raising future productivity. For the owners of small businesses and farms (who have difficulty borrowing from banks), more income is available to purchase machines and thereby expand operations.

Improved income distribution tends to reduce spending on luxuries and to increase spending on wage goods and other necessities, so that less is spent on imported goods, making more foreign exchange available for importing machinery and other foreign goods essential for economic development. Purchasing power is expanded for domestically produced industrial goods, thereby raising scale economies and productivity. If too much income is paid to upper-income groups and too little to middle- and lower-income groups, political stability is jeopardized, and domestic and foreign investments may decline. But there is such a thing as distribution being too equal, as in the case of China and other Communist countries. Economists in these countries complain that incomes are too equally distributed to serve as incentives for work.

There are various measures of income inequality, each with features that make them appropriate for certain purposes. Gini coefficients are used in the following discussion mainly because statistical offices usually use them in their publications, and accordingly, they have become the most convenient measure for international comparisons. The Gini is not necessarily the best measure, since it does not give various points of the total distribution; various Gini values are published for the same distribution, depending on how detailed the Lorenz curve is measured; its decomposition is difficult.

More troublesome in the study of income distribution is the limited availability of the statistics themselves (although in Asia the data are more plentiful than in other developing regions and more reliable). Data must be obtained from sample surveys of households, which are expensive to conduct in developing countries because of the large number of illiterate persons without the ability to keep books, and because of the necessity for large numbers of interviewers. In Japan, Taiwan, South Korea, Hong Kong, and Singapore, respondents are literate and keep daily accounts of spending. Thus East Asian data are much more reliable than data for other countries, which must be used with caution and can be used only for testing broad and simple issues, not for fine-tuned hypotheses. Even in East Asian surveys, upper incomes (subject to income taxes) may be grossly understated.

Income distribution in Asia tends to be less unequal than in Latin American countries, where huge haciendas support the very high incomes of the rural elites. In densely settled monsoon Asia, the farms are small, and variations in the income generated by agriculture are limited. Similarly, the importance of small and medium-sized industries and services keeps urban income inequalities lower than in Latin America, with its large urban enterprises. But compared to the developed countries of the West, Asian distributions tend to be more unequal because of (1) much less mechanized agriculture, so that income per farm worker is much lower than in industry, (2) greater prevalence of underemployment in monsoon agriculture, (3) more unskilled workers and low-income proprietors, and (4) the small transfer payments received by lower income families (figure 9.1).[1] The focus of the following discussion is on trends, and this is done in relation to Simon Kuznets's well-known hypothesis, which is simple enough to be tested by Asian income data.

## KUZNETS'S LONG SWING IN INCOME DISTRIBUTION

Kuznets's hypothesis asserts that in the course of economic growth income inequalities rise in the early stages of development and fall in the later stages. The upward movement is a gradual, long-run process, which in the West took place in the nineteenth century. The downward phase occurred in the twentieth century, with the peak sometime around the turn of that century, or in its early decades.[2]

Kuznets thought long-term forces accounted for the U.S. decline during the post–World War I period. He referred to the following factors: (1) the decline in disparity in output per worker between agriculture and nonagriculture, mainly because of farm mechanization, (2) the decline in the size of the entrepreneurial or proprietor class because of the fall in handicraft production and farm mechanization, (3) the increase in white-collar workers relative to the blue-collar workers, especially unskilled blue-collar workers, (4) the fall in the share of property incomes at the top, and (5) the shift in government policies toward welfarism and egalitarianism.[3] The lessening in inequalities was clear-cut and occurred not only in the United States but also in Western European countries. Kuznets was puzzled by the decline in so many countries, since he thought that

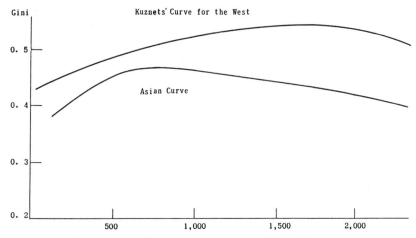

FIG. 9.1. Income distribution trends, Asia and the West (stylized).

distributive shares were subject to a wide variety of forces, some raising shares and others lowering them, with the net balance uncertain.[4]

It may be that Kuznets was not aware of the unique character of the post–World War I period. He wrote before historical research had established the enormous impact on the economy of the shift from the steam-operated technologies of the nineteenth century to the electric- and gas-operated technologies of the 1920s. This technological shift from the first industrial revolution to the second resulted in the mechanization of agriculture with internal combustion engines, such as tractors and electric-powered equipment reducing the farm work force while raising output per worker closer to that of nonagriculture. In industry, cheap, small electric machines were affordable for small firms, unlike the costly steam-powered equipment, and replaced a large number of unskilled workers. Moreover, housewives found employment in factories because electric power made possible small machines, which women could handle, and this increased the number of earners in low-income families.[5]

In other words, the decline in inequalities in the West in the twentieth century was due to special circumstances related to the changeover of technologies from the first to the second industrial revolutions.[6] By the early decades of the twentieth century, Western economies had become industrialized by utilizing the technologies of the second industrial revolution. Per capita income was about $2,000 in 1972 prices.[7] In contrast, in the postwar decades, Asian countries moved directly from agrarian economies based on traditional handicraft technologies into electric-powered technologies, skipping the stage of steam-powered technologies. At the time when the Ginis in Asia were falling, per capita incomes in U.S. 1972 dollars were low, $100 or less in Bangladesh, Sri Lanka, India, and Taiwan, $170 in the Philippines, $200 in Singapore, $300 in Indonesia, $400 in Hong Kong, $650 in Malaysia, and $1,000 in Thailand.

Less known are Kuznets's views concerning the rise of inequality in the early stages of development. In 1975, he pointed out "that the transition from the preindustrial to the modern industrial epoch was a relatively painful process. Groups of the population were displaced off the land, a number of traditional crafts and trade groups were adversely affected by competitive pressures of new factories, and there were marked effects on the relative distribution of income among groups attached to the several production sectors, with technological unemployment marking several decades in the transition." All this was accompanied by a rapid rise in population, as death rates fell and birth rates rose, with an unfavorable impact on income distribution. When this situation continues for long, disruptions are likely to occur, with the danger of a breakdown in national consensus and unity.[8] As examples of breakdowns, Kuznets cites the United States in the Civil War, Europe in the nineteenth century, and several of the less developed countries after World War II.

### INCOME DISTRIBUTION IN ASIAN DEVELOPMENT

Even though the downward turning point in income distribution trends did not come in the later stages of development, it is possible to detect a downward turning point in the early stages of Asian development. The following list shows the trends of Ginis:[9]

**Japan**

| | |
|---|---|
| 1962 | .37 |
| 1965 | .34 |
| 1970 | .41 |
| 1975 | .36 |
| 1980 | .33 |
| 1985 | .35 |

**Taiwan**

| | |
|---|---|
| 1953 | .56 |
| 1959–60 | .44 |
| 1964 | .36 |
| 1970 | .32 |
| 1975 | .31 |
| 1980 | .30 |
| 1985 | .32 |
| 1987 | .33 |

**Singapore**

| | |
|---|---|
| 1966 | .50 |
| 1972 | .44 |
| 1974 | .43 |
| 1979 | .42 |
| 1984 | .47 |

**Malaysia**

| | |
|---|---|
| 1957–58 | .45 |
| 1967–68 | .48 |
| 1970 | .51 |
| 1973 | .52 |
| 1979 | .49 |
| 1984 | .48 |
| 1988 | .44 |

**Indonesia**

| | |
|---|---|
| 1970 | .45 |
| 1976 | .49 |
| 1978 | .51 |
| 1982 | .45 |
| 1987 | .37 |

**Sri Lanka**

| | |
|---|---|
| 1953 | .50 |
| 1963 | .49 |

| | |
|---|---|
| 1970 .37 | 1975–76 .43 |
| 1973 .35 | 1980–81 .45 |
| 1981 .31 | 1985–86 .50 |
| 1985 .43 | 1988 .43 |
| | 1990 .40 |

**Pakistan**

| | |
|---|---|
| 1963–64 .39 | **Philippines** |
| 1966–67 .36 | |
| 1970–71 .33 | 1956 .49 |
| 1980 .51 | 1961 .51 |
| 1984 .44 | 1965 .51 |
| | 1971 .47 |

**South Korea**

| | |
|---|---|
| 1966 .34 | 1985 .45 |
| 1971 .36 | 1988 .45 |
| 1976 .37 | **Bangladesh** |
| 1980 .39 | 1963–64 .36 |
| 1982 .36 | 1966–67 .34 |
| 1985 .41 | 1968–69 .29 |
| 1987 .46 | 1973–74 .36 |
| | 1976–77 .45 |

**Hong Kong**

| | |
|---|---|
| 1957 .48 | 1981–82 .39 |
| 1963–64 .50 | 1983–84 .35 |
| 1966 .49 | 1988 .39 |
| 1971 .44 | |
| 1973–74 .42 | **India** |
| 1976 .44 | 1956–57 .34 |
| 1979–80 .40 | 1964–65 .42 |
| 1981 .48 | 1967–68 .48 |
| | 1975–76 .41 |

**Thailand**

| | |
|---|---|
| 1962–63 .41 | **Nepal** |
| 1968–69 .43 | 1976–77 .50 |

In Thailand, in 1962–63, the Gini was very low at a time when the per capita income was US$125. At this time, Thailand was still very much a traditional Asian economy with a very limited spread of industrialization and farm commercialization. Similarly, Bangladesh had per capita incomes of less than US$100, with a rising Gini. The Ginis were highest in India, with a per capita income of US$80, in Sri Lanka with US$80, in the Philippines with US$140, and in Taiwan with US$145. These peak Ginis suggest that, if there were surveys in the period before these peak years, the Ginis may have been rising, as was true in Thailand, Bangladesh, India, Malaysia, and Hong Kong in surveys before the peak.

The tendency for Ginis to rise and then fall after the peaks may be indicative

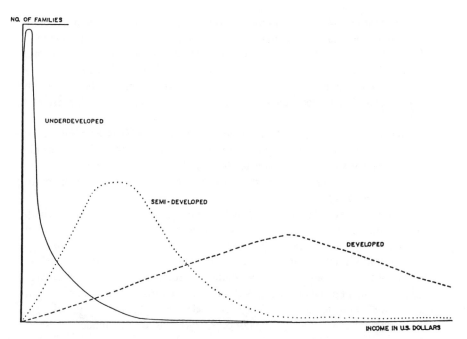

NO. OF FAMILIES

UNDERDEVELOPED

SEMI - DEVELOPED

DEVELOPED

INCOME IN U.S. DOLLARS

FIG. 9.2. Asia: income distribution by stage of development (stylized). *Source:* Harry T. Oshima and Bruno Barros "Trends in Growth and Distribution of Income in Selected Asian Countries," *Philippine Economic Journal* 15 (1976).

of a stylized, generalized curve for Asian countries, rising in the early period and then falling much earlier in terms of per capita income levels than in the West (figure 9.2). The curve is shaped like a small mountain, with a falling slope to the right of the peak. Kuznets designated the Western curve as a long swing; it was others who labeled it an inverted U curve. The Asian curve reaches a peak at per capita dollar incomes (in 1972 prices) under $1,000, most of them under $500, in contrast to the Western curve's $2,000 or so. At such a level of per capita income, Western economies had already become industrialized, with the industrialized sector employing more than twice the work force of the agricultural sector. In contrast, in 1950 agricultural employment was about three times industrial employment in Taiwan and six or seven times in South Korea.

Kuznets noted that he did not have enough data to ascertain whether there was a rising trend in the United States and other Western countries before World War I. "No adequate empirical evidence is available for checking this conjecture of a long swing in income inequality; nor can the phases be dated precisely."[10] But he noted that there was some evidence that, in the United States, England, and Germany, the widening inequality seemed to have started in the nineteenth century, especially around the middle of the nineteenth century. He thought that the rise and then fall in income inequality was related to the long swing in the population growth rate. The upward swing was due to a slowing in the death rate. The downward swing was due to a slowing in the birth rate. Rapid urbanization, migration, type of technology in the nineteenth vis-à-vis the twentieth century, and the low rate of national savings in the nineteenth century and higher rate in the twentieth century all contributed to the rise and fall.

The beginning portion of the Asian curve (figure 9.2) is also somewhat speculative, as data are not available for the prewar decades or for the decade after the end of World War II. The justification for assuming inequality to rise in the beginning is the assumption that the premodern, traditional distribution of income in Asia is fairly equal.

Thailand's 1962–63 rural income distribution curve (a very high, sharp mode at the extreme left and a short tail to the right) signifies the prevalence of self-subsisting peasants farming less than two hectares of land (typical in monsoon Asia), a much smaller number of middle-income peasants, who sell to urban markets, and an even smaller number of high-income people with large farms and other businesses (figure 9.3). Thailand's 1962–63 urban curve is flat, with a small mode to the right of the rural mode, a short tail to the right, close to the horizontal axis but above the tail of the rural curve. This mode represents

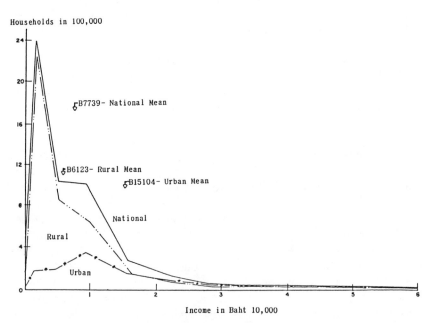

FIG. 9.3. Thailand: size distribution of household income, 1962 to 1963. *Source:* See Figure 9.2.

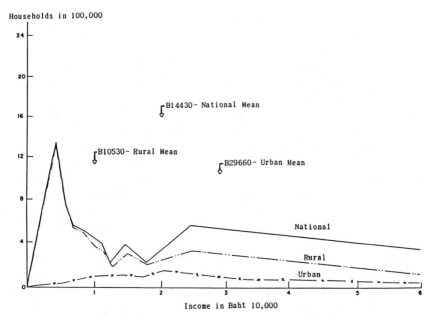

Fɪɢ. 9.4.  Thailand: size distribution of household income, 1968 to 1969. *Source:* See Figure 9.2.

proprietors of cottage industries and small stores and stalls, with their unpaid family helpers. The higher income groups are represented in the long tail and are the mercantile class (merchants, wholesalers, moneylenders), urban landowners, professionals, and public servants.

To get a notion of the relative size of the income groups, we can look at the Thai economy of 1937, when it was basically undeveloped. Nearly 90 percent of the labor force was in agriculture, fishing, and forestry; 3 percent was in manufacturing, mining, construction, and transport; and 7 percent was in commerce and services. At the end of World War II, the number of textile spindles amounted to only 10,000; at the end of 1968 there were 333,000.[11] Incomes were not highly unequal.

Figure 9.4 depicts income distribution in Thailand in 1968–69.

In a traditional economy, modern economic growth is likely to widen income disparity. If modernization begins in urban areas (especially large cities) with the introduction of modern industries, inequalities may rise because the already high incomes of mercantile and import-substitution industrial groups may increase faster than the incomes of those in old industries, and incomes in large cities will grow faster than those in small cities. In rural areas, the increase in demand for agricultural products will benefit farms near large cities, which are usually large and owned by people in the upper-income brackets. Thus only high-income groups in rural and urban areas are favorably affected by modernization: their share of total incomes rises, while the share of the lower income quintiles (those whose incomes remain unchanged) falls.

Modernizing may begin in rural areas. New agricultural technologies such as high-yielding cereal crops and plantation and industrial crops may raise the incomes of those adopting the new technologies. But at the outset, only a small group of farmers adopt them—those better situated vis-à-vis the market and those with the requisite physical and financial resources. These are likely to be farmers with large incomes, not the small, subsistence-level peasants located far from the market and government agencies. The upshot of this is that the share, if not the amount, of incomes of small peasants declines, while that of the upper-income brackets rises. As modernization proceeds, more farmers modernize, but the impact is still peripheral. Most peasants fail to take advantage of the improved cereal varieties and technologies due to lack of roads, irrigation, and other infrastructure, to insufficient credit and suitable land, to insufficient knowledge and information, and to insufficient government service extension and other assistance. Their income position may even worsen if, with a rising population, the size of their holdings declines. Accordingly, income inequality tends to worsen in rural areas.

In urban areas, the spread of modern technology (in protected, import-substituting industries) is not constrained by lack of infrastructure, capital, knowledge, institutions, and government assistance. If industrial growth is so rapid that the service and commerce sectors decline relative to the industrial sector, urban inequalities may lessen. Average income is highest in the commerce, public service, and professional service sectors. Moreover, these sectors are considerably larger than the industrial sector in terms of employment. A major reason for the high income in these sectors is the low proportion of employees per proprietor or manager compared with modern industries in manufacturing. In factory industries, large skilled and unskilled work forces are brought together in large establishments, supervised by a few proprietors or managers. Traditional services and traditional industries are conducted in small shops, stores, and offices, usually on a family basis.

Industry in the twentieth century has tended to equalize income in the urban sector, because its electric-powered machines tend to eliminate the simplest processes and skills—usually low-paying jobs. Because of the greater productivity of machine production, modern industry can pay higher wages to its employees than can cottage industries and other nonmechanized industries. On the other hand, it replaces by its own handling of marketing and distribution the mercantile proprietors who dominate marketing and financing for cottage and traditional industries.

Because Western industrial technologies (e.g., textiles, shoes, food canning, wood products, household utensils) are more adaptable than Western agricultural technologies, and because urban institutions are more flexible than agricultural institutions, income inequality diminishes earlier in urban areas than in rural areas. In sum, the slow modernization of rural areas, together with the difficulties in such rural institutions as tenancy and landownership, is responsible for the growing inequality in the nationwide distribution of income. Although urban inequalities may increase in the early stages of growth, the spread of modern industry soon stabilizes or reduces them. At some point, diminishing income inequalities in urban areas more than offset rising rural income inequalities. Then, nationwide inequalities begin to fall.

Western income inequalities were due to the industrial revolution of the nineteenth century. Besides the displacement of the rural population with the enclosure of large farms, the destruction of handicrafts resulted in extensive unemployment in urban areas, and steam-powered technologies generated a proletariat doing menial, unskilled jobs in factories. Property incomes rose. Asian countries, with the exception of Japan, came too late to industrialization to be affected by the first industrial revolution.

In the twentieth century, with the spread of the technologies of the second industrial revolution—with its small and numerous machines—Western inequalities fell as farms and industries mechanized. This eventually brought Western inequalities below Asian levels. Asia's industrialization was much slower, especially in the first half of the twentieth century—with the exception of Japan, which eventually caught up with the West toward the end of the twentieth century.

Income distribution data for seventeen Western industrialized countries in the latter 1970s and early 1980s show that their average Gini coefficient was about 20–25 percent lower than the average of twelve Asian countries.[12] Japan's Gini was lower than most Western countries, the exceptions being Belgium and the Netherlands, very small countries with limited regional heterogeneities. In contrast, Australia, a large country relative to the size of its population, has the highest Gini among industrialized countries. Although there is some resemblance to Kuznets's hypothesis of upward and downward swings of inequality, the timing of the peak in terms of per capita dollar incomes in Asian countries is different. Because the peak occurred when Asian economies were predominantly agricultural, the forces and mechanism by which inequalities fell in Asia differed from those of the West.

## THE LONG SWINGS IN ASIAN INCOME INEQUALITY

### East Asia (Excluding Japan)

Taiwan has the lowest income inequality in Asia and one of the lowest in the capitalist world.[13] Inequality probably rose in the late 1940s with the entry of large numbers of refugees from China, which increased population by 10 percent and raised unemployment. The decline in inequality started in the early

1960s with a successful rural development program that raised farm income nearly to the level of nonfarm income with land reform, irrigation, multiple cropping, mechanization, improved seeds, credit, farmers' associations, extension services, and marketing institutions. Tenancy as a legacy from the prewar colonial period was reduced from 44 percent in 1948 to 17 percent in 1960. Off-farm employment for farm families began to rise in the 1970s. Rural unemployment and underemployment were wiped out, and the farm Gini fell from a low of .32 in 1966 to .28 in 1970.

In the urban sector, Ginis fell from .32 in 1966 to .20 in 1974 due to the growth of labor-intensive industries (especially food, textiles, and garments). These industries were protected in the 1950s but became efficient in the later 1960s and were able to export. The mechanization of industry reduced the number of low-paid unskilled workers, and with full employment, marginal and menial service workers, such as domestics, found other employment. Sustained full employment raised the wages of unskilled workers in construction and services, and labor shortages enabled housewives to obtain employment, raising the number of earners in low-income households.[14] In the 1980s, income inequality tended to rise with the establishment of capital-intensive industries (steel, cement, petrochemicals) and the expansion of the service sector (banks, real estate, and business services).

Land reform and labor-intensive industrialization began in South Korea in the 1950s. Both of these expanded employment opportunities and kept income inequalities low in the 1950s and into the 1960s. South Korea began to shift to capital-intensive industrialization in the 1970s and neglected rural development, small industries, and services, since it channeled all its resources to the heavy industry sector. Wages and salary differentials widened as the demand by capital-intensive industries for skilled workers rose and the demand by smaller firms for unskilled workers fell. This situation continued into the 1980s, and South Korea was unable to wipe out unemployment until the late 1980s. In addition, the severe shortage of capital kept interest rates high because the credit needs of the smaller enterprises could not be satisfied.

The South Korean and the Taiwan experiences show that the early decline in the Gini is related to the development of small farms and labor-intensive industries. A policy of heavy industrialization, with neglect of the farm sector, raises the Gini.[15]

Since agriculture was not important in the city-states, Hong Kong and Singapore depended on full employment to reduce inequalities. This was readily accomplished by accelerating industrial exports, which expanded job opportunities in the export sector. Workers from traditional and marginal services (domestic services, peddling, informal eating places, and low-paying handicrafts) shifted to modern industrial sectors, where wages were higher. With sustained full employment into the 1970s and 1980s, the demand for female

workers rose, enabling housewives to find jobs in the factories. Female participation rates rose from 37 percent in 1961 to 44 percent in 1977 in Hong Kong,
and from 30 percent in 1970 to 47 percent in 1980 in Singapore. The wages of
unskilled workers rose faster than those of skilled workers, as labor shortages
occurred and mechanization accelerated.

### Southeast Asia

In Malaysia, the Gini rose in the 1960s as a result of policies to speed up
industrialization after Malaysia's separation from Singapore. Modern infrastructures were built in the major cities, to which factories, financial and trading
firms, and government offices moved. The population of the ten largest cities
increased from 1.3 million to 1.9 million between 1957 and 1970, and the urban
Gini rose from .35 to .46. The largest enterprises were superimposed on the
small, traditional enterprises, creating a dual structure. The fall in the share of
the lowest income quintile from 15.7 percent to 11.7 percent was due to the
agricultural sector, in which rural development policies promoted large plantations (rubber and palm oil) and large farms (sugar, cocoa, tapioca, maize). The
income generated by large urban firms and large farms rose faster than other
income.[16] The main beneficiaries were the British plantations and the urban
Chinese, not the Malay peasants.

In an effort to reverse these tendencies and bring down the Gini, new policies
were adopted in the early 1970s. Farmland was hacked out of forests and
distributed to the Malay peasants; by 1983, 250,000 hectares were made available. Industrial estates and export zones were established in an effort to disperse
industries, thus creating jobs for rural families. Irrigation was provided to farms
in the north for multiple cropping. These were targeted to poor farmers and the
unemployed to raise the income of the lowest income group. Primary health
care, universal primary education, and low-cost housing were also provided,
contributing to the decline in the Gini in the latter 1970s and into the 1980s.

In Thailand, income disparities fell slightly in 1975–76, rose in 1980–81,
and declined in 1988. The slight fall in 1975–76 may not be statistically
significant as a trend, considering the year-to-year fluctuations of the Gini (as
may be seen in the Japanese experience) and the crudeness of the data.[17] The
Thai economy grew slowly in the 1950s. Growth speeded up in the 1960s,
when modern physical infrastructure (modern roads, concrete buildings, public
utilities) were more widely available. Modern industry and services were introduced into the Bangkok-Thonburi area, generating much higher incomes than
in the traditional handicrafts and services of other parts of Thailand, making for
regional income disparities. In addition, agriculture rapidly commercialized,
especially near Bangkok. Only 9 percent of farms used chemical fertilizers in
1963. This usage had tripled by 1969, and exports of agricultural products rose

50 percent as exports of maize and sugar tripled.[18] Tenancy also increased, as the ratio of rented land to total holdings rose from 3.6 percent in 1963 to 11.9 percent in 1971.[19]

But most parts of Thailand away from the cities and large rivers were unaffected by the commercialization of agriculture and remained basically subsistence economies with low incomes. The Gini rose to a peak of .47 in 1985–86. Agricultural prices fell, affecting especially the northeast, while Bangkok incomes rose. Unemployment rose from 0.9 percent of the labor force in 1980 to 3.5 percent in 1986. In 1988, with prices improving and unemployment falling, the Gini fell. With the further fall of unemployment and underemployment after 1988, and with the approach to full employment in 1990, a further fall in Gini may be expected. The exceptional feature underlying the Thai trend in income disparity is the extreme concentration of the industrial and service sectors in Bangkok, the only major city in Thailand. Bounded on the west, north, and east by land, Thailand's only coastline is in the south, near Bangkok. Incomes were lowest in the northeast and north, with their poor soils and little water. Regional development has thus been uneven.[20]

Income data for Indonesia up to 1978 are based on household expenditure surveys, which show increasing income inequality in the 1960s and 1970s due to the rapid rise of modern industries and services, most of which were highly protected.[21] Nonagriculture production tripled between 1960 and 1975, compared to a 50 percent increase in agricultural production. Public utilities, transport and communication industries, mining, manufacturing, construction, petroleum companies, commerce, banking, and government all grew. These were superimposed on handicraft industries of low productivity, and most were located in Jakarta, where the average income rose two or three times more than in rural areas, so that regional disparities increased.

Because of the severe land shortage in densely populated Java, there was increased land tenancy and landlessness in the 1960s and 1970s, as population growth accelerated. Tenants increased from under half a million in 1973 to more than two million in 1980. Migration to the cities grew, but jobs were scarce. The inflation of the 1960s and 1970s may have hurt low-income groups more than upper-income groups, with falling real wages. The reduction in Indonesian income disparities in the 1980s may have been due to improved agricultural production, with the use of high-yielding rice seeds, the extension of modern industries and commerce to other parts of Indonesia, and the reduction in unemployment and underemployment—especially the latter, which dropped from 38 percent of the labor force in 1980 to 13 percent in 1986. From about the mid-1980s, efforts were made to reduce regulations and move to a more open economy.

The Philippine trend is the most puzzling. No country in Asia has shown a trend as stable and unchanging (almost a straight line), even though there are few countries in Asia with so much economic and political instability. There may be problems in the data, since the 1985 and 1988 surveys were conducted on a small budget, permitting only two survey rounds, one in July (covering the first six months) and another in January (covering the last six months). The usual practice is to conduct four rounds, one for each quarter, since it is difficult for respondents to recall what their incomes and expenditures were for a six-month period. This may be the reason why only about half of personal income (as estimated from the national accounts) was reported, while in Taiwan and South Korea, surveys covered 80 percent or so. Large surveys in the 1970s (not comparable with the 1960s and 1980s surveys) show higher disparities.[22] It may be speculated that there was a rise in inequality in the 1950s, after independence came in the mid-1940s. Land was increasingly concentrated in the hands of landlord groups, accompanied by increasing tenancy and landlessness. Capital-intensive industries protected by import substitution policies were established by U.S. businesses and Filipino landlords, who also moved into banking and other financial ventures.

### South Asia

The fall in income inequality in Bangladesh during the early years of separation from Pakistan probably reflects its greater stability after the disorganization caused by the war of independence. The rise in inequality from 1968–69 to its peak in 1976–77 was the result of unemployment and a fall in real wages in the rural sector due to the concentration of landownership. Inequality was reduced after 1977, as employment increased with the growth of cottage industries, public works, higher cropping intensities, and expanding farm acreage.

Income distribution became more equal in Sri Lanka in the 1960s and 1970s because of the adoption of extensive welfare policies, which benefited idle workers, the sick, and the old, while subsidies reduced the cost of education and housing. Its rural development program was moderately successful in distributing land, credit, and the building of infrastructure. But income inequalities rose in the 1980s with the reduction of welfare benefits, greater unemployment, and civil strife.

In India, policies promoting heavy industrialization adopted by Nehru in the late 1950s benefited only those employed by big industries and their suppliers. These heavy industries failed to create jobs but drained public resources away from agriculture and small industries. In the late 1970s and into the 1980s, income inequality fell as small farmers increased their share relative to large and medium-sized farmers. Several Indian states enacted minimum wage laws for the agricultural sector, and this raised the share of agricultural wages. Such laws benefited landless farm workers with the lowest incomes.

### Japan

Unlike other Asian countries, Japan began to modernize and move into industrialization in the late nineteenth century. Accordingly, the Japanese income trends resemble those of the West, with a long upward swing from the 1890s to the 1940s and a downward swing after World War II. According to various estimates brought together by Professor Toshiyuki Mizoguchi of Hitotsubashi University, income inequality began to rise around the time Japan began to industrialize in the late nineteenth century and up to the 1940s.[23]

Inequality between the agricultural and nonagricultural sectors began to widen in the 1890s. After feudalism, Japan entered the modern era with land reform, but heavy taxes levied on farmlands contributed to indebtedness and loss of land by farmers. With rice prices low, income inequalities within the farm sector rose in the 1920s and 1930s. Inequality increased among nonagricultural families because of widening wage differentials between skilled and unskilled workers. The establishment of heavy industries raised the demand for—and the wages of—skilled workers, who were in short supply. But due to the rise of population and the migration of rural workers, there was a surplus of unskilled workers, which prevented their wages from rising. Income differentials among regions may have increased with the introduction of modern industry in the major cities and with the inadequate network of roads and other infrastructure in the pre–World War II period.

In the postwar period, Japan started with low income disparities because of a series of institutional changes (land reform, democratic industrial relations, unionization of labor, *zaibatsu* dissolution). There were tendencies toward rising inequalities in the 1950s, but with the disappearance of labor surpluses in the 1960s, this tendency disappeared. Full employment contributed to income equalization by reducing wage differentials, since small firms had to raise wages to retain their workers. Labor shortages in urban areas forced firms to move to rural areas, creating employment opportunities for members of farm families. The mechanization of farming accelerated, freeing male workers to take off-farm jobs. Except for a temporary rise in disparities during the recession years of 1970–71, they have been stable at levels lower than in the West during 1970s and 1980s.

The long swing in Japanese income disparities resembled the Western experience, even though the peak was reached at an income level much lower than in the West. As in the West, the number of farmers and farm workers fell sharply in the 1960s, and income per farm worker rose faster than in industry with farm mechanization, multiple crops, and off-farm employment. In industry, there was a drop in the number of the lowest paid workers (day laborers and family workers) relative to total employees. With technologies imported from the West, mechanized work rapidly replaced handwork not only on small farms but in small firms in industry and services, thus raising the productivity of the lowest paid workers.

## Summary

There is a tendency for income inequality in Asia to rise to a peak and then fall. This peak is reached much earlier in the development stage in Asia than it is in the West, where a fall in income inequality began in the 1920s, after per capita incomes had passed US$2,000. In Asia, the peak was reached well before US$1,000, when the agriculture sector was predominant. Hence the forces and mechanism in Asia were different from those in the West. In Asia, agriculture led the way; in the West, industry did.

It was fortunate that the decline in inequality started early in the postwar period, because it enabled economic growth to proceed without much political and social instability. South Korea became very unstable as income inequality rose in the 1980s. Falling inequality means a lower incidence of poverty.

## THE INCIDENCE OF POVERTY

A cross-country comparison of poverty incidence in different countries depends on data based on a uniform definition of poverty. The World Bank in 1985 defined *poverty* as US$275 per capita annual income for the very poor and US$370 per capita for the poor.[24] The proportion of the population who are poor and very poor is 20 percent in East and Southeast Asia, 51 percent in South Asia, 42 percent in sub-Sahara Africa, 31 percent in Middle East and North Africa, and 19 percent in Latin America and the Caribbean.

The United Nations defines *poverty* as "that income line below which a minimum nutritionally adequate diet plus essential nonfood requirement are not affordable."[25] It shows poverty incidence in Asia during 1980–88 as lowest in East Asia and highest in South Asia. Poverty incidence in East Asia was highest in South Korea, at 16 percent of total population. In Southeast Asia it was highest in the Philippines, with 51 percent. In South Asia it was highest in Bangladesh, with 86 percent. In most Asian countries, poverty incidence was higher in the rural areas than in the urban areas, with the exception of South Korea and Pakistan. Many of the urban poor were migrants from rural areas.

Rural poverty was highest in the Philippines, Indonesia, Bangladesh, India, and Nepal, countries where landless workers, tenants, subtenants, tribal groups, and coastal fishermen were large. Within each country, poverty followed an uneven pattern, with concentrations in certain provinces and regions. Poverty was highest in Bicol, Visayas, and parts of Mindanao in the Philippines, the north and northeast regions of Thailand, and in Bihar, Uttar Pradesh, West Bengal, and Orissa in India.

The major factor associated with decline in poverty is the growth of GDP per capita, which generates jobs, and the growth of productivity, which raises wages and other incomes. With the sustained growth of GDP per capita, jobs are created for the unemployed labor force, and in due time even unskilled workers obtain jobs. When full employment is approached, attained, and sustained, wages of even the lowest paid workers rise, and families in the lowest income bracket benefit. Thus improvements in the employment and income of the lowest income groups reduce the incidence of poverty.

Besides income and employment growth, other forces contribute to the reduction of poverty, especially in the long run. A slowdown in population growth reduces poverty, because the poor tend to have larger families. An increase in education and skills and an improvement in nutrition and health contribute to the employability and productivity of the lower income groups. Thus the lower incidence of poverty, and even its eradication in East Asia, are related to its higher GDP, lower population growth, and higher life expectancies and literacy.[26]

Poverty incidence generally fell in all Asian countries, as shown in the following list.[27]

**Korea**

|  |  |
|---|---|
| 1965 | 41% poverty |
| 1970 | 23% |
| 1976 | 15% |
| 1980 | 5% |
| 1982 | 8% |

**Singapore**

|  |  |
|---|---|
| 1953–54 | 19% |
| 1972–73 | 7% |
| 1977–78 | 2% |
| 1982–83 | 3% |

**Thailand**

|  |  |
|---|---|
| 1962–63 | 57% |
| 1968–69 | 39% |
| 1975–76 | 31% |
| 1980–81 | 23% |
| 1985–86 | 30% |
| 1988 | 25% |

**Malaysia**

|  |  |
|---|---|
| 1970 | 49% |

|  |  |
|---|---|
| 1975 | 44% |
| 1976 | 40% |
| 1980 | 29% |
| 1983 | 30% |
| 1984 | 18% |
| 1985 | 24% |
| 1987 | 17% |

**India**

|  |  |
|---|---|
| 1972 | 54% |
| 1977 | 50% |
| 1983 | 43% |
| 1987 | 30% urban, 34% rural |

**Pakistan (rural)**

|  |  |
|---|---|
| 1963–64 | 45% |
| 1968–69 | 46% |
| 1969–70 | 36% |
| 1971–72 | 43% |

**Hong Kong**

|  |  |
|---|---|
| 1971 | 21% |
| 1976 | 14% |

**China**

| | |
|---|---|
| 1979 | 27% |
| 1986 | 11% |
| 1988 | 14% |

**The Philippines**

| | |
|---|---|
| 1961 | 75% |
| 1965 | 67% |
| 1971 | 62% |
| 1985 | 58% |
| 1988 | 49% |

**Indonesia**

| | |
|---|---|
| 1970 | 57% |
| 1976 | 50% |
| 1978 | 48% |

| | |
|---|---|
| 1980 | 40% |
| 1984 | 34% |
| 1987 | 17% |

**Bangladesh**

| | |
|---|---|
| 1973–74 | urban 81%, rural 83% |
| 1981–82 | urban 66%, rural 74% |
| 1983–84 | urban 66%, rural 57% |
| 1985–86 | urban 56%, rural 51% |

**United States**

| | |
|---|---|
| 1960 | 22% |
| 1970 | 13% |
| 1978 | 11% |
| 1980 | 13% |
| 1985 | 14% |
| 1987 | 14% |

Data were not available for Sri Lanka, but it appears that poverty there fell until the early 1980s and rose thereafter because of the sharp rise in unemployment with the beginning of civil disturbances. Even though income disparities did not improve in some of the countries, poverty did decline in most countries. This is because the poverty cutoff was fixed in the earlier period, so that as long as there was some improvement in the lowest incomes, poverty incidence fell, even though the upper incomes might have risen faster. It is not unusual for growth to favor upper-income groups over the low-income groups when there is high unemployment. Below, details of the trend in poverty are analyzed for each country. For East Asia, as recent poverty data are not available, reasons are given for the view that poverty may have been eradicated by 1990.

*East Asia*

Poverty incidence in Japan and Hong Kong was reduced substantially with full employment in the 1950s. In Hong Kong, emigration from China was under control by the 1950s, but in the 1960s emigration began to increase, and unemployment in 1975 rose to a peak of 9 percent of the labor force. Nevertheless, poverty fell sharply from 1963–64 to 1973–74. The factors behind this were (1) the export boom, which raised real wages in each industry, (2) structural shifts to higher income industries and higher occupations, (3) increased numbers of earners per family, with the increased availability of jobs for women and the young, and (4) the shift from short-term, casual, and seasonal employment to longer term employment.[28]

The quality of employment in Hong Kong improved with a tightening of the labor market due to better paying industries, higher level occupations, more permanent jobs, rising real wages, and more employment for women and the young. Thus the relation between poverty and employment goes beyond unemployment rates, which may rise—as they did in Hong Kong in 1975 to a record 9 percent. The explanation for this lies in the fact that poverty is a household phenomenon. Though unemployment may be rising, if the labor force is growing rapidly, employment is also likely to be rising, and earners per family stay the same and bring home larger incomes.

In the 1980s Hong Kong, like other East Asian countries, was faced with severe labor shortages. It brought workers from China and the Philippines, an indication that even the lowest paid Hong Kong workers were too affluent to take the lowest paying jobs. When maids are difficult to hire, full employment is reached and poverty is reduced. Maids come from the poorest families, and housework is low paying, with long hours spent away from home. As jobs become plentiful, housewives among middle-class families are able to find good jobs, and the demand for maids rises, although at the same time women from poor homes are able to find better jobs than housework.[29]

In Japan the number of families spending more than 50 percent of their incomes on food (the Engel coefficient) fell from half of all families in 1955 to a fourth in 1960. Japan, unlike urban Hong Kong, had first to solve the problem of rural poverty, which was extensive in the prewar period. This was done by comprehensive land reform in the late 1940s, which gave land, credit, and services to farmers. More work became available in the dry months. Peasant incomes grew rapidly in the 1950s not only because of these jobs but also because of the increased productivity resulting from greater use of fertilizer and insecticides and the mechanization of plowing and harvesting. By 1960 only 2 percent of farm households spent more than 50 percent of their income on food, compared to 34 percent in nonfarm households. Farming incomes were higher than nonfarm incomes.

In the 1960s and 1970s, the development of heavy industries and technology-intensive industries in Japan generated jobs that were better paying than those in the labor-intensive industries of the 1950s. Poverty was also reduced as higher wages and jobs in higher paying industries and occupations became available. Earners per family rose as more female members joined the work force. Low-paying jobs could not be filled by local workers, who could find better positions. Sustained full employment produced labor shortages. Foreign workers came from lower income countries as the jobs of local workers were upgraded.

Poverty is reduced rapidly after full employment is reached. If growth proceeds on a full-employment path long enough, poverty can be virtually wiped out. After a prolonged period of extremely low unemployment, as in Hong Kong during the 1960s and the first half of the 1970s, a slight increase in unemployment rates, as in Hong Kong in the 1980s, is not likely to make any impact on poverty incidence, because of accumulated savings, other wealth accumulation, and social security benefits. Between 1976 (when 14 percent were reported to be poor) and 1988, per capita incomes in Hong Kong more than doubled.[30]

Taiwan reached full employment in 1968, when unemployment and under-employment fell to 2 percent. Both the proportion of the poor and the poverty index peaked in 1968; they began to fall with full employment, until 1973, when they began to rise. Unemployment reached its lowest level in 1973 and then began to rise.[31] Taiwan attained full employment in the late 1960s, about the time when the multiple-cropping index rose to 1.9 crops per hectare. This high level of cropping generated jobs not only in agriculture but also in non-agriculture through higher rural purchasing power for urban production. Taiwan grew with the tight labor market it had had since 1968, and wages rose rapidly as capital-labor substitution accelerated (as in the case of Japan a decade earlier). By 1988, the lowest decile of families was receiving US$5,000 per year, nearly fourteen times the poverty cutoff of US$370. In 1975, poverty incidence was 10 percent, only 25 percent of households owned color television sets, and only 40 percent owned washing machines; by 1987, only 4 percent did not have TVs and 80 percent had washing machines.[32]

Singapore and South Korea attained full employment somewhat later than Japan, Taiwan, and Hong Kong, mainly due to the political confusion in Singapore in the 1950s and the war in Korea. But Singapore caught up through a massive public housing and infrastructure program, which generated jobs for the unemployed and provided housing for slum dwellers. Poverty incidence in Singapore declined sharply in the 1970s as a result of accelerated employment generation, which reduced unemployment by nearly half and put the economy on a full-employment path in the late 1970s. Average weekly earnings in all industries, including construction, doubled during the 1970s, as productivity rose. In the 1980s, except for 1985 and 1986, Singapore's GDP grew at 8–9 percent per year, so that poverty by the end of the 1980s was probably eradicated.

The ravages of the Korean War set back economic progress by half a decade, but later growth enabled South Korea to catch up by the end of the 1970s, when unemployment fell to 3 percent. Unemployment increased to 5 percent during the global recession of 1980, but rapid progress later whittled this down to the record low of 2.5 percent, attained in 1988. South Korea's slower progress in poverty eradication, compared to Taiwan, was also due to its premature shift into a whole range of costly heavy industries in the 1970s, which left few resources for developing irrigation and other rural infrastructure for agriculture, thereby retarding the growth of diversified agriculture and the reduction of unemployment. Thus in the period 1977–86, poverty incidence was 17 percent.

After 1985, when full employment was reached, real wages rose at a rate of 6 percent per year, and poverty incidence probably fell below the 5 percent level of 1982. By 1986, the lowest income families were earning about twice the

US$370 cutoff. Between 1986 and 1989, South Korean GDP grew at the unprecedentedly high rate of 11 percent, generating greater employment in lower income families.

China achieved low levels of poverty even with low per capita incomes. That is to say, China reduced poverty not by growth but by redistribution. Under Mao, there was a drastic reduction in income disparities through the establishment of uniform urban incomes, land reform and farm collectivization, guaranteed employment, and other policies. In the 1980s under Deng's administration, peasants were allowed to move out of their villages, unlike under Mao, and were encouraged to supplement their agricultural incomes by working in towns and rural industries. Off-farm incomes rose rapidly. Poverty incidence in the very large rural sector fell by more than half between 1979 and 1986, as peasants found additional sources of income to supplement their agricultural incomes.[33]

Besides vigorous growth and job creation, other factors were favorable to poverty reduction. Population growth slowed in East Asia, including China, reducing the number of dependents in families at all income levels. Important also was the fall in income disparities during most of the period, contributing to better nutrition and to health and life expectancies. The establishment of mass public education early in the postwar decade meant that opportunities for literacy and skill training became available to lower income groups. Poor families benefited from all these, and in turn, more jobs and training increased the productivity of the poor.

### Southeast Asia

Poverty incidence in Southeast Asia is the lowest in Malaysia, which has the highest per capita income. (Indonesia's incidence is as low as Malaysia's, but Indonesia's income cutoff is much lower.) Malaysia's daily caloric supply of 2,700 calories per capita places it at a level not far from the 2,800 level of East Asia. Malaysia's poverty incidence declined impressively, from 49 percent in 1970 to 17 percent in 1987. By 1984 it was down to 18 percent, as unemployment fell from 7.5 percent of the labor force in 1970 to 3.6 percent in 1983. It rose to 24 percent in 1985, when the recession pushed up unemployment rates to 6.7 percent. GNP growth accelerated toward the end of the 1980s, and unemployment began to fall.

Poverty levels in Malaysia are low due to a number of factors. Rural underemployment is low, because there is a minimonsoon in the early months of the year, which together with summer rains brings enough water to sustain perennial crops, such as rubber and palm oil trees. Malaysia is not as densely populated as other Asian countries, and agricultural land per farm population is one of the largest in Asia. Accordingly, Malaysia's farm sector is one of the richest and most productive in monsoon Asia. Malaysia's human development index is the highest in Southeast Asia.

In the 1970s and early 1980s, the Malaysian government generated work for rice peasants by double cropping through irrigation and drainage programs, by expanding the size of farms through land clearing and resettlement, and by establishing about a hundred industrial estates and free-trade zones with infrastructure to attract local and foreign enterprise, especially in textiles and electronics. Fertilizer and rice prices were subsidized for rice peasants, the ownership of boats and modern equipment for deep-sea fishing was promoted, the replanting, rehabilitation, and intercropping of small coconut farms were encouraged; extension, processing, marketing facilities, and credit assistance were made available to all farmers.[34]

Although unemployment continued to be high (about 8 percent even in 1988), more than 70 percent of the unemployed were young high school and university graduates under twenty-five years old and most of them were jobless for less than a year. Those unemployed for more than three years composed only 5 percent of the total unemployed. Thus the impact of unemployment on poor families was not large, and poverty fell. In addition, efforts were made to shift the educational emphasis from academic to vocational and technical education, while inservice training was encouraged through a double tax deduction incentive scheme.[35] The low poverty in Malaysia was also related to the virtual absence of tenancy, since land was plentiful.

In Thailand, poverty has declined over the decades, with the exception of 1985–86, when unemployment rose, and the first half of the 1980s, when poverty rose because of the oil shocks (slowing down GNP growth) and the 1981–86 decline in farm prices. The rise in poverty incidence in 1985–86 was only in the rural sector; it continued to fall in the Bangkok area.[36] Unemployment has been low in Thailand for some time; as a result, poverty has declined in Bangkok, since unemployment is largely an urban phenomenon. The poverty of the rural sector is concentrated mainly in the northeast and north, where the lack of irrigation during the dry months leaves many without work. Underemployment among the Thai labor force is very large, as much as 20 percent of the labor force.[37]

Thailand's Fifth National Economic Plan (1982–86), aimed at alleviating rural poverty by generating jobs during the dry season through rural public works, created some 1.2 million jobs through 160,000 projects.[38] But this effort was not enough to counteract the sharp decline in farm prices, and poverty incidence rose to 29 percent in 1985–86. The Sixth Plan (1987–91) attempted to create off-farm jobs by promoting light industries in the rural area. Poverty alleviation was further boosted by the improvement of farm prices and exports in 1987. Employment opportunities rose as a large number of foreign enterprises came to Bangkok, and GDP accelerated to 10 percent in 1987–89.

Thailand's fertility rate and population growth are the lowest in Southeast Asia, while its human development is almost as high as Malaysia's.

The Philippines began the postwar era with a rebellion of poor peasants, most of whom were tenants and landless workers. The roots of poverty in that country date back to the Spanish period, when the landed oligarchy emerged with the takeover of land from the free peasants, forcing them into various types of tenancy. By 1948, 27 percent of the arable land was cultivated by tenants.[39] Population grew rapidly as poor peasants tried to increase their incomes in the only way they could—with a larger number of children to earn money and to offset high infant mortality rates. The surplus population moved into the cities, but jobs there were difficult to find, because the highly protected, inefficient, capital-intensive industries failed to expand. With GDP growth rates averaging 6 percent in 1965–80, it is plausible to have expected the poverty incidence to have declined before 1980. But in 1985 it continued to decline after a series of low growth years, perhaps because of the decline in income inequality. During 1982–85, average growth was −1.6 percent per year (−6 percent in 1984 and −4.3 percent in 1985), with unemployment and underemployment reaching double-digit levels.

With the improvement in employment and income, poverty incidence fell from 59 percent in 1985 to 49 percent in 1988. Incomes increased 12.5 percent in real terms over 1985 for the nation as a whole, and for every region the share of wages and salaries in total incomes rose from 30.6 percent to 36.3 percent. The Engel coefficient (food expenditures) declined from a share of 51.9 percent in 1985 to 50.8 percent in 1988, with a larger decrease in rural than in urban areas.[40] The real growth rate of GDP rose from a −4.3 percent in 1985 to 4.7 percent in 1987 and to 6.4 percent in 1988. Underlying the improvement in income was the decline in unemployment, which fell from 12.1 percent in 1985 to 8.5 percent in 1988. Underemployment fell in the second quarter of 1986 and throughout 1987 and 1988, in both urban and rural areas.[41] Average real family income and employment rose between 1985 and 1988 in Bicol, the region with the heaviest concentration of poor families, in the Visayas, and in western and central Mindanao.[42]

In Indonesia, poverty incidence has fallen consistently since 1970, when it was 57 percent. It declined to 27 percent in 1988, with income disparities falling sharply from a .49 Gini in 1976, to .45 in 1982, and .37 in 1987. Other factors were low unemployment in the 1970s and 1980s and the reduction of rural underemployment from 45 percent in 1976 to 13 percent in 1986. But poverty in Indonesia is too low relative to that of other Southeast Asian countries. The cutoff around US$100 is lower than Thailand's US$200 and Malaysia's and the Philippines' US$300. The most significant contribution to poverty alleviation was made by the rural development program in the 1970s and 1980s. Agricultural products grew by 4.2 percent per year between 1976 and 1984—the highest in East and Southeast Asia—with the use of high-yielding varieties and subsidized fertilizer. Employment grew by 3 percent during the 1970s, contributing nearly 30 percent to the increase in total employment.[43] Employment in both rural and urban construction projects increased during the dry season. Farm family women work in trade and service occupations when they are unable to work on the farms, and off-farm incomes have been rising. The increase in tree-crop production has also raised off-farm jobs through the expansion of processing industries. Migration from Java to the outer islands in the 1980s raised incomes of migrants, who found work on the larger farms outside Java.

The increased employment resulting from Indonesian rural development has been favorable to the lower income rural groups. A study of income distribution between 1969–70 and 1981 shows that the share of personal income of the lowest income groups (the bottom 40 percent in the rural sector) rose from 19.4 percent to 22.2 percent, while the share for the higher groups declined.[44] Further declines in poverty may be expected as foreign investments and the GNP growth rate continue to rise and population growth slows.

### South Asia

The incidence of poverty has generally fallen in most of the economies of South Asia, despite sluggish growth in this region and a large pool of idle workers. Poverty estimates are not available, but the exceptions may be Sri Lanka and Burma, where civil strife has disrupted economic activities. There is not much reliable information from Burma, but official estimates of per capita GDP growth indicate that it was zero from 1986 to 1988.

In Sri Lanka, GDP growth was only 1.5 percent, with unemployment rising from 13 percent in 1973 to 18 percent in 1986. In 1978 poverty incidence (households having less than 300 rupees per month at their disposal, regarded as the minimum needed to meet basic human needs) was 64 percent.[45] Poverty incidence probably fell during the decade 1963–73, when the Gini coefficient fell from .49 to .41 under extensive welfare policies, which included heavily subsidized food, medical care, housing, and transportation. But poverty incidence probably rose after 1981, with the Gini climbing to .49 in 1978–79 and then to .52 in 1981–82. Sri Lanka's Engel coefficient (the percentage of food purchases in total expenditures) rose from 52 percent in 1969–70 to 70 percent in 1981–82.[46]

It is not likely that Sri Lanka's poverty incidence has declined since 1981–82; its per capita food production index dropped from a peak of 102 in 1985 to 91 in 1988.[47] Sri Lanka has tried to overcome poverty with welfare policies to help low-income groups through handouts. These huge subsidies were financed through heavy taxation of British-owned plantations, which were left with little to invest and thus to create jobs with. Sri Lanka's inefficient industries (most of them government owned) have not generated much employment. Young people educated for white-collar jobs have refused to take blue-collar work, opting instead to live on unemployment relief payments. Thus welfare policies intended to eradicate poverty have also become the source of poverty.

No country in the world has more poor people living below the poverty line than India, with about a quarter of a billion poor. One can sense the severity of Indian poverty from the sight of masses of homeless, hungry-looking, poorly dressed, barefoot people living in the streets of Indian cities. The rural poor spill over into the cities, arriving as squatters and later becoming slum dwellers. Without land reform, the villages are dominated by the landed oligarchy, and the dispossessed become landless workers, who eventually end up in the cities. But urban jobs are scarce, as too many resources have been put into capital-intensive, poorly managed large industries.[48] Most of these poor find low-paying casual or domestic work or take to hawking, peddling, cart pulling, shoe shining, and the like.

The rural poor, about four-fifths of the total poor, are uneducated, under-employed, or landless and spend about 70 percent of their income on food.[49] During the drought of 1986–87, agricultural production declined, but the decline was more than compensated for in 1988 by a bumper crop, suggesting that poverty declined substantially in 1988. The decline in poverty in the 1980s was largely the result of a shift to a liberalized, deregulated industrial policy and to greater attention to agricultural development.

The unemployment concepts used in Indian surveys are different from those in other countries' surveys. One study estimates that in 1983 unemployment and underemployment affected about a fourth of the labor force. An equally important factor underlying Indian poverty is the low productivity characteristic of those performing menial jobs in cities and on small farms. Since poverty incidence is much greater than unemployment or underemployment, it is the low-income levels of existing work that is responsible for the poverty of some of the population, especially tribal groups and the lower castes.[50]

Poverty incidence in Bangladesh rose in the 1960s and early 1970s, as unemployment climbed, but then it declined from a high of 82 percent in the early 1970s to 52 percent in 1985–86. The fall in poverty was largely due to the drop in unemployment and underemployment, from as high as 41 percent of the labor force in 1973 to 12 percent in 1986. Income inequality has been falling since the late 1970s. But severe floods in 1987 and 1988 may have raised the poverty incidence, since the agricultural production index fell from 114 in 1986 to 109 in 1988, with agricultural GDP dropping from 39.3 billion taka in 1986 to 38.4 in 1988.[51]

Jobs were generated in Bangladesh through the construction of infrastructure for agriculture and through public works and food programs. In addition, rising agricultural productivity increased acreage and cropping intensity, and higher real wages for unskilled workers in agriculture and industry raised purchasing power and demand for the products of cottage and service industries. Increased employment and wages affected day laborers and others below the poverty cutoff, including female workers heading the poorest households—and who are badly discriminated against.[52] All this has contributed to the expansion of employment in handicraft and service occupations.

Pakistan's poverty problems are less serious than those of other countries in South Asia. Lying outside the main monsoon zone, it is not as densely populated. The average size of a farm is around five hectares instead of the usual one or two hectares, and its wheat crop is much larger than its rice crop. Its rainfall is the lowest in Asia. Poverty in rural Pakistan fell throughout the 1960s and into the 1970s. Although we have no data for the 1980s, poverty may have risen in the first half of the decade, when unemployment and underemployment climbed. Such a rise would have been moderate, since Pakistan was better off through the first half of the 1980s than other countries in South Asia. For example, its average GDP growth rate of 7 percent between 1980 and 1986 was better than India's. Unemployment in Pakistan has been falling since 1985, and the country was a leading beneficiary of job openings in the Middle East during the late 1970s and early 1980s, when 6–7 percent of its labor force emigrated, remitting a portion of their earnings to Pakistan.

One of the highest poverty incidences is found in Nepal, which together with Bangladesh has the lowest per capita calorie supply, largely due to meager farmland.[53] Besides its meager natural resources, Nepal is hampered by a feudal land tenure system. Open unemployment is nearly 6 percent, and of the days available for work per family, 63 percent were underutilized in the rural sector and 45 percent in the urban sector. The Planning Commission of Nepal estimated poverty incidence to be 42 percent, using a per capita income of US$110. A figure of US$200 would mean an incidence of 60 percent, and if the poverty cutoff used for Malaysia were adopted, the figure would be higher than the average per capita income of the whole of Nepal. In the current plan, poverty eradication by the year 2000 through the extension of irrigation for increased multiple cropping and the development of labor-intensive industries are principal goals, along with a rural public works program. Under the present plan, Nepal has enjoyed greater success than in the past, with the economy growing at a rate of 4.7 percent between 1980 and 1987—or more than double the 2 percent figure for the previous decade.

CONCLUDING NOTES

An attack on poverty is one of the best ways to improve the distribution of income. Reducing poverty by raising GNP and employment, by slowing population growth, and by extending educational and health services will improve productivity. Thus a cycle is established whereby reduction of poverty and income inequalities slows population growth (with lower infant mortality and employment of housewives), raises employment and GNP through higher purchasing power, and improves income distribution.

As to policies, the East Asian experience is instructive. Because of rural poverty in Japan, Taiwan, and South Korea, where tenancy and landlessness were extensive, these countries in the early postwar era undertook comprehensive land reform (with supporting credit and extension services) and rural development (with the construction of roads, irrigation, drainage, electrification, and reforestation). These together with multiple cropping and off-farm employment eventually wiped out underemployment and poverty in the rural sector—for the first time in monsoon Asia. The rise in rural productivity raised rural purchasing power for the output of urban industries and lowered the cost of food for industrial workers.

Poverty is not only highest in the rural sector, but many of the urban poor originate in agriculture. Unable to find enough work in agriculture, the rural poor migrate to the cities. Hence, rural development can wipe out most of the nationwide poverty.

In urban areas, small and medium-sized industries, which are more labor-intensive and less skill-intensive than large firms, should be promoted. Not only should trade and industrial policies discriminating against such industries be abolished, but policies should be enacted to assist them. Frequently, the poor remain unemployed because they do not have the skills that new jobs require. Vocational and technical training should be given in the public high schools and in training centers for youths not attending school. Adult education courses and on-the-job-training are also helpful.

The fall in poverty in several countries of South and Southeast Asia should not make for complacency. Not only do the dollar cutoffs in the definitions vary, but they may be too low. Many of the cutoffs are based on an income level corresponding to total expenditure levels centered on a calorie intake of 2,100. As economies grow, they move into higher stages of development, with more sophisticated life-styles and consumption patterns. With greater commercialization, agricultural mechanization, urbanization, industrialization, and modernization, ways of working and living are transformed. With these changes, basic food needs go beyond carbohydrates and include meats, vegetables, and fruits; also needed are more and more varied clothing, household equipment, and such services as education, health, transport, and personal care. Some of these are required for urban work and living. Thus the basket of consumer goods and services required for a minimum level of living expands.

To be more useful for policy purposes, the poverty cutoff should be reviewed and upgraded from time to time. The old definition could be kept as a cutoff for the very poor and for time-series comparisons. For each region, new cutoffs should be adopted—for example, for East Asia, a per capita income of US$700, for Southeast Asia US$400, and for South Asia US$200. In the United States the cutoff is around US$11,000, and a debate is going on as to whether it should be raised. The new cutoffs depend on the extent of assistance that each country can afford to allocate to the poor, but higher levels may be justified by the rise of per capita income since the old levels were established.

Also for policy purposes, there may be a need to define poverty not only by income level but by the duration of this level. For those previously unemployed, higher incomes due to a year or two of transitional employment may not pull them out of the slums and other poverty conditions (as in the Philippines, when jobs became plentiful in 1988) if these persons lose their jobs the following year. And the lower incomes of farmers for one or two years due to falling farm prices may not make them poor (as in the case of Thai farmers in 1985–86) if prices rise in the following years. People can be tided over one or two bad years by their savings from good years, and their living standards can be more or less maintained.

# CHAPTER 10

# Toward the Pacific Century: The Role of Government

It is abundantly clear from the foregoing chapters that the role of government in Asian development is of utmost importance, especially during the agroindustrial transition. Even in the next transition, from industry to services, government's role will be important, as the East Asian experience shows. The exception there is Hong Kong, where government intervention was minimal; but even in Hong Kong, more involvement may have reduced earlier some of the undesirable features of its growth, such as dilapidated and crowded housing, traffic congestion, and long hours of work. If Hong Kong had had a good industrial policy, its shift to higher technology industry and away from textiles would have raised per capita income nearer to those of Japan—after all, Hong Kong began to export and grow as early as Japan—in the early 1950s.

But in an economy dominated by a highly sophisticated service sector, the role of government can be minimal, since services do not need to be regulated as much as industry, with its large wage-earning class and numerous small firms, nor do they need to be assisted, as agriculture does, with its large number of low-income and poor farmers. This is why, as economies develop to the level of the West, the role of the market begins to supersede that of the government. If this is so, the Singapore government intervened unnecessarily with labor regulations, social security, family planning, and nationalization.[1] Governments tend to intervene too much or too little, depending on the demands of the vested interests.

Governments in monsoon agriculture have a greater role to play than in other regions: land is scarce, and many farmers own little or no land, so agrarian reform is needed. Rents charged to tenants and interest rates on loans tend to be high, requiring regulation. But often governments fail to intervene, fearing the landowning class, which in India and the Philippines possess private armies. Irrigation is needed to supply water during the dry season, and drainage is needed in the wet season. Industry in monsoon Asia is characterized by large numbers of small firms, unlike Latin America or elsewhere. This is true even in Japan. To become efficient, these small firms need government help with credit, technology, marketing, and managerial advice.

During the early stages of the agroindustrial transition, there are other functions to be performed by government. Government is crucial in the construction of modern physical infrastructure, the import and supervision of technologies, the development of human and natural resources, the mobilization and channeling of savings, and the reduction of unemployment and poverty. Moreover, traditional institutions must be modernized, and the foundations of new organizations, such as labor unions, farmers' cooperatives, industrial and commercial associations, and banks, must be laid.

There are some who are impatient with the inefficiencies of government and want to shift to the market, which they consider the most efficient allocator of resources. But the market is only as efficient as the forces making up the market. It took some time for the West to evolve and nurture these forces.[2] Indeed, an important historical function of government in the process of development is to mold these forces so that the market becomes an efficient resource allocator. It is true that Hong Kong was able to grow with a laissez-faire government, but this was because it started early in the postwar era with a large number of very experienced Shanghai manufacturers, who spearheaded the early growth of Hong Kong.

One reason for the rapid growth of East Asian countries was the efficiency of their governments. Not only were their bureaucracies less corrupt than those in Southeast and South Asia, but they were more effective in raising productivity, in promoting saving, in generating employment through agricultural diversification, multiple cropping, and off-farm employment, and in developing human resources. In addition, they supplied the necessary urban infrastructures such as roads and public utilities (unlike Thailand), secured political and social stability (unlike the Philippines, Malaysia, Sri Lanka, and Burma), and motivated the populace to work energetically to develop the economy (unlike India, Bangladesh, and Indonesia). The governments of East Asia did all this without disturbing the market unduly or weakening market forces through excessive taxation (which Sri Lanka did). One reason for the better performance of their governments may be the influence of Confucianism, whose teachings are oriented to the proper behavior of bureaucrats and rulers. No similar political values can be discerned in the teachings of other Asian religions.

In this chapter, government expenditure patterns are analyzed. Government policies are then summarized. In the concluding section, the emerging Pacific century is viewed against the background of the present Atlantic century and its accomplishments.

## THE SHARE OF GOVERNMENT IN GROSS DOMESTIC PRODUCT

*Government share* is defined as the share of the total receipts of general government net of subsidies in GDP.[3] The United Nations publishes *A System of*

*National Accounts and Supporting Tables;* this account, on the current receipt side, shows the amounts taken directly or indirectly from GDP by the government through indirect taxes, income from property (net rent, interest, and dividends from government ownership of physical and financial assets), income from entrepreneurship (receivables from government enterprises), direct taxes (including social security contributions), current transfers from households and private nonprofit institutions (such as school fees, fines, and penalties), and current transfers from the rest of the world (such as cash and in-kind grants received from abroad for consumption purposes). It would have been desirable to leave out the last item (as it originates in foreign GDPs), but few countries report in-cash and in-kind gifts separately. In any case, the item is of minor importance for most countries (in the Philippines it is less than 0.1 percent of GDP). Subsidies paid out, as shown on the expenditure side of the consolidated government account, are subtracted from total receipts, since GDP at market prices excludes subsidies. Government current receipts minus subsidies as a percentage of GDP compose the GDP share going to the government. Items in the capital reconciliation accounts of the government are not flows from the current production of GDP and are left out of the share. In the next section, Asian governments' shares of GDP are shown and are compared with those of industrial countries, where it is widely believed that amounts of GDP taken by government are excessive and have an unfavorable impact on private activities.

On the other side of the consolidated government account (or the disposition of current receipts) are the current expenditures of government (wages and purchase of goods and services), subsidies, current transfers to households and abroad, and savings. The expenditures can be classified by function (such as general administration, defense, education, and health), and the data are used to determine which expenditures underlie the trend in government share.

To throw further light on the trend in the share, the productivity of government activities relative to the productivity in the private sector is looked at. If government productivity rises as rapidly as private productivity, the government share need not be as large. The trend in wages and salaries originating in public administration and defense is estimated, using data on income originating in industries shown in the supporting tables of the national accounts and data on employment in industries from population censuses and labor force surveys. A broader concept of government productivity is obtained by including employees in public schools and hospitals and dividing into employee compensation from the consolidated government account's government consumption expenditures.

Institutionally, general government comprises all central and local government agencies, including social security agencies, public schools, and hospitals, but not public enterprises selling goods and services, such as nationalized industries, the post office, housing authorities, and printing and publishing establishments. But to the extent that agencies produce exclusively for the government, such as its publishing arm and its statistical office, they are included in general government as auxiliary units. The distinction is often difficult to draw in practice, and the size of these agencies and their organizational and accounting structure may determine how they are classified. Although public enterprises are not part of general government, their surpluses (or deficits) are receivables included in the general government account. In industry's income and employment, only that part of general government confined to public administration and defense (as defined by the International Standard Industrial Classification system) is included. Employees in public education and hospitals are excluded.

One advantage in defining concepts within a system of national accounts is that it is easier to work out alternatives and proxies. If the consolidated government account is not worked out, as is the case in several Asian countries, total current receipts minus subsidies can be approximated by taking government consumption expenditures from the national account and adding to them current transfers from households and from the rest of the world and savings (or surplus on current account) from the budgets in the statistical yearbooks. For broader productivity estimates, government consumption expenditures can be divided by the public administration and defense, labor force, public school-teachers, and public hospital employees, as shown in statistical yearbooks. A still broader productivity estimate using total current revenue or total disposal of current revenue of general government is not possible, as there is no way to meaningfully deflate current transfers to households and to the rest of the world, net interest, and subsidies paid by general government—notwithstanding attempts to do so, using the consumer price and other indexes.[4]

### Trends in Government Share in GDP

The government share in GDP in Western countries rose slowly during the nineteenth century. It picked up after the 1910s, when these countries moved quickly into the second industrial revolution, whose technology called for increased expenditures for education, infrastructure, and the military. In 1938 and the early postwar years, government share in current prices was less than 20 percent in the following countries: Ceylon (19 percent in 1938 and in 1948–54), Indonesia (14 and 15 percent in 1938 and 1948–54, respectively), Burma (12 percent and 15 percent), Malaysia (14 percent in 1949–54), the Philippines (7 percent in 1948–54), and India (8 percent in 1948–54). Japan's share was 22 percent (1948–54). These Asian shares compare with those of the major industrialized countries (the United States and Europe) of 25 percent and over, and as high as 35 percent for the United Kingdom.[5]

For most Asian countries for which data were obtainable, the share of government receipts in GDP has been rising, as can be seen in table 10.1.

TABLE 10.1

Government Receipts in Gross Domestic Product, 1950s to 1980s (current prices)

| Country | Per Capita Gross National Product, 1988 (US$) | Per Capita Government Receipts, Early 1980s (US$)[a] | Government Receipts in Gross Domestic Product (percent) | | | |
|---|---|---|---|---|---|---|
| | | | 1950s | 1960s | 1970s | 1980s |
| Japan | 21,020 | 2,678 | 19.5 | 19.8 | 22.1 | 30.0 |
| Taiwan | 5,520 | 632 | 23.3 | 21.8 | 23.2 | 22.1 |
| South Korea | 9,000 | 363 | 13.7 | 17.8 | 17.1 | 24.3 |
| Singapore | 9,070 | 1,328 | | 17.7 | 21.8 | 27.0 |
| Philippines | 630 | 98 | 9.6 | 11.0 | 14.2 | 14.5 |
| Thailand | 1,000 | 100 | 10.5 | 13.8 | 13.6 | 14.2 |
| Malaysia | 1,940 | 615 | 14.0 | 26.9 | 26.6 | 33.1 |
| Indonesia | 440 | 130 | 15.0 | 7.1 | 19.9 | 23.7 |
| India | 340 | 47 | 8.0 | 9.0 | 16.4 | 17.3 |
| Sri Lanka | 420 | 72 | 18.4 | 21.2[b] | 20.2 | 21.7 |
| Bangladesh | 170 | 28 | | | 15.8 | 17.6 |
| Nepal | 180 | 12 | | 4.4 | 6.4 | 9.3 |

*Source:* Official national accounts and yearbooks; World Bank, *World Tables;* United Nations, *Yearbook of National Accounts;* World Bank, *World Development Report;* Asian Development Bank, *Key Indicators;* Donald Snodgrass, *Ceylon: An Export Economy in Transition* (New Haven: Economic Growth Center, Yale University Press, 1966).

[a] Government receipts divided by population and converted into dollar values using average exchange rates for the early 1980s.

[b] 1963–69.

Taiwan's high share of receipts in the 1950s was due to the large U.S. grants to help Taiwan maintain a huge military force against mainland China. In the 1950s, these grants were 5.5 percent of GDP, falling to 1.2 percent in the 1960s, and virtually disappearing to 0.04 percent thereafter. If these grants were left out, Taiwan's government share would also show an upward trend. Similarly, in South Korea, U.S. grants for military expenditures were 6.4 percent in the 1950s, 3.3 percent in the 1960s, and 0.2 percent thereafter; the upward trend in government share would have been more pronounced if the grants were left out. Hence, if we take, as in figure 10.1, not receipts (which include grants) but revenues, the trend is clearly upward in South Korea and Taiwan.

Japan's and Singapore's shares in the early 1980s were as high as those of Western European countries in the early 1950s, although Japan's share throughout the postwar decades and into the early 1980s was the lowest of all shares in the industrialized countries.

Indonesia's share was higher than those of the Philippines and Thailand, even though its per capita GDP was lower than theirs. Both Indonesia and Malaysia are oil-producing countries and receive large revenues from oil ex-

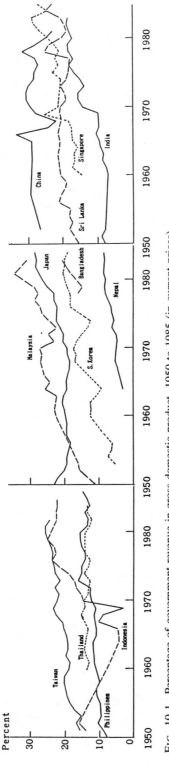

Fig. 10.1. Percentage of government revenue in gross domestic product, 1950 to 1985 (in current prices). *Source:* Official national accounts; United Nations, *Yearbook of National Accounts. Note:* Government revenue excludes transfers from the rest of the world.

ports and from their extensive export-oriented plantation sectors. Malaysia's share was the highest in all Asia in the 1970s and early 1980s, even though its per capita GDP was lower than those of East Asian countries.

In South Asia, the highest share was in Bangladesh, which has the lowest per capita GDP, while India had much higher shares than Sri Lanka despite lower levels of per capita GDP. This is in line with findings that the association of per capita GDP and government shares is not as strong as previously thought.[6]

In Sri Lanka, the upward trend was slight: In the 1950s, Sri Lanka spent large amounts on health, food subsidies, housing, transportation, and other welfare consumption. Because the British plantations (tea, rubber, and coconut) were highly efficient and profitable in the 1950s, the government paid for these large social expenditures by heavily taxing the plantations and their exports. Throughout the 1950s, this spending was about half of total current budget expenditures and led to large balance of payments deficits in the early 1960s, forcing the government to hold spending levels only slightly higher than 1950 levels.[7]

Government share of receipts rose in all Asian countries. East Asian countries spent less than receipts, generating surpluses in the 1980s, but South and Southeast Asian governments spent more than receipts.[8]

*The Functional Distribution of Current Expenditures*

In using the distribution of current government expenditures by function, the underlying assumption is that the demand for government services governs the share the government takes from current production. This may not always be the case, since some government services may be too costly, given expected revenues (as was the case of welfare expenditures in Sri Lanka in the 1970s and educational expenditures in the Philippines in 1987). On the other hand, even if revenues are expected to be more than expenditures, there must be a good justification for raising spending on a particular program. Without such a justification, excess revenues may go into savings, or become surpluses carried over to next year's budget, or used to retire debts.

Within the limits imposed by the GDP, there can be wide variations in government share, since the limits are flexible—a band rather than a line. South Korea and Malaysia have similar levels of per capita GDP but a large difference in shares; the same is true of Nepal and Bangladesh, and of Indonesia and the Philippines. Part of the explanation for these differences is the nature of the source of revenues. Indonesia and Malaysia have large revenues from oil exports, while South Korea, the Philippines, and Taiwan do not. Politically, it is more difficult to raise taxes from internal sources than from oil exports. Table 10.2 shows the distribution of government expenditures by function.

Sri Lanka's lack of a rise in government receipts after the 1950s is associated with a decline in social services and welfare spending from the 1970s. Such

TABLE 10.2

Government Expenditures, 1970s, 1980s (percent)

| Country | 1970 | 1972 | 1974 | 1976 | 1978 | 1980 | 1982 | 1984 | 1986 |
|---|---|---|---|---|---|---|---|---|---|
| **Japan** | | | | | | | | | |
| General public services | 27.6 | 27.5 | 26.8 | 27.2 | 27.1 | 26.9 | 26.5 | 26.4 | 27.1 |
| Defense | 9.9 | 9.7 | 8.7 | 8.4 | 8.5 | 8.6 | 8.7 | 9.2 | 9.4 |
| Education | 36.8 | 36.6 | 36.9 | 37.9 | 37.9 | 37.2 | 37.2 | 36.4 | 35.8 |
| Health | 4.5 | 4.3 | 4.4 | 3.9 | 3.6 | 3.8 | 3.9 | 4.3 | 3.7 |
| Social security and welfare | 3.9 | 4.2 | 4.8 | 4.8 | 4.9 | 5.0 | 5.2 | 5.2 | 5.7 |
| Housing and community amenities | 3.8 | 4.5 | 5.2 | 5.1 | 5.2 | 5.7 | 5.7 | 5.7 | 5.7 |
| Recreational, cultural, and religious affairs | 1.3 | 1.4 | 1.6 | 1.6 | 1.8 | 2.0 | 2.2 | 2.2 | 2.3 |
| Economic services | 12.0 | 11.5 | 11.5 | 10.8 | 10.6 | 10.5 | 10.2 | 10.2 | 9.8 |
| Other | 0.2 | 0.3 | 0.3 | 0.3 | 0.3 | 0.4 | 0.4 | 0.4 | 0.4 |
| **South Korea** | | | | | | | | | |
| General public services | 26.9 | 26.1 | 92.1 | 93.3 | 94.1 | 93.7 | 91.9 | 27.0 | 25.7 |
| Defense | 60.3 | 63.6 | | | | | | 42.5 | 43.6 |
| Education | 3.4 | 3.5 | 3.0 | 3.1 | 2.6 | 2.7 | 4.0 | 21.7 | 22.3 |
| Health | 0.8 | 0.7 | 0.5 | 0.5 | 0.5 | 0.5 | 0.4 | 1.5 | 1.4 |
| Social security and welfare | 1.6 | 1.1 | 0.9 | 0.7 | 0.8 | 0.6 | 0.6 | 1.7 | 1.8 |
| Housing and community amenities | 0.3 | 0.1 | 0.2 | 0.2 | 0.2 | 0.2 | 0.2 | 0.6 | 0.7 |
| Recreational, cultural, and religious affairs | 1.1 | 1.5 | 1.1 | 0.9 | 0.8 | 0.6 | 0.4 | 0.7 | 0.8 |
| Economic services | 5.7 | 3.3 | 2.4 | 1.4 | 1.0 | 1.7 | 2.5 | 4.3 | 3.7 |
| **Taiwan** | | | | | | | | | |
| General administration and defense | 56.6 | 53.9 | 51.4 | 55.3 | 55.0 | 53.2 | 40.0 | 46.4 | 44.5 |
| Justice and police | 4.8 | 4.1 | 4.4 | 5.0 | 4.7 | 4.5 | 5.2 | 6.2 | 6.5 |
| Education and research | 16.2 | 16.8 | 17.8 | 18.9 | 18.0 | 17.5 | 21.9 | 18.8 | 18.9 |
| Health | 1.5 | 1.7 | 1.8 | 2.3 | 2.3 | 2.4 | 2.6 | 2.4 | 2.4 |
| Social security | 2.3 | 2.3 | 2.7 | 3.0 | 3.2 | 2.4 | 5.3 | 16.0 | 15.2 |
| Economic development | 4.5 | 4.7 | 5.0 | 3.6 | 6.2 | 5.5 | 6.0 | 6.1 | 6.8 |
| Transport and communication | 1.4 | 1.4 | 1.5 | 1.4 | 2.6 | 1.8 | 1.7 | 2.4 | 3.1 |
| Other | 12.7 | 15.1 | 15.4 | 10.6 | 8.1 | 12.8 | 17.4 | 1.7 | 2.6 |
| **Thailand** | | | | | | | | | |
| General public services | 30.2 | 28.9 | 27.0 | 25.2 | 23.7 | 26.4 | 26.4 | 26.6 | 26.2 |
| Defense | 41.3 | 39.7 | 39.0 | 38.1 | 43.7 | 39.6 | 38.2 | 38.2 | 39.8 |
| Education | 19.1 | 21.9 | 25.0 | 24.7 | 24.1 | 25.8 | 26.4 | 26.2 | 25.3 |
| Health | 3.6 | 4.1 | 3.9 | 4.3 | 4.6 | 5.1 | 5.5 | 6.0 | 6.1 |
| Social security and welfare | 0.6 | 0.6 | 0.6 | 0.5 | 0.5 | 0.4 | 0.5 | 0.5 | 0.5 |

*(continued)*

TABLE 10.2 (*Continued*)

| Country | 1970 | 1972 | 1974 | 1976 | 1978 | 1980 | 1982 | 1984 | 1986 |
|---|---|---|---|---|---|---|---|---|---|
| Housing and community amenities; recreational, cultural, and religious affairs, and economic services | 4.8 | 4.4 | 4.2 | 6.7 | 2.9 | 2.3 | 2.2 | 1.8 | 2.1 |
| Other | 0.3 | 0.4 | 0.4 | 0.5 | 0.4 | 0.4 | 0.7 | 0.7 | |
| **Sri Lanka** | | | | | | | | | |
| General public services | 19.0 | 18.5 | 23.5 | 24.0 | 30.9 | 27.9 | 41.8 | 37.7 | 23.0 |
| Defense | 5.5 | 9.9 | 6.2 | 6.1 | 5.8 | 8.8 | 6.6 | 11.3 | 34.3 |
| Education | 28.1 | 27.2 | 21.7 | 28.3 | 20.8 | 17.6 | 18.0 | 17.2 | 15.0 |
| Health | 14.0 | 13.4 | 10.9 | 13.8 | 10.8 | 11.1 | 9.2 | 9.9 | 7.5 |
| Social security and welfare | 10.9 | 12.6 | 11.1 | 13.2 | 13.2 | 11.3 | 11.6 | 12.6 | 13.3 |
| Housing and community amenities | 0.1 | 0.1 | 0.8 | 1.0 | 0.8 | 0.9 | 0.8 | 0.8 | 0.3 |
| Recreational, cultural, and religious affairs | 1.4 | 1.3 | 0.4 | 0.6 | 0.5 | 0.6 | 0.5 | 0.5 | 0.4 |
| Economic services | 21.1 | 17.1 | 25.4 | 12.9 | 17.3 | 21.9 | 11.6 | 10.0 | 6.2 |
| **India** | | | | | | | | | |
| General public services | | | 15.3 | 13.8 | | 12.9 | 15.4 | 13.5 | |
| Defense | | | 17.8 | 17.6 | | 14.8 | 14.6 | 14.7 | |
| Education | | | 13.9 | 13.5 | | 13.8 | 13.9 | 14.2 | |
| Health | | | 2.9 | 2.9 | | 3.5 | 3.5 | 3.4 | |
| Social security and welfare | | | 2.5 | 2.1 | | 2.9 | 3.2 | 3.3 | |
| Housing and community amenities | | | 3.0 | 3.2 | | 4.5 | 4.2 | 4.3 | |
| Cultural, recreational, and religious affairs | | | 0.9 | 1.0 | | 1.1 | 1.1 | 1.2 | |
| Economic services | | | 42.2 | 44.8 | | 45.6 | 43.3 | 44.9 | |
| Other | | | 1.4 | 1.1 | | 0.9 | 0.9 | 0.7 | |
| **Nepal** | | | | | | | | | |
| General public services | | 13.4 | 17.4 | 10.9 | 11.8 | 12.0 | 11.5 | 11.1 | |
| Defense | | 7.1 | 6.8 | 7.1 | 6.5 | 6.7 | 5.4 | 6.3 | |
| Education | | 7.1 | 9.5 | 12.2 | 10.4 | 9.9 | 9.9 | 11.3 | |
| Health | | 4.7 | 4.9 | 6.7 | 5.3 | 3.9 | 4.5 | 4.4 | |
| Social security and welfare | | 0.4 | 0.7 | 0.7 | 0.6 | 0.5 | 0.4 | 0.6 | |
| Housing and community amenities | | 0.3 | 0.5 | 0.6 | 2.5 | 1.2 | 3.9 | 2.6 | |
| Other community and social services | | 1.2 | 1.3 | 1.6 | 1.1 | 0.6 | 1.9 | 0.8 | |
| Other | | 8.1 | 4.2 | 8.4 | 6.6 | 6.5 | 9.4 | 7.9 | |
| Economic services | | 57.7 | 54.7 | 51.8 | 55.2 | 58.8 | 53.1 | 55.0 | |

(*continued*)

TABLE 10.2 (*Continued*)

| Country | 1970 | 1972 | 1974 | 1976 | 1978 | 1980 | 1982 | 1984 | 1986 |
|---|---|---|---|---|---|---|---|---|---|
| Malaysia | | | | | | | | | |
| General public services | | 6.7 | 7.6 | 5.1 | 4.6 | 5.3 | | | |
| Defense | | 18.5 | 17.9 | 15.3 | 14.6 | 14.6 | | | |
| Education | | 23.4 | 22.7 | 20.3 | 21.2 | 18.0 | | | |
| Health | | 6.8 | 6.6 | 5.8 | 6.3 | 5.0 | | | |
| Social security and welfare | | 3.4 | 3.2 | 2.6 | 3.9 | 3.9 | | | |
| Housing and community amenities | | 1.0 | 0.9 | 0.4 | 0.7 | 2.9 | | | |
| Other community and social services | | 2.1 | 2.0 | 1.6 | 1.9 | 0.6 | | | |
| Other | | 24.0 | 24.0 | 33.6 | 28.5 | 20.2 | | | |
| Economic services | | 14.2 | 15.0 | 15.4 | 18.2 | 29.4 | | | |
| Indonesia | | | | | | | | | |
| General public services | | | 19.9 | 20.8 | 29.0 | 33.2 | 29.8 | 33.7 | 32.4 |
| Defense | | | 17.7 | 16.6 | 15.8 | 13.5 | 13.9 | 13.6 | 9.3 |
| Education | | | 7.2 | 7.8 | 9.2 | 8.3 | 8.5 | 11.9 | 8.5 |
| Health | | | 1.9 | 1.9 | 2.1 | 2.5 | 2.5 | 2.7 | 1.9 |
| Housing and community amenities | | | 0.4 | 0.9 | 1.2 | 1.8 | 1.1 | 1.4 | 1.4 |
| Other community and social services | | | 0.5 | 2.0 | 0.9 | 1.0 | 1.2 | 1.2 | 0.7 |
| Other | | | 21.8 | 12.9 | 11.8 | 7.0 | 11.8 | | 26.6 |
| Economic services | | | 30.7 | 37.0 | 30.1 | 32.6 | 31.3 | 35.6 | 19.3 |
| Singapore | | | | | | | | | |
| General public services | | 15.5 | 12.5 | 10.2 | 10.1 | 0.7 | 13.2 | 11.1 | 12.1 |
| Defense | | 35.3 | 29.4 | 27.2 | 26.8 | 24.9 | 22.9 | 20.1 | 19.0 |
| Education | | 15.7 | 19.3 | 18.5 | 14.4 | 14.4 | 19.2 | 20.2 | 18.2 |
| Health | | 7.8 | 9.4 | 7.7 | 8.5 | 6.9 | 6.4 | 6.2 | 4.1 |
| Social security and welfare | | 0.5 | 1.7 | 1.4 | 1.2 | 1.3 | 1.4 | 0.9 | 1.6 |
| Housing and community amenities | | 3.4 | 5.8 | 7.2 | 8.4 | 6.2 | 6.8 | 5.6 | 14.3 |
| Other community and social services | | 1.5 | 1.7 | 1.8 | 1.4 | 1.4 | 1.5 | 1.9 | 0.5 |
| Other | | 10.3 | 11.0 | 12.2 | 17.0 | 17.6 | 14.4 | 18.9 | 10.4 |
| Economic services | | 9.9 | 9.1 | 13.8 | 12.2 | 17.5 | 14.2 | 15.0 | 19.9 |
| Philippines | | | | | | | | | |
| General public services | | 13.0 | 7.3 | 16.1 | 20.0 | 16.1 | 16.8 | 12.6 | 13.5 |
| Defense | | 14.6 | 15.3 | 19.4 | 12.9 | 12.6 | 11.8 | 9.5 | 7.0 |
| Education | | 21.8 | 13.5 | 11.6 | 13.0 | 10.4 | 16.2 | 14.3 | 13.7 |
| Health | | 4.3 | 3.7 | 4.4 | 4.0 | 3.7 | 4.6 | 4.0 | 4.2 |
| Social security and welfare | | 4.8 | 2.3 | 2.4 | 2.7 | 1.1 | 0.8 | 1.3 | 1.4 |

(*continued*)

TABLE 10.2 (*Continued*)

| Country | 1970 | 1972 | 1974 | 1976 | 1978 | 1980 | 1982 | 1984 | 1986 |
|---|---|---|---|---|---|---|---|---|---|
| Housing and community amenities | | 1.0 | 1.2 | 1.0 | 2.1 | 4.2 | 2.9 | 2.1 | 1.4 |
| Other community and social services | | 0.2 | 0.5 | 0.6 | 0.4 | 0.7 | 0.7 | 0.9 | 0.6 |
| Other | | 16.8 | 5.8 | 3.7 | 6.2 | 5.7 | 7.4 | 15.8 | 19.4 |
| Economic services | | 23.5 | 50.3 | 40.9 | 38.7 | 45.6 | 38.9 | 39.6 | 38.5 |

*Source:* Official national accounts and yearbooks; International Monetary Fund, *Government Finance Statistics Yearbook.*

*Note:* The definition of each function is in International Monetary Fund, *Government Finance Statistics Yearbook.*

spending fell from about 75 percent of the budget in 1970 to 50 percent in 1982. The political leadership that came into power in 1982 reduced free rice rations, housing, and transport subsidies, which went to everyone, and introduced higher fees for health and education. They had no alternative, since budget and trade deficits of the early 1960s were too large to be sustained.[9] But defense expenditures rose with the Tamil rebellion, offsetting the decline in social welfare spending.

Japan's low government receipt shares are similar to those of Western industrialized countries and are traceable to its low defense spending. In contrast, Western countries spent 20–30 percent. The United States, with the highest defense expenditure, took care of Japan's defense, since limits were imposed on Japan's (and Germany's) military expenditures.[10] What made Japanese government receipt shares the highest in Asia was its spending for education, higher than that of France (29 percent) and the United States (24 percent) in 1967–69. Japan's rising trend of total government shares was not due to education but social expenditures (social welfare, housing, recreation, culture, health), which nearly doubled, from 12 percent to 23 percent.

The changes in government share in Taiwan and South Korea were fairly steady due to the rise in social expenditures being offset by the decline in defense expenditures. Social expenditure shares in both countries in the early 1980s was low, perhaps due to the need to maintain large military establishments. Despite broadly similar spending patterns in the two countries, South Korea spent much less than Taiwan on education—due to the much larger private education sector in South Korea (attesting to the strong commitment of South Koreans to pay for private education).

After rising from the 1950s, the Thai share of government receipts in GDP kept steady at around 13 percent, the lowest in Southeast Asia. This stability was due largely to the offset between declining defense and rising educational expenditures. The low share of receipts was related to low spending on social expenditures. In contrast to Thailand, Malaysia's share was the highest in

Southeast Asia and was related to its high expenditures on education, health, social welfare, and housing. Malaysia is a welfare state, like Sri Lanka, and like Sri Lanka, established a number of government enterprises, which—like those in Indonesia and the Philippines—were inefficient and costly.

The Philippines' defense expenditures were among the lowest in Southeast Asia, largely the result of U.S. bases in Subic and Clark, which made large expenditures unnecessary. Its expenditures for economic purposes were the highest in Southeast Asia, reflecting the increasing entry and intervention into business activities by the Marcos regime. Indonesia's economic service expenditures were nearly as large as the Philippines', as the Suharto regime also established large numbers of government enterprises.

India's economic expenditures were the largest in Asia, exceeding those of the Philippines and Indonesia. India's growth strategy strongly emphasized the development of a wide range of costly heavy industries whose inefficient operation has been a big drain on current revenues.[11] Because of large economic expenditures, the share spent by India on education, especially lower education, was one of the lowest.

The high current and capital expenditures on economic services of India, Indonesia, the Philippines, and Malaysia contrast strikingly with the low current and capital spending in Thailand, Singapore, South Korea, and Taiwan. Singapore's capital-intensive industries are paid for by multinational companies. Singapore, like Malaysia, spent a lot on social services (education, health, social security, welfare, housing and community services), and is probably the leading welfare state in Asia, since its share of government receipts is twice that of Hong Kong.[12]

Variations in the uses made of government revenues are considerable. The distribution pattern of budget expenditures is dominated by spending on defense, education, and other social and economic services, with general administration expenditures varying much less. Defense shares are small if a country is not threatened externally or internally or is protected by foreign military bases, as are Japan and the Philippines. Educational expenditures are low if a country's private educational facilities are extensively developed, as in South Korea and the Philippines. Other social expenditures are high if the country's political leadership espouses social welfare philosophies, as in Sri Lanka, Singapore, and Malaysia. Likewise, economic expenditures are low where governments rely on market mechanisms for resource allocation.

Over time, defense expenditures tend to fall with improvements in foreign relations, while educational expenditures tend to rise with the increasing demand for an educated work force, as agriculture, industry, and services become more modern and complex. Social and economic expenditures also expand with industrialization, urbanization, and modernization. It may be that there are strong relations between the size of functional expenditures in each country. Faced with the need to build up defenses against threatening forces from the outside, Taiwan and South Korea were compelled to give military expenditures top priority—and because of rapid economic growth could not give low priority to education. Hence social welfare spending was kept low.

Historical forces also contribute to the pattern of expenditures, such as the lesser need for public spending on education in countries where religious groups establish private schools, as the Catholics did in the Philippines, the Protestants in South Korea, the Muslims in Indonesia, and the Buddhists in Burma. Because of ethnic rivalries, Malaysia's political leadership is opposed to private schools, thereby preventing the Chinese from setting up their own schools. Confucians do not like social welfare doles as much as the Muslims and the Theravadan Buddhists, although Singapore and Thailand are exceptions.[13]

### Trends in Government Productivity

It would have been desirable to work out government production per worker on a much broader basis than in table 10.3, but data for employees in public hospitals, schools, social service agencies, and economic organs that matched the classifications in general government expenditures were not available for most countries. As it is, data were available for only six countries. Average annual GDP for public administration and defense in constant prices was divided by number of employees over the years shown, and the percentage change over these years was computed. Growth in government production was lowest in administration and defense, lower than that of the slow-growing service sector.

In the Philippines and South Korea, government productivity declined throughout the period. This slow growth of government production is to be expected, as most government workers have job security and are eventually promoted, less by merit than by seniority, and government agencies are not exposed to competition.[14]

If the same amount of government services could be produced with fewer employees, the public wage bill would be lower. The public wage bill tends to be high relative to number of employees because public employment, as in most service industries, comprises more white-collar jobs than commodity production does. Accordingly, public jobs tend to be more education-intensive. The issue of whether wages paid by the government for comparable occupations are higher than in the private sector is difficult to resolve, because public workers in most Asian countries receive more than the statutory pay. In 1979 the share of government wages to national income at market prices was low in the Philippines, even lower than in Sri Lanka and India. Filipino government workers received income from extensive moonlighting, graft, and corruption, besides special allowances and fringe benefits.[15] Such outside incomes are also common, although to a lesser extent, in other Asian countries. Thus low growth

TABLE 10.3

Government Product per Worker, 1960s to 1980s (thousands of national currency)

| Country | 1960s | 1970s | 1980s | Growth 1960s to early 1980s (percent) |
|---|---|---|---|---|
| Japan | | | | |
| Administration and defense | 31,115 | 34,906 | 41,867 | 34.6 |
| Agriculture | 6,001 | 8,765 | 9,897 | 64.9 |
| Industry | 16,320 | 31,225 | 43,333 | 165.5 |
| Social services | 18,244 | 29,747 | 34,200 | 87.4 |
| Thailand | | | | |
| Administration and defense | 12.5 | 16.2 | 17.2 | 37.6 |
| Agriculture | 2.6 | 3.8 | 4.3 | 65.4 |
| Industry | 23.7 | 37.2 | 47.7 | 101.3 |
| Social services | 14.8 | 26.8 | 28.9 | 95.3 |
| Philippines | | | | |
| Administration and defense | 4.2 | 4.1 | 3.8 | −9.5 |
| Agriculture | 2.2 | 2.4 | 2.7 | 22.7 |
| Industry | 7.2 | 9.3 | 11.9 | 65.3 |
| Social services | 6.6 | 7.0 | 6.9 | 4.5 |
| Korea | | | | |
| Administration and defense | 3,220 | 3,003 | 2,646 | −17.8 |
| Agriculture | 961 | 1,143 | 1,533 | 59.5 |
| Industry | 1,869 | 3,039 | 4,410 | 136.0 |
| Social services | 2,666 | 3,322 | 3,026 | 13.5 |
| Taiwan | | | | |
| Administration and defense | 150.7 | 180.3 | 215.8 | 43.2 |
| Agriculture | 62.1 | 74.0 | 102.3 | 64.7 |
| Industry | 169.1 | 234.6 | 318.1 | 38.1 |
| Social services | 214.0 | 273.0 | 333.1 | 55.6 |
| United States | | | | |
| Administration and defense | 10.0 | 10.3 | | 3.0 |
| Agriculture | 21.3 | 28.3 | | 32.9 |
| Industry | 14.3 | 16.6 | | 16.1 |
| Social services | 15.8 | 16.8 | | 6.3 |

*Sources:* Official national accounts and yearbooks.

of productivity per worker together with a higher wage bill tends to keep the share of government receipts in GDP high, as economic development calls for increasing public services.

### THE ROLE OF GOVERNMENT IN ECONOMIC GROWTH

Kuznets pointed out that the role of the nation-state in "modern economic growth with its continuous technological and social innovations and its rapid rate of structural change . . . is an important factor in modern economic growth," and asked whether the delay in the rise of a modern nation-state was a factor in the failure of underdeveloped countries to enter the modern growth process.[16] According to Abramovitz,

> the process includes the displacement and redistribution of population among regions . . . the abandonment of old industries and occupations, and the qualification of workers for new, more skilled occupations . . . and extension of education. [The growth of] very large-scale enterprise . . . establishes new types of market power and alters the relations of workers and employees. [These] imply a great change in the structure of families and in their roles in caring for children, the sick, and the old. [These and other changes] alter the positions, prospects and power of established groups. Conflict and resistance are intrinsic to the growth process [and] to resolve such conflict and resistance in a way which preserves a large consensus for growth, yet does not impose a cost which retards growth unduly, a mechanism of conflict resolution is needed. . . . The national sovereign state necessarily becomes the arbiter of group conflict.[17]

Thus these leading students of modern economic growth have concluded that the expansion of the role of government was inevitable since it was (up to a certain point) essential to the growth of productivity in the private sector and that the cost must be paid for, immediately or ultimately, through taxes. Hence it is to be expected that government expenditures have risen. But they have risen faster than revenues in South and Southeast Asia, so that debts have piled up. There is now a need to ask whether the costs of governments are too much for the private sector—that is, do the costs to the private sector reduce private productivity more than government spending raises productivity? This is difficult to show, as benefits from public spending on education, social security, health, defense, and administration are not easily quantifiable. Not only the level of government spending but the pattern and efficiency of that spending need to be taken into account.

Japan's postwar economic growth was substantially higher than that of other industrialized countries, and the share of GDP taken by its government was the lowest. This is the result not only of low defense expenditures but also of its low expenditures for health, social security, and welfare.[18] The high growth rates of the other East Asian countries (GDP per capita of about 6 percent, 1950–83) were not associated with low shares of government receipts in GDP except for Hong Kong. These shares in Taiwan and South Korea were high in large part due to high defense expenditures, although these were offset in part by low expenditure shares for health, social security, welfare, and economic services. If these had not been low, the high shares for defense and education would have raised total receipt shares considerably. As to the city-states, the contrast between government roles in Hong Kong and Singapore is notable, with Hong Kong's share less than half that of Singapore's. Hong Kong does not publish functional expenditures, but its expenditures for defense and social and economic services may have been very low and its educational expenditures may be fairly high, since average years of school completed for the labor force (eight years) were almost as high as those of Taiwan and South Korea, and higher than those of Singapore (six years).[19] Singapore, faced with low growth, substantially reduced its social security contributions and economic interventions. Current and capital expenditures on economic services were lower in these countries than in India, Indonesia, and the Philippines. Apparently, these countries leave much of the operation of the economy to private enterprises.

In Southeast Asia, Thailand, with the highest economic growth rate, had the lowest share of government receipts in GDP. This is notable even though Thailand's per capita income during the late 1970s and early 1980s was about the same as that of the Philippines. The Philippine share was low because many of its defense needs were taken care of by the United States and its educational needs by private schools, which means that the parents of students paid for the costs. Unlike the Philippines, Malaysia, and Indonesia, the Thais have not invested in costly public enterprises. Nor does Thailand have large social and welfare programs, as Malaysia does. Thailand should have spent more on education and physical infrastructure (roads, public utilities, housing). It is now faced with insufficient infrastructure and public education, as it moves into double-digit growth.

In South Asia, all the governments were burdened with large expenditures for economic services as a result of public enterprises, most of which were inefficiently operated. Even in the 1980s, Sri Lanka had a large social welfare program and the largest general public services spending in Asia. These expenditures, especially for slow-growing public enterprises, contributed to the low growth in South Asia. Unlike Japan, Taiwan, South Korea, Thailand, and Malaysia, all of which at one time or another spent substantial amounts to get their agriculture moving, South Asia's agricultural productivity is low and its growth is slow, because these socialist republics follow a growth strategy based on nationalized industries, while East and Southeast Asia depend largely on private industry. The latter (except for the Philippines) spend much more on education than South Asia (except for Sri Lanka).

As a whole, the Asian share of central government current revenues in GDP tends to be lower than that of other countries with per capita GDP of less than $1,500 (15 percent for Asia and 20 percent for the others).[20] But this share is rising and is expected to continue to rise as industrialization, urbanization, and social modernization accelerate with modern economic growth. It is essential that it rise if Kuznets and Abramovitz are correct. But it is important that such increases be used to enhance productivity. Level of government expenditures is not as important as where and how they are spent. If spending is large for social welfare, as in Sri Lanka, and for public enterprises and regulations, as in the Philippines, India, and Indonesia, then the impact of this spending on economic growth may not be favorable. Without productivity growth, spending on education, health, and social welfare cannot be sustained, since budget and balance of payments deficits will rise. Abramovitz argued that excessive government costs may have constrained productivity growth in the United States and European countries since the 1970s, when GDP per worker fell substantially.[21] Here, too, it may not be just the level of spending but the type of spending that matters. Military expenditures and the huge benefits paid by social security systems in the United States and Europe throw government budgets out of balance and upset the fiscal systems.

Japanese leaders, aware of the changes in the United States and Europe and worried that the needs of modern economic growth will make the same demands on Japanese society, prepared for the problems that an aging society will pose. They seek better solutions than those of the West, which call for vast government spending, entailing a tax intake of as much as half of GNP. They fear that such government demands will blunt people's vitality and competitiveness and their desire to work and save. Western industrialized countries have found that marginal taxes as high as half of personal income tend "to reduce the supply of labor, especially among the highly paid," while the long lag of benefits behind payments tends to cut savings.[22] Because social security benefits reduce the need to save for ill health and old age, and the dependence on government leads to entitlement expectations, the social values of diligent work work and saving may be weakened.

The beginnings of the welfare state in the West were evident in the pre–World War II decades, especially in the 1930s, when social security systems were established to cope with unemployment. The rapid increases in social security, education, and health expenditures took place after World War II. These were in part due to unemployment in the first postwar decade and to the problems of poverty, congestion, noise, pollution, and environmental changes, which came with growth and technological progress. In the past, some of these problems were taken care of within the family system, but the structure and functions of families eroded under the impact of modern growth, and there is now a tendency to shift to the state what used to be the family's concerns. The problem Asia must face is how to avoid or mitigate the negative effects of growth without disrupting the social consensus needed for sustained growth—or how to get the private sector to shoulder some of these tasks.

Basic to reducing the negative effects of growth is the development strategy undertaken by the state. A full employment strategy in East Asia wiped out unemployment and underemployment and accelerated growth without increasing income inequality. Hence the pressure for welfare measures was minimal in East Asia, as lower income groups had jobs and regular income increases. East Asia reached full employment through an emphasis on agricultural development, supplemented by labor-intensive industrialization. In monsoon Asia, except in the city-states, full employment is difficult to attain without starting out with a strong agricultural sector, where most of the low-income and under-employed groups are found. In the West, many years of unemployment and low income in the 1930s, 1940s, and into the early 1950s left a large group of low-income families insecure and worried about the future even when employment and income began to rise in the late 1950s and the 1960s. Their need for a more secure future led to a full-blown welfare state in some Western countries, even though the 1960s saw exceptionally high growth rates and full employment.

Modern economic growth leads to declining birth and death rates and longer life expectancies, all of which produce an aging population. The problem of security for old age comes to the fore as modern growth tends to break extended families into nuclear ones. The traditional value of caring for old parents weakens as family ties loosen, particularly in cities with their high costs of housing, food, and medical care. The West opted to let the state take care of the aging population through old age pensions and health insurance. One alternative is to maintain traditional family values (still strong in Asia) through mass media and schools and through initiating ways of taking care of the aged population that are cheaper and more wholesome than care via government payments. Another alternative is to encourage private firms and voluntary organizations (with subsidies from the state) to establish insurance schemes that better match premium payers and benefactors. Some Western European countries, faced with huge deficits in their social security funds, are considering restricting payments to lower income groups and to those without private pensions and health schemes, or else paying a flat, standard amount not linked to income.[23]

To reduce government spending for economic services, many Asian governments are looking at the denationalization and deregulation of industries, letting market forces take over. As to privatization, many nationalized industries are too inefficient to be easily sold at reasonable prices. Nevertheless, it may be better to get rid of them even with large losses than to keep them. Resistance comes from workers and management of these public enterprises and from bureaucrats with vested interests in them. Over the long run, more employment may be created by turning these enterprises over to the private sector. The public would benefit from unsubsidized, cheaper, and better products from more efficient operations.

Deregulation may be beneficial in most industries, since market mechanisms can better allocate resources than government agencies can. In some cases, more than just deregulation is needed. Where markets are controlled by monopolies, as in diversified agriculture, the government should dismantle these monopolies and promote cooperatives. In the Philippines, the landed oligarchy is too dominant and tenants and workers too weak to enable the market to function efficiently.[24] In China, a hasty shift to market mechanisms in urban areas resulted in a chaotic situation, with illegal imports, bribery, black marketing, overproduction, shoddy goods, cheating, and monopolization. Where the market forces on both sides of the bargaining table are not developed, the government should intervene to develop and strengthen market forces with the view to making deregulation effective. Just as in the West, antitrust laws are necessary for the efficient operation of commodity markets. In developing countries, deregulation can work only if monopolies and monopsonies are eliminated in the input, financial, and commodity markets.

It is unwise to reduce spending on education and training, since this spending will have only to be increased when Asian countries reach levels of growth requiring a better trained labor force.[25] Governments should encourage the establishment of private educational institutions—not ban them, as Malaysia has. Government resources become increasingly inadequate as the demand for education outruns the GDP growth. Of course, private schools need to be regulated and helped with modest subsidies to maintain high levels of education. Private education enables those who can afford it to shift from public education, leaving room for others, and those who cannot pass the exams for public schools to get an education even though of lower quality.

Government should use the radio, television, and newspapers for educational purposes, since these mass media are relatively inexpensive ways to disseminate information. The adult populations in South and Southeast Asia include families that have migrated from rural areas or never had a chance to acquire an education. Adult education programs can reduce illiteracy, upgrade skills, improve public health, and modernize social values. But to be effective, governments must spend sufficiently on good mass media programs, attractive enough to hold the attention of the audience.

Because there are few natural resources in most Asian countries, they have not been important to the discussion in this volume. But precisely because of their meagerness, natural resources should not be wasted. More attention needs to be paid to natural resources and the environment, whose degradation has been extensive. It is understandable that in the early stages of development there was a need to concentrate on economic growth, but now both East Asia and Southeast Asia can afford to improve the natural environment. In fact, the traffic jams, pollution, and overcrowding in major Asian cities have become so serious that they are beginning to retard economic growth and affect living standards.

Policies should go beyond the construction of roads, housing, and other urban facilities, which may encourage more migration to the cities. Economic opportunities in rural areas—both in agriculture and in nonagricultural activities—should be expanded. This will call for the decentralization of industrial activities away from the metropolis and for the expansion of agricultural activities.

The International Rice Research Institute has urged a large increase in rice production to "avert a potential famine."[26] The reason for this is that the rice surpluses in the 1980s made for complacency through false impressions that the world rice problems were solved. Robert Chandler, the first director of IRRI, noted that the demand for rice in Asia by the year 2000 will be about 570 million metric tons. On the basis of Asia's past performance, Chandler estimated that production will fall short by 50 million metric tons. It will be difficult to meet the projected demand because, despite efforts of plant breeders to improve varieties, "the greatest gains in yield potentials have already been made. . . . It is impossible at this stage to predict what advances will come from genetic engineering and from other areas of biotechnology."[27] Every effort must therefore be made to improve rice yields through liberal credit to farmers, more extension services, irrigation, and above all, the intensification of cultivation with more labor. To induce farm families to stay on the farm and put more labor into rice growing, the price of rice must be high enough to pay for their labor. Where land reform is needed, redistribution can raise the intensity of cultivation and yields.

A major source of farm income can be multiple and diversified cropping, but, for this, irrigation and other investments are needed. Investments in agriculture and irrigation by national governments and the World Bank have declined since 1979: the share of total lending by the World Bank for irrigation purposes in South and Southeast Asia fell from 24 percent in 1977 to 12 percent in 1986–87.[28]

In addition, off-farm work in nearby cities and towns to which the farm population can commute daily can keep farm workers residing at home. This will require investment in transportation facilities. To further slow the movement of rural youth to the city, amenities such as schools, radio, television, and movie houses should be made available in smaller towns.

Since in most instances, military expenditures are externally influenced, they are difficult to reduce. But they are the most unproductive expenditure from an economic point of view.[29] With the failure of communism, the time has come to cut back sharply on military expenditures, not only in the West but in Asia. Military expenditure is the largest single item in central government budgets in nearly all Asian countries (see table 10.2), and reductions can release resources for education and infrastructural construction.

Popular participation in the decision-making process is most important. Japanese governance promotes such participation through groups like labor unions, farmers' cooperatives, trade associations, and consumer unions. In Hong Kong, British officials consult widely with industry councils and associations. In Taiwan, peasants in farmers' associations make the decisions regarding agricultural activities. However, popular participation in the Philippines grew slowly under pre- and post-Marcos democracies because the landed oligarchs kept the peasants under control and barred them from effective participation. And in India, the caste system excludes the lower classes from participation in many activities. Without the broad participation of the masses, many mistakes are made in policy making and implementation. Nor can people be motivated to work toward higher productivity without being part of the decision-making process.

Civil servants, the police, agricultural extension agents, schoolteachers, tax collectors, and others in the bureaucracy execute land reform, manage traffic, maintain law and order, teach schoolchildren, and collect taxes. But the efficiency of bureaucracies varies considerably from country to country. In East Asia, the bureaucracies are relatively efficient and have a minimum of corruption. Influenced by the practices of the Japanese or British bureaucracies of the prewar decades or by their Confucian heritage, these countries execute policies in a businesslike way, which contributes to their favorable investment climate and the smooth conduct of their public functions. The Malaysian civil service exhibits the virtues of the British civil service, under which it was trained. This cannot be said of the Philippine civil service, which steadily departed from American practices, ending up as one of the most corrupt and inefficient in Asia.[30] Likewise, the Indian civil service, once one of the best examples of British training, has lost its reputation for efficiency. The Thai bureaucracy, which started out as a traditional Asiatic institution in the nineteenth century, has steadily improved over the postwar decades to become one of the best outside of East Asia.

What policies are adopted and how they are executed depend to a large extent on the ruling elites, who dominate policy making, and on the higher echelons of the executive branch, which set the tone for the lower echelons. Prewar Japan was ruled by the landed and the financial oligarchs who, together with the civilian and military bureaucracies, made the decisions to wage war. After the war, the oligarchs were purged by the Allied occupation, land reform took power away from the landlords, and the big family monopolies were dismantled.[31] After World War II, the liberated governments of Taiwan and South Korea conducted extensive land reform, and the landlords remaining from the period of the Japanese occupation were wiped out.

In Thailand, landlord power was destroyed when the monarchy freed the slaves and serfs who composed the work force for the nobility; without the workers, the lands of the nobles reverted to the monarchy, which turned them over to the peasants. In Indonesia, Dutch planters lost their estates to the Indonesian government after World War II. Sri Lanka broke up its large landholdings. There was land reform in Bangladesh. The Communist countries of China, Vietnam, Laos, and Cambodia nationalized agricultural land. Burma carried out a comprehensive land reform at one stroke by abolishing all tenancy, but the military government failed to provide credit and other support, so most peasants lost their land to the moneylenders.[32]

Only limited land reform was undertaken in parts of India and the Philippines, and landlords are still very powerful, despite attempts at agrarian reform. In the presentday democracy of the Philippines, the executive and legislative branches of the government are dominated by the landed oligarchy, which together with the highly protected industrialists and monopolistic banks are unable to generate enough jobs through stable and vigorous growth. To comply with the demands of aid donors, upon which they are highly dependent (the International Bank for Research and Development, the International Monetary Fund, the United States, and Japan), they go through the motions of reforming their agrarian and tariff structures, always stopping short of success. This activates the middle classes through the armed forces and the impoverished lower classes through the Communist parties to revolt. Thus it is difficult to make democracy work when the oligarchs are powerful and there is pressure for authoritarian rule. This was the experience of the early 1970s, when Marcos declared martial law—but it did not take long for Marcos to find out that the old oligarchs were too powerful to buck, and he soon joined them in the plunder.[33]

Ruling elites dominated by the landlord class are likely to constrain modern economic growth, as in Ricardian England, when landlords raised tariffs on imported wheat and raised rents. Such elites are anachronistic to the modern economy, belonging as they do to the ancient Asiatic mode of production. In countries where landlords are powerful, there is a tendency for industrialization to be capital-intensive, requiring large subsidies and extended protection. In the Philippines, the traditional landlords opted for capital-intensive industries in the early postwar decades, as only they had the wealth to invest in them. Such industries are complex and difficult to run efficiently, especially for traditional landlords, who belong to the leisure class. They were unable to manage them efficiently, and protection continues into the present, perpetuating inefficiencies. In Taiwan, South Korea, Thailand, and early postwar Japan, where land reform has been undertaken, the rural elites were poorer and more populist, and industrialization started out with predominantly labor-intensive, light industries, which after a short period of protection were efficient enough to export.

In countries where landlords dominate the ruling elites, the currencies tend to be overvalued to keep the costs of imported materials and equipment for the capital-intensive industries low. Since the owners are not interested in exporting, higher export prices do not matter much. But overvaluation makes it difficult for labor-intensive industries to export and slows down industrialization. Capital-intensive industries tend to stagnate when the limits of the domestic markets are reached. The Philippines and India chronically face balance of payments deficits. Where land reform was undertaken, the Japanese yen, the Taiwanese dollar, and the South Korean won were undervalued as part of an export-oriented growth strategy. Landlords are not enthusiastic about family planning to reduce population growth or about measures to attain full employment, as both would raise rural wages.

In sum, the governments of East Asia contributed to growth through appropriate strategies and policies.

### THE NORTH ATLANTIC BASIN AND THE PACIFIC CENTURY

Although frequent references to the Pacific century have been made, it is not clear what it is or what it takes for the center of economic growth to shift from the North Atlantic to the Pacific basin countries. I undertook to explore these conceptual issues in a 1983 article, but I now realize that that study needs to be supplemented by other considerations.[34] This can best be done by examining the Atlantic century, which dominated during most of the twentieth century.

The countries of the North Atlantic basin, comprising the United States, Canada, the United Kingdom, France, Germany, the Benelux countries, and Scandinavia, made this the most outstanding century in mankind's history. It was they who converted the primitive mechanized technologies of the nineteenth century into the more powerful, faster, and precise gas- and electric-powered technologies and succeeded in mechanizing most of the operations in agriculture, industry, and services, thereby raising productivity and wages, wiping out most of the unskilled occupations, and opening up many job opportunities for females. The status of women was raised, and the net value of children fell, resulting in a slower population growth. The reduction in unskilled occupations and the employment of wives lowered income disparities, and the complexity and pervasiveness of the new technologies forced parents to educate their children beyond primary levels. Democratic institutions became more firmly established with universal education, the rise in women's status, and the equalizing of income.

In these North Atlantic countries, the physical, biological, and social sciences, and the humanities were developed to the highest levels.[35] Life expectancies were raised to unprecedented heights, as death rates fell and nutrition and health services improved. Poverty was reduced with unemployment insurance, health insurance, and old age pensions. North Atlantic countries were home to a number of institutions that became the foundation of a truly democratic and humane society: labor unions, farmers' cooperatives, agricultural extension services, and local governments. Widespread university education and adult education became commonplace. Mass media reached every family, and freedom of speech, press, and religion came to be taken for granted.

Thus the contributions of the Atlantic century to the progress of humankind are immense, extending beyond high per capita income. Thus more than income level is involved if the countries of the Pacific basin are to enter the twenty-first century with the banner of the Pacific century. The contributions made by the North Atlantic countries are not easily matched by East Asian countries, which have become affluent only recently. It took much of the nineteenth century and the early decades of the twentieth century for the West to evolve into mature societies.

Japan has made good progress toward becoming a democratic, humane society. Many of the institutions noted above are in place, poverty has been eradicated, life expectancies are the highest in the world, and Japan is now making major contributions to poorer nations. But the other East Asian countries and Southeast Asia have just begun to adopt democratic ways; it was only recently that national elections were held in South Korea and Taiwan. Singapore has been holding elections for some time—but not Hong Kong, which is still a colony of Britain. In all of these, much has to be done before politics and society can come up to the democratic standards of the North Atlantic community.

In 1988, average per capita (PPP) dollars was about US$15,000 for OECD countries, most of which were Western European countries. (PPP dollars are currencies of various countries converted into U.S. dollars by their purchasing power parities.) In 1988, the average per capita PPP$ in the NIEs was about half of the OECD average; the ASEAN Four's average was about one-fifth of this average. Assuming growth rates of 7–8 percent for the 1990s, it will take a decade for the NIEs to approach the 1988 OECD per capita income average and at least two decades for the ASEAN Four to reach this figure.

Although the NIEs grew 7–8 percent a year in the 1980s and early 1990s and may be expected to continue at this rate, it is uncertain that such a rate could be sustained into the latter half of the 1990s. After all, these high growth rates have gone on for over three decades, during which time (in the mid-1970s) the per capita income of these countries surpassed that of Japan's. Japan's growth at that time fell to about 5 percent, so a possibility of a slowdown in the NIEs cannot be dismissed. This is not only because of the protectionism and slowdown in Western economies but because of internal forces within the NIEs.

Capital formation in the NIEs lagged by about half or more in the 1980s. The reason for this was not only the global recession of the early 1980s but also the completion of the construction of their basic infrastructure. By the early 1990s, most of their production processes became mechanized. When this occurs, technological progress increasingly takes the form of old machines being replaced by new machines. But this process is slower than the substitution of machines for labor, because entrepreneurs hesitate to replace old machines that are in good condition merely because they have become technologically obsolete.

More important, it will not be long before many of their industries will be approaching the technological frontier. Countries tend to import the machines for which they do not own the technology embodied in the machines. In Taiwan and South Korea around the late 1980s, the import growth of machines slowed—in the former from 13 percent to 11 percent of GNP and in the latter from 16 percent to 14 percent. Under the circumstances, the NIEs have no choice but to raise their R and D spending, whose share in GNP in Taiwan and South Korea is comparable to the shares in developed countries. The generation of new technologies through R and D is much slower than through imports; thus as the technology frontier is approached, technological progress is likely to slow down.

With the slowdown in capital formation, the NIEs became creditor nations, with chronic excess savings. These excess savings must be invested abroad. In a closed economy, savings and investment are always equal, but in an open economy, excess savings going abroad take the form of excess exports over imports or the form of net foreign investment (including repayments of debt). But if excess savings are sent abroad, they contribute to the productivity and growth of other countries. The interests and dividends that these foreign investments earn are relatively small compared to total investments abroad—about 10 percent. Most of the earnings from investment abroad are in the form of wages and salaries, which are paid and spent abroad. During the period when Britain was sending savings abroad in the latter part of the nineteenth century (e.g., to build railroads in the United States), British productivity growth fell from 1.5 percent per year to 0.6 percent.[36] The United States had a similar experience in the late 1960s.

A major source of growth among the NIEs in the past was the shift of the labor force from low-income agriculture to high-income industry and services. This source is drying up as the agricultural sector shrinks, employing in 1990 only 10 percent of the labor force in Taiwan and 17 percent in South Korea. Moreover, the service sector is becoming increasingly important. In Taiwan in 1990, about twice the number of workers were found in services than in industry; in South Korea, about equal numbers were employed in the two sectors. Modern technology, especially machines, is more readily applicable to material and commodity production than to services.

Other tendencies may also slow growth in these countries in the future. There is a demand for greater democratic governance and participation in decision making after decades of autocratic demands for discipline, belt tightening, and sacrifice. Through their unions, workers are demanding higher wages and better working conditions, and are pressuring the government to spend more for health care, old age pensions, and housing. Moreover, Hong Kong's imminent reversion to China, South Korea's accommodation with North Korea, and Taiwan's concerns for independence from China will, on the whole, dampen growth. Hence the approach to the frontier of technology, the shift of savings to investment abroad, sluggish structural changes, and demands for better working conditions and social security are likely to slow growth rates from 9–10 percent to 5 percent in the 1990s.

Fortunately, there is a good chance that the growth of the ASEAN Four will accelerate, perhaps to replace East Asia as the dynamic center of development in the 1990s. Thailand has grown at about 10 percent per year in the late 1980s, Malaysia at 9 percent, and Indonesia at 7 percent between 1988 and 1991. The total population of these three countries is three times the population of the

NIEs, while the Thai and Malay populations roughly equal them.

Of course, the acceleration of growth in Thailand, Malaysia, and Indonesia has been due to the massive investments from Asian countries, in particular Japan and Taiwan. Nevertheless, these countries have probably developed their internal capabilities enough to sustain high growth throughout the 1990s, even if foreign investments taper off. In the 1960s and 1970s they developed their agricultural sectors at a rate of 5 percent, exceptionally high for this sector. This rate is indicative of these countries' ability to supply cheap food for industrial workers, to supply experienced rural workers for factories, to supply savings for industrial investments, to provide markets for industrial products, and to earn foreign exchange through exports of agricultural products. Thus agricultural development is an important prerequisite to industrial development.

The years of education attained by the labor force of these three countries averaged five years by the mid-1980s and six years by the 1990s, which is as high as in the heavily industrialized East Asian countries during the early 1970s. Adult literacy was somewhat higher by the end of the 1980s, averaging about 80 percent (compared to the NIEs' 70 percent). Since the 1950s, their labor force has accumulated experience with industrialization and with the workings of the market. By the late 1980s, exports of manufactured commodities overtook agricultural exports.[37] By the end of the 1980s, their confidence in their ability to cope with external competition was manifested by trade liberalization. Their competitive ability should grow further now that full employment has been attained, since productivity gains should accelerate with rising wages, compelling entrepreneurs to substitute capital for labor.

Income distribution improved in all three countries by the end of the 1980s, with declining incidence of poverty. This not only improved the purchasing power of lower income groups but, together with the reduction of unemployment, contributed to political stability. After a shaky start in the early postwar decades, the three countries have been politically stable for several decades. Military coups have not affected the underlying economic stability of the Thais, whose monarchy has been a strong symbol of unity and solidarity. Military leaders have been careful not to interfere in the economy, nor have the occasional ethnic flare-ups disturbed the firm political grip of the Malay majority since 1969. Indonesians, under military rule since the mid-1960s, have overcome the chronic confusion of the Sukarno era.

Thus it may be safe to conclude that by 2010 both the NIEs and the ASEAN Four will catch up to the 1990 per capita income levels of OECD countries. But the catch-up process can be speeded up with closer cooperation between all of East Asia and Southeast Asia, a cooperation that will be in the interest of all Pacific rim countries, as it will sustain the vigor of the region. This cooperation has already begun, with the massive flow of East Asian investment into Southeast Asia. But more should be done to hasten the restructuring and transformation of the region. Japan, Taiwan, and South Korea should buy more of Southeast Asia's agricultural and industrial products. While Japan's agricultural purchases from the United States, Taiwan, and South Korea rose substantially in the late 1980s, its purchases from Southeast Asia fell: a 10 percent decline in Malaysia's total exports to Japan between 1984 and 1987, 40 percent in Thailand's, 5 percent in the Philippines', and 50 percent in Indonesia's. Japan's tariff rates on agricultural products rose between the early 1960s and 1982, although they have fallen considerably since then.

By 1988, Japan's overall average tariff rates fell below those of the United States and the European Community. There also has been a relaxation of nontariff barriers: quotas, import surcharges, restrictive standards, administrative guidance, customs procedures, and the like (although even by the end of 1986, the percentage of Japan's imports subject to "hard core" nontariff barriers was 29 percent, the same as in 1981). Taiwan also began to open its markets. But the benefits from this relaxation have gone to the United States and Europe, not to Southeast Asia, since it affects mainly Western products such as meat and citrus fruits, and not Southeast Asian products such as bananas and pineapples. The improvement in Japan's quotas and tariffs is also not applicable in the main to Southeast Asian agricultural products, and very little of ASEAN manufactured products are imported into Japan.[38] If East Asia does not buy more from Southeast Asia, the latter will be unable to purchase the machines and equipment needed for rapid industrialization; its balance of payments deficits are already increasing.

One frequent complaint among these countries is that, in joint ventures, private Japanese firms have not been willing to transfer their knowledge of technologies. The reasons for this are several: the language barrier, the short visits of Japanese experts to Southeast Asia, and Southeast Asia's low absorption capability and lack of qualified local personnel and supporting industries. In part, this problem can be rectified by the establishment of a technology transfer center in Southeast Asia staffed by specialists, who may be retired from companies and institutes and who will stay long enough to assist with the identification, modification, and adoption of Japanese technologies and to train others to use them. Such a center may be particularly useful for the numerous small and medium-sized enterprises in Southeast Asian countries. Such a center should assist with both modern technologies and craft technologies. The center could also include marketing specialists, who could help with marketing problems, which are formidable in Japan, with its many-tiered distribution system.

There will also be a need for academic and scientific cooperation between Japan and Southeast Asia. In the past, the Ford and Rockefeller foundations had university development programs in Southeast Asia, but these have ended. Small projects still exist, such as those of the Japan Foundation. A large-scale project involving more universities and institutes would help to expand research and training programs. This project should include the exchange of research and teaching personnel between Japanese and Southeast Asian universities and institutes. If Southeast Asian economies grow to double-digit levels, there may be a shortage of high-level manpower if training is not expanded now, since such manpower takes a long time to train.

With a large influx of foreign investments in the coming years, there will be a severe shortage of technical and vocational workers for the more sophisticated industries. Lacking trainers for these skills, Southeast Asian schools have not been turning them out in sufficient numbers. Japan can establish a technical and vocational training center in Southeast Asia staffed with experienced teachers well equipped to train the trainers, who would then return to their factories to teach their technical workers. The center should also include a training program to improve agricultural products, which could be imported to Japan. Also, Japan's immigration policies should be relaxed to permit foreign workers to work for awhile and acquire skills and experience in higher technology industries.

A center for comparative development studies staffed by Southeast Asian specialists in comparative growth, public finance, labor, agriculture, industry, population, and so on—and complementing the work of Japanese institutes—could be established to feed into the work of a core of comparative policy specialists in the foregoing fields. With the participation of experienced bureaucrats, the center could hold conferences to evaluate policies. It could contribute to the progress of various social science research and policy institutes established only recently in Asian countries. A major concern of the comparative studies center should be the alleviation of poverty, the historic problem of densely populated Asia. East Asia has demonstrated that poverty can be eradicated, and the end of the Cold War should free resources for an all-out attack on the problem.

The United States, bogged down with domestic problems, can no longer play the role it played in previous decades. But Japan, the powerhouse of Asia, can take the place of the United States. It can take the lead in assisting Southeast Asian growth. The example set by East Asia in trade liberalization and institutional development can influence Southeast Asia to do likewise. Then all of these countries can help the rest of Asia. Thus Japan's role is crucial, as it can set the tone for the rest of Asia to follow, similar to what the Marshall Plan did for Western Europe in the early postwar era. But since there is a limit to what donors can do, Southeast Asian countries should adopt more outward-looking policies and improve their growth performance.[39]

I am aware of how difficult this role will be. In trade liberalization, it entails the phasing out of monsoon Asia's small peasant farms, whose sheer numbers deter political leaders in Japan, Taiwan, and South Korea from forthright action. And yet this should be carried out if the constraints imposed by the monsoons are to be overcome and if the minifarms are to be converted to large-scale farms with enhanced labor productivity. But this is just the right moment in history to make these changes because of the slowdown in the West, currency realignments, and labor shortages in East Asia.

The contribution Japan can make in taking the initiative to liberalize trade and investments in other Asian countries will improve the prospects for the United States as it struggles to overcome its massive trade deficits and avoid further protectionism. This, together with assistance to develop human resources, should lessen the backlash effects, as Japan's foreign investments begin to dominate many Southeast Asian economies. The foreign policies of Japan have paid too much attention to the West and not enough to its neighbors. The time has come for Japan to "take its place in the circle of its Asia-Pacific neighbors . . . and construct some designs for Japan's responsibility in the region."[40]

And Southeast Asia could do more to catch up. East Asia is growing as fast as can be expected, and its potential for increasing its growth rate is minimal. But the potential of Southeast Asia is large and should be exploited more fully in the 1990s. Improvement of the foreign investment climate can be speeded up in Indonesia and the Philippines. For example, these countries do not permit foreign department stores to be built, unlike Thailand, Malaysia, Singapore, and Hong Kong. By banning foreign competition, they are missing the opportunity to create more jobs in their manufacturing industries. The experts employed by Japanese department stores that locate in other countries assist local manufacturers to improve the products that they sell to the department stores, enabling these local producers to make products they can export. This benefit is in addition to the benefits to local consumers, who find their local department stores improving with foreign competition.

Thailand and Indonesia should develop their physical infrastructure, especially transportation, and spend more on secondary education—with emphasis on technical and vocational training. In the meantime, South Asian countries should shift more resources into the development of agriculture and human resources, so that by the end of the twentieth century they will be in a position to benefit from the development of East and Southeast Asia.

A CONCLUDING NOTE

With the participation of Pacific countries such as the United States, Canada, Australia, and New Zealand, the march to the Pacific century has begun. The center of civilization, which moved westward to eastern and southern Europe from traditional China in the middle of the second millennium, and then to Baltic Europe, and finally to the North Atlantic in the nineteenth century, may be moving across the western Pacific, completing a full circle of the globe.

But recent events show that the West cannot be so easily counted out. With western Europe moving toward a huge common market, eastern Europe converting into market economies, and the end of the Cold War freeing vast resources for development, a rejuvenated West can regain the momentum of the past. If so, it may be that we may again see the rise of two major centers of economic growth, which can compete to make the twenty-first century a century of unprecedented human progress.

# NOTES

CHAPTER 1: INTRODUCTION

1. *Processes* are defined as "systematic series of actions directed to some end" (*Random House Dictionary of the English Language,* unabridged, 1967).

2. R. C. O. Matthews et al., *British Economic Growth* (Stanford: Stanford University Press, 1982); they cite the works of Nerlove (1967), Nadiri (1970), and Kennedy and Thirwall (1972). See also E. Malinvaud et al., *French Economic Growth* (Stanford: Stanford University Press, 1975).

3. In nowhere else in the world is the change from the wet season to the dry season so clear-cut and extensive. This and the next section are brief summaries of Harry Oshima, *Economic Growth in Monsoon Asia: A Comparative Survey* (Tokyo: University of Tokyo Press, 1987), chap. 1.

4. Harry Oshima, "The Growth of Factor Productivity in the U.S.: The Significance of New Technologies in the Early Decades of the Twentieth Century," *Journal of Economic History* 44 (1984).

5. World Bank, *World Development Report;* Asian Development Bank, *Key Indicators;* Oshima, *Economic Growth in Monsoon Asia.*

6. Islam reduced the work force by demanding that females be kept in the homes.

7. From 1880 to 1930, Java's population doubled. Nena Vreeland et al., *Area Handbook for Indonesia,* 3d ed. (Washington, D.C.: American University, 1975), 27. Indonesia's outer islands have many natural resources per capita (land, oil, minerals), but the Javanese resist moving to these islands.

8. The slowdown in population growth, as childhood education and female employment increased, raised the opportunity costs of children. The slow rise of the labor force further intensified the process toward full employment, accelerating the growth of labor productivity and reducing income disparities.

CHAPTER 2: DIFFERENTIAL PRODUCTIVITY TRENDS

1. Product per worker is equal to GDP divided by the working population; product per capita is equal to GDP divided by total population.

2. Gross domestic product data are from World Bank, *World Development Report.*

3. Simon Kuznets, *The Economic Growth of Nations* (Cambridge: Harvard University Press, 1971).

4. Moses Abramovitz, "Economic Growth in the United States," *American Economic Review* (1962) reviews Edward Dennison's *The Sources of Economic Growth in the U.S., and the Alternatives Before Us* (New York: Committee for Economic Develop-

ment, 1962). Also see Abramovitz, *Why Growth Rates Differ* (Washington, D.C.: Brookings, 1970); and John Kendrick, ed., *International Comparisons of Productivity and Causes of the Slowdown* (Cambridge: Harvard University Press, 1984).

5. Another measure widely used in the West is product per man-hour, which is more a measure of efficiency. Man-hour data for the economy as a whole are difficult to find in most Asian countries.

6. World Bank, *World Development Report 1987*, 270–71. Per capita dollar product in 1980 computed by the purchasing power method was twice or more than those estimated from exchange rates for India, Indonesia, the Philippines, Sri Lanka, and Pakistan, but for Japan it was about 5 percent lower in 1980. Since then the margin has widened 20 to 30 percent, because the yen has doubled in value: exchange rates are related more to balance of payments than to purchasing power.

7. Output per worker is equal to yield per hectare multiplied by size of farm per worker.

8. Harry Oshima, "East Asia's High Growth," *Singapore Economic Review* (1986).

9. Simon Kuznets, *Modern Economic Growth* (New Haven: Yale University Press, 1966), 85.

10. For a detailed discussion of the agroindustrial service transition, see Oshima, *Economic Growth in Monsoon Asia,* chap. 2. The agroindustrial transition is completed when sector *I* employment begins to exceed sector *A* employment. The industrial-service transition is completed when sector *S* employment begins to exceed sector *I* employment.

11. For details, see Oshima, "East Asia's High Growth."

12. Ibid. For detailed studies on agricultural productivity, see V. Ruttan, Y. Hayami, and H. M. Southworth, eds., *Agricultural Growth in Japan, Taiwan, South Korea and the Philippines* (Honolulu: University Press of Hawaii for the East-West Center, 1979).

13. *Business World,* Manila, February 1, 1988; *Thailand Statistical Yearbook, 1985–1986;* Food and Agriculture Organization, *Production Yearbook, 1986*. The rapid spread of Thai mechanization was partly due to the extremely large female participation in farm work, which favors the use of machines to do heavy work, and also to the small number of landless workers, since large tracts of new land were opened up in the 1960s and 1970s for farming.

14. Data from the special issue on multiple cropping in Asian development, *Philippine Economic Journal* (1975).

15. For data see Harry Oshima, "Levels and Trends of Farm Families' Non-agricultural Incomes at Different Stages of Monsoon Development," in *Rural Industrialization and Non-Farm Activities of Asian Farmers*, ed. Y. B. Choe and Fu-chen Lo (Seoul: Korea Rural Economic Institute; Kuala Lampur: Asian and Pacific Development Center, 1986), table 1.

16. Harry Oshima, "Postwar Growth in the Service Sector in Asian Countries: A Macro-Comparative View," *Philippine Review of Economics and Business* (1979), table 1.

17. Oshima, *Economic Growth in Monsoon Asia,* 163.

18. Harry Oshima, "Human Resources in Macro-Comparative Productivity Trends in Asia," in *Development Strategies and Productivity Issues in Asia,* ed. Shinichi Ichimura (Hong Kong: Asian Productivity Organization, 1988).

19. The U.S. national accounts do not estimate government capital formation. Also, a larger percentage of total investment went into residential construction in the United States (28.3 percent, compared to Japan's 24.1 percent).

20. The average age of U.S. industrial capital stock was 11 years compared to 7.6 years in Japan. See *Japan Economic Journal,* Tokyo (July 28 1990). This also reflects the shortage of Japanese labor, which forced entrepreneurs to substitute new machines for old ones.

21. *Nikkei Weekly,* Tokyo, August 3, 1991.

22. International Labor Organization, *Yearbook of Labor Statistics, 1988.*

23. *International Comparison of Labor Productivity* (Tokyo: Japan Productivity Center, September 1991). In fact, Japan ranked tenth in the world in 1988 in GDP per employed person, behind all OECD countries except Spain. The reason for this was low agricultural productivity, along with low wholesale and retail trade. Even in manufacturing, Japan ranked sixth, behind the United States, the United Kingdom, Italy, Belgium, and Canada.

24. *Japan, Statistical Yearbook, 1963; Japan, 1955 Population Census.*

25. *Japan, Statistical Yearbook, 1983, 1987.*

26. W. Galenson, ed., *Foreign Trade and Investment: Economic Development in the Newly Industrializing Asian Countries* (Ithaca: Cornell University Press, 1985), 47; *Statistical Abstract of the Republic of China, 1959;* S. P. S. Ho, *Economic Development of Taiwan, 1860–1970* (New Haven: Yale University Press, 1978); *Korea, Statistical Yearbook, 1970; Korea, Census of Population 1955, 1965.*

27. *Comparative Information on Productivity Levels and Changes in APO Member Countries* (Tokyo: Asian Productivity Organization, 1991), tables 1, 2, 3.

28. World Bank, *World Development Report, 1988.*

29. *Statistical Yearbook of China, 1986,* 583.

30. World Bank, *World Development Report, 1988; Statistical Yearbook of China, 1987; International Herald Tribune,* Tokyo, February 3, 1988.

31. *Statistical Yearbook of China, 1987.*

32. Anthony Tang and Agnes Quisumbing, "Chinese Agricultural Reforms and Their Rationale," in *Research in Asian Economic Studies,* vol. 2 (Greenwich: JAI, 1990).

CHAPTER 3: CAPITAL FORMATION AND TECHNOLOGICAL CHANGE

1. E. N. Wolff, "Capital Formation and Productivity Convergence," *American Economic Review* (June 1991), pertains to the long-run data of developed countries.

2. Robert Solow, "A Contribution to the Theory of Economic Growth," *Quarterly Journal of Economics* (February 1956); R. F. Harrod, *Towards a Dynamic Economics* (New York: St. Martin's, 1948).

3. Harry Oshima, "Capital-Output Ratios in Underdeveloped Countries," in *Proceedings of the International Statistical Institute Conference* (Tokyo, 1960). At the time of the controversy, data on capital were scarce, and postwar growth had not been going on for long. We now have both the data and the hindsight.

4. K. Ohkawa and M. Shinohara, eds., *Patterns of Japanese Economic Develop-*

*ment, A Quantitative Appraisal* (New Haven: Yale University Press, 1979), 154; official national accounts.

5. Official national accounts. Left out from the calculation were the recession years of 1974, 1975, and 1982 for Taiwan and 1980 for South Korea, when GNP growth was negative. Professor Toshiyuki Mizoguchi of Hitotsubashi University pointed out to me that the low construction levels in Taiwan and Korea were due to the fact that Japan had built railways, roads, and other infrastructures in its colonial period.

6. United States, *Statistical Abstract, 1986;* J. B. De Long and Laurence H. Summers, "Equipment Investment and Economic Growth," *Quarterly Journal of Economics* (May 1991).

7. Official statistical yearbooks and national accounts. Heavy industries include paper, chemicals, petroleum, metallic and nonmetallic industries, fabricated metal products, and machinery.

8. See Harry Oshima, "Problems of Heavy Industrialization in Asian Development," *Philippine Review of Economics and Business* 20 (1983). Capital-output ratios are affected by capacity utilization, because output in the denominator is low if there is unused capacity. In contrast, in East Asia and Thailand, factories were often operated day and night.

9. Kuznets, *Capital in the American Economy* (Princeton: NBER, 1961); Moses Abramovitz, "Nature and Significance of Kuznets Cycles," *Economic Development and Cultural Change* (April 1961). On construction swings, see Moses Abramovitz, *Evidence of Long Swings in Aggregate Construction since the Civil War* (New York: NBER, 1964), which contains extensive references to the literature. Miyohei Shinohara found long swings in the Japanese data, tracing them back to the early decades of this century, a time when the economy was still predominantly agricultural; see Miyohei Shinohara, *Structural Changes in Japan's Economic Development* (Tokyo: Kinokuniga, 1970), chap. 7.

10. Moses Abramovitz, "Passing of the Kuznets Cycle," *Economica* (November 1968).

11. Abramovitz, *Economic Development and Cultural Change.* See also his press interview in Manila, in *Businessday* (Manila), October 6, 1977.

12. For data on money supply, prices, and public finance, see Asian Development Bank, *Key Indicators, 1987.*

13. *Personal Income Distribution in Taiwan Area of the Republic of China, 1983; Thailand, Report on Socio-Economic Survey, 1985;* Harry Oshima, "Perspectives on Trends in Asian Income Distribution," in *Ekonomi dan keuangan, Indonesia* 30 (1981); Harry Oshima, "Changes in Philippine Income Distribution in the 1970s," *Philippine Review of Economics and Business* 20 (1983).

14. Harry Oshima, "Debt Repayment and Business Cycles," *Review of Economics and Statistics* 40 (1958); *Hong Kong, Annual Digest Statistics, 1984; Singapore, Economic and Social Statistics, 1960–1962, 1983.* Taiwan is least troubled by external debt, as it has amassed one of the largest amounts of foreign assets—perhaps the largest in Asia on a per capita basis.

15. Note, however, that the residual in the production function used is not just technological change.

16. Robert Solow, "Total Factor Productivity of the Manufacturing Industries in Thailand, 1963–1975," Seminar Paper Series 1982–83, National University of

Singapore; E. K. Y. Chen, "Factor Inputs, Total Productivity and Economic Growth: the Asian Case," *Developing Economies* (June 1977); and M. Ezaki, "Growth Accounting of the Philippines: A Comparative Study of the 1965 and 1969 Input–Output Tables," *Philippine Economic Journal*, no. 29 (1975). For Japan, see K. Ohkawa and H. Rosovsky, *Japanese Economic Growth* (Stanford: Stanford University Press, 1972); and Z. Griliches and I. Mairisse, "R & D and Productivity Growth: Comparing Japanese and U.S. Manufacturing," Working Paper 1778 (NBER, December 1985).

17. Z. Griliches, "Productivity and Technical Change," *NBER Reporter* (Spring 1988): 3.

18. *Japan, Statistical Yearbook, 1978, 1980, and 1987.*

19. M. Peck and S. Tamura, "Technology," in *Asia's New Giant*, ed. H. Patrick and H. Rosovsky (Washington, D.C.: Brookings, 1976).

20. Paitoon Wiboonchutikula, "Japanese Direct Investment and Technology Transfer to Thailand," *TDRI Quarterly Newsletter*, Bangkok (September 1987).

21. Computed from Asian Development Bank, *Key Indicators, 1988.*

22. Asian and Pacific Center for Transfer of Technology, *Technology Policies and Planning*, Country Study Series (Bangalore, 1986).

23. S. Urata, "The Impact of Imported Technologies in Japan's Economic Development in 1950s and 1960s," paper prepared for the Japan-Korea Comparative Study Project, East-West Center, Honolulu, April 1987.

24. Asian and Pacific Center for Transfer of Technology, *Technology Policies and Planning.*

25. For a detailed discussion of agricultural technology, see Hiroshi Kakazu, *Industrial Technological Capabilities and Policies in Selected Asian Developing Countries* (Manila: Asian Development Bank, 1990).

26. Oshima, "The Growth of Factor Productivity in the U.S."

27. For example, the Philippines and Sri Lanka had sufficient educated manpower to handle the labor-intensive technologies in the 1960s and 1970s, but there was little need to save labor when there was so much surplus labor.

28. Peck and Tamura, "Technology."

29. Urata, "The Impact of Imported Technologies."

30. *Joint Conference on the Industrial Policies of the Republic of China and the Republic of Korea, 1984, and 1987*, Conference Series 4 and 6 (Tapei: Chung Hua Institution for Economic Research, 1985, 1987).

31. Asian and Pacific Center for Transfer of Technology, *Technology Policies and Planning*. In the Philippines, a technology import division was added to the Science and Technology Council only recently. In Indonesia, there is no information on payment for technology import.

32. Peck and Tamura, "Technology."

33. South Korea and Taiwan are approaching the technology frontier in many of their export industries. South Korea is finding that it is falling behind Japan and Western countries in technology in the heavy industries, such as automobiles, iron, and steel. It will have to spend huge amounts for R and D to keep up. Thus as these countries come closer to the technology frontier, their growth will slow down.

CHAPTER 4: PERSONAL SAVINGS AND CONSUMPTION

1. In the United States, for example, 1970 capital consumption allowances were 50 percent larger than personal saving, and by 1986 they grew 300 percent. *U.S. Survey of Current Business* (October 1987). In Japan, with the increase of corporate activities, depreciation allowances have grown to equal personal savings.

2. See Harry Oshima, "Meiji Fiscal Policy and Agricultural Progress," in *The State and Economic Enterprise*, ed. W. W. Lockwood (Princeton: Princeton University Press, 1955). This essay argues that the amount of forced saving was too large and was detrimental to the development of agriculture, eventually leading to Japan's invasion of China in the 1930s, as the peasantry sought more land to cultivate.

3. W. W. Rostow, *The Stages of Economic Growth* (New York: Cambridge University Press, 1971); and Arthur Lewis, *Economic Development with Unlimited Supply of Labor* (Manchester: Manchester School, 1954).

4. For a concise summary, see Chen Sun and Min-yi Liang, "Savings in Taiwan 1953–1980," paper prepared for the Conference on Experiences and Lessons of Economic Development in Taiwan, Taipei, December 1981.

5. Sun and Liang, ibid., point out that regression analyses of income theories of savings do not adequately explain why Taiwan's savings rate is the highest in the world. They also find factors such as income distribution, interest rates, and inflationary expectations inadequate. These theories of savings were intended to explain cyclical movements, not long-term trends.

6. *Japan Economic Journal* (April 1987). France's rate was 13 percent, West Germany's was 12.7 percent, Canada's was 11.5 percent, and Sweden's was less than 1 percent. The U.S. rate of 5–6 percent is not defined the same as in the UN system of accounts.

7. Harry Oshima, "Consumer Asset Formation," *Economic Journal*, London (March 1961); Oshima, "Debt Repayment and Business Cycles." Debt repayments by consumers were three times the debt repayments by business and governments.

8. Bank of Japan, *1986 Survey;* Central Bank of Taiwan, *Economic Outlook Quarterly* (April 1986); Bank of Korea, *Saving Survey 1984, 1985, 1986.* Japanese savers are unable to buy homes because of the exorbitant prices and higher down payments; instead, they purchase consumer durables and travel.

9. See A. W. Wright and D. S. Nivision, ed. *Confucianism in Action* (Stanford: Stanford University Press, 1959).

10. "The Role of Savings in Economic Development," *Conference on Economic Development in the Republic of China on Taiwan,* Conference Series 7 (Taipei: Chung Hua Institution for Economic Research, 1987).

11. Charles Horiuchi, "Importance of Saving for Education in Japan," *Kyoto University Economic Review* (April 1985); Charles Horiuchi, "Cost of Marriage and Marriage-Related Saving in Japan," *Kyoto University Economic Review* (April 1987).

12. See figures 7.4, 7.5, and 7.6. This contrasts sharply with the United States, where savings come almost entirely from upper-income groups.

13. For a discussion of this problem, see Moses Abramovitz, "Welfare Quandaries and Productivity Concerns," *American Economic Review* (March 1981); Moses Abramovitz, *Catching Up and Falling Behind* (Stockholm: Trade Union Institute of Economic Research, 1986).

14. Asian Development Bank, *Key Indicators, 1991.*

15. Abramovitz, *Evidence of Long Swings in Aggregate Construction since the Civil War.*

16. Estimates based on official national accounts.

17. International Labor Organization, *Yearbook of Labor Statistics 1988; Statistical Yearbook of the Republic of China, 1989;* Oshima, *Economic Growth in Monsoon Asia.*

18. In Taiwan (1987) and South Korea (1985), fixed capital formation in the service sector was about half of the industrial sector; in Japan it was only a third. Data from official national accounts.

19. Angus Maddison, *Phases of Capitalist Growth* (Oxford: Oxford University Press), chap. 2.

20. Ibid. Gross national savings began to fall in the United Kingdom in the late decades of the nineteenth century; see R. C. O. Matthews, C. H. Feinstein, and J. C. Odling-Smee, *British Economic Growth* (Stanford: Stanford University Press, 1982), chap. 2.

21. Ibid., 210.

22. Estimates based on data from Abramovitz, "Welfare Quandaries and Productivity Concerns"; United States, *Economic Indicators.* No data are available for the Netherlands.

23. Data from Bank of Japan, *Flow of Funds 1988,* Special Paper 180, appendix table 2; *Japan, Statistical Yearbook, 1987.*

24. *Statistical Yearbook of the Republic of China, 1989;* Asian Development Bank, *Key Indicators, 1989; Korea, Statistical Yearbook, 1987.* In 1986, Korea's returns on investments were US$812, compared to payments of US$4,020.

25. Official national accounts.

26. United States, *Statistical Abstract, 1989.*

27. Ibid.; and United States, *Historical Statistics, 1970.*

28. Kuznets, *Modern Economic Growth,* 429.

29. Simon Kuznets and A. Bergson, eds., *Economic Trends in the Soviet Union* (Cambridge: Harvard University Press, 1963).

30. $GY \equiv \Delta C + \Delta S \equiv \Delta Y/Y \equiv \Delta C/C \, (C/Y) + \Delta S/S \, (S/Y)$. If $C$ in the first term and $S$ in the second term are canceled out, we have remaining $\Delta C + \Delta S$, which is equal to $\Delta Y$, because of the Keynesian identity $S = I$.

31. See M. K. Bennett, *The World's Food* (New York: Food Research Institute, 1954), 64, 65.

32. Left out from the discussion is the lower consumption due to having fewer children, leaving more savings for education, thereby enabling quality to substitute for quantity of children. This is discussed in Andrew Mason, *National Saving Rates and Population Growth: A New Model and New Evidence,* Population Institute Reprint 215 (Honolulu: East-West Center, 1987). Also, smaller families permit women to go out to work, thus increasing incomes.

33. In Taiwan between 1955 and 1985, the share of population in cities and towns with more than 100,000 doubled, while the number of college and high school graduates rose fivefold. See *Statistical Abstract of the Republic of China, 1987.* Similar changes occurred in Japan between 1950 and 1980 and in South Korea from 1955 to 1985. For the city-states, even though the growth of urbanization was moderate, the upward changes

in occupational and educational structure were as large as in the other East Asian countries.

34. These data are from Japan's nutrition surveys and give lower figures than those estimated from food balance sheets. See Harry Oshima, "Food Consumption, Nutrition, and Economic Development in Asian Countries," *Economic Development and Cultural Change* (July 1967), for details.

35. Oshima, *Economic Growth in Monsoon Asia*, chap. 4.

36. The reduction in per capita caloric intake in Japan and Taiwan was largely at the expense of rice consumption. The Japanese Ministry of Agriculture reported that per capita annual rice consumption fell after 1962, when a peak of 183 kilograms was reached. In 1985 it was down to 74.6 kilograms. The younger generations eat a more diversified diet than their elders, and bread is more appropriate with Western meals. Hence, with growth and modernization, the prevalence of simple meals, such as salted fish with lots of rice, disappeared, so that from the demand side the importance of monsoon paddy agriculture declined—a new phenomenon in the history of monsoon Asia. Per capita rice intake has been falling in Taiwan since the 1970s but has not yet fallen in South Korea.

37. *Bangladesh, Household Income and Expenditure Survey, 1985–86.*

38. Data from *Historical Statistics of the United States: Colonial Times to 1970; Statistical Abstract of the United States, 1987.*

CHAPTER 5: UNDEREMPLOYMENT AND UNEMPLOYMENT

1. Ragnar Nurske, *Problems of Capital Formation in Underdeveloped Countries* (New York: Oxford University Press, 1953); Arthur Lewis, *Economic Development with Unlimited Supply of Labor* (Manchester: Manchester School, 1954); Harvey Leibenstein, *Economic Backwardness and Economic Growth* (Berkeley and Los Angeles: University of California Press, 1957); Gustav Ranis and John Fei, "A Theory of Economic Development," *American Economic Review* (September 1961).

2. Harry Oshima, "Underemployment in Backward Economies," *Journal of Political Economy* (June 1958); Harry Oshima, "The Ranis-Fei Model of Economic Development," *Journal of Political Economy* (June 1963).

3. Harry Oshima, "Labor Absorption in East and Southeast Asia: Summary Perspective and Prospects," *Philippine Economic Journal* 15 (1976).

4. World Bank, *World Development Report, 1987.*

5. Harry Oshima, "Malaysia's Labor Force Trends and Unemployment Problems in Comparative Perspective," *Malaysian Journal of Economic Studies* (December 1988).

6. Asian Development Bank, *Key Indicators, 1987.*

7. Ibid.

8. Much of the discussion from this point on is a brief summary of Oshima, *Economic Growth in Monsoon Asia.*

9. Oshima, "East Asia's High Growth."

10. Harry Oshima, "Sector Sources of Philippine Postwar Economic Growth," *Journal of Philippine Development*, no. 1 (1983).

11. The mismanagement of the Philippine economy came to a head in the 1980s,

when per capita GNP declined substantially in two consecutive years (1984 and 1985), unprecedented in postwar Asia. Unemployment has always been worrisome in the Philippines, although kept under control in the late 1970s with large loans from the Middle East, which were used to prime the economy. On the theory of insecurity and high fertility, see Simon Kuznets, "Notes on Population Trends in LDC's," *Philippine Economic Journal* 3 (1977).

12. Oshima, *Economic Growth in Monsoon Asia,* chap. 8. The fall in fertility of Communist countries is related to the welfare portions of their programs, which reduced uncertainty as to jobs, old age, health, and other basic needs.

13. *Business World, May 23, 1988.*

14. Oshima, "Malaysia's Labor Force Trends."

15. Perhaps Thailand was a bit too cautious. If it had borrowed to construct roads and other infrastructure, it would not be so severely short of infrastructure.

16. Land reform, started in 1947 and completed in 1950, was comprehensive, transferring nearly 4 million hectares of land and limiting absentee landlords to 1 hectare of land. Japan's land reform became the precedent; Taiwan and South Korea followed in the early 1950s. See T. Ogura, ed., *Agricultural Development in Japan* (Tokyo: Fuji Publications, 1963).

17. *Japan, Statistical Yearbook.*

18. Oshima, *Economic Growth in Monsoon Asia.*

19. Harry Oshima, "Reinterpreting Japan's Postwar Growth," *Economic Development and Cultural Change* (October 1982).

20. Data from Shintani, "Estimates of Average Man-Days per Crop in Agriculture, 1872–1970," *Kezai Kenkyu,* Tokyo (July 1974). These man-days are lower than Taiwan's because of the use of more equipment in Japan.

21. Data from Ministry of Agriculture and Forestry.

22. Shintani, "Estimates of Average Man-Days."

23. M. Umemura et al., *Long-Term Statistics of Japan,* vol. 9, *Agriculture and Forest* (Tokyo: Toyo Keizai Shimposha, 1966), 227.

24. The ratio of improved area to cultivated area was 55 percent in 1940 and 90 percent in 1960. See Y. Hayami, *A Century of Agricultural Growth in Japan* (Tokyo: University of Tokyo Press, 1975), 172.

25. *Japan, Farm Household Economy Survey, 1959.*

26. *Japan, Statistical Yearbook.*

27. Harry Oshima, "The Industrial and Demographic Transitions in East Asia," *Population and Development Review* (December 1983).

28. *Labor Force Surveys of Taiwan;* Harry Oshima and Wen Hui Lai, "Labor Absorption in Taiwan," *Philippine Economic Journal,* nos. 1, 2 (1976): 142. Paul Liu, *Labor Welfare, Income Distribution, and Export-Led Industrialization: The Experience of Taiwan* (Nankang: Academia Sinica, 1987), 12, worked out underemployment rates, adjusted for unused man-days in agriculture plus the unemployed (including those who intended to work but were not seeking work) and got the lowest levels in 1967–68.

29. *Statistical Yearbook of the Republic of China, 1987.*

30. *Yearbook of Labor Statistics, Republic of China, 1978, 1987.*

31. Earlier studies date the absolute decline in agricultural employment to 1970, but later figures indicate that it started earlier. See Teng-hui Lee, *Agricultural and Economic*

*Development in Taiwan,* vols. 1, 2 (Taichung: Joint Commission on Rural Reconstruction, 1983).

32. Y. M. Mao, "Land Reform and Agricultural Development," in *Agricultural Development in China, Japan, and Korea,* ed. C. Hou and T. S. Hou (Nankang: Academia Sinica, 1982), 748.

33. In the late 1960s, the share of irrigation to total arable land in Taiwan was the second highest in Asia, next to that of Japan, but in 1982 it was equal to Japan's. See Harry Oshima, "Food and Agriculture in Asia Towards the Year 2000," in *Asia Toward the Year 2000* (Kuala Lumpur: APDC, 1988).

34. *Philippine Economic Journal,* nos. 1, 2 (1975).

35. Ibid. Exporters received rebates for duty they paid on certain imports; export zones were established; above all, measures were taken to promote education and training, especially vocational schools and institutions, in the mid-1960s; later, on-the-job training was instituted. For data on the capital-labor intensity of Taiwan industries, see *Taiwan, Industry and Commerce Census.*

36. Oshima, *Economic Growth in Monsoon Asia;* Shirley Kuo and John Fei estimated that direct and indirect labor used by total exports as a share of labor used by total final demand in 1961 and 1971 was 12 percent and 33 percent, compared to 88 percent and 67 percent of domestic demand. See Kuo and Fei, "Export Expansion in the Republic of China," in *Foreign Trade and Investment.*

37. Paul Kuznets, "Labor Absorption in Korea," *Philippine Economic Journal,* nos. 1, 2 (1976), showed the pronounced seasonality of employment.

38. National Statistics Bureau, Taipei.

39. *South Korea, Statistical Yearbook; South Korea, Economically Active Survey.*

40. Oshima, "The Industrial and Demographic Transitions in East Asia," fig. 3.

41. Korea Institute for Population and Health, *Population and Family Planning in Korea, 1986.*

42. S. H. Ban, P. Y. Moon, and D. H. Perkins, *Rural Development: Studies in the Modernization of Republic of Korea* (Cambridge: Harvard University Press, 1980), 53. To get labor input per hectare, the growth rate of cultivated land was deducted from the growth rate of labor used.

43. *South Korea, Statistical Yearbook.*

44. World Bank, *World Development Report, 1986.*

45. Ban, Moon, and Perkins, *Rural Development.* For example, the government decreed the use of HYVs for all farms, but it soon found that HYVs could not resist blast, and large crop losses were incurred in the late 1970s.

46. Ibid.

47. *South Korea, Statistical Yearbook, 1986.* Rice imports dropped substantially in 1984 and 1985, to $2–3 million.

48. Ibid.

49. Oshima, "East Asia's High Growth." During the Korean War, the managers, technicians, and skilled workers from the north fled in large numbers to the south.

50. I was unable to find estimates for the 1980s. These are from Hak-Chung Choo, "Economic Growth and Income Distribution," in *Human Resources and Social Development in Korea,* ed. Chong-kee Park (Seoul: Korean Development Institute, 1980).

51. Laurence Chau estimated unemployment rates at 16 percent in 1954; Chau,

"Industrial Growth and Employment in Hong Kong," *Philippine Economic Journal*, nos. 1, 2 (1976). The article includes details of labor absorption in Hong Kong in the 1950s, 1960s, and early 1970s.

52. World Bank, *World Development Report, 1987*.

53. More details on this technological-educational approach to fertility are found in Oshima, *Economic Growth in Monsoon Asia*.

54. World Bank, *World Development Report, 1987*.

55. The 1959 census of population indicates that the unemployment rate was 13 percent. See K. F. Yin and D. H. Clark, "Labor Absorption and Economic Growth in Singapore," *Philippine Economic Journal*, nos. 1 and 2 (1976). The full-time equivalent unemployment of 11 percent for 1966 takes into account those working part-time. For details, see Harry Oshima, "Growth and Unemployment in Singapore," *Malayan Economic Review* (October 1967). Excluding part-time workers, the open unemployment rate was 9 percent.

56. Asian Development Bank, *Key Indicators, 1984, 1987*.

57. On this, see Yin and Clark, "Labor Absorption and Economic Growth in Singapore." They point out that the nuclear family became more prevalent in Singapore than in Hong Kong because of the more extensive housing of families in high-rise apartment buildings. And full employment made it difficult to find domestic help in both countries.

58. B. Rao and M. Ramakrishnan, "Structural Changes and Change in Income Distribution," in *Income Distribution by Sectors and Overtime in East and Southeast Asia*, ed. H. Oshima and T. Mizoguchi (Quezon City: University of the Philippines; Tokyo: Hitotsubashi University, 1978).

59. Data from *Singapore, Yearbook of Statistics, 1985–86*.

CHAPTER 6: AGRICULTURAL DIVERSIFICATION AND STRUCTURAL CHANGE

1. The chapter uses sections of Harry Oshima, "Agricultural Diversification in the Philippines Recovery Program," *Philippine Review of Economics and Business* (July 1986); and Harry Oshima, *Underemployment and Off-Farm Employment in Indonesia* (Jakarta: BIDE/DAI project for Bappenas, 1987). It also draws from *Philippine Economic Journal*, nos. 1, 2 (1975).

2. See, for example, data from Food and Nutrition Research Institute, Philippines, *Nationwide Nutrition Survey, 1978, 1982*.

3. This section on food consumption is based on Harry Oshima, "Food and Agriculture in Asia Toward the Year 2000," in *Asia Toward the Year 2000* (Kuala Lumpur: APDC, 1988).

4. United Nations, *World Population Prospects, 1985*.

5. Ernesto Pernia, *Implications of Urbanization for Food Policy Analysis in Asian Countries* (Tokyo: Population Research Institute, Nihon University, 1986).

6. L. A. Gonzales, "An Economic Perspective of Crop Diversification in Rainfed Areas: Implications for National and Regional Planning," *Philippine Journal of Crop Science* 9 (1984). Corn, the most important diversified crop, was suited to 1.5 million hectares.

7. Ibid., 9. These measures, as in other quantitative indexes, do not take into account qualitative aspects. But in the long run, the quality of Philippine products can be improved, particularly under conditions of better institutional mechanisms, so that foreign exchange saved from import substitution and earned from exports can rise.

8. Irrigation designed for rice growing is not ideal for diversified crops, and experiments are under way using furrow and sprinkler systems.

9. But in many countries, the institutional constraints on diversification may be more serious. In countries like the Philippines, with many big landlords, land reform becomes necessary. Landlords traditionally do not receive rents from diversified cultivation, and they are likely to oppose it on the grounds that the fertility of the land is lowered. Without cooperatives and other farmer organizations, collection, marketing, financing, and transporting may be too expensive, since powerful groups of trader-truckers can exercise monopsonistic powers over small farmers.

10. Oshima, "Agricultural Diversification in the Philippines Recovery Program."

11. *Taiwan, Agricultural Yearbook, 1985.*

12. Kuznets, *Economic Growth of Nations*, 275–302.

13. For data on the labor intensity of the production of crops other than fruits, see Oshima, "Agricultural Diversification in the Philippines Recovery Program."

14. Without these supports, land reform will fail, as shown by the experience of the U.S. occupation of the Philippines in the prewar period and in the Burmese land reform under Ne Win in the 1960s.

15. Kuznets, *Modern Economic Growth*, 85.

16. Kuznets, *Economic Growth of Nations*, table 22.

17. Oshima, *Economic Growth in Monsoon Asia*, chap. 1.

18. This was especially true in Nehru's India, in Mao's China, and in the Philippines. See ibid., chaps. 7, 8, 9.

19. This section updates Harry Oshima, "Notes on Differential Growth and Structural Changes in Postwar Asia," *Philippine Economic Journal*, no. 3 (1977), which also contains the sources of data for the 1980s; and Harry Oshima, "Postwar Growth of the Service Sector in Asian Countries."

I follow Kuznets's classification by including transportation and communications in the secondary sector instead of the tertiary sector. He argues that the high capital requirements of transportation and communications make them closer to public utilities. Also, as in the secondary sector, they are characterized by scale economies.

20. Asian Development Bank, *Key Indicators, 1987.*

21. Calculated from K. Ohkawa and M. Shinohara, *Patterns of Japanese Economic Development*, table A21.

22. UNIDO, *India* and *China,* Industrial Development Review Series.

23. M. T. Lim, "An Evaluation of the Performance of the Steel and Cement Industries," *Philippine Economic Journal*, nos. 3, 4 (1981); UNIDO, *Philippines*. Industrial Development Review Series.

24. UNIDO, *Malaysia* and *Indonesia,* Industrial Development Review Series.

25. Household survey data from Sri Lanka (1973), Malaysia (1967–68), and the Philippines (1971) indicate the Gini coefficient to be higher in the $S$ sector than in the $I$ and $A$ sectors.

26. U.S. data from *Historical Statistics of the U.S.: Colonial Times to 1957.*

27. Thailand's 1937 census of population. The Philippine 1903 census also shows a larger number of merchants, about 137,000, or 4 percent of the total labor force.

28. See Oshima, "Postwar Growth in the Service Sector in Asian Countries," table 2. About half of the urban labor force and about a third of the rural labor force are in the S sector. But with the decline of agriculture, the S sector's labor force share rises, especially in personal services.

29. International Labor Organization, *Yearbook of Labor Statistics, 1985;* Taiwan data came from its statistical yearbook.

30. The general practice of relating total population to total land is inappropriate for our purpose, because urban countries like Singapore and Hong Kong will have the highest density in Asia.

31. Of course, the technology of rice production became increasingly labor-intensive in the 1920s with the new rice seeds from Japan, which required chemical fertilizers, insecticides, and more careful cultivation. And even more labor per hectare was needed for the high-yielding varieties of the International Rice Research Institute.

CHAPTER 7: OFF-FARM EMPLOYMENT AND MACROPRODUCTIVITY

1. This chapter integrates and updates two papers, one written for a conference held in Chiang-Mai, Thailand, in August 1983, and the other written for a seminar in Seoul, Korea, in April 1985. See Harry Oshima, "Off-Farm Employment and Income in Postwar East Asian Growth," in *Off-Farm Employment in the Development of Rural Asia,* ed. R. T. Shand (Canberra: National Centre for Development Studies, Australia National University, 1986); and Harry Oshima, "Levels and Trends of Farm Families' Non-agricultural Income at Different Stages of Monsoon Development."

2. S. Hymer and S. Resnick, "A Model of Agrarian Economy with Nonagricultural Activities," *American Economic Review* (September 1969): 493. This concept emphasizes substitution, ignoring the forced idleness due to the dry weather by citing brush fallowing—which, however important it may be in Africa south of the Sahara, is of no importance in monsoon Asia.

3. Definitions are in Food and Agriculture Organization, *Production Yearbook.*

4. One other figure may be noted, that of 22 percent for small farms in Zambia in 1966–68.

5. Norton Ginsberg, ed., *The Pattern of Asia* (Englewood Cliffs: Prentice-Hall, 1958), 54, 374, 496. The monsoons do not reach most parts of Hokkaido, Manchuria, northern and western China, Pakistan, Punjab, and Irian Jaya, which are in nonmonsoon Asia, where the main staple crop is not rice. Monsoon Asia is where more than 90 percent of Asia's population lives. There are considerable variations in the rain patterns for long narrow countries like the Philippines, Japan, and Indonesia and for large countries like India and China.

6. Oshima, "Problems of Heavy Industrialization in Asian Development."

7. Oshima, *Economic Growth in Monsoon Asia,* chap. 5.

8. Official national accounts and United States, *Statistical Abstract.* But farm income figures exclude the income of nonresident farm operators (*Historical Statistics of the United States*).

9. This section is based on an article in Swapna Mukhopadhyay and Chee Peng Lim, eds., *Development and Diversification of Rural Industries in Asia* (Kuala Lumpur: APDC, 1984); Mukopadhyay and Lim, eds., *The Rural Non-Farm Sector in Asia* (Kuala Lumpur: APDC, 1985); R. T. Shand, *Off-Farm Employment in the Development of Rural Asia.*

10. Samuel Ho, "Rural Nonagricultural Development in Asia: Experience and Issues," in Mukhopadhyay and Lim, *The Rural Non-Farm Sector in Asia.*

11. R. Islam, "Productivity and Equity Considerations in Policies for Rural Industrialization: An Analysis Based on Some Asian Experiences," in Mukhopadhyay and Lim, *The Rural Non-Farm Sector in Asia;* M. Hossain, "Employment Generation through Cottage Industries," in Mukhopadhyay and Lim, *Development and Diversification of Rural Industries in Asia.*

12. H. M. G. Herath, "An Exploratory Study of Off-Farm Employment and Incomes in Sri Lanka," in Shand, *Off-Farm Employment in the Development of Rural Asia,* vol. 2.

13. For wage data, see G. K. Chadha, "Agricultural Growth and Rural Non-Farm Activities: An Analysis of Indian Experience," in Mukhopadhyay and Lim, *Development and Diversification of Rural Industries in Asia;* Islam, "Productivities and Equity Considerations"; and Herath, "An Exploratory Study of Off-Farm Employment and Incomes in Sri Lanka."

14. For a discussion of the shift in Japan from hand looms to semiautomatic and fully automatic power looms in the first three decades of the twentieth century, see R. Minami and F. Makino, "Conditions for Technological Diffusion: The Case of Power Looms," *Hitotsubashi Journal of Economics* 23 (1983). In 1907, 98 percent of the weaving was by hand looms, declining to 63 percent in 1920 and to 50 percent in 1938.

15. Kosit Panpiemras, "Rural Industrialization in Thailand," in Mukhopadhyay and Lim, *Development and Diversification of Rural Industries in Asia;* R. Fabella, "Rural Nonagricultural Employment," in Mukhopadhyay and Lim, *Development and Diversification;* and P. Kasryno, "Structural Changes in Rural Employment and Agricultural Wages in Indonesia," in Shand, *Off-Farm Employment in the Development of Rural Asia.*

16. Y. B. Choe, "Seminar Report on Rural Industries and Off-Farm Employment," Seoul, 1983; *Taiwan, Family Income and Expenditure, 1975; Japan, Employment Status Survey, 1962.*

17. *Japan, Statistical Yearbook, 1969.* For Taiwan, see A. Speare and Paul Liu, *Urbanization and Labor Mobility in Taiwan* (Taipei: Academica Sinica, 1977). The authors find that a fourth of the workers in the smaller cities preferred to live on the farms nearby, since commuting "enabled them to help with farming and housekeeping on weekends" besides providing them cheaper living costs.

18. In my visits in 1985 to two factories in Ansung, one producing grinders and the other roller chains, employers cited cheaper wages as the major attraction of the town.

19. *Japan, Establishment Census, 1981.*

20. *Japan, Employment Status Survey, 1962, 1968, 1979.*

21. Benjamin White, *Rural Non-Farm Employment in Java* (Jakarta: UNDP/ILO, 1986); R. T. Shand, "Agricultural Development, Nonfarm Employment, and Rural Income Distribution in Kelantan," in Shand, *Off-Farm Employment in the Development of Rural Asia.*

CHAPTER 8: HUMAN RESOURCE DEVELOPMENT

1. Agricultural population per hectare of arable land in Asia is three times that of the world, eight times that of Europe, eighteen times that of North America, and thirty times that of South America; see Oshima, *Economic Growth in Monsoon Asia,* 23. Asia is also poor in fuel, minerals, and chemical resources. See Chira Hongladarom et al., "The Economic and Social Impact of Declining Fertility: A Case Study of Thailand," *Asia-Pacific Population Journal* (June 1987).

2. World Bank, *World Development Report;* International Labor Organization, *Yearbook of Labor Statistics 1978, 1983, 1986, 1988; Statistical Yearbook of the Republic of China, 1987.*

3. Fertility rates and incomes from World Bank, *World Development Report, 1988;* World Bank, *World Tables.*

4. *Population and Development Review* 12 (1986), supplement.

5. This section is based on Harry Oshima, "Manpower Quality on Differential Postwar Asian Growth," *Philippine Economic Journal* (October 1981).

6. Kuznets, *Modern Economic Growth,* 6.

7. A. F. Wright, ed., *Confucian Persuasion* (Stanford: Stanford University Press, 1960); Wright and Nivision, *Confucianism in Action;* A. F. Wright and D. Twitchett, eds., *Confucian Personalities* (Stanford: Stanford University Press, 1962). In Japan and other East Asian countries, Confucian doctrines were taught in moral education courses throughout the primary and secondary schooling. For the Tokugawa period, see Robert Bellah, *Tokugawa Religion: The Values of Pre-Industrial Japan* (New York: Free Press, 1957).

8. World Bank, *World Development Report, 1980, 1987, 1988;* International Labor Institute, *Yearbook of Labor Statistics, 1978, 1983, 1986, 1988; China, Statistical Yearbook, 1987;* UNDP, *Human Development Report, 1990.*

9. Asian Development Bank, *Key Indicators, 1988.*

10. *Far Eastern Economic Review,* July 12, 1990.

11. Nena Vreeland et al., *Area Handbook for the Philippines* (Washington, D.C.: American University, 1975), 107. A Japanese mission sent to Europe in the early Meiji period to learn about capitalist institutions was impressed by the dynamism of the northern parts of Europe, where Protestantism prevailed, and by the stagnancy of Spain and southern Italy, where Hispanic Catholic priests dominated.

12. As reported in *Newsweek International,* November 11, 1991.

13. Samuel Ho, *Economic Development of Taiwan, 1860–1970* (New Haven: Yale University Press, 1979), 99–102; N. F. McGinn et al., *Education and Development in Korea* (Cambridge: Harvard University Press, 1980), 80–85.

14. See World Bank, *World Development Report, 1978,* for literacy data. J. S. Furnival points out that in 1939 about a fifth of the Philippine budget was spent on education, a figure greater than any other South or Southeast Asian country: see J. S. Furnival, *Educational Progress in Southeast Asia* (New York: Institute of Pacific Relations, 1943), 112.

15. J. W. Henderson et al., *Area Handbook for Thailand* (Washington, D.C.: American University, 1971), 109, 113.

16. Harry Oshima, "Human Resources in Macro-Comparative Productivity Trends in Asia," table 5.

17. The following discussion is based on ESCAP, *Economic and Social Survey of Asia and the Pacific, 1986.*

18. Asian Development Bank, *Education and Development in Asia and the Pacific, 1988;* UNESCO, *Statistical Yearbook, 1987.*

19. *Business Week,* September 19, 1988. It may be that social values regarding learning, together with saving propensities, may have weakened in the United States.

20. "On the Down Grade," *Far Eastern Economic Review,* July 8, 1989.

21. In many parts of the Philippines the dropout rates are close to half of the pupils enrolled. See A. Herrin, "Human Resource Development in the Philippines: Policy Issues and Research Directions," in *Human Resource Policy and Economic Development, Selected Country Studies* (Manila: Asian Development Bank, 1990).

22. ESCAP, *Economic and Social Survey of Asia and the Pacific, 1986,* 128.

23. This is hard to believe. Four decades of teaching tells me that if the class has forty or fifty students instead of twenty or thirty, there is much less time for each student to take part in class discussions; nor is it easy to assess the ability of each student or to give each student enough individual time and effort. It may be that lecturing is no more difficult for a large class than for a small class, but for primary schools, lectures are not the main method of teaching.

24. Hong Kong, Singapore, and South Korea had a literacy rate of about 70 percent; Taiwan's was 54 percent. World Bank, *World Development Report, 1978.*

25. U.S. employers complain that high schools are not turning out workers with enough math and science to work out problems. This is traced to poor teaching of math and science in the primary schools. Japanese high school students perform better in math and science than U.S. and European students.

26. Japan has established a center for the retraining of teachers in math and science at the University of the Philippines.

27. Filipino students scored 12 percent better on math and science tests after student-textbook ratios rose from 10:1 to 2:1. World Bank, *Education Policy Paper, 1980,* 35.

28. See ESCAP, *Economic and Social Survey of Asia and the Pacific, 1986,* 156, for data on the growth of the enrollment ratio, which has been much faster at the tertiary level than at the primary level in every country except Pakistan. The enrollment ratio is the proportion of the total age group enrolled. But when economic growth speeds up, shortages develop, as it has in Thailand with large influxes of direct foreign investment from Japan and Taiwan. But the shortage may also be due to the slow growth of Thai secondary education, especially vocational and technical training. See S. Chalangphob et al., "Human Resource Problems and Policy Priorities in Thailand," in *Human Resource Policy and Economic Development, Selected Countries* (Manila: Asian Development Bank, 1990).

29. ESCAP, *Economic and Social Survey of Asia and the Pacific, 1986,* 154.

30. Official statistical yearbooks of Japan, Taiwan, and South Korea. See also Japan, National Council on Educational Reform, *Educational Reform,* Final Report, August 1987.

31. See *Far Eastern Economic Review,* April 6, 1989, for the problems faced by Japanese educators in trying to make the changes.

32. For details on skill formation, see ESCAP, *Human Resource Development: Its Technological Dimensions* (Bangkok, 1988), and a number of UNESCO publications, such as *Technical and Vocational Education in Asia and the Pacific, 1980.* It is possible

to train workers for different types of skills as the Japanese do in their in-service programs. But this is not possible if labor unions in collective bargaining contracts demand specifications for each job, as in the United States.

33. The social values of traditional Japan, rooted in the feudalistic past, emphasized loyalty to employers—even more than to family.

34. German and Japanese firms hesitate to invest in the Philippines because of the shortage of skilled workers. Those they undertake to train are hired away by other firms. *Business World,* August 21, 1989.

35. L. P. Jones and Il SaKong, *Government, Business and Entrepreneurship in Economic Development: the Case of Korea* (Cambridge: Harvard University Press, 1980).

36. In socialist countries (Vietnam, China, and North Korea), socialism has weakened Confucian social values with policies of employment guarantees, social security, and public enterprises. But it is not clear that the values have been permanently destroyed. The Chinese immigrating to Hong Kong appear to be able to adjust after awhile to a hectic pace.

37. Food and Agriculture Organization, *Fifth World Food Survey.*

38. World Bank, *World Development Report.*

39. UNDP, *Human Development Report, 1990,* table 7. See also U.S. Food and Drug Administration, dietary studies.

40. China's policies illustrate the attempt to solve these problems with "barefoot doctors" and through an emphasis on preventive health strategy, on improved nutrition, sanitation, and water supply, and on a combination of Western and traditional medicines. This section on health is largely based on ESCAP, *Economic and Social Survey of Asia and the Pacific, 1986.*

## CHAPTER 9: FAMILY INCOME DISTRIBUTION AND THE ALLEVIATION OF POVERTY

1. Family income is personal income, defined in the national accounts to include wages, salaries, net receipts of family enterprises, net interests, rents, transfer receipts, commissions, tips, bonuses, and honoraria.

2. It was not the sharp upward and downward movement suggested by later writers.

3. Kuznets, *Modern Economic Growth,* 206–17.

4. Simon Kuznets, *Economic Growth and Structure* (New York: Norton, 1965), 257–87.

5. See Warren O. Divine, Jr., "From Shafts to Wires: Historical Perspectives in Electrification," *Journal of Economic History* (June 1983); Oshima, "The Growth of Total Factor Productivity in the U.S."

6. With the shifting of these technologies to electronic technologies, inequalities may begin to rise, as they have in the United States. See T. Smeeding and G. Duncan, "Whither the Middle Class," Syracuse University, N.Y., 1990.

7. In the 1920s, per capita income was actually about $700; prices rose three times by the 1970s. See U.S. Bureau of the Census, *Historical Statistics of the U.S., 1972.*

8. Simon Kuznets, introduction to *Income Distribution, Employment, and Econom-*

*ic Development in Southeast and East Asia*, vol. 1 (Tokyo: Japan Economic Research Center; Manila: Council for Asian Manpower Studies, 1975).

9. The following unpublished papers are from Hitotsubashi Institute of Economic Research: Toshiyuki Mizoguchi, "Economic, Sociological, and Institutional Factors Related to Changes in the Size Distribution of Household Income: Japan's Experience in a Century"; Shirley Kuo, "Income Distribution in Taiwan"; Laurence C. Chau, "Economic Growth and Income Distribution of Hong Kong since the Early 1950s"; Tzon-biau Lim, "Growth, Equity, and Income Distribution Policies in Hong Kong." Also see Hak-chung Choo, "Estimation of Size Distribution of Income and Its Sources of Changes in Korea, 1982," *Korean Social Science Journal* 12 (1985); T. Iwamoto, "Distribution of Income and Wealth in Korea," *Azia Keizai* (February 1991); V. V. Bhanoji Rao, "Income Distribution in East Asian Developing Countries," *Asian-Pacific Economic Literature* 2 (March 1988); V. V. Bhanoji Rao and M. K. Ramakrishnan, "Income Distribution in Singapore, 1966–1973," *Malayan Economic Review* (1976); Yukio Ikemoto, *Income Distribution in Thailand* (Tokyo: Institute of Developing Economies, 1991); Abuzar Asra, "Distributional Impacts of Economic Growth: The Case of Indonesia, 1969–70 to 1981," Ph.D. diss., 1988, Griffith University; H. N. S. Karunati-lake, "Long-Term Changes in Income Inequalities in Sri Lanka," *CAMS-JERC* 2 (1985); Lee Shen-Yi, "Income Distribution, Taxation, and Social Benefits in Singapore," *Journal of Developing Areas* 14 (October 1979); S. R. Osmani and A. Rahman, *Study of Income Distribution in Bangladesh*, BIDS Research Report 53 (November 1986); A. Rahman, S. Mahmud, and T. Haque, *A Critical Review of the Poverty Situation in Bangladesh in the Eighties*, BIDS Research Report 66 (May 1988); *Taiwan, Survey of Personal Income Distribution, 1986, 1987; Philippines, Family Income and Expenditure Survey, 1988* (preliminary and highlights); *Fifth Malaysian Plan, 1986–1990; Sri Lanka, Labor Force and Socio-Economic Survey, 1985–86;* National Council of Applied Economic Research, *Changes in Rural Income in India, 1968–69 to 1970–71* (New Delhi, December 1975); NCAER, *Household Income and Its Disposition* (New Delhi, January 1980); NCAER, *Changes in Household Income, Interclass Mobility, and Income Distribution in Rural India, 1970–71 to 1981–82* (New Delhi, April 1986).

10. Simon Kuznets, "Economic Growth and Income Inequality," *American Economic Review* (March 1955).

11. *Thailand, Census of Population, 1937.*

12. World Bank, *World Development Report, 1989, 1990.*

13. For details, see Harry Oshima, "Trends in Growth and Distribution of Income in Selected Asian Countries," *Philippine Economic Journal* 15 (1976), from which most of the data in this section are taken.

14. For a detailed discussion, see Kuo, "Income Distribution in Taiwan."

15. Hak-chung Choo, *A Comparison of Income Distribution in Japan, Taiwan, and Korea* (Seoul: Korean Development Institute, 1989).

16. Yukio Ikemoto, "Income Distribution in Malaysia, 1957–1980," *Developing Economies*, Tokyo (December 1985).

17. But see Ikemoto, *Income Distribution in Thailand*, 14–19, where he argues that rural development policies, the commodity boom, and minimum wage laws were favorable to falling inequalities in the early 1970s.

18. See *Thailand, Agricultural Statistics of Thailand.* Piron Chantaworn, "Decomposition of Measures of Inequality of Income Distribution in Thailand," Master's thesis,

University of Philippines, shows that between 1963 and 1969 Ginis in the rural sectors of four regions were rising.

19. Medhi Krongkaew, "Agricultural Development, Rural Poverty and Income Distribution in Thailand," *Developing Economies*, Tokyo (December 1985). He also notes that the rice tax system adversely affected income distribution.

20. Suganya Hutaserani and Somchai Jetsuchon, *Thailand's Income Distribution and Poverty Profile and Their Current Situation* (Bangkok: Thailand Development Research Institute Foundation, 1988), 19; decomposition analysis shows that the differentials in per capita income between agricultural and nonagricultural and between rural and urban regions is the underlying factor in the worsening of income disparities. Also see Oshima, "Trends in Growth and Distribution of Income in Selected Asian Countries."

21. Sam Poli, *Over-Time Changes in Living Standards and Poverty in Indonesia, with Special Reference to 1964/65, 1969/70, and 1976*, National Socio-Economic Survey (Hasanuddin: Hasanuddin University, 1978). On protection and income inequality, see K. Yoneda, "A Note on Income Distribution in Indonesia," *Developing Economies*, Tokyo (December 1985).

22. Oshima, "Changes in Philippine Income Distribution." In talking to the heads of Philippine statistical surveys, I was told that very little from the late 1970s surveys was published because President Marcos did not want the great inequalities in the country publicized. It is difficult to suppress the suspicion that the 1970s surveys were devised to prevent comparisons with the 1960s surveys. See also Y. Terasaki, "Income Distribution and Development Policies in the Philippines," *Developing Economies*, Tokyo (December 1985).

23. Mizoguchi, "Economic, Sociological and Institutional Factors Relating to Changes in the Size Distribution of Household Income."

24. World Bank, *World Development Report, 1990*.

25. U.N., *Human Development Report, 1991*.

26. Ibid.

27. Swapna Mukhopadhyay, ed., *The Poor in Asia: Productivity-Raising Programmes and Strategies* (Malaysia: APDC, 1985), 267, 473, 475, 567, 605, 608; World Bank, *The Philippines: The Challenge of Poverty* (1988), 125; Sang Mok Suh, unpublished papers; Laurence L. C. Chau, "Economic Growth and Reduction of Poverty in Hong Kong," *Philippine Economic Journal* 18 (1978): 590; Lim Chong Yah et al., *Policy Options for the Singapore Economy* (Singapore: McGraw-Hill, 1988), 394; World Bank, *Poverty Alleviation*, vol. 2 (1988); Oey Astra Meesook, "Income Consumption and Poverty in Thailand, 1962–63 to 1974–75," Working Paper 364, World Bank (1979), 59; Suganya Hutasirani and Somchai Jitsuchon, "Thailand's Income Distribution and Poverty Profile and Their Current Situation," Thailand Development Research Institute Foundation (1988), table 4.4; A. Balisacan, *Rural Poverty in the Philippines* (Asian Development Bank, forthcoming); *Far Eastern Economic Review* (1989); *Mid-Term Review of the Fifth Malaysia Plan, 1986–1990;* World Bank, *World Development Report, 1990;* World Bank, *Poverty Alleviation*, vol. 2; World Bank, *Bangladesh: Recent Economic Development and Short-Term Prospects;* United States, *Statistical Abstract 1987, 1989*.

28. Chau, "Industrial Growth and Employment in Hong Kong."

29. While my family was in Tokyo in 1959, we were able to hire a live-in maid, but

she left the next year for a factory job. We then hired a neighborhood housewife, who came for a few hours in the morning and afternoon. But in 1961, she too left for a factory job, and we were unable to get a replacement. The same thing happened during our stay in Singapore in 1968.

30. Asian Development Bank, *Key Indicators, 1989.*

31. C. C. Chen, "Poverty in Asia," *Philippine Economic Journal* 18 (1979).

32. Taipei, *Report of the Survey of Personal Income Distribution, 1988;* Harry Oshima, "Preface: Notes on Some Poverty Research Issues," *Philippine Economic Journal* 18 (1979).

33. These policies probably increased overall income inequality in the 1980s, especially within the rural sector.

34. For details, see H. Osman-Rani, "Employment and Poverty," *Philippine Review of Economics and Business* (September-December 1987).

35. *Mid-Term Review of the Fifth Malaysian Plan, 1986–1990.*

36. Hutaserani and Jitsuchon, *Thailand's Income Distribution and Poverty Profile.* Income disparities fell in 1988, when farm prices rose.

37. World Bank, *Thailand: Growth with Stability.* A large number of seasonally unemployed workers are left out of the labor force totals.

38. Medhi Krongkaew, "Economic and Social Impact of Thailand's Rural Job Creation Program," *Philippine Review of Economics and Business* (September-December 1987).

39. There may be problems in the 1985 and 1988 surveys of family income and expenditure, which were conducted in only two rounds, compared with the usual four rounds in surveys of this type. Comparability of these surveys with earlier ones may be questionable.

40. *Philippines, Highlights of the 1988 Family Income and Expenditure Survey.*

41. *Philippines, Labor Force in the Philippines, 1989.*

42. Ibid.; *Philippines, Third Nutrition Survey, 1987.*

43. World Bank, *Indonesia: Strategy for Economic Recovery.*

44. Asra, "Distributional Impacts of Economic Growth."

45. H. N. S. Karunatilake, "Poverty in Sri Lanka," *Philippine Economic Journal,* no. 4 (1979).

46. USAID, *Country Development Strategy, Sri Lanka, 1985;* 45 percent of total households were found to be consuming less than 2,160 calories in 1980–81.

47. Asian Development Bank, *Key Indicators, 1989.*

48. M. M. Verna, ed., *Planning for the Poor* (New Delhi: Gitanjali, 1986).

49. World Bank, *Report of the Poverty Task Force,* vol. 2. Daily per capita calorie supply in India is only 2,200; the large share of income spent on food denotes low income levels.

50. S. R. Hashim, "Employment Strategies for Accelerated Economic Growth," Asian and Pacific Development Center.

51. Asian Development Bank, *Key Indicators.*

52. Rahman, Malmud, and Hague, *A Critical Review of the Poverty Situation in Bangladesh in the Eighties.*

53. *A Survey of Employment, Income Distribution and Consumption Patterns in Nepal, 1976/77.*

CHAPTER 10: TOWARD THE PACIFIC CENTURY: THE ROLE OF GOVERNMENT

1. Lim Chong Yah et al., *Policy Options for the Singapore Economy* (New York: McGraw-Hill, 1988).

2. Note the difficulties the socialist countries are encountering in shifting from a planned to a market economy. It will take some time before market forces are developed, especially the ability of entrepreneurs to finance and market their production.

3. Data in this section are from United Nations, *A System of National Accounts and Supporting Tables*.

4. For example, Morris Beck, "Public Sector Growth: A Real Perspective," *Public Finance*, no. 3 (1979).

5. See Harry Oshima, "Share of Government in GDP of Various Countries," *American Economic Review* (June 1957), for the prewar figures. For Asia and Latin America, they rose slightly from 1938. For industrialized countries, see OECD, *National Accounts, 1962–1979, 1972–1984*, vol. 2.

6. A. A. Tait and Peter S. Heller, *International Comparisons of Government Expenditures*, Occasional Paper 10 (Washington, D.C.: International Monetary Fund, 1982).

7. Donald Snodgrass, *An Export Economy in Transition* (New Haven: Economic Growth Center, Yale University, 1966).

8. For data on budget deficits, see IMF, *International Financial Statistics, 1988*. See Asian Development Bank, *Asian Development Review, 1987*, for a special issue on the public sector.

9. The Ceylon government was advised by a team of well-known British economists sent by Clement Atlee's welfare-oriented Labor government. Whatever may be the rationale for industrialized countries to indulge in large welfare programs, a low-income country such as Ceylon could not sustain such programs, which crowded out expenditures on investment and growth. See Snodgrass, *An Export Economy in Transition*.

10. In 1967–69, U.S. defense expenditures absorbed 43 percent of the central budget, compared to Japan's 9 percent and West Germany's 21 percent; while Italy, France, and the United Kingdom spent 30 percent. OECD, *Expenditure Trends in OECD Countries, 1960–1980*.

11. Oshima, "Problems of Heavy Industrialization in Asian Development."

12. Data on Hong Kong from IMF, *Government Finance Statistics Yearbook*, table B, which also shows very high economic service shares for Nepal (about one-half) and Burma (about one-third in the early 1980s).

13. See Tait and Heller, *International Comparisons of Government Expenditures*, chap. 3, for a study of about ninety countries around 1977. Their regression results (with low $R^2$) are difficult to interpret, as the study includes a wide variety of countries— ranging from the industrialized countries to the tribal societies of Africa and city-states such as Singapore to vast agricultural countries such as Brazil. Furthermore, they lump together proximate and ultimate determinants. The meaning of per capita national income or GNP data of predominantly tribal societies, as in Africa, and of large agricultural countries, such as Indonesia, Brazil, and India, is discussed in Harry Oshima, "National Income and Product and the Price System," *Review of Economic Statistics* (August 1951).

14. For data on government wage shares in national income, see P. S. Heller and

A. A. Tait, *Government Employment and Pay: Some International Comparisons* (Washington, D.C.: IMF, 1983); they also discuss conceptual and statistical difficulties in the measurement of public employment.

15. Productivity has been falling since the early 1950s. See José A. Bulao, "The Growth of Government Services Sector in the Philippines, 1947–1976," Master's thesis, University of the Philippines, 1981.

16. Kuznets, *Economic Growth of Nations*, 346–47.

17. M. Abramovitz, "Welfare Quandaries and Productivity Concerns," *American Economic Review* (March 1981): 2.

18. Tait and Heller, *Government Employment and Pay,* table 10.

19. Hong Kong's social security and welfare benefits in 1982–83 were less than 1 percent of GDP. *Hong Kong Annual Digest of Statistics, 1984.*

20. World Bank, *World Development Report, 1986,* table 23.

21. Abramovitz, "Welfare Quandaries and Productivity Concerns."

22. *Japan in the Year 2000.*

23. *International Herald Tribune,* May 15, 1987.

24. R. N. Bautista, "Rapid Agricultural Growth Is Not Enough: the Philippines, 1965–1980," International Food Policy Research Institute, July 1990.

25. In OECD countries, despite high educational expenditures in the 1950s, educational expenditures (in constant prices) had to be increased by about 7 percent per year in the 1960s. OECD, *Social Expenditures, 1960–1990.*

26. International Rice Research Institute, *1990 Annual Report.*

27. Robert Chandler, speech before the Thirtieth Anniversary of IRRI, Los Baños, September 20, 1990.

28. Ibid. The statistics are attributed to Randolph Barker and Duane Chapman.

29. Saadet Deger, *Military Expenditures in Third World Countries: the Economic Effects* (London: Routledge and Kegan Paul, 1986).

30. The evidence of Philippine corruption is in the poor construction of public roads, perhaps the worst in Asia. Also the tax effort (revenues collected as a percentage of GNP) is the lowest in Asia, attesting to the widespread graft of tax collectors. Filipino taxpayers, aware that much of the taxes they pay is siphoned off by politicians and bureaucrats, try to evade paying taxes by bribing tax collectors.

31. For details, see Oshima, *Economic Growth in Monsoon Asia,* chap. 4.

32. This was also the case in Meiji Japan when land was redistributed without follow-up provisions, and in prewar Philippines when the United States distributed church lands. Peasants became heavily indebted and soon lost their land to the landlords.

33. *Far Eastern Economic Review,* July 12, 1990; Benedict Kerkvliet and Tria Kerkvliet, *Everyday Politics in the Philippines: Class and Status Relations in a Central Village* (Berkeley and Los Angeles: University of California Press, 1990).

34. Harry Oshima, "On the Coming Pacific Century: Perspective and Prospects," *Singapore Economic Review* (October 1983).

35. It is not by chance that four-fifths of the Nobel Prizes (1901–85) have gone to citizens of North Atlantic nations.

36. Matthews, *British Economic Growth.*

37. Asian Development Bank, *Key Indicators, 1991.*

38. *Business World,* November 4, 1987; World Bank, *World Development Report,*

*1987;* Aurora Sanchez, "Non-Tariff Barriers and Trade in ASEAN," *Asian Economic Bulletin* (July 1987).

39. On this, see G. R. Tecson, "Export Markets for Philippine Diversified Agriculture and Labor-Intensified Industries," *Philippine Review of Economics and Business* (September/December 1986).

40. Miyohei Shinohara, "Japan as Growth Pole in the Asian Pacific Region," *Asian Economic Journal* (March 1987).

# INDEX

GDP, 57; education, prewar, 185–86; factors contributing to idleness, 108; growth in 1980s, 8; income inequality, 211; off-farm incomes, Stage I, 162; poverty incidence, 222

Indonesia: Center for Agribusiness Development, 129–30; entrepreneurial competition, 193; factors contributing to idleness, 107, 109; growth in 1980s, 9–10; income inequality, 210; poverty incidence, 220–21

Industrialization strategy: in East Asia, 8; in India and Sri Lanka, 8; in Philippines and China, 8

Industrial revolution, Asia, 4–5

Infrastructure, 133–34; policies for, 134–35

In-service training (on-the-job), Japan and Singapore, 192

Inverted U-curve, Kuznets, 2–3

IRRI: HYV, 126; Robert Chandler, 244–45

Japan: agricultural productivity growth, 31; calorie intake, 92; construction and GDP, 55; education, postwar, 186–89; education, prewar, 184–85; excess savings, 76; farm family income and savings, 170–71; full employment, 111–13; income inequality, 211–12; in-service training, 192; off-farm incomes, 156–57, 160–61; off-farm incomes, Stage III, 164, 165–66; off-farm policies, 172–73; personal savings, 73; population growth, 178–79; poverty incidence, 216; reasons for saving, 73; second industrial revolution, 4–6; service sector, 139–41; share of government receipts, 236; structural change, 136–37; technology policies, 66

Japan Productivity Center, data, 34, 259

Java: growth in 1980s, 9; rural population density, 148–49

Landlords: in India, 108; in Japan, 111–12; in the Philippines, 107

Land reform: income distribution, 208; in Japan, 111; relation to agricultural pro-

ductivity, 30–31; in South Asia, 211; in South Korea, 118; in Taiwan, 115

Lee, T. H., 114, 265–66

Lewis, Arthur, 4; growth theory, 99

Life expectancy, 195–96

Lim, Chee-Peng, 161, 270

Literacy levels, 187

Maddison, Angus, 81, 263

Malaysia: calorie intake, 92; education, prewar, 185; export-led growth, 36; factors contributing to idleness, 105–7; income inequality, 209; off-farm incomes, 159–60; off-farm incomes, Stage II, 164; poverty incidence, 218–19; rural population density, 149; share of government receipts, 236–37; structural change, 137; underemployment, 105

Mason, Andrew, 263

Matthews, R.C.O., 257

Medical services, 195–96

Migration to cities, 165

Mizoguchi, Toshiyuki, income inequality, Japan, 213

Monsoon agriculture, productivity, 32

Monsoon Asia: countries included, 1; data on, 7; non-monsoon areas in Asia, 10–11; service sector, 139–40; technological revolutions, 4–6

Monsoon patterns, 154–56

Moon, P. Y., 118–19, 266

Moral education, 185–90

Mukhopadhyay, S., 161, 270

Muslim: education, prewar, 186; social values, 182

Nepal: calorie intake, 93; off-farm income, Stage I, 162; poverty incidence, 223

NIE: creditor nations, 250; greater democracy, 250; growth slowdown, 249–50

Non-monsoon areas in Asia, 10–11

Nurkse, Ragnar, 4

Nutrition: data, 194–95; importance, 194; South and Southeast Asia, 194–96

Off-farm employment: agro-industrial transition, 161–63; concepts, 152–53; data, 154–55; impact on economic growth,

*Designed by Nighthawk Design*

Composed by The Composing Room of Michigan, Inc.,
in Times Roman text & Gill Sans display

Printed on 50 lb. Booktext Natural
and bound in Holliston Roxite Vellum
by Bookcrafters